02/15

Encountering
Genocide

Encountering Genocide

Personal Accounts from Victims, Perpetrators, and Witnesses

Paul R. Bartrop

ABC-CLIO

Santa Barbara, California • Denver, Colorado • Oxford, England

Library of Congress Cataloging-in-Publication Data
Encountering genocide : personal accounts from victims, perpetrators, and witnesses / [compiled by] Paul R. Bartrop.
        pages cm
    ISBN 978-1-61069-330-1 (hardback)—ISBN 978-1-61069-331-8 (ebook)
1. Genocide. 2. Genocide—Case studies. I. Bartrop, Paul R. (Paul Robert), 1955-
    HV6322.7.E525 2014
    364.15'1—dc23   2013047636

ISBN: 978-1-61069-330-1
EISBN: 978-1-61069-331-8

18 17 16 15 14   1 2 3 4 5

This book is also available on the World Wide Web as an eBook.
Visit www.abc-clio.com for details.

ABC-CLIO, LLC
130 Cremona Drive, P.O. Box 1911
Santa Barbara, California 93116-1911

This book is printed on acid-free paper ∞
Manufactured in the United States of America

To the memory of

Don Bartrop (1918–1974)
Barbara Bartrop, *née* Page (1920–2013)
Eugene Jelinek (1901–1984)
Edith Jelinek, *née* Kleinová (1913–1985)

Each, in his or her own way, simultaneously victims and
witnesses of the Century of Genocide

Contents

Preface and Acknowledgments

Just as I was in the throes of finishing my previous book, *A Biographical Encyclopedia of Contemporary Genocide: Portraits of Evil and Good,* my then editor at ABC-CLIO, Maxine Taylor, approached me with the idea to compile a book of firsthand accounts of people who, in some way, had experienced genocide—either as victims, perpetrators, or witnesses. It took me very little time to agree that this would be a project worth pursuing. Personal accounts provide the most intimate view of any experience, and where genocide is concerned there can be little doubt that, through those who were actually there, we see the darkest side of the human journey, related by genuine experts. If we cannot discern what genocide really means by reference to those who have undergone its trials, we never will.

This project started while I was still enjoying the honor of being the Ida E. King Distinguished Visiting Professor of Holocaust and Genocide Studies at Richard Stockton College of New Jersey. I cannot speak highly enough about this institution and its Holocaust and Genocide Program, and the encouragement the College gave me to pursue serious academic scholarship while I was there. Among those I am pleased to recognize are Carol Rittner RSM for her ongoing inspiration; Maryann McLoughlin, for providing me with the fruits of her outstanding work in rescuing Holocaust memoirs; and the former dean of the School of General Studies, G. Jan Colijn, who provided me (and you) with a gift in translating from Dutch the account by Els de Temmerman that appears in this volume. My graduate assistant at Stockton, Joanna Seremba, combined the rigors of her own advanced studies in genocide with my research demands at the outset of the project, and I am very grateful to her for the efforts she made on my behalf.

Since moving to Florida Gulf Coast University, my students have been the chief beneficiaries of several of the accounts reproduced in this volume, and I have been delighted with their responses. In classroom discussions, they have often helped me to discern fresh insights into the content of the testimonies we have studied. It might well be said, in this respect, that the teacher has learned from his students.

A number of colleagues and friends have also helped me in various ways. Silva Nercessian provided the account of her grandmother, Sevly Krickorian, and translated it especially for this volume from Armenian into English. Sargon Donabed was a very accommodating colleague who, from a chance meeting at a conference in San Francisco, led me to the account by Reverend Joseph Naayem (via another colleague, Hannibal Travis). And, through an even more chance meeting—a cab ride in Melbourne—I was fortunate in meeting "Amer," who agreed to relate, for this volume and for the very first time anywhere, his concentration camp experiences in Bosnia and Serbia.

At every stage, and at every level, I have been blessed with the company of my friend and colleague Michael Dickerman. Mike played a big part in keeping me focused on the project during the difficult time of transition between institutions (Stockton College to Florida Gulf Coast University), states (New Jersey to Florida), and countries (the United States to Australia, then back again). For his sake, I hope that the current work is sufficiently "Bartropian" to pass muster.

My editors at ABC-CLIO, Maxine Taylor and Padraic (Pat) Carlin, have been as professional and accommodating as one could ever want. I am delighted to be part of the ABC-CLIO family of authors, and have found nothing but fulfilment in my relationship with this excellent publisher.

As with all my books, my definitive acknowledgment goes to my dear wife Eve. In an earlier book I wrote of her that she is my muse, and nothing has changed in that regard. And that is *my* personal testimony.

Paul R. Bartrop
Fort Myers, 2014

Introduction

Firsthand accounts of genocide play the most crucial role in forming our understanding of what life was like during the most horrific times in the human experience. Whether we are considering accounts from survivors, perpetrators, or witnesses, these are our primary links to genocide as seen and experienced at "ground level."

Where survivors are concerned, testimonial accounts have a special status as firsthand narratives written by people who lived through genocidal barbarities. As such, it can be argued that all accounts, regardless of their artistic quality or historical accuracy, are vitally important documents that must be considered and respected as historical data.

Witnesses to genocide are often placed in the difficult position of reporting what they have seen without necessarily being able to ease the suffering of those around them. We frequently identify frustration, anxiety, and anger in such accounts, as those who are spectators to genocide can usually only report what they are seeing, without becoming directly involved. In the case of diplomatic observers, this is compounded by the very real issue of having to communicate government policy—in which case, they must suppress even their personal feelings when dealing with the perpetrators.

Additionally, we need to consider the nature of perpetrator accounts during genocide. It is rare, indeed, that we find those who commit genocide admitting their wrongdoing, and all too often they devote themselves to statements of self-justification rather than confession. Indeed, more often than not the only form of admission we find from perpetrators is one in which they explain why they have had to engage in their heinous actions. This can, of course, make it difficult to establish the accuracy of a situation, as perpetrator accounts are sometimes written for the purpose of clearing their author of responsibility, rather than shedding light on a specific situation.

As the majority of testimonies in this work have been produced by survivors, it is worthwhile to spend a little time deliberating the nature of their accounts. Survivor testimonies, by virtue of their special status as firsthand narratives written by people who have lived through barbaric treatment at the hands of their persecutors, are our primary links to the perpetrators as viewed from the victims' perspective. As such, all accounts are vitally important documents. Put simply, it can be argued that there is merit in every survivor account.

We therefore need to examine how testimonies may be assessed as sources of history. After all, such accounts are written or delivered after the fact, presumably when the victims are safely away from the scenes of their victimization. Moreover, such accounts are, for the most part, not recounted by practiced writers. Usually, a sifting process has taken place in an author's (or interviewee's) mind or by an editor's hand; some elements of memory are sacrificed for the sake of publication, while others are retained and possibly even enhanced for the same reason.

Such considerations alert us to a type of memoir that needs to be read differently from other forms of historical documentation. Survivor accounts chronicle events either directly witnessed by their authors or told to them by others at the time of their ordeals. It is these events—and, more universally, the truth—that genocide survivors attempt to impart to their readers. What is the historian, often coming onto the scene much later, to do with such material?

It might be said that there is a certain dimension of truth in survivor testimony that is absent in other forms of memoir literature. Once the dry statistical data of a victim's experience are known—the "why" and "where" aspects, which generally differ from one person to another—we see that survivors aim simply to convey the essence of what they went through to their audience.

In a court of law, such evidence serves a different purpose from that gathered by the historian. To those who would argue that the only standard of proof to be adopted by a scholar should be that found in a courtroom, it must be pointed out that the evidence a judge is looking for is altogether different from what the historian seeks. In a courtroom, the prosecution, defense, judge, and jury are all looking for specific evidence of a precise type—they need the kind of evidence that will either acquit or convict a person against whom a certain charge has been brought. The questions asked, therefore, are of a very special nature. Generally speaking, they do not look for the textures, smells, sights, and contours of a person's experience, nor do they explore the wider contextual backdrop against which things occurred. The historian of genocide and massive human rights violations, on the other hand, not only uses all these things in an effort to reach an understanding of the past; he or she also permits the survivors to discuss what made a special impression on them at the time of the nightmares they were experiencing. Such testimony is thus based on an entirely different attitude toward events than that found in a courtroom. Even if it would not always pass for "the truth" as a court would require it, it is nonetheless often more valuable for the historian than the kind of response that questions from a judge or attorney might elicit.

The historian cannot dismiss a survivor's impressions of an incident once it is firmly established that the survivor saw the incident take place. Especially in the field of genocide, there are cases where only one witness has survived. Nevertheless, or even because of this fact, the evidence that person brings is of value, often immensely so. What may we know of such things when no one survived to tell the tale? How does one establish what happened in a community where a population that perhaps once numbered several thousand has been totally obliterated? From whom does one obtain eyewitness testimony if all the eyewitnesses have been killed? How does one examine written records where none were kept? How did genocide manifest itself in these communities? We may never know, but the use of testimony, however fragmentary it might be, will start the process of rescuing history from oblivion, and for this reason alone *all* testimonial accounts are of use.

Above all, survivors are mostly interested in conveying to their readers a sense of what happened to *them,* as *they* remember it. Do they wish to be seen in a particular light? Perhaps. Is their intention to tell the "truth," as they understand it? Certainly. Do they hope to compose a particular set of images concerning their persecutors, or humanity in general? Yes. These are the broad realities. Overall, however, the reflections and reminiscences of genocide survivors are intimate accounts of individual experiences, which the survivors wish to share with others.

Implanted within this need to tell the story as they know it is a particular consciousness of what surviving is all about. Where genocide survivors are concerned, the need to bear witness is often a necessary part of the reason for survival itself. Survival is a specific kind of experience, and surviving in order to bear witness is one of its forms. It permits the survivor to allow the dead their voice; it serves as a call to humanity, a signal to all those observing the power of radical evil, a warning for future generations. Thus, many survivors identify a powerful duty to get their story down as accurately as possible.

Except in rare cases, survivors do not ask us to try to "imagine" their experiences. For the most part, that is not what they are attempting to achieve. For many, it is sufficient merely to tell their story, to record, to bear witness, to show that the ordeal through which they lived was in fact all too real. The challenge is not one of "imagining." Rather, it is one of conveying to the world an understanding of what the survivor went through, of explaining the essence of the evil that one group of people inflicted on another, as seen from the perspective of one who was there as a participant-observer-victim. Testimonial literature does not attempt to make magic, nor does it ask us to imagine the unimaginable. Survivors simply try to tell the story from their own individual perspectives, as the accounts in this volume make clear. Here, we frequently come across searing accounts of the most hideous encounters with the vilest expressions of human malevolence. More often than not, the survivors have not sought to impress us or embellish their accounts beyond the facts of their experiences. They simply want to share with us what happened to them, their families, their neighbors, and their communities.

Encountering Genocide has been constructed in such a way as to enable users to make the most use of it as a learning tool, having been planned to be both practical and more than just a reference work. The intention is that, beyond those in schools and universities, it will also be accessible to a general audience interested in the nature of survival in the face of human evil. The book looks at a variety of experiences involving a wide range of people on four different continents, across the century from 1904 and 2003.

This volume considers 10 case studies of modern genocide: the Hereros of German South-West Africa, 1904–1907; the Armenian Genocide, 1915–1923 (incorporating the concurrent genocides of the Assyrians and the Anatolian and Pontic Greeks); the Holocaust (*Shoah*) of the Jews by Nazi Germany, 1933–1945; the Cambodian Genocide, 1975–1979; the Guatemalan Genocide, 1982–1983; the East Timor Genocide, 1975–1999; the Kurdistan Genocide, 1988; the Rwandan Genocide, 1994; the Bosnian Genocide, 1992–1995; and the Darfur Genocide, 2003–2010.

Each of the accounts in this volume is introduced briefly, in a contextual statement that explains who wrote it, when, where, and so forth. The account itself follows. These range from diary entries to interviews, memoirs, military orders, witness statements, confessions, compilations, and other forms of personal accounts in which the accent is on narrative reportage. Each account is followed by a scholarly commentary on its content and nature, in which an attempt is made to consider the themes, dependability, and environment running through the document. As an aid to teachers, a number of discussion questions follow; these can be employed in the classroom.

Firsthand accounts of genocide, whether they are those of victims, perpetrators, or witnesses, provide us with a glimpse into the murderous darkness that is just as much a part of the human experience as is the illumination that acts of goodness can bring. Personal accounts are not easy to read; indeed, our natural inclination might be to avert our eyes, close the book, or skip to the next page. Yet they are the reminiscences of men and women whom circumstances decreed should be persecuted—or engage in persecution, or witness it—under conditions that had no guarantee of survival. They came from all walks of life, and from all corners of the globe. Their accounts were produced from the perspective of a few months or after the reflection of many years. And because they—and we—are human, their accounts deserve to be read.

1. The Herero Genocide

The German assault against the Herero people from 1904 to 1907, in Germany's colonial possession of South-West Africa (now Namibia), can be termed the first true instance of genocide in the twentieth century. During this time, the destruction of up to 80 percent of the total population took place. The devastation was not isolated, as at least 50 percent of the Nama, or "Hottentot," population, was also wiped out at this time.

In late 1903, Herero leaders learned of a proposal the Germans were considering that would see both the construction of a railway line through Herero territory, and the consequent concentration in reservations of Herero living in that territory. In response, in January 1904, the Hereros rebelled with the intention of driving the Germans out of Hereroland altogether. At the time, according to the best estimates, the Hereros numbered some 80,000.

After a German counterattack, reinforcement, and widespread campaign of annihilation and displacement that forced huge numbers of Hereros of both sexes and all ages into the Omaheke (Kalahari) Desert, tens of thousands perished. The situation was exacerbated by the policy of German general Lothar von Trotha (1848–1920), who ordered that all waterholes be located and poisoned in advance of the arrival of those Hereros who—by a miracle—might have survived the desert.

The roots of the genocide can be found in several areas. These include colonialism, Christian missionizing, economic self-interest, labor recruitment and slave labor, militarism, nationalism, and racism.

In 1883, Franz Adolph Eduard Lüderitz (1834–1886), a German businessman and merchant, purchased a strip of land from the Nama people at what would later be called Lüderitzbucht ("Lüderitz Bay"). A small settlement was established there, and within a year Lüderitz managed to have the area declared a protectorate of the German government. By 1885 a treaty of protection against the neighboring tribes was signed between the Herero chief Kamaharero (1820–1890) and the then colonial governor Heinrich Ernst Göring (1839–1913), father of the future Nazi leader Hermann Göring (1893–1946). The treaty was renounced in 1888 after repeated German violations, but reinstituted in 1890 by Kamaharero's son Samuel (1856–1923), who ceded large tracts of land to the Germans in return for their help with his becoming *Ovaherero* ("Paramount Chief").

As the colony grew, Göring was replaced by Theodor Leutwein (1849–1921), whose policies included unsuccessful attempts to mediate between the German colonists and the native peoples. Continuous tribal conflict, which threatened the safety and economic potential of the German colony, led Germany to send *Schutztruppe* ("Protection Troops") to pacify the area. Increasingly, however, the Germans exploited the native laborers (often transforming them into de facto slaves), raped their women, and encroached onto their lands without compensation.

In 1903, the Nama people, under the leadership of Hendrik Witbooi (c. 1830–1905), rose in revolt, and the following year the Hereros joined them in increasing numbers, driven by the continuing loss of their lands to the German settlers. An attack that same year resulted in the deaths of 150 Germans and found Leutwein unable to quell the rebellion. Under the circumstances, he was forced to request more troops from Germany. On June 11, 1904, Lieutenant-General Lothar von Trotha, who had already established a reputation for ruthlessness because of his suppression of rebellions in German East Africa and in China during the Boxer Rebellion, arrived with more than 14,000 troops. An avowed racist, von Trotha saw the only military solution as being one of extermination and annihilation. His infamous *Vernichtungsbefehl* ("Extermination Order"), issued on October 1, 1904, demonstrated this quite clearly.

At the Battle of Waterberg on August 11 and 12, 1904, von Trotha defeated 5,000 Herero fighters using a tactic of advancement on three sides, leaving as the only escape route one that led into the Omaheke Desert, where the remaining fighters and their families would die of exposure and lack of food and water. Some of those who managed to survive the desert experience, including Samuel Maharero, escaped to British Bechuanaland. Others survived, only to be captured and killed on von Trotha's direct orders, without mercy.

Von Trotha was indeed successful in meeting the terms of his orders to put down the uprising in South-West Africa, but his means of doing so generated criticism both within Germany and outside of it. In 1907, his orders were cancelled, a gesture robbed of much of its meaning, as he had already experienced ferocious success in putting down the rebellions. He was recalled to Germany in 1905 and, in 1910, he was made a full general in the German infantry. Von Trotha died on March 31, 1920, in Bonn, his place in history guaranteed—he was the first twentieth-century perpetrator of what would later come to be deemed genocide.

Before his return to Germany, von Trotha was responsible for the deaths of thousands of Nama people, with over half the population destroyed during 1905 alone. However, it was primarily under both his and Leutwein's successor's—Governor General Friedrich von Lindequist (1862–1945)—leadership that stage two of the genocide would take place, through the implementation and institution of *Konzentrationslager* ("concentration camps") and *Arbeitslager* ("work camps"). Together, these might more appropriately be termed *Vernichtungslager,* or "death camps."

The best-known (and most notorious) of the concentration camps were at Bondelslokation, Karibib, Keetmanshoop, Lüderitz, Okahandja, Omaruru, Swakopmund, and Windhoek; the worst of the work camps were at Okomitombe, Omburo, Otjihaenena, and Otjosongombe. A camp which many have since termed a death camp was located at Shark Island, adjacent to the town of Lüderitz. Shark Island prisoners were used as forced labor on infrastructure projects such as railroad construction and the development of the nearby harbor. Most prisoners sent to Shark Island died, though the population was replenished constantly. The main reasons for death included diseases (such as typhoid), malnutrition, extreme overwork, and constant brutality.

By the time the uprising was considered to be over, the Herero and Nama populations had been destroyed by military action, starvation and thirst, disease, and overwork in the concentration and labor camps. Evidence exists of medical experiments having been carried out, and of sexual crimes having been committed against Herero women. In 1911, when a count was made of the surviving Hereros, only about 15,000 could be found. The vast majority of the rest had been killed, either directly or indirectly, by German forces over the preceding half-dozen years, though most of the killing had taken place from 1904 to 1905.

PETER MOOR

Peter Moor was a German naval infantryman from Kiel. He served as a foot soldier during the Herero war in German South-West Africa in 1904–1905. As one of the first of the reinforcements sent from Germany after the outbreak of the rebellion, he was in the thick of the initial phases of the conflict and the subsequent pursuit of the Hereros into the Kalahari Desert. He related his experiences to a well-known writer of patriotic novels, Gustav Frenssen (1863–1945) in 1906. The book was translated into English by Margaret May Ward in 1908, and sections of it were later incorporated into the British government's Report on the Natives of South-West Africa and Their Treatment by Germany *(London: His Majesty's Stationery Office, 1918).*

The next morning we ventured to pursue the enemy. We left our unmounted men with the sick and wounded in camp and set out towards the east, two hundred horsemen in number. But our horses were weak, half-starved, or sick, and the region into which we were advancing was a waterless land and little explored. The ground was trodden down into a floor for a width of about a hundred yards; for in such a broad, thickly crowded horde had the enemy and their herds of cattle stormed along. In the path of their flight lay blankets, skins, ostrich feathers, household utensils, women's ornaments, cattle and men dead and dying and staring blankly. A shocking smell of old manure and of decaying bodies filled the hot, still air oppressively.

The further we went in the burning sun, the more disheartening became our journey. How deeply the wild, proud, sorrowful people had humbled themselves in the terror of death! Wherever I turned my eyes lay their goods in quantities; oxen and horses, goats and dogs, blankets and skins. And there lay the wounded and the old, women and children. A number of babies lay helplessly languishing by mothers whose breasts hung down long and flabby. Others were lying alone, still living, with eyes and noses full of flies. Somebody sent out our black drivers and I think they helped them to die. All this life lay scattered there, both man and beast, broken in the knees, helpless, still in agony or already motionless; it looked as if it had all been thrown down out of the air.

At noon we halted by water-holes which were filled to the very brim with corpses. We pulled them out by means of the ox-teams from the field pieces, but there was only a little stinking, bloody water in the depths. We tried to dig deeper, but no water came. There was no pasturage, either. The sun blazed down so hot on the sand that we could not even lie down. On our thirsting, starving horses, we thirsting and starving men rode on. At some distance crouched a crowd of old women, who stared in apathy in front of them. Here and there were oxen, bellowing. In the last frenzy of despair man and beast will plunge madly into the bush somewhere, anywhere, to find water, and in the bush they will die of thirst.

We rode on till evening. . . .

Toward evening, when I was ordered to ride in the bush with four men as a flank protection,—for we were shot at now and then, —we chanced to see a Cape wagon behind some high bushes, and we heard human voices. Dismounting, we sneaked up and discovered six of the enemy sitting in animated conversation around a little camp-fire. I indicated, by signs, at which one of them each of us was to shoot. Four lay still immediately; one escaped; the sixth stood half erect, severely wounded. I sprang forward swinging my club; he looked at me indifferently. I wiped my club clean in the sand and threw the weapon on its strap over my shoulder, but I did not like to touch it all that day.

The ground was everywhere bare, yellowish brown and stony; the sparse grass had been eaten, burned, or trodden down. Dead cattle lay about everywhere. The hoarse bellowing of dying oxen quavered horribly through the air. The bush got thinner, often opening into a great clearing.

Entirely forsaken in the scorching sun lay a two-year-old child. When it caught sight of us, it sat up straight and stared at us. I got down from my horse, picked the child up and carried it back where there was a deserted fireplace near a bush. It found at once the remainder of a root or a bone, and began to eat. It did not cry; it did not show fear, either; it was entirely indifferent. I believe it had grown there in the bush without human help. . . .

When it came to my turn to watch and I went outside, the night was so bitter cold that I made all sorts of motions to keep a little warmth in my body. I even climbed twice on a low, tumble-down anthill and watched the fires which here and there in the distance shone through the darkness. While I was thus gazing, however, I was struck by the fact that one fire was burning not far from us in the thick bush. I remembered when I was relieved, and told the lieutenant, who was sitting on the ground by our burned-out fire.

Before dawn we got up, discovered the exact place in the bush, and stealthily surrounded it. Five men and eight or ten women and children, all in rags, were squatting benumbed about their dismal little fire. Telling them with threats not to move, we looked through the bundles which were lying near them and found two guns and some underclothing, probably stolen from our dead. One of the men was wearing a German tunic which bore the name of one of our officers who had been killed. We then led the men away to one side and shot them. The women and children, who looked pitiably starved, we hunted into the bush. . . .

We rode on. The guardsman pointed once or twice into the bushes; I looked over there. Then we reached the summit and then looked attentively out over the plain, which lay in boundless extent an absolute stillness, like a yellowish grey sea. The long rays of the setting sun lay upon it like strips of thin, bright shining cloth.

We sprang off our horses, loosened the girths, and lay down on the ground. The guard's horse began to sniff at his face, but he did not notice it; he was already asleep. The lieutenant stood up again and said to me: "Get up! If we fall asleep, we shall sleep all night and then we are lost." I rose, and we both stood awhile with benumbed senses in a state between sleeping and waking. The sun sank in a dull glow; the air grew cooler, and the horses got somewhat more lively and began with weary steps to nibble a few little bushes.

After a while the Afrikaner woke and asked in a woe-begone voice if I had a drop of water. I said: "No." He said: "The lieutenant has some, then." Again I said: "No." Then he said he could hold out no longer without water—he had trusted too much to his strength, he should have to die here. The lieutenant, who had dozed standing by his horse and holding onto the saddle, woke and said consolingly: "Cheer up! We shall start at once. Then we are off for home, for the war is now really over." "Yes," said the guardsman, "it is over; forty thousand of them are dead; all their land belongs to us. But what good does all that do to me? I must die here." He begged mournfully: "Have you not a single drop of water?" The lieutenant shook his head: "You know I have none. Rest a little longer; it is night, and that will refresh us." The guardsman got up with difficulty and went with bent back down the slope to one side where there were some bushes. I said: "What does he want? I believe he is out of his senses and wants to search for water."

At that moment there came from the bushes into which he had vanished a noise of cursing, running, and leaping. Immediately he reappeared, holding by the hip a tall thin negro dressed in European clothing. He tore the negro's gun from his hand and, swearing at him in a strange language, dragged him up to us and said: "The wretch has a German gun, but no more cartridges." The guardsman had now become quite lively, and began to talk to his captive, threatening him and kicking him in the knees. The negro crouched, and answered every question with a great flow of words and with quick, very agile and remarkable gestures of the arms and hands. "He says he has not taken part in the war." Then he asked him some more questions, pointing towards the east; and the negro also pointed towards the east, answering all sorts of things of which I understood nothing. The guardsman said: "He is stuffing me with lies." This went on for some time. I can still hear the two dry, shrill voices of the German and the native. Apparently the guardsman at last learned enough, for he said: "The missionary said to me, 'Beloved, don't forget that the blacks are our brothers.' Now I will give my brother his reward." He pushed the black man off and said: "Run away!" The man sprang up and tried to get down across the clearing in long, zigzag jumps, but he had not taken five leaps before the ball hit him and he pitched forward at full length and lay still.

I grumbled a little; I thought the shot might attract to us the attention of hostile tribes who had perhaps stayed behind. But the lieutenant thought I meant it was not right for the guardsman to shoot the negro, and said in his thoughtful, scholarly way: "Safe is safe. He can't raise a gun against us any more, nor beget any children to fight against us. The struggle for South Africa will be a hard one, whether it is to belong to the Germans or to the blacks."

Source: Gustav Frenssen, *Peter Moor's Journey to Southwest Africa: A Narrative of the German Campaign* (London: Constable, 1908), 189–193, 204–205, 229–232.

Commentary

Germany's assault on the Herero and Nama peoples in the early part of the twentieth century initiated the century of genocide. In January 1904, in response to increasing German settler encroachments on Herero land, the Hereros rebelled with the intention of driving the Germans out of their territory. In what was considered to be an outrageous assault against German national pride, Kaiser Wilhelm II (1859–1941; reigned 1888–1918) replaced the colonial governor, Theodor Leutwein, with Lieutenant-General Lothar von Trotha, a commander already known for his brutality because of his fierce suppression of African resistance to colonization in German East Africa. When von Trotha arrived in South-West Africa on June 11, 1904, the war against the Hereros had already been in progress for five months, though the German forces had not been able to achieve much success against the guerrilla tactics of the Hereros. Von Trotha brought with him an army of 10,000 heavily armed men and a plan for war.

The plan called for the concentration of the Hereros in a central place that would be surrounded on three sides, with a fourth—the base of Waterberg Mountain—left open as a means of escape. The chosen site of salvation led into the Kalahari (Omaheke) Desert in eastern South-West Africa. The Hereros were to be harried and given no peace until, having been drawn deeper and deeper into the desert, they would expire by exposure, hunger, and, above all, thirst. It seemed as though everyone left alive in the entire Herero nation fled into the desert, en route to British Bechuanaland (modern-day Botswana).

The German forces were paid well to pursue the Hereros into this forbidding environment. Along the way they were also ordered to poison the few water holes they encountered. By August 14, 1904, however, they had returned to the Waterberg, with soldiers and horses suffering from exhaustion, hunger, and thirst. While subsequent efforts were made to resume the hounding of the Hereros, the plan was eventually abandoned at the end of September. Ultimately, owing to the inhospitable climate and terrain, it was deemed impossible to keep the troops and horses in peak condition.

The German military presence during the war comprised 11,000 soldiers of all ranks. Sickness was the primary cause of casualties, with some 57 percent on sick call due to the effects of lack of water and sanitation, as well as the effects of typhoid fever, malaria, jaundice, and chronic dysentery.

The account given by Peter Moor provides evidence of just how extensive this general malaise was. Throughout his statement, as indeed throughout his entire book, he grumbles continually about the heat, the thirst, and the fatigue accompanying his every step. While his physical ordeal was probably legitimate, it becomes somewhat tedious to read of his ongoing stress when we realize that the situation of the Hereros was clearly much worse. This is confirmed by Moor himself: "How deeply the wild, proud, sorrowful people had humbled themselves in the terror of death! . . . And there lay the wounded and the old, women and children. A number of babies lay helplessly languishing by mothers whose breasts hung down long and flabby. Others were lying alone, still living, with eyes and noses full of flies." Within this tragic scene, the German authorities saw the need to put people out of their misery. Thus, "somebody sent out our black drivers and I think they helped them to die"—that is, they were murdered. There is, of course, an irony here: the Germans, in this case, were using the dispossessed in order to kill others who were also dispossessed.

In another incident, Moor took part in an action in which several Hereros were ambushed. Four of them were killed immediately and another escaped, but "the sixth stood half erect, severely wounded. I sprang forward swinging my club; he looked at me indifferently." Following the man's death, Moor "wiped my club clean in the sand and threw the weapon on its strap over my shoulder." He was, however, unable to touch the weapon for the rest of the day. This suggests a particularly human dimension of killing: while he could shoot his victims from a distance through the impersonal means provided by a gun, he found clubbing a very personal and intimate act, which distressed him.

Despite this, it is clear that Moor had little regard for human life, other than from his own self-regarding point of view. When the Afrikaner accompanying his unit was begging for water—at a time when there was none to be had, and all the soldiers were equally thirsty—Moor observed that his lieutenant attempted to console the man: "Cheer up! We shall start at once. Then we are off for home, for the war is now really over." The Afrikaner's response was indicative of the attitude prevailing among the attackers: "Yes . . . it is over; forty thousand of them are dead; all their land belongs to us." Referring to his thirst, he then asked, "But what good does all that do to me? I must die here." The matter-of-fact way in which Moor describes this exchange is a solid indication of how he viewed life and death during the campaign.

The theme is continued a little later, when the same Afrikaner shoots a captive in the back after having already released him. Moor's response is one of disapproval—not, as he tells us, because of any moral qualms, but because he thinks the shot might attract enemy attention. His lieutenant takes it the wrong way, believing that Moor is expressing some sort of ethical condemnation. The lieutenant's response, instead, neatly encapsulates the German view of the entire war: "Safe is safe. He can't raise a gun against us any more, nor beget any children to fight against us. The struggle for South Africa will be a hard one, whether it is to belong to the Germans or to the blacks." It is, indeed, a succinct statement of rationalization by those representing a genocidal regime.

Questions

1. What was Peter Moor's greatest area of concern during his military experience: attacks from the Hereros or the possibility of catching disease?
2. What was Moor's attitude toward life and death? Did it change during his military service?
3. Do you think Moor ultimately found his experience as a soldier during Germany's conflict with the Hereros a rewarding one?

LOTHAR VON TROTHA

The German commander-in-chief of military forces in South-West Africa between 1904 and 1907, Lieutenant-General Lothar von Trotha had a single aim in mind for his role: to destroy utterly the Herero people, while at the same time crushing their rebellion and intimidating other local peoples into not following the Herero example. On October 2, 1904, he issued an order calling for the Hereros' extermination; in the three years that followed, not only was the Herero uprising put down, but the Herero people were effectively destroyed as a viable population. The account here depicts his "Vernichtungsbefehl" ("Extermination Order") and adds some of his other comments relating both to it and to the conflict in general.

I, the great general of the German troops, send this letter to the Herero People. Hereros are no longer German subjects. They have murdered, stolen, they have cut off the noses, ears, and other bodily parts of wounded soldiers and now, because of cowardice, they will fight no more. I say to the people: anyone who delivers one of the Herero captains to my station as a prisoner will receive 1000 marks. He who brings in Samuel Maharero will receive 5000 marks. All the Hereros must leave the land. If the people do not do this, then I will force them to do it with the great guns. Any Herero found within the German borders with or without a gun, with or without cattle, will be shot. I shall no longer receive any women and children; I will drive them back to their people or I will shoot them. This is my decision for the Herero people.

The Great General of the Mighty Kaiser

This order is to be read to the troops at quarters with the additional statement that even if a trooper captures a captain of the Hereros he will receive the reward, and the shooting of women and children is to be understood to mean that one can shoot over them to force them to run faster. I definitely mean that this order will be carried out and that no male prisoners will be taken, but it should not degenerate into killing women and children. This will be accomplished if one shoots over their heads a couple of times. The soldiers will remain conscious of the good reputation of German soldiers.

* * *

There is only one question for me: how to end the war? The ideas of the governor and the other old African hands and my ideas are diametrically opposed. For a long time they have wanted to negotiate and have insisted that the Hereros are a necessary raw material for the future of the land. I totally oppose this view. I believe that the nation as such must be annihilated or if this is not possible from a military standpoint then they must be driven from the land. It is possible by occupying the waterholes from Grootfontein to Gobabis and by vigorous patrol activity to stop those trying to move to the west and gradually wipe them out. . . . My knowledge of many central African peoples, Bantu and others, convinces me that the Negro will never submit to a treaty but only to naked force. Yesterday before my departure I ordered the execution of those prisoners captured and condemned in the last few days and I have also driven all the women and children back to the desert to carry the news of my proclamation. . . . The receiving of women and children is a definite danger for our troops, to take care of them is an impossibility. . . . This uprising is and remains the beginning of a racial war.

* * *

The mighty and powerful German Emperor will grant mercy to the Hottentot people and will spare the lives of those who voluntarily surrender. Only those who at the beginning of the uprising murdered whites or ordered others to do so will forfeit their lives in accordance with the law. I announce this to you and further say that those few who do not submit will suffer the same fate that befell the Hereros, who in their blindness believed that they could carry on successful war with the mighty German Emperor and the great German people. I ask you where are all the Hereros today, where are their chiefs? Samuel Maherero, who once called thousands of head of cattle his own, is now harried like a wild beast and driven over the border into English territory. He has become as poor as the poorest field Herero and possesses nothing. It is the same with the other chiefs, the majority of whom have lost their lives, and the Herero people too have been annihilated—part of them dying of hunger and thirst in the desert and part murdered by the Ovambos. The Hottentots will suffer the same fate if they do not surrender and give up their weapons. You should come with a white piece of cloth on a stick together with your whole village and nothing will happen to you. You will get work and receive food until the war ends at which time the Great German Kaiser will regulate anew the conditions in this land. He who believes that mercy will not be extended to him should leave the land for as long as he lives on German soil he will be shot—this policy will go on until all such Hottentots have been killed. For the following men, living and dead, I set the following price: Hendrik Witbooi – 5000 marks; Stürmann – 3000; Cornelius – 3000; for the other guilty leaders – 1000 each.

Source: German Federal Archives, Imperial Colonial Office, Vol. 2089, 7 (recto).

Commentary

Under General Lothar von Trotha's command, his 10,000-strong army advanced into Hereroland on three fronts, pushing the Hereros toward the desert while at the same time blocking their opportunities to escape. On October 2, 1904, he issued an order calling for the Hereros' extermination. In the three years that followed, not only had the Herero uprising been put down, but the Herero people, as previously understood, had effectively been destroyed. Prior to the uprising, by best accounts, the Herero population had numbered around 80,000; after it, no more than about 15,000 could be counted.

Some have asked whether or not von Trotha's actions constituted a new form of colonial warfare or if they were, in fact, genocide. To assess this, it is useful to consider the events occurring between 1904 and 1907. An important fact to note is that von Trotha arrived after the main part of the rebellion had already ceased. The Hereros rose up in the early months of 1904, but they were soon defeated by the technologically and tactically superior Germans. When von Trotha's force attacked the Herero encampment at Waterberg on August 11, 1904, many of the Hereros were there to sue for peace, not to engage the Germans militarily.

The German attack at Waterberg led to a massacre, but it was not the end of the affair. Von Trotha forced the survivors to retreat into the Omaheke Desert (that is, the Kalahari), where it was intended that they would die from hunger and thirst. The Germans set up a perimeter to ensure that no Hereros would manage to return from the desert, leading to a situation in which any Herero man, woman, or child was destined for death if sighted by the Germans. The subsequent campaign resulted in the notorious extermination order of October 2, 1904.

Von Trotha's "*Vernichtungsbefehl*" was quite explicit:

> The Hereros are no longer German subjects. . . . All the Hereros must leave the land. If the people do not do this, I will force them to do it with the great guns. Any Herero found with or without a gun, with or without cattle, will be shot. I shall no longer receive any women or children. I will drive them back to their people or I will shoot them.

In a supplemental order handed to his officers, von Trotha made a pretense to spare the Herero women and children by shooting over their heads so they would "run faster." However, that additional message seems to have been little other than a pretext to announce that the German army was full of men who do not kill women and children. Von Trotha confirmed this intention in a letter to his general staff, in which he claimed that diseases present among the Hereros were a potential danger to the Germans. This was, of course, simply an overt justification for the killing; his underlying racist attitude, though obvious to everyone, was not mentioned. Individuals who were never in a state of rebellion, such as women and children, were thus being persecuted to their destruction.

Looking at the language of von Trotha's order gives us little doubt that he intended to commit genocide. He was clear: he stated that if the Hereros did not leave as demanded, they would be forced to do so, after which any found would be shot on sight.

The language employed in von Trotha's statements is culturally arrogant and demonstrates total disdain for the Hereros. His words are also intended to demonstrate absolute power over a subject people, presuming some sort of an ordained right to kill. His description of the Herero leader Samuel Maharero (1856–1923), recognized by the German colonial authorities as the paramount chief of the Hereros, goes beyond simple propaganda. Von Trotha is not merely trying to demoralize the Hereros by remarking on the weakness of their leader; rather, he seems intent on their outright humiliation.

Von Trotha also extends his wrath toward the Nama. The Nama, from the southern part of the country, joined the rebellion alongside the Hereros, with devastating results. Following the military defeat of the Hereros, von Trotha turned his attention to quelling the Nama, and on April 22, 1905, he issued orders, in unequivocal terms, that the Nama should surrender or they would face immediate extermination if found at large in German-controlled areas. In short measure, over half the Nama, some 10,000, were murdered. Of those remaining, most were captured and confined in what the Germans referred to officially as *Konzentrationslager*, or concentration camps. Following the appalling carnage wrought on the Nama population, survival and slow recovery resulted in a regrowth of the overall Nama population, though the trauma remains in popular lore today.

Overall, it can be said that Lothar von Trotha's statements regarding the Hereros and the Nama were clearly declarations of genocidal intent. Statements such as "I believe that the nation as such must be annihilated"; "as long as [a rebel] lives on German soil he will be shot"; and "no male prisoners will be taken" are affirmations that von Trotha had no other intention but mass murder, with no quarter given. It is for this reason that he can be labeled the first *génocidaire* of the twentieth century, and a model that others, intentionally or not, would follow.

Questions

1. In your opinion, is von Trotha's "Extermination Order" a warrant for genocide? Why or why not?
2. Was there any opportunity in this account for the Hereros or the Nama ("Hottentots") to avoid their fate?
3. Overall, could it be said that von Trotha was responsible for war crimes, crimes against humanity, or genocide—or a combination of some (or all) of these?

HENDRIK FRASER AND DANIEL ESMA DIXON

When South Africa, acting at the request of the British government in 1918, produced a report detailing Germany's treatment of its colonial subjects in South-West Africa, a series of interviews took place with a variety of people who had witnessed the genocide of the Herero and Nama peoples between 1904 and 1907. The report provided an opportunity to take statements under oath from some 50 African witnesses and victims, as well as several others. These were later incorporated into the British government's Report on the

Natives of South-West Africa and Their Treatment by Germany. *Hendrik Fraser was listed as a "Bastard" (of the tribe of descendants of Cape Afrikaner men and indigenous African women), and hailed from Keetmanshoop. Daniel Esma Dixon, a transport driver, came from Omaruru.*

HENDRIK FRASER:

When I got to Swakopmund I saw very many Herero prisoners of war who had been captured in the rebellion which was still going on in the country. There must have been about 600 men, women and children prisoners. They were in an enclosure on the beach, fenced in with barbed wire. The women were made to do hard labour just like the men. The sand is very deep and heavy there. The women had to load and unload carts and trolleys, and also to draw Scotch-cart loads of goods to Nonidas (9–10 kilos. away) where there was a depôt. The women were put in spans of eight to each Scotch-cart and were made to pull like draught animals. Many were half-starved and weak, and died of sheer exhaustion. Those who did not work well were brutally flogged with sjamboks. I even saw women knocked down with pick handles. The German soldiers did this. I personally saw six women (Herero girls) murdered by German soldiers. They were ripped open with bayonets. I saw the bodies. I was there for six months, and the Hereros died daily in large numbers as a result of exhaustion, ill-treatment and exposure. They were poorly fed, and often begged me and other Cape boys for a little food. . . . The soldiers used the young Herero girls to satisfy their passions. Prisoners continued to come in while I was there; but I don't think half of them survived the treatment they received.

After six months at Swakopmund I was sent to Karibib towards the end of September 1904. There I also saw an enclosure with Hereros waiting for transport to Swakopmund. Many were dying of starvation and exhaustion. They were all very thin and worn out. They were not made to work so hard at Karibib, and appeared to be less harshly treated. . . .

In March 1905 I was sent from Karibib and accompanied the troops of Hauptmann Kuhne to the Waterberg. I then saw that the Germans no longer took any prisoners. They killed all men, women and children whom they came across. Hereros who were exhausted and were unable to go any further were captured and killed. At one place near Waterberg, in the direction of Gobabis, after the fight at Okokadi, a large number of (I should say about 50) men, women and children and little babies fell into the hands of the Germans. They killed all the prisoners, bayoneted them.

On one occasion I saw about 25 prisoners placed in a small enclosure of thorn bushes. They were confined in a very small space, and the soldiers cut dry branches and piled dry logs all round them—men, women and children and little girls were there—when dry branches had been thickly piled up all round them the soldiers threw branches also on top of them. The prisoners were all alive and unwounded, but half starved. Having piled up the branches, lamp oil was sprinkled on the heap and it was set on fire. The prisoners were burnt to a cinder. I saw this personally. The Germans said, "We should burn all these dogs and baboons in this fashion." The officers saw this and made no attempt to prevent it. From that time to the end of the rising the killing and hanging of Hereros was practically a daily occurrence. There was no more fighting. The Hereros were merely fugitives in the bush. All the water-holes on the desert border were poisoned by the Germans before they returned. The result was that fugitives who came to drink the water either died by poisoning or, if they did not taste the water, they died of thirst. . . .

DANIEL ESMA DIXON:

I was present at the fight at Gross Barmen, near Okahandja, in 1904. After the fight the soldiers (marines from the warship *Habicht*) were searching the bush. I went with them out of curiosity. We came across a wounded Herero lying in the shade of a tree. He was a very tall, powerful man and looked like one of their headmen. He had his Bible next to his head and his hat over his face. I walked up to him and saw that he was wounded high up in the left hip. I took the hat off his face and asked him if he felt bad. He replied to me in Herero, "Yes, I feel I am going to die." The German marines, whose bayonets were fixed, were looking on. One of them said to me, "What does he reply?" I told him. "Well," remarked the soldier, "if he is keen on dying he had better have this also." With that he stooped down and drove his bayonet into the body of the prostrate Herero, ripping up his stomach and chest and exposing his intestines. I was so horrified that I returned to my wagons at once.

In August 1904, I was taking a convoy of provisions to the troops at the front line. At a place called Ouparakane, in the Waterberg district, we were outspanned for breakfast when two Hereros, a man and his wife, came walking to us out of the bush. Under-officer Wolff and a few German soldiers were escort to the wagons and were with me. The Herero man was a cripple, and walked with difficulty, leaning on a stick and on his wife's arm. He had a bullet wound through the leg. They came to my wagon, and I spoke to them in Herero. The man said he had decided to return to Omaruru and surrender to the authorities, as he could not possibly keep with his people who were retreating to the desert, and that his wife had decided to accompany him. He was quite unarmed and famished. I gave them some food and coffee and they sat there for over an hour telling me of their hardships and privations. The German soldiers looked on, but did not interfere. I then gave the two natives a little food for their journey. They thanked me and then started to walk along the road slowly to Omaruru. When they had gone about 60 yards away from us I saw Wolff, the under-officer, and a soldier taking aim at them. I called out, but it was too late. They shot both of them. I said to Wolff, "How on earth did you have the heart to do such a thing? It is nothing but cruel murder." He merely laughed, and said, "Oh! These swine must all be killed; we are not going to spare a single one."

I spent a great part of my time during the rebellion at Okahandja, loading stores at the depot. There the hanging of natives was a common occurrence. A German officer had the right to order a native to be hanged. No trial or court was necessary. Many were hanged merely on suspicion. One day alone I saw seven Hereros hanged in a row, and on other days twos and threes. The Germans did not worry about rope. They used ordinary fencing wire, and the unfortunate native was hoisted up by the neck and allowed to die of slow strangulation. This was all done in public, and the bodies were always allowed to hang for a day or so as an example to the other natives. Natives who were placed in gaol at that time never came out alive. Many died of sheer starvation and brutal treatment. . . . The Hereros were far more humane in the field than the Germans. They were once a fine race. Now we have only a miserable remnant left.

Source: Union of South Africa, *Report on the Natives of South-West Africa and Their Treatment by Germany* (London: His Majesty's Stationery Office, 1918), 100, 66–67.

Commentary

On August 22, 1916, after the South African conquest of German South-West Africa in May 1915, a British Major, Thomas Leslie O'Reilly, was appointed as the military magistrate for the Omaruru District of central South-West Africa. He was later given the task of acting as the lead investigator for a Blue Book—that is, an official report containing specific information on a particular subject—on Germany's colonial record in South-West Africa. By the end of 1917, the report had been drafted, and in 1918, with the Great War seemingly coming to an end, the British government ordered the South African government to go ahead with the report's preparation. The subsequent *Report on the Natives of South-West Africa and Their Treatment by Germany,* prepared by the South African Administrator's Office in Windhoek in January 1918, was published in London by His Majesty's Stationery Office. The Blue Book was presented to both Houses of Parliament in London in August 1918.

The Blue Book was based on witness statements taken under oath, combined with numerous German colonial documents. This combination produced what is arguably one of the most damning documents of colonial history, an indispensable source document on the nature of German colonial rule in South-West Africa.

The accounts of Hendrik Fraser and Daniel Esma Dixon were two of those taken by the investigators. The descriptions of the hardships and atrocities committed against the Hereros could well have been written about the treatment of other victim peoples in situations of genocide. Each contains material emblematic of the suffering experienced under a regime of persecution.

Thus, when Hendrik Fraser describes the appalling situation of women who were yoked together and made to draw wagons "like draught animals," he is describing a situation that could have been seen in Ravensbrück under the Nazis in 1942. Or when, a little further along, he describes having seen six young Herero women who were "ripped open with bayonets" and murdered by German troops, he could have been describing a similar situation in Rwanda in 1994.

In a catalogue of horrific events, Fraser's account of the fate of some 25 Herero prisoners—"men, women and children and little girls were there" —is particularly gruesome. Placed in an enclosure made of thorn bushes, the soldiers cut dry branches and piled dry logs all around them, then added kindling and combustible material to the mix. He notes that the prisoners "were all alive and unwounded, but half starved." This human bonfire was then set ablaze, and, as Fraser testifies, the prisoners "were burnt to a cinder." He adds, "I saw this personally," and, "The officers saw this and made no attempt to prevent it."

After this, "there was no more fighting," which was not surprising considering that the military phase of the Herero Uprising had ended several months prior, and the German military was responsible by this point for harassing, mopping-up, and destroying Hereros wherever they could be found (owing largely to von Trotha's "extermination order" of October 2, 1904). From then on, "the killing and hanging of Hereros was practically a daily occurrence," and the Hereros "were merely fugitives in the bush."

Daniel Esma Dixon's accounts, in their way, are equally as grisly as those of Fraser. Witnessing the murder of an already-wounded Herero, he notes that the soldier who committed the murder "stooped down and drove his bayonet into the body of the prostrate Herero, ripping up his stomach and chest and exposing his intestines." This, clearly, was not conventional warfare, especially given that the wounded man lay face down and was in no position to be able to continue fighting. Dixon, the transport driver, writes, "I was so horrified that I returned to my wagons at once."

On another occasion, Dixon saw the cold-blooded killing of two elderly Hereros by a junior under-officer and a soldier under his command. When Dixon objected, his protest was met with laughter and the comment that "these swine must all be killed; we are not going to spare a single one."

Dixon spent much of his time during the rebellion at Okahandja, which in 1904 was a small but growing town in the central part of the country, near the meeting place between the Herero and Nama peoples. Here, "the hanging of natives was a common occurrence"; Hereros could be hanged without trial on the order of a German officer, even if the order was founded "merely on suspicion." Dixon witnessed one such hanging. Seven Hereros were hanged in a row, with the Germans using fencing wire. The situation would be repeated by their descendants, the Nazis, who were known to use piano wire for the execution of their most reviled victims.

Accounts of this kind, based on sworn testimony, provide evidence given by a witness who has made a commitment to telling the truth. The essential purpose of such a declaration is to recite the facts of a situation. In an inquiry such as that which led to the compilation of the Blue Book, the facts in question rely on individual memories. A government-appointed official wrote down the Blue Book testimonies.

Hendrik Fraser's testimony is somewhat straightforward and descriptive, with little in the way of concern about what was being done to the Hereros. As is required in the delivery of sworn testimony, he does his best not to intrude personally into the account he is delivering. Dixon's account, on the other hand, includes his efforts to help the Hereros and his expressions of disgust at what the Germans were doing before his very eyes. He concludes that the Hereros were more humane than the Germans as soldiers in the field, but, as he views it, "Now we have only a miserable remnant left."

In 1926, a year after Germany was readmitted to the world of "respectable" nations as a result of the Locarno Treaties, the British and South African governments ordered the destruction of the Blue Book as an act of reconciliation between British South Africa and the German-speaking population of South-West Africa. The main reason given was that the Blue Book had become an "embarrassment" in the new post-war environment.

Questions

1. Are the testimonies of Fraser and Dixon useful in helping to describe the German campaign in South-West Africa?
2. Describe Fraser's attitude toward the killing of women and girls. Can you identify how he feels about what he witnessed?
3. What is Dixon's view of German behavior toward the Hereros?

2. The Armenian Genocide

Genocide was committed against the Armenian population of the Ottoman Empire by the regime of the Committee of Union and Progress (*Ittihad ve Terakki Jemyeti*), also known as the "Young Turks," in the period following April 24, 1915. According to most accounts, at least one million—though, on the balance of probabilities, closer to one and a half million—Armenians were slaughtered as a direct result of deliberate Turkish policies seeking the Armenians' permanent eradication.

Massacres of Armenians had already been carried out by different regimes of the Ottoman Empire during two time frames, between 1894 and 1896 and in 1909. In the first, Sultan Abdul Hamid II (1842–1918; reigned 1876–1909) carried out a series of anti-Armenian pogroms, with the worst occurring in 1895. Estimates of those killed range widely, from 100,000 to 300,000, with thousands more maimed and rendered homeless. Most of those killed were men. The killings took place in open areas, in the full sight of the community, and they seemed to be designed to intimidate the Armenian population rather than destroy it wholesale. This was an attempt to quash talk of autonomy and the spread of a distinctive nationalist (perceived to be anti-Ottoman) identity.

The massacre of 1909, by contrast, which occurred in the region surrounding the city of Adana, was largely the result of civil strife between supporters of the sultan and the Young Turk reformers. Armenians appeared to be scapegoats for both sides. The Adana massacres claimed up to 30,000 victims. Both persecutions—the 1894–1896 massacres (also referred to as the "Hamidian Massacres," after the sultan) and the 1909 Adana massacres—seemingly prepared the Turkish population to accept the genocide that was undertaken from 1915 on. They must be seen as physical and psychological precursors to that event.

The reasons for the persecutions are varied. As the size of the Ottoman Empire shrank during the nineteenth century, conditions deteriorated for the Christian minority populations (Armenians, Assyrians, and Greeks), and they, along with the sultanate, became scapegoats for the deterioration of the Empire. With the weakening of the sultan's authority and respectability, a militant group of Turkish nationalists calling themselves the Young Turks) launched a revolution in 1908. Their goal was to create a modern, revitalized, and pan-Turkic empire that would stretch all the way to Central Asia. The revivified Turkish state would thus need to be modernized;

to achieve this, the Young Turks determined that the state would have to become militarized, industrialized, and much more nationalistic. Led by the triumvirate of Minister of Interior Mehmet Talaat Pasha (1874–1921), Minister of War Ismail Enver Bey (1881–1922), and Minister of the Navy Ahmed Djemal Pasha (1872–1922), the new regime instituted a plan that would devise an "inclusive-exclusive" approach for the Empire's future. This would leave out the Christian Armenians, Assyrians, and Greeks, fulfilling a strategy that would transform the multicultural Ottoman society into a much more homogeneous Turkish and Islamic one.

The year 1915 saw a massive military defeat for Turkey at the hands of the Russians at the Battle of Sarikamish (December 22, 1914 to January 17, 1915) in the Caucasus Mountains, followed by defeats in Egypt and Sinai in February. When, on April 25, 1915, British, French, Indian, Australian and New Zealand (ANZAC), and Newfoundland troops landed on the Gallipoli Peninsula, the Young Turk leadership feared that the regime—indeed, the Empire—was in peril. Earlier, on April 20, an Armenian revolt occurred in the city of Van, motivated by fears of deportation and certain death.

Under these tumultuous wartime conditions, the Young Turk government, feeling besieged and looking for a scapegoat, responded swiftly and forcefully. They implemented confidential plans that had been formulated in secret party meetings several months earlier. On the night of April 24, 1915—a date commemorated to this day as the Armenian Genocide Remembrance Day—some 250 Armenian leaders in Constantinople were arrested. Most would be murdered soon after their arrest, in an action that precipitated the genocide to follow. With these measures set in train, at a time when Turkish military forces were waging war against Russians in the northeast and British, French, and ANZAC forces at Gallipoli, scarce military resources were diverted to the campaign of murdering the Armenian and other Christian populations. These measures were far more extensive than any previous anti-Armenian massacres. All relevant government agencies now had the singular aim of totally destroying the Armenian population.

That the genocide took place under cover of war was more than just a coincidence. The war was, in reality, a crucial part of the genocide's so-called success. By conducting deportations of Armenians to places far off the beaten track, forcing many victims (primarily women and children, including babies) into underpopulated regions of the Empire, the Turks were able to exploit the war situation to achieve their genocidal aims. Technology, in the form of modern telecommunications and transportation, was employed in order to coordinate the killing activities and speed up the process, while other minorities supportive of the Turks' aims, in particular some Kurdish and Arab allies, assisted in carrying out the murders.

At the same time that the Armenian Genocide was taking place, the Young Turks also carried out genocides against two other Christian peoples in the Empire, the Pontic and Anatolian Greeks, and the Assyrians. As with the Armenian Genocide, a large proportion of the fatalities occurred as a result of death marches from homelands into the Syrian Desert. Most of those who died were the victims of heat, starvation and thirst, exposure, and incessant brutality at the hands of their captors. It might thus be more appropriate to refer to the Turkish campaign more broadly, calling it genocide against the Christian population of the Ottoman Empire rather than dividing the three national experiences into their constituent parts. After all, the three populations were subjected to the same experiences (massacre, deportation, dismemberment, torture, and other atrocities), largely for the same reasons based on difference. Whole cities were depopulated. When not killed outright, the inhabitants were deported to their deaths.

The eventual result was a loss of life, in a relatively short space of time, of what had hitherto been unimagined proportions. The worst of the killing was over within about 18 months, but this was only because the ferocity of the Turks' campaign led to a shortage of potential victims. This did not, however, stop the killing, and Armenian and other communities in various parts of the Empire, when they were found, continued to be attacked until the early 1920s.

SAYIED AHMED MOUKHTAR BAAS

Ottoman lieutenant Sayied Ahmed Moukhtar Baas, who, like many other Ottoman citizens, was against the genocide and even tried to save Armenians, was sickened by the atrocities he witnessed. In a document presented to the British War Cabinet on December 26, 1916, the account by Baas was described as a "Report by an Eye-Witness." As a report written by a Turkish officer involved in the genocide, the account has a special voice, given that Baas was opposed to the project from the start. Although the word genocide did not yet exist, there is little doubt that Baas held the view that what was happening fit all the criteria of complete group destruction.

In April 1915 I was quartered at Erzeroum. An order came from Constantinople that Armenians inhabiting the frontier towns and village be deported to the interior. It was said then that this was only a precautionary measure. I saw at that time large convoys of Armenians go through Erzeroum. They were mostly old men, women and children. Some of the able-bodied men had been recruited in the Turkish Army and many had fled to Russia. The massacres had not begun yet. In May 1915 I was transferred to Trebizond. In July an order came to deport to the interior all the Armenians in the Vilayet of Trebizond. Being a member of the Court Martial I knew that deportations meant massacres.

The Armenian Bishop of Trebizond was ordered to proceed under escort to Erzeroum to answer for charges trumped up against him. But instead of Erzeroum he was taken to Baipurt and from there to Gumush-Khana. The Governor of the latter place was then Colonel Abdul-Kadar Aintabli of the General Staff. He is famous for his atrocities against the Armenians. He had the Bishop murdered at night. The Bishop of Erzeroum was also murdered at Gumush-Khana.

Besides the deportation order referred to above an Imperial "Iradeh" was issued ordering that all deserters when caught, should be shot without trial. The secret order read "Armenians" in lieu of "deserters." The Sultan's "Iradeh" was accompanied by a "fatwa" from Sheikh-ul-Islam stating that the Armenians had shed Moslem blood and their killing was lawful. Then the deportations started. The children were kept back at first. The Government opened up a school for the grown up children and the American Consul of Trebizond instituted an asylum for the infants. When the first batches of Armenians arrived at Gumush-Khana all able-bodied men were sorted out with the excuse that they were going to be given work. The women and children were sent ahead under escort with the assurance by the Turkish authorities that their final destination was Mosul and that no harm will befall them. The men kept behind, were taken out of town in batches of 15 and 20, lined up on the edge of ditches prepared beforehand, shot and thrown into the ditches. Hundreds of men were shot every day in a similar manner. The women and children were attacked on their way by the ("Shotas") the armed bands organised by the Turkish Government who attacked them and seized a certain number. After plundering and committing the most dastardly outrages on the women and children they massacred them in cold blood. These attacks were a daily occurrence until every woman and child had been got rid of. The military escorts had strict orders not to interfere with the "Shotas."

The children that the Government had taken in charge were also deported and massacred.

The infants in the care of the American Consul of Trebizond were taken away with the pretext that they were going to be sent to Sivas where an asylum had been prepared for them. They were taken out to sea in little boats. At some distance out they were stabbed to death, put in sacks and thrown into the sea. A few days later some of their little bodies were washed up on the shore at Trebizond.

In July 1915 I was ordered to accompany a convoy of deported Armenians. It was the last batch from Trebizond. There were in the convoy 120 men, 700 children and about 400 women. From Trebizond I took them to Gumish-Khana. Here the 120 men were taken away, and, as I was informed later, they were all killed. At Gumish-Khana I was ordered to take the women and children to Erzinjian. On the way I saw thousands of bodies of Armenians unburied. Several bands of "Shotas" met us on the way and wanted me to hand over to them women and children. But I persistently refused. I did leave on the way about 300 children with Moslem families who were willing to take care of them and educate them. The "Mutessarrif" of Erzinjian ordered me to proceed with the convoy to Kamack (*sic*). At the latter place the authorities refused to take charge of the women and children. I fell ill and wanted to go back, but I was told that as long as the Armenians in my charge were alive I would be sent from one place to the other. However I managed to include my batch with the deported Armenians that had come from Erzeroum. In charge of the latter was a colleague of mine Mohamed Effendi from the Gendarmerie. He told me afterwards that after leaving Kamach they came to a valley where the Euphrates ran. A band of Shotas sprang out and stopped the convoy. They ordered the escort to keep away and then shot every one of the Armenians and threw them in the river.

At Trebizond the Moslems were warned that if they sheltered Armenians they would be liable to the death penalty.

Government officials at Trebizond picked up some of the prettiest Armenian women of the best families. After committing the worst outrages on them they had them killed.

Cases of rape of women and girls even publicly are very numerous. They were systematically murdered after the outrage.

The Armenians deported from Erzeroum started with their cattle and whatever possessions they could carry. When they reached Erzinjian they became suspicious seeing that all the Armenians had already been deported. The Vali of Erzeroum allayed their fears and assured them most solemnly that no harm would befall them. He told them that the first convoy should leave for Kamach, the others remaining at Erzeroum until they received word from their friends informing of their safe arrival to destination. And so it happened. Word came that the first batch had arrived safely at Kamach, which was true enough. But the men were kept at Kamach and shot, and the women were massacred by the Shotas after leaving that town.

The Turkish officials in charge of the deportation and extermination of the Armenians were: At Erzeroum, Bihas Eddin Shaker Bey; At Trebizond, Naiil Bey, Tewfik Bey Monastirly, Colonel of Gendarmerie, The Commissioner of Police; At Kamach, The member of Parliament for Erzinjian. The Shotas' headquarters were also at Kamach. Their chief was the Kurd Murzabey who boasted that he alone had killed 70,000 Armenians. Afterwards he was thought to be dangerous by the Turks and thrown into prison charged with having hit a gendarme. He was eventually executed in secret.

Source: National Archives, London, PRO FO 371/ /2768/1455/folios 454–458. Available online at http://www.armenian-genocide.org/br-12-26-16_1.html.

Commentary

The role of the Turkish military forces during the Armenian Genocide was both crucial and substantial. While the military leaders of the Young Turk party directed the genocide from the highest levels, it was the officers and soldiers "on the ground" who—willingly or unwillingly—had to carry out the orders they received. For many, the orders went beyond what a soldier's duty should be, prompting an order from Minister for the Interior Talaat Pasha, dated September 16, 1916, to government representatives in Aleppo. Referring to the fate of the Armenians up to that point, Talaat stated: "An end must be put to their existence, however criminal the measures taken may be, and no regard must be paid to either age or sex, nor to conscientious scruples."

Consequently, Turkish soldiers were ordered not only to arrest, contain, and transport Armenian civilians. They were also obliged to escort Armenian civilians, under arms, through cities, towns, and villages, through the desert, and to their ultimate deaths.

Soon, reports arrived on the desks of Allied and neutral officials, many of which were made public through the press or in government statements. Newspaper coverage of the genocide, while it was in progress, was ongoing and, because of a continuous supply of government information, detailed. In the British Parliament, information was discussed with some frequency; politicians often learned of events through their contacts in neutral countries such as Switzerland, the United States, and Spain, as well as through dispatches from the Foreign Office. Formal debates were sometimes organized, and papers were occasionally tabled in the House of Commons or House of Lords.

One such paper was the testimony of Lieutenant Sayied Ahmed Moukhtar Baas. Baas was more than just an eyewitness; he was in charge of a caravan of deportees, even though he, like many other Ottoman subjects, was actually opposed to the genocide. Certainly, he was under no illusions as to the promises, made by the authorities, that they would protect the deportees. He was highly aware of the forced nature of the deportation of women, children, and the elderly, and conscious of it becoming transformed into a death march accompanied by extreme violence and deprivation. These deportations seemed to be caravans to nowhere. Frequently, the deportees would just wander in the desert—under close military supervision—until they died of starvation, thirst, or exhaustion.

The testimony of Lieutenant Baas, as presented to the British War Cabinet on December 26, 1916, recounts almost all of the strategies used by the Turks to exterminate the Armenians. These included the murder of the intellectual and cultural leaders of the Armenian community, which first took place on April 24, 1915; the dissemination of military orders to kill Armenians; the "legalization" of the killings; the separation of women and children from the men; the mass killing of the men; the use of armed bands of civilians organized by the Turkish government to attack women and children; mass deportations of Armenians; and mass rape of Armenian women as a weapon of genocide.

There is a clear recognition that the word "deportation" was a euphemism. Baas, "being a member of the Court Martial," was aware that "deportations meant massacres," and with that in mind he considered the implication of the order that "all deserters when caught, should be shot without trial"—and the implication of a secret order substituting "Armenians" for "deserters." Further, "the children that the Government had taken in charge were also deported and massacred," a statement that places direct and unequivocal responsibility for such a reprehensible act at the feet of the government. To underpin his accusations of full government accountability, Baas finishes his account with a roll call of the Turkish officials who had local responsibility for the extermination of the Armenians.

Baas's account also brings up the issue of the willingness of the Armenians to believe the Turks' assurances that they would be safe. At the start of the deportation from Erzurum ("Erzeroum"), the Armenians brought their cattle and whatever possessions they could carry. The Vali (governor) of Erzurum assured them that "no harm would befall them." With such a promise, the Armenians proceeded, not knowing that the men and women of the first caravan had already been murdered.

Such deception is, of course, seen in many examples of genocide. The human instinct to hope often results in victims deceiving themselves into thinking that they will be safe and can trust the authorities, which perpetrators exploit to their own murderous advantage.

Mass murder was not only conducted by the regular army, another feature of the genocide we learn from Baas's account. Shostas ("Shotas"), irregular forces accompanying death marches, were given the authority to rape and dismember women. They were sent to ensure that the women and children progressed toward their final destination in the Syrian Desert, but Baas notes that they also engaged in "the most dastardly outrages" before "they massacred them in cold blood." As a final indictment, he notes that "the military escorts had strict orders not to interfere" with their vicious actions.

Interestingly, in view of the circumstances and the period, even the Turkish administration could find the behavior of the Shostas too much to bear. At Kemah ("Kamach"), a town in Eastern Anatolia, a Shosta headquarters was located. The Shosta chief, a Kurd named Murza Bey ("Murzabey"), "boasted that he alone had killed 70,000 Armenians," a record the Turkish authorities considered dangerous for discipline and morale. Murza Bey was imprisoned on the convenient charge of having struck a Turkish gendarme. He was later executed.

The value of Sayied Ahmed Moukhtar Baas's testimony lies in his disclosure of the full extent of the Turkish measures against the Armenians. His references to the many strategies employed by the Turks in the destruction of Armenian communities align with other eyewitness accounts from the time, which cover similar territory on the mass murder of Armenian civilians by Ottoman troops. The fact that Baas was a military officer with responsibility for carrying out the deportations gives his account added distinction, as perpetrator testimonies such as his are relatively rare.

Questions

1. In view of the fact that he was a perpetrator, why do you think Lieutenant Baas provided his testimony?
2. What was Lieutenant Baas's attitude toward the "Shotas," irregular militias sanctioned by the Turkish authorities?
3. Do you think that Lieutenant Baas should have been tried for crimes against humanity? Why or why not?

FRANCES GAGE

Frances Gage, an American who was the Young Women's Christian Association's secretary for Turkey, had been a university professor before she agreed to serve as a missionary in the heart of Asia Minor. Her work on behalf of the Armenians led to many lives being saved, and her letters and reports back to the United States, both unofficially and formally through U.S. Ambassador Henry Morgenthau, Sr. (1856–1946), raised awareness of the atrocities she had witnessed personally or learned about on the scene. What follows is part of a report written by Miss Gage. It was communicated to the U.S. State Department by the American Committee for Armenian and Syrian Relief, which in turn passed it on to the American Relief Committee.

About eight months after the beginning of the war, a notice was served on all Armenians that they must give up their arms. The reason for this was stated to be that there were so many more Armenians than Turks left in the country and that the nation was known to be revolutionary. This political difficulty was being anticipated by the Government, which was in no condition to meet an inter-racial revolution.

At other times, just before a massacre, arms had been demanded from the Armenians, and so when this order was given great fear took possession of the people. The Government promised in public and private that no harm should come to the Armenians, and that this was only a war measure and a legitimate protection to the nation. The Armenians, however, gave up their arms very reluctantly and very slowly.

But suddenly one night a batch of about 20 men were arrested and sent, after a day or two's imprisonment, to {Sivas}, the seat of the Vali for the whole province.

This was immediately followed by the imprisonment of other leaders among the Armenians of the city. These men were tortured cruelly. Meanwhile what was going on in {Marsovan} was being duplicated in all other cities. I saw some of the men who had been released, after they had been exhausted by torture. They had been thrown into a dungeon and kept without food, then beaten on their backs and the soles of their feet, and, when the flesh was sensitive, hot water had been poured on them and they had been beaten again—all this in order to make them reveal the whereabouts of the hidden arms. When they would not tell, they were made to kneel and their arms and feet were bound together; their mouths were filled with manure and all kinds of indignities were poured upon them. Some died under the process; many went mad. Eyes and nails were torn out. Some were let go, whether they had confessed anything that satisfied the Government or not, but many others disappeared entirely. This sort of inquisition went on until late June.

Some bombs were found in a field, and it is claimed that they had been hidden in the houses in the city and then, in fear, transferred to this field, where the Government soon afterwards found them.

The Missionaries approached the Government, asking that a Committee from the different Armenian communities—Catholic, Gregorian and Protestant—might be formed, to collect arms. The Government gave permission for this, and promised again that no trouble should be given to the Armenians if they gave up their arms. The Government told the Committee how many rifles ought to be delivered from that city, and claimed to know who had most of them. Representatives of the Committee spoke to the people in the churches, and promised that if they would deliver their arms to them their names would not be given to the Government. The requisite number of rifles were soon collected, but, almost immediately, the order for deportation was given.

First the men were taken, usually from their homes at night, and imprisoned in empty barracks. About 400 men were taken the first time. The next morning their families were notified that they were to be deported, and that, if they wished, they could furnish them with food and clothing. So the women got together their supplies and carried them to their husbands, hoping that they were providing for their needs on a long journey. They sold everything they could lay their hands on, and provided money for the men. After a few days the men were sent away. They were sent at night, bound in fours, about 50 a night. The barracks were continually filled with recruits from the city. I do not know what became of these men, but I do know that, within six hours of the city, there are long ditches and deep wells filled with the bodies of Armenians. Their clothing was taken from them, as well as those supplies that the women had so pathetically prepared, and all their money.

Officers of the Government have told our friends that the official figure for the number of men killed at {Marsovan} is over 1,300. People like to tell stories in Turkey, and it may be that this is not true.

On the 4th July the deportation order for the women came. It had been hoped that they would be allowed to remain. At the same time, it was publicly announced that people could save themselves if they would become Mohammedans. Large numbers, it is said 1,000 families, put in petitions to the Government. Only a small number of these petitions were accepted; the rest of the women and children were rapidly sent away.

Ox-carts were provided, and in some cases wagons, by the Government, but the people had to pay the carriage hire; if not, they had to walk. Some people could get donkeys, but, of course, the poor went on foot. It was difficult to get wagons and carts, and so the people were not all sent out at once. The Government scheduled the houses of those who were to go in each company, and gave them notice two or three days beforehand.

Sometimes they were taken in batches of from three to four hundred up to a monastery, about an hour from the city. Here they were imprisoned, and the Turkish men and women went to take away the women and girls who could be persuaded to become Turks and live in their harems. This was said to be the only way to save their lives, for they were all assured over and over again that, if they were not killed by the gendarmes or the wild villagers, they would die from the privations of the journey. . . .

It is generally understood that, on the 29th of August, an order went out from Constantinople to all the vilayets stopping the further deportations of the Armenians, but yet the deportation has been continuing ever since. Only four weeks before I left {Marsovan}, a company of young Armenian brides with their little boys, all of whom had become Mohammedans, were sent away. The order had come privately, not to the Governor but to the police, that women who had boys, no matter if they were babies in arms, should be deported with their children. Of that category there were perhaps three or four hundred in the city, and about 60 wagonloads were chosen out at this time to go. No warning was given to the people beforehand; the ox-carts were simply driven to their doors in the morning. They had made no preparation, and the women, especially mothers-in-law (who have a good deal of influence in this country) were very angry. They went to the Governor and said: "See! We have given our pearl necklaces to your wife in order to save our lives; we paid one hundred liras to be saved; we have become Mohammedans. We have sold our souls and have given our money, and now you take our lives. We will not go." One woman stood up on her cart and shouted all the Mohammedan prayers she had learned, to prove that she was a Mohammedan. It was a time of general frenzy. But they grabbed the women—bound them to the carts in many instances—and took them to the Armenian monastery. There they were imprisoned, but after much petitioning they finally got permission to send a representative from each family to the city to prepare food and get money for their journey. They sold their personal effects and in this way provided for themselves. This whole batch was killed in the mountains, on the other side of the city. Their birth certificates were found, and the burial had been so badly done that the bodies of little children were left on the ground, and the arms and legs of the corpses in the ditches protruded. Stories of this kind can, of course, be duplicated in all parts of the country, but I am only telling the things I can personally vouch for. . . .

Many stories of wonderful bravery are told of the people who went away. . . . In a mountain village there was a girl who made herself famous. Here, as everywhere else, the men were taken out at night and pitifully killed. Then the women and children were sent in a crowd, but a large number of young girls and brides were kept behind. This girl, who had been a pupil in the school at {Marsovan}, was sent before the Governor, the Judge and the Council together, and they said to her: "Your father is dead, your brothers are dead, and all your other relatives are gone, but we have kept you because we do not wish to make you suffer. Now just be a good Turkish girl, and you shall be married to a Turkish officer and be comfortable and happy." It is said that she looked quietly into their faces and replied: "My father is not dead, my brothers are not dead: it is true you have killed them, but they live in Heaven. I shall live with them. I can never do this if I am unfaithful to my conscience. As for marrying, I have been taught that a woman must never marry a man unless she loves him. This is part of our religion. How can I love a man who comes from a nation that has so recently killed my friends? I should neither be a good Christian girl nor a good Turkish girl if I did so. Do with me what you wish." They sent her away, with a few other brave ones, into the hopeless land. Stories of this kind can also be duplicated. . . .

Whatever may be said about the revolutionary intentions of the Armenian people, a rebellious nation is not executed by its government, but is fought in fair fight, and those of us who have loved the Turks and believed that they would, in the end, work out a government that could be respected, grieve almost more over this great failure of theirs than over the suffering of their unfortunate subjects.

Source: James Bryce and Arnold Toynbee, *The Treatment of Armenians in the Ottoman Empire, 1915–1916: Documents Presented to Viscount Grey of Fallodon by Viscount Bryce* (London: Hodder and Stoughton, 1916), 350–355.

Commentary

American missionaries operating throughout the Ottoman Empire witnessed anti-Armenian atrocities firsthand, and frequently worked to protect and save the lives of those being persecuted. They were the first foreign eyewitnesses of the genocide. Their actions helped to mobilize relief efforts back in the United States and elsewhere.

These Protestant missionaries were evangelizing to a community that was already Christian, trying to help reform and modernize its path to Jesus. Over time, given the extent of their network, the missionaries managed to create an extensive system of schools, orphanages, hospitals, and colleges for Armenians throughout the Empire. Americans staffed these institutions, which became rich repositories from which witness statements could emerge. In fact, missionaries were second only to U.S. consuls in the Ottoman Empire when it came to providing *in situ* accounts of the genocide. Despite the wartime situation, missionaries were permitted to remain in the Ottoman Empire until 1917, owing to the neutrality of the United States.

Almost every mission sent reports regarding anti-Armenian persecutions, frequently through the U.S. Embassy in Constantinople. Often, these were then forwarded to the Department of State in Washington at the behest of Ambassador Henry Morgenthau, Sr. The missionaries' reports were crucial in assisting the Armenians, as they generated influence in the United States that could result in assistance and expertise—particularly medical aid and humanitarian help—wherever such was permitted by the Turkish authorities.

Soon after war broke out in 1914, Viscount James Bryce (1838–1922), a British intellectual, ambassador, and politician, busied himself with collecting evidence of Turkish contraventions of international law. In 1915 the British government assigned him the task of gathering whatever could be found on the developing Armenian Genocide. Through his contacts in the U.S. State Department, he was able to tap into American dispatches from Constantinople, both formal and informal; these, together with other documents, Bryce entrusted to a young historian, Arnold Toynbee (1889–1975), to edit into a government Blue Book. The Blue Book was a devastating indictment of the deportation and extermination of the Armenian people at the hands of the Young Turk regime. Lord Bryce's collection was published as *The Treatment of Armenians in the Ottoman Empire, 1915–1916*, and was presented to the British parliament by the foreign secretary, Viscount Grey of Fallodon (1862–1933). Many of the documents in the collection included accounts from missionaries who witnessed the genocide.

When the Blue Book was first published, there were a number of blank spots that transmission had left incomplete, as the names of many people and places had been deliberately obscured in order to safeguard sources still in the Ottoman Empire. After an enormous forensic effort to track down these sources, British scholar Ara Sarafian pieced together a definitive edition in 2000. A second edition, from which the current account has been taken, appeared in 2005. As Sarafian filled in the gaps, he inserted "curly brackets" (that is, {}), which is how the text appears here.

Miss Frances Gage was one of the American missionaries whose correspondence was picked up by Ambassador Morgenthau and sent to Washington. A highly articulate woman, Miss Gage made observations and gave reports with much to offer. Right from the beginning of her account, for example, we see a number of strategies employed by the Turks in order to harass the Armenians. These included disarming the Armenian men, torture, and—in a common occurrence during the genocide—the expropriation of Armenian property and valuables. The genocide served as a means of redistributing wealth from the Armenians to the Turks, which created an incentive to Turkish peasants to participate in the killing.

After the men had been deported, it was the women's turn. Miss Gage notes that it had been hoped the women would be allowed to remain, and this seemed possible—on the condition that they converted to Islam. Sadly, she notes, this was a charade: while up to 1,000 families sought such a change to their status, only a small number of requests were actually granted. "The rest of the women and children were rapidly sent away" in ox-carts and wagons; those who used them were obliged to pay for the privilege or walk. Most of the women would die on the deportation journey, for "they were all assured over and over again that, if they were not killed by the gendarmes or the wild villagers, they would die from the privations of the journey." The consensus view was that the only way the women and girls could be saved was for them to convert to Islam, join Turkish families, then give themselves up to live in harems—that is, in sexual servitude.

The fate of these communities, of both men and women, is described in detail. Miss Gage's testimony charges the Turks with duplicity after the fact, in that they did not respect the conversions and instead continued harassing and killing Armenians in spite of their new status.

She describes the "many stories of wonderful bravery" on the part of the deportees. Her account of the young Armenian girl who refused to betray her faith and the memory of her family—all of whom had already been murdered—had already become legendary by the time of Miss Gage's report. In light of the suffering she witnessed, Miss Gage's final words are especially telling: "Those of us who have loved the Turks and believed that they would, in the end, work out a government that could be respected, grieve almost more over this great failure of theirs than over the suffering of their unfortunate subjects."

The missionaries were devastated, both physically and emotionally, by the genocide of the Armenians. During this encounter with the worst of human horrors, they worked valiantly to give succor to those whose care they had elected to uphold, but at every turn, not surprisingly, they faced opposition from the perpetrators. Knowing this only serves to place the account of Frances Gage into sharper relief, a point not lost on Ambassador Morgenthau, who saw fit to forward her dispatches to Washington in the hope that some greater good might come from them.

Questions

1. Given that Armenians belong to the oldest Christian nation in the world, do you think it was appropriate for Christian missionaries from western countries to be among the population before the genocide?

2. What were the implications of deporting women and children from Marsovan?
3. The story of the Armenian girl who refused to convert to Islam in order to save her life is the stuff of legends. Would you have done it? Why or why not?

SEVLY KRICKORIAN

Sevly Krickorian (née Kouyoumdjian) was born sometime in the spring of 1911, in the Armenian village of Jibin. As a child, she was given up for protection by her mother to a Turkish woman, who promised to safeguard Sevly's life for as long as she lived—the presumption being that the obligation would not be a lengthy one. The motive of the Turkish woman in making this offer is uncertain. Perhaps she made it out of pity, perhaps to obtain a daughter, or perhaps it was meant to gain a source of cheap household labor. Regardless, Sevly's life was saved through the woman's action. Interviewed in 1972 in Sydney, Australia (to which she migrated many years after her childhood experiences), Sevly shows a remarkable recollection of detail as seen through a child's eyes.

[At the start of the genocide] I was only a small girl, about four years old. I remember that a Turkish lady came to my mother and said to her: "Give me this child so I can look after her when you go. When you go 'there,' you're all going to die, but at least this child won't die." This much I know.

It was towards evening; my mother picked me up and gave me to this lady. The lady put me on her back and took me to her village. Four days later, I got the measles. The lady had two sons who were older than me. They said to her: "We don't want this *gavur* here. We're going to take this *gavur* and throw her into the Euphrates." The lady said: "She's sick. Wait until she dies, and then you can throw her in." They said: "No, we'll throw her in now." The river wasn't far away from the house, and so the lady told her sons: "Give her back to me, and I'll give it [her] to someone else." She fought with them to take me back, and then hid me in a little alcove in some rocks, just big enough for me to fit into. She put down hessian for me to sit on. To cover me, she put some rocks in front as a "door," so no one could see me and so that stray dogs could not get to me. I remained there but at the time I didn't know how long I would be there.

The children of my father's sister lived in the same village. My cousins were older than me, and knew where I was. They said "Let's go and see if Sevly's still alive." They came to the alcove; not only did they find me alive, but there were two dogs with me, licking my face!

Seeing that I hadn't died, my cousins returned home. The next day the Turkish lady came and put ointment onto my measles spots. She said "You're still alive. When you've died I'll throw you into the river." I stayed there for a month. My cousins told me this afterwards; this is how I know how long I was there for.

One day the Turkish lady came to see me again. Seeing that I was still alive, she decided to take me back home with her. But her sons still didn't like me being there. She had a small kitchen with no windows and no light. She wrapped me up in that place in potato sacks. I was still sick; altogether I remained sick for about a year. After this, wherever the Turkish lady went, she would put me on her back and take me with her. This kept me away from her two sons. She must have been a God-fearing woman; I don't know. But from then on, I would help her in her daily chores, while she would always protect me.

When I was about seven years old she said to me: "Go and get me some water from the Euphrates." I went down to the river with a little bucket, and saw things floating in the river. They looked like people floating, but that didn't register. There was another little girl next to me, and in Turkish I said to her: "What are these?" She responded: "These are *gavurs*." She said that when the Turks threw *gavurs* into the river, or people threw themselves in, they came floating down to here. The Turks would stand on the bank of the Euphrates with a hook on a stick, and drag the dead bodies to the shore to loot them. I saw this. If there was any gold, they would take it and then throw the bodies back in. After seeing this, I dropped my little bucket and ran into the water. The little Turkish girl said: "All the *gavurs* are going, you should go there too." She motioned with her hands the direction I should go.

So I screamed, and ran back crying to the Turkish lady. I just left the bucket somewhere in the water. When I told her I had lost the bucket, she came down with me to retrieve it. Pointing to the bodies, I said to the Turkish lady: "Mama, what are these?" She said: "These are *gavurs*." Then she took me home.

When I was eight years old, I had been there for four years. By this stage I didn't remember anybody from my family. I didn't know my mother or father or anyone else. One day I saw a lady come to the house. She wanted to hug me; she said: "I am your mother." I said: "I don't know you. This is my mother," pointing to the Turkish lady. She tried very hard to get me to come to her and hug and cuddle her, but I kept running back to the Turkish lady's side. My mother came back three or four times, but the Turkish lady didn't want to give me up, either. When my mother came back the fourth time, the Turkish lady said: "She was sick for a year and I took care of her. Now she belongs to me."

My natural mother's name was Goldie. The next time she came, she brought some candy with which to try to bribe me. She told the Turkish lady: "I concede that she's yours. But can I take her for a couple of days? I'll bring her back." The Turkish lady said: "Since you're desperate, you can take her for a couple of days and then bring her back." Remember, I'm eight years old. I know what's happening. I said to my natural mother in Turkish, "are you going to bring me back in two days' time?" Goldie said, "If you can see behind your ear, I'll take you back home." The Turkish lady let me go for a couple of days. I was crying, and tried to look behind my ear so I would go back. Then I was on the road out of the village.

When I realized that I was not going to go back, I cried. Goldie took me to her little house. There was nothing in it. The Turks had taken away everything. We slept on grass matting. The next day the Turkish lady and her two sons came to take me back. Goldie convinced them that I would only stay with her for a couple of days, so they went away again.

In Aintab, where we were, there were donkey-drawn carts going back and forth all day carrying people; there were no buses in those days. Goldie, looking for a way to escape with me, sent word to my step-brother Jack (Hagop), saying: "I rescued your little sister from these people. They are trying to take Sevly away from me. I need to find an escape route to get her out of here." Jack immediately wrote back: "Don't dilly dally, send her here to the Aintab orphanage." My godfather then tried to smuggle me onto a donkey taking a load through Aintab, but it didn't work—so he agreed to take me on his back to the orphanage in Aintab.

This was a two day journey from the village where we were. But when we arrived and he handed me over to Jack, he learned that all the orphanages were already full of displaced children. After a desperate search, he found a refuge (not an orphanage) for women and children who had been ravished by the Turks. This was a reception center for displaced people. You only got food once a day, and the camp was packed to the brim. Many of these people had come from previously affluent families, but they were now crammed into this awful space.

Jack managed to leave me there for safety's sake. Fortunately, the doorkeeper was a relative, a cousin. Jack entrusted me to the care of an older Armenian woman, a widow, and left. I don't know how long I was in that camp.

One day Jack arrived and said to me: "Come with me, little sister. I've found an orphanage for you." In that orphanage I was safe and happy. We eat, we drink, we sleep comfortably. We know we've been rescued from the atrocities. Then, out of the blue, bombs came. Aintab was attacked. The war against the Armenians had arrived in Aintab, as the Turks began dropping bombs onto the orphanages. The Turks knew the orphanages contained women and children, and they were trying to kill us in order to make sure the Armenians wouldn't breed into the next generation. We children were herded into underground cellars for safety. Here, there was little food. All we had were small quantities of raisins—and a single walnut for each child. The baking kilns were outside, so we couldn't get any bread, nor could we get any water. I don't know how long we stayed in these bunkers.

Soon after this it was decided to evacuate Aintab. We had to wait until sunset. They gave us special sandals for our feet and on our backs a sling bag, into which they put food which we were to eat on the road: koftas, walnuts and some raisins. Our transport was carts used by stonemasons, into which were placed ten girls and one adult for supervision. We had to travel through a cemetery, each of us in a line as we passed through. It was very emotional, but we sang a made-up song to keep our spirits up and give us courage. I don't remember it exactly, but the gist of it was "Bad Turks, go away," or something like that.

We had gone some distance when we got word that the bridge we had to cross into safety had been pulled down, and we were surrounded. We were taken out of the carts and sent up a nearby hill to hide. With us were other families, including men. By daylight the able-bodied men had repaired the bridge enough to enable us to cross, carts and all, with us inside them again.

The Chetes, local militia forces employed by the Turks, were now after us, too. We knew the Chetes were out to kill us. Then we saw four Allied planes above us; they bombed the Chetes, and we managed to continue our journey. We went to Kilis, a village in Cilicia, and they put us in a church—there were no beds and nothing to cover us, but we got lovely fresh bread and cheese, brought by the Armenian townsfolk of Kilis. That night we slept under the columns of the Armenian Church.

In the morning we woke up and were told we would be catching a train to Aleppo. Two days later, we boarded the trains, but we didn't travel in the carriages; we were in the wagons set aside for donkeys and cattle to travel in. It was about dawn when we arrived in Aleppo. We thought that would be our final destination, but, staying only one night, we passed through it instead en route to Beirut. When the people of Aleppo heard that the orphanage children had been saved, and they came out to greet us with lots of food for the trip. We ate with happiness. We didn't know how much food we could consume; we were just so happy to eat.

The next morning, we continued on to Beirut. When we got there, there were no houses for us, just big tents. Each and every one of us was given something to drink (I didn't know what it was, but we had to drink it; I think it was a medicine of some sort). For the next twenty-four hours, we all slept. Maybe that's what the drink was, a sleeping potion of some sort. We were all so scared, all nervous and frightened, that we needed something to calm us. . . . Soon we moved to a proper orphanage. . . .

This is my life. But what my mother went through was tenfold worse.

Source: Interview by Hasmig Ziflian with Sevly Krickorian, Chatswood (Sydney, Australia), 1972, in the possession of Mrs. Krickorian's granddaughter, Silva Nercessian. Translation by Silva Nercessian, July 8, 2012. Used by permission of Silva Nercessian.

Commentary

Sevly Krickorian's testimony describes an occurrence that was not uncommon during the Ottoman Genocide of the Armenians (or indeed, during any genocide)—namely, the surrender by mothers of their children to members of the perpetrator group, in the hope that this would spare the child's life.

At the beginning of Sevly's account we are told that she was only a four-year-old child. This immediately brings up a matter of both interest and concern: how much could one so young both take in the events around her, and recall them later? The account occurs between the ages of what she identifies as four and eight (though the ultimate age of nine is more likely, given the context). We can, perhaps, expect that some of the things she recalled as she got older had a greater sense of authenticity for Sevly than their reality reflected. On the other hand, traumatic images can certainly stay in the forefront of memory for even the youngest children—and there can be no doubt that Sevly faced some harrowing moments.

The threat to her life was surely one of these. While being handed by her mother to "the Turkish lady" did not appear to be anything out of the ordinary for Sevly (perhaps suggesting that the two women had known each other previously), Sevly certainly recalled the tug-of-war between "the Turkish lady" and her two sons over her fate. Although the details might have blurred over time, Sevly could also have retained the vivid memory of being deposited, sick, in a rock fissure.

Beyond that, we are left to wonder how Sevly responded to both separation from her birth mother and adoption by "the Turkish lady." From the perspective of historical distance, we see from this one example that not all Turks were bloodthirsty killers (as often portrayed), as "the Turkish lady" was willing to look beyond stereotypes of race or religion in order to save the child's life. Sevly even forgot her birth mother (who, as we learn, was named Goldie), and eventually called "the Turkish lady" Mama.

The other important recollection we have of Sevly's experience relates to her awareness of the difference between herself and those around her. She knew, because she was told continually, that she was a *gavur,* an offensive, derogatory name employed by Muslims in Turkey for non-Muslim "infidels." This term is used a number of times in Sevly's account, indicating that she was aware that it meant her relative to everyone else. When she visits the river and is confronted by a mass of bodies in the water, she is able to recognize that the fate of *gavurs* is death. She understands that this will also mean her at some point.

Sevly's recollection of the time her mother returned to reclaim her is remarkable for its level of detail, but, given the nature of oral testimony, it is probably ex post facto in several instances. Nonetheless, by the time she was older the images in her memory might well have been retained vividly.

Recalling the bombing of Aintab, for example, is likely to have been undemanding, even if the details were skewed. The so-called Siege of Aintab was a military engagement between Turkish Nationalist forces and those of the French army. It lasted from April 1920 until the city's capitulation in February 1921, and it did involve bombing of the kind described by Sevly. However, there had already been substantial anti-Armenian measures adopted by the Turks two years prior, with one contemporary account from April 1918 describing the depopulation of the city's Armenians. Sevly's recollection of the Chetes (irregular Turkish militia forces) might have come from this earlier time.

Moreover, as Sevly was undergoing her final evacuation to safety in Lebanon, she recalled passing through the southern Turkish city of Kilis, from which she boarded a train to Aleppo, then Beirut. The direction would have been accurate, though it might only have been the names of the towns that Sevly recalled.

Thus, through a child's eyes, it is likely that the order of events could have become mixed up somewhat. But Sevly's account provides enough detail that readers can attempt to make some sort of sense of the horror that ensued.

The main elements of Sevly's story are the small points of memory that would stay in the mind of a child growing to maturity: ointment, bucket, river, *gavurs*, donkey-cart, orphanage, raisins, "a single walnut," stone-mason's cart, fear. Broader issues might or might not also have been present, but details could well have been conveyed to Sevly later, either by others (for example, her cousins) or through subsequent knowledge transmitted in other ways.

From a historical point of view, we are reminded in Sevly's testimony of the establishment of orphanages to shelter Armenian children both during and after the genocide. This key piece of data plays an important role in the history of the Armenian Genocide, as it was in these orphanages that the majority of the genocide survivors—that is, the children—sought sanctuary. At first in the outlying regions of southern Anatolia, then, increasingly, in Lebanon, thousands of Armenian children found themselves freed from continued persecution. Although inadequate from a modern perspective, these places were all they had, which is no small matter in a time of war, persecution, and the aftermath of both.

Sevly's account, while problematic in a number of ways (the most important of which is the quality and extent of her childhood recollections), is nonetheless highly evocative of the period of the genocide. It captures something of the horror experienced by a small girl in response to the events swirling around her. It is also a deeply intimate recounting of a single experience, which, regardless of its complications, is nevertheless another tiny piece in the jigsaw that can help us to generate some small measure of understanding.

Questions

1. Do you think Sevly's young age presents any problems regarding accuracy of her account? What might they be?
2. Why do you think "the Turkish lady" agreed to take Sevly in?
3. Sevly experienced many threatening situations. What, in your view, was the singular event that saved Sevly's life?

GRIGORIS BALAKIAN

A priest and later bishop in the Armenian Apostolic Church, Grigoris Balakian (1875–1934) was one of 250 Armenian community leaders from Constantinople who were arrested and deported by the Ottoman Turkish government on April 24, 1915. The event precipitated the Armenian Genocide. His memoir, Armenian Golgotha, *was translated into English in 2009 by his great-nephew Peter Balakian (b. 1951) and Aris Sevag (1946–2012), bringing to a broad audience one of the most important eyewitness accounts of the genocide. Balakian was one of the few surviving leaders of the Armenian community able to provide an account of the deportations as they were both endured and observed.*

By giving the customary bribe, I managed to get special permission to go into town again, unattended by a police soldier, in order to purchase things our companions had requested.

Wanting a bowl of soup, I went into a Greek restaurant that faced the railroad station. As it was long before noon, I had to wait quite a while, since nothing had been prepared yet. Sitting in a corner next to a window, I was observing the passersby, looking for Armenian survivors, when a little hand that was reduced to skin and bones suddenly passed through the half-open window. It was the hand of an eight-year-old boy whose skin had turned to black leather from the desert sun. He was not only bare-headed and barefoot but practically naked, for the rags hanging from the poor lad's shoulders didn't cover half his body.

He was obviously starving; his skin bore the yellow spots characteristic of those dying from hunger. His facial features had become so disfigured that he looked more like a monkey than a human being. In fact, this was not a human being but a human ghost, resurrected from the grave; a desiccated, moving shadow. Even those like us on the road to Der Zor, deserving no less sympathy, would have had to pity this hapless boy. As we were heading toward our graves, this living skeleton seemed to be returning from his. . . . In a barely audible voice he begged in Turkish, "Give ten paras for the souls of your deceased ones" [*Effendi, olurerin jane ichun on par aver*]. Yes, he had returned from the grave and was begging for a crust of bread in the name of the dead. . . .

I was so moved that, despite thinking that this poor little boy was an orphaned Muslim, I gave him five piasters so he wouldn't disappear from my sight . . . for my tormented soul couldn't take seeing him anymore; and then I thought I too would be like this tomorrow. But I had barely put the money into his hand when he raced over to his sister, who had been waiting just ten steps away, and shouted with all the breath he could summon, "Zarug, the priest [*Der baba*] gave me five piasters. Go over to him—he'll give you money, too, for sure!"

I was pierced with grief, for the little boy I had taken for a Muslim turned out to be Armenian . . . and the shriveled-up shadow standing off in the distance, barely twelve years old, was his sister, Zarug. . . . She could hardly stand, swaying like a stalk of wheat. Encouraged by her little brother Hagop, she slowly walked toward the window and, in turn, extended her leathery, bony hand, saying, "*Der babas,* give ten paras for the souls of your deceased ones . . . we haven't eaten anything for two days." Like her brother, the little girl was a living skeleton, a moving shadow, who might be able to drag her worn-out body around for another day or two.

For the sake of truth, I must mention that she was practically naked; the remnants of a dress hanging off her body didn't even cover her private parts, and the lascivious Turkish passersby made fun of her nakedness, uttering lewd curses. . . . The innocent little girl was telling me all this as she was crying.

After looking around and making sure that there were no Muslims in the restaurant—as a matter of fact, there was no one else there because of the hour—I invited the two orphans to come to my window, and I asked them questions. Little Zaruhi related the following, in a schoolgirl's proper Armenian, of which this is a brief summary.

> *Der baba*, my brother and I are natives of Adapazar; my father was a merchant and one of the city's prominent men. I was attending the Hayuhyats [Armenian girls' school]; there were fourteen members of our family: my father, my mother, my sisters, my brothers, my maternal aunts and maternal uncles. All of them, in turn, died in exile, especially in Islahiye, and there are only the two of us left . . . how I wish [*keshge*] we hadn't survived. . . .

Unable to continue, she began to cry, sobbing. Her little brother Hagop said, "Don't cry, Zarug," and encouraged her [to continue]. "Oh, *Der baba,* we too were rich; we had houses, stores, and gardens. Now we don't have anything, and my brother and I live by begging." At this point two Armenian soldiers with sunburned faces entered the restaurant, greeted me, and came over and sat down. They had come from Der Zor and were coachmen in the military administration. I continued asking questions, and Zarug continued her story.

> Oh, my *Der baba,* wherever we went, they threw us out. Through the windows we would enter the houses left empty by Armenians and sleep there at night, but now those houses are filled with Turkish refugees, so we go to the stables of the *khans* and bury ourselves in the refuse and sleep. But often they don't let us sleep in those places either, and so we go and bury ourselves in the dry garbage dumped in the gardens to sleep, with just our heads showing. When winter came, there were many Armenian orphans trying to live by begging; however, all of them died and we are the only ones remaining. Now I am too sick; I got it from the Turkish

youths and now I have no energy and am done for. . . . Oh, *Der baba,* can't you send us back to Adapazar? We have many properties; we can make a living there. Wherever we go, the Turks throw us out. If you can't send us back, take Hagop and me wherever you go so we can be free from this place; we would want to eat the scraps in the streets but now the dogs won't let us.

While this forlorn orphan was telling her story, one of the two Armenian soldiers, a native of Malatya, began to cry, like a boy having been bastinadoed: "If one of my children has survived," he exclaimed, "who knows where he is begging like these. . . . My God, what a deplorable state we have reached! They've made us worse than the Gypsies."

So moved were we by these children that we hadn't noticed the many customers of various nationalities who had entered as lunchtime approached and were watching in amazement. After we gave what money we could to the two orphans, we sent them on their way, convinced that a few days later our paths would meet in eternity.

I was then left alone with the two Armenian soldiers, who expressed amazement at their luck in finding an Armenian clergyman still alive. . . . The one from Malatya, a brave young man, fairly educated, told me the following:

Hayr sourp [Reverend Father], what can I say? It's what is known to everybody. Don't think that there are any Armenians left, and if there are any hanging on, they won't last. . . . It's true, the Turks are finished, but these detestable people have finished us off too, along with themselves.

How can I tell you so that you will understand? It is impossible for human language to describe what those who went to Der Zor experienced. Thousands of families put on the road from Aleppo, to be sent to Der Zor; of these, not even five percent reached Der Zor alive. Because bandits in the desert, called Yeneze, in groups on horseback and armed with spears, attacked these defenseless people; they killed, they abducted, they raped, they plundered, they selected those appealing to them and carried them off, subjecting those who resisted to horrific tortures, before picking up and leaving. Because it was forbidden and impossible to turn back, those who survived had no choice but to go forward and were subjected to new attacks and plundering. Not even five percent reached Der Zor.

We saw caravans of women, completely naked because the Yeneze bandits who greeted the caravans had taken even their undergarments. We came across thousands of corpses as naked as the day they were born and with eyes gouged out; all their limbs had been cut off for sport and their bodies swollen; their entrails were spilled out; during the daytime, the vultures would descend on these corpses and feast, while it was the wild animals' turn at night. Reverend Father, where is the God of the Armenians? . . . Where is the Jesus you preach about? . . . Could it be that he doesn't see this unheard-of wretchedness and suffering?

If these stones, fields, and desert sands could speak, what stories they would tell. . . . If only you had been here and seen the tribulations of the Armenian people! . . . Reverend Father, they killed people who were hungry and thirsty. . . . They sold God's water for money only to those who could pay a lot. . . . The poor people were willing to drink even fetid water, and even this water was sold for money. And wasn't it their intention to kill us anyway!

Now I'll tell you, but you won't believe it, that while transporting goods across the deserts by military vehicle, many, many times I saw half-naked women and children gathered around dead and stinking animals or camels, and eating the corpses. . . . I saw mothers gone mad who had thrown their newly deceased little children into the fire then eating them half cooked or half raw . . . and those who ate rotten corpses got poisoned and died.

I asked him whether there weren't police soldiers with the caravans of deportees to defend them. He replied, "What are you saying? It was the police soldiers accompanying the deportees who sent word to the bandits and then joined in with them. The police soldiers robbed the helpless people and directed the bandits to the beautiful girls, as well as to those with gold or diamond jewelry and coins.

"Reverend Father, it's a shame for you to throw your life away at such a young age. Don't go beyond this point; look after yourself. It's a shame for you and the nation both. As it is, there are so few of us left." . . .

Yes, it was necessary to flee. All those who had tried to convince me that those who had fled had managed to stay alive were right.

For sure, taking just one step forward was foolish; determination was required. What I had seen and heard that day convinced me that I had to take advantage of opportunity. I had decided to flee; now I had to follow through, because there was no time to waste.

Therefore, I got to work planning my escape, occupying myself with the most tediously minute details, for I knew that a seemingly insignificant detail could abort the most serious plan. If I failed to escape, clearly I would end up dead.

Commentary

The generally recognized date on which the Armenian Genocide began is April 24, 1915. This was the night when approximately 250 Armenian intellectuals and community leaders were arrested in Constantinople and moved by Minister of the Interior Talaat Pasha to two holding centers near Ankara. They included clergymen, physicians, editors, journalists, lawyers, teachers, and politicians. Under the so-called Tehcir Law of May 27, 1915, which authorized the deportation of the

Ottoman Empire's Armenian population, they were expelled into the Syrian Desert. Most did not survive.

During the genocide that followed, an estimated 4,000 Armenian bishops and priests were murdered. The full force of the anti-Christian measures fell on the Armenian Apostolic Church, the Armenian national church (and the world's oldest). Among the other Christian communities, the Armenian Catholic Church would see 19 eparchies (dioceses) and hundreds of Catholic churches, missions, schools, monasteries, and convents destroyed. Bishops, priests, nuns, and as many as 100,000 Armenian Catholics died.

Grigoris Balakian, a *vartabed,* or celibate priest, in the Armenian Apostolic Church, was born in Tokat, a city in the mid-Black Sea region of northern Anatolia. Sanassarian College, from which he graduated, was his jumping-off point for the higher degree in civil engineering he later obtained in Germany. On the night of April 24, 1915, he was among those arrested in Constantinople.

Over the next four years, Balakian made it his priority to record what he saw and heard. The need to bear witness would be one of the major motivations behind his resolve to stay alive—he intended to recount his observations after the horror had come to an end and justice could, hopefully, proceed.

The first line of Balakian's account suggests a society in which, if genocide or persecution did not necessarily prevail, at least corruption did. By giving "the customary bribe," Balakian was able to leave his confinement and enter a more populated area unguarded. This gave him access to travel; it also allowed him to obtain much-needed items that assisted him in his struggle to stay alive. Once in the town, he entered a realm where accounts of starvation, torture, and death ruled. The tragic story of the little boy and girl he encountered was compounded by the social status from which they came: "My father was a merchant and one of the city's prominent men" in the densely populated northern Anatolian city of Adapazari. Emphasizing their tragedy was how far they had fallen, as Zaruhi, the little girl, testified: "We too were rich; we had houses, stores, and gardens. Now we don't have anything, and my brother and I live by begging." This memory was, of course, of little comfort. Orphaned, starving, and the only remaining members of a much larger family, these children only had each other left. Because of their debilitated state, their future seemed dubious, at best.

Fr. Balakian was among the deportees who were marched in the direction of Deir ez-Zor in the Syrian Desert. This was known as the final destination for many of the deportation caravans. It was here that scores of thousands of Armenian men, women, and children were systematically murdered during 1915 and 1916. In his account, Balakian engages in discussions with two Armenian soldiers serving as coachmen in the military administration. (How they had survived to this point, and in government service, is not explained.) They had come from Deir ez-Zor, and from them he learns the true horror of what has been happening to the Armenian deportees.

The testimony they offer, in the words of one of the soldiers, depicts how "impossible" it was "for human language to describe what those who went to Der Zor experienced." The horrors the soldiers then proceed to relate were, indeed, shockingly graphic. These included references to "not even five percent" of those sent to Deir ez-Zor reaching their destination alive; to "these defenseless people" being killed, abducted, raped, and plundered; to "caravans of women, completely naked" because "bandits had taken even their undergarments"; and to "thousands of corpses as naked as the day they were born and with eyes gouged out; all their limbs had been cut off for sport and their bodies swollen; their entrails were spilled out; during the daytime, the vultures would descend on these corpses and feast, while it was the wild animals' turn at night."

In a rare discussion—or condemnation—of religion, one of the soldiers then challenges Father Balakian regarding any divine purpose in the Armenians' suffering: "Reverend Father, where is the God of the Armenians? . . . Where is the Jesus you preach about? . . . Could it be that he doesn't see this unheard-of wretchedness and suffering?" Such a comment, within the context of the devout Armenian religious tradition, may be considered unusual, but given what these soldiers had witnessed, it is obvious that they were in a state of shock: "If these stones, fields, and desert sands could speak, what stories they would tell." Among those stories would be one of how, "while transporting goods across the deserts by military vehicle, many, many times I saw half-naked women and children gathered around dead and stinking animals or camels, and eating the corpses." Another would be a reference to "mothers gone mad who had thrown their newly deceased little children into the fire then eating them half cooked or half raw."

One of the biggest ongoing questions relates to the Turks' ultimate ambition. As one of the soldiers asked, "Wasn't it their intention to kill us anyway?" Further, although "the Turks are finished," they had "finished us off too, along with themselves."

After this, Fr. Balakian had one final revelation: he would have to flee both in order to save his life and to serve the remnants of the Armenian nation. As he saw it, "If I failed to escape, clearly I would end up dead." As it turned out, Balakian's efforts to stay alive paid off. He witnessed immense savagery, rape, forced conversion to Islam, and the theft of Armenian property. Learning about the government's plan to exterminate the entire Armenian population, he worked on various projects on the Baghdad railway. He was helped by German engineers, and he finally succeeded in escaping from Constantinople to Paris.

His full testimony, *Armenian Golgotha*, was written in Armenian in Vienna in 1922 and translated into French in 2002. An English version, recognized as a much more accessible (and definitive) firsthand account of the genocide, appeared in 2009, to much acclaim around the world.

Questions

1. Was the experience of the children in Fr. Balakian's account believable? Why or why not?
2. In the discussion Fr. Balakian had with the two soldiers, what clues do we find that the Turks' ultimate ambition was the annihilation of the Armenians?
3. What finally prompted Fr. Balakian's decision to flee? Why do you think he had not done so earlier?

WILLIAM S. DODD

Dr. William S. Dodd was the chief physician of the American Red Cross hospital in Konya, located in a semi-arid region of central Anatolia. In this letter from Dodd to U.S. Ambassador Henry Morgenthau, Sr., dated September 8, 1915, he attempts to describe conditions in the town and in nearby Eregli. So taken was Ambassador Morgenthau by the content of the letter that he transmitted it to the State Department in Washington, D.C., to the attention of the secretary of state.

The conditions are so bewildering here that it is hard to know how to present a general view of the situation. The deportation is still going on in full force, and yet shows unaccountable stoppages and delays. I suppose that the *vis a tergo* emptying out the population is so out of proportion to the executive ability to keep the channels of travel open that the result is this great damming back of the current that has filled the cities from Eski Shehr to the Taurus mountains. Beyond that I know very little. Exemptions and delays are granted with no apparent reason, often, however, with the plainest of reasons, viz., the encircling of the police. The amount of extortion practised must extend into thousands of liras.

Dr. {Wilfred M. Post} will tell you of what he has seen on the way here. I will try not to duplicate what he says. The information that I have from {Eregli} is reliable. The Protestants of {Konia} who were there have all returned here, though many difficulties were thrown in their way. There were about 15,000 exiles in {Eregli}, but there has been a steady stream pouring in that direction and the number must be larger now, except for the number sent on into the mountains from there. How many there are at Bozanti, the terminus of the railway, I have not been able to learn. Whether they are now being sent on to Tarsus and Adana, I cannot learn with certainty. Reports have it that travel beyond Adana is cut off, and so the exiles are not being sent, as before, beyond Aleppo.

In {Eregli} the exiles are encamped in the open fields in the neighbourhood of the railway station. No protection is provided for them, and they have none, except such tenting as they can make up for themselves out of carpets, coarse matting, cloaks, gummy [*sic*] sacks, sheets, cotton cloth, tablecloths, or handkerchiefs, all of which I have seen used here in {Konia}. There are no sanitary arrangements for this horde, and every available spot is used for depositing excrement. The stench of the region is described as appalling. Here in {Konia} I have seen how the adjoining field, entirely open as it was, was so thickly covered with excrement that it seemed impossible to step anywhere, while women and girls, as well as others, were defecating there in the daytime simply because there was absolutely no screen or protection anywhere. While it is considered that diarrhœa and dysentery are rife, you can imagine the results. The region there, as well as here, is exceedingly malarial, and this is the time of year for it. I have no knowledge of how many deaths have taken place.

After a time, large numbers of the exiles at {Eregli} were allowed to find shelter in the town, where they rented houses and for a time were better off. But they were not allowed to rest in quiet. Suddenly the order would come from the police that all were to leave for Bozanti, and the whole number who were in the town, perhaps 5,000, would be driven (and I mean literally driven under the lash) into the streets with all their goods and be rushed to the encampment. There perhaps 100 wagons would be ready and 500 people find places and be sent off. The rest were then left to stay in the encampment or bribe their way back to the town again and re-rent their houses, until another alarm and driving forth. Every such onslaught meant several medjids of expense for every family for transporting their goods and bedding to and fro, and this in addition to the bribes paid to the police for the privilege of going back to the town. Such bakshishes had to be paid to the police for every favour asked, from medjids to liras. No one could go to present a petition to the Governor without bribing the police first. In the encampment the police would come along in the morning and order all tents in a certain section to be taken down, saying they were to start for Bozanti, and this order would be enforced instantly with scourge and club. The terror of the people, from the reports they had of that journey "beyond"—of pillage, murder, outrage, stealing of girls and starvation—was such that they were always ready to purchase a few days' respite if they had any money to do it with. No wagon or train is ready, so when enough money is brought out, the people are graciously allowed to put up their tents again twenty feet away from their former site. The sick, the aged—none were respected. The people have described to me the terror of that constantly recurring order, "Down with the tents!" with the whip behind it.

For those who did have to start, the conditions were still worse. They must hire wagons brought there for them, and the drivers charge four times the ordinary price. It must be paid, or they will be driven out to go on foot, and, of course, in that case, can take no bedding and hardly any food with them. The drivers acknowledge afterwards that the police take one half of the price paid. It is impossible for me to tell you all the means of extortion employed. I know of a family here who had to pay nineteen liras to hire a wagon and hamals and get permission from the police to move from the filthy encampment to a small, horribly crowded hotel near by. The hotel-keepers charge a lira a day for a little room with three or four dirty beds in it, and then share this with the police.

Protestants are supposed to be freed. The story of my contest with the officials here, before the Vali arrived, shows how they had planned to get all sent away before his arrival by concealing the order for exemption.

The Protestants who were already in {Eregli} were notified that they were free, yet had to pay fifty liras to the police to get their permit to leave. At the station, where they went to get third-class tickets, they were told that there were no third-class coaches left and that they must take second-class. After purchasing these tickets two-thirds of them were put into third-class coaches after all. It was merely a trick to separate them from more of their money. Of course, they were glad to have third-class coaches, for, coming here first, the exiles were compelled to pay the full fare and then packed forty or fifty together in box-trucks, cattle-trucks, or even open flat trucks. The Railway seems to be as conscienceless in wringing the money out of them as the Government or the Turks.

The whip and the club are in constant use by the police, and that upon women and children too. Think what it is for people, many of them cultivated, educated, refined, to be driven about in this way like dogs by brutes. I have seen women black and blue from the beating they have received. A woman with a fractured thigh at the station was being helped by friends intending to bring her to the hospital. A commissary of police came along and ordered her to be dragged back into the carriage. A boy yesterday in the encampment here was struck on the head by a policeman and killed. The pastor of the church at {Isnik (Nicomedia)} was beaten with a whip and his forehead cut open, in a great gash, by a blow from a club, for saying that he was a Protestant and asking for his freedom. He is not freed yet in {Eregli}. Two of his daughters we took into the hospital as nurses when the family first passed through here. . . .

The Armenians of {Ilghin} sent here were forced to come by wagon. The Circassians of the region knew of it and followed after and robbed them, and shot one girl. Gendarmes were sent out after the Circassians, but only took their turn in completing the stripping of the party.

Another party was sent in the same way and was attacked at night by Circassians, and one of the men was shot through the thigh—a horrible wound. He died here in the hospital a few hours later. We have one boy and one girl here in the hospital who were run over by trains, compelling the amputation of the leg. Three hundred families from Baghtchedjik are in Eski Shehr. About two hundred of the men were in market, nearly a mile from the encampment, when the police came on them and drove them out at once to start on foot for {Konia}, without letting them go back to their families or get money. They are here now, begging me to try to communicate with their families. The mail is closed to all such communications. Telegrams innumerable are given in at the office, the money received and the telegram never sent—(witness two long telegrams I sent you).

During the last four days the inhabitants of the villages above Baghtchedjik have been poured in here, and are filling the encampment. They come from a cool and well-watered region. They are thrown out here in this burning heat, without shelter and with a water supply so scanty that there is a constant struggle at the fountain to get their jars filled. The sickness that we are seeing among them is heart-rending. Many are simply overcome with the heat. Our dispensary floor is covered all day with sick in all stages. A little girl died here this morning. Others, moribund, will perhaps hardly get back to their tents. We are trying to refresh them with yoghourt and water-melons. They are too sick to take bread. . . .

The saddest part of all this is our utter impotence to do anything to stay the awful deeds that are being perpetrated.

Source: James Bryce and Arnold Toynbee, *The Treatment of Armenians in the Ottoman Empire, 1915–1916: Documents Presented to Viscount Grey of Fallodon by Viscount Bryce* (London: Hodder and Stoughton, 1916), 421–425.

Commentary

Konya, a city in south-central Anatolia, is arguably the most religiously conservative city in Turkey. The home of the famed "Whirling Dervishes" (the Mevlevi Order, a devout Sufi sect), Konya was the capital and principal city of the *vilayet* (province) of the same name. Konya—known as the "citadel of Islam"—was an important stop on the railway that traveled from the port city of Smyrna in the far west. Its people were (and remain) proud of the city's reputation for piety and religious zeal.

William S. Dodd, an American medical doctor working with the United States Red Cross in 1915, was particularly involved with the Protestant community of the Armenian Evangelical Church, a denomination that was officially established in 1846 after Patriarch Matteos Chouhajian excommunicated those seeking reform within the Armenian Patriarchate of Constantinople. Dodd's account of developments in Konya and the nearby town of Eregli is taken from a letter to U.S. Ambassador Henry Morgenthau, Sr., dated September 8, 1915. It was included in the British Blue Book and, as with the account by Frances Gage above, it was researched by British scholar Ara Sarafian in order to produce a definitive rendition of the document.

In his observations of the conditions at Konya, Dodd notes that things "are so bewildering here that it is hard to know how to present a general view of the situation." The deportation of the Armenians was progressing with little let-up, and there was also an enormous amount of corruption on the part of the guards. The only way to explain the large number of exemptions and delays in carrying out the deportations, he concludes, is that the "amount of extortion practised must extend into thousands of liras." The pressures building up behind the scenes—he uses the Latin term *vis a tergo*—to get the job done must have been considerable. As Dodd sees it, the policy of deporting the Armenian population gave the Turks performing the task an opportunity for personal enrichment along the way.

Dodd mentions the Armenians who were deported from the nearby town of Eregli, which was used as a staging point on the road to further deportation. Eregli was a large village before the railway reached it from Konya in 1904, after which it grew quickly into a bigger town of some importance. A center of textile manu-facturing based on cotton grown on the Adana Plain (another center of the Arme-nian population), Eregli was also linked by road with Konya.

Dr. Wilfred M. Post, a colleague of Dodd's at the American Hospital in Konya and a long-term resident of the Red Cross mission there, provided Dodd with ad-ditional information about conditions at Eregli. The deportees were dumped into open fields near the train station, with neither protection from the elements nor sanitary arrangements made on their behalf. Beyond Eregli, all was in a state of uncertainty. Dodd could not ascertain how many Armenians there were at Bozanti, a bleak and windy place then in the process of having a railroad terminus built (it was finally completed in 1917). In an indication of what the fate might have been for the deportees—an accurate projection, as it turned out—Dodd notes that he has been alerted to reports that "travel beyond Adana is cut off, and so the exiles are not being sent, as before, beyond Aleppo." It was this city, in northern Syria, that served as the main conduit through which scores of thousands of Armenian depor-tees from across the Ottoman Empire were sent on their forced marches to places such as Deir ez-Zor, and to ultimate death.

Dodd's account provides a description of the horrendous conditions in which the Armenian deportees were held. In Konya, for example, he observes how the area was "so thickly covered with excrement that it seemed impossible to step any-where, while women and girls, as well as others, were defecating there in the day-time simply because there was absolutely no screen or protection anywhere." Here we have an important reminder of how it was that many of the deaths suffered by Armenians at the hands of the Turks were caused by sickness resulting from the conditions. Debility from dysentery significantly reduced the possibilities of con-suming food, leading to disease-induced starvation.

One of the points of frustration for Dodd concerned the tortures brought on the Armenian community by those who acted on behalf of the Turkish authorities, who were neither army nor gendarmes. He refers specifically to the Circassians, the largest Muslim group in Turkey after the Turks themselves. Originally from the North Caucasus, in the middle of the nineteenth century they moved to the

Ottoman Empire from Russia—at which point the Ottoman government exploited them as a means to repress the Empire's Christian minorities. In this capacity, the Circassians played an active role during the Armenian Genocide. Dodd's account describes them as robbers and wanton murderers, and mentions specific situations in which they shot men and children who were brought into his hospital for treatment. All too often, those men and children arrived too late and succumbed to their wounds.

On August 4, 1915, the German consul-general in Constantinople, Dr. Johann Heinrich Hermann Mordtmann (1852–1932), sent a dispatch to Berlin regarding the deportation and expulsion of the Armenians. Included was a digest of reports he had received from around Turkey. One referred specifically to Baghtchedjik, generally recognized as a completely Armenian town of about 10,000 inhabitants. Noting that Baghtchedjik was a town of mixed Christian denominations (Catholic and Protestant, as well as Armenian Orthodox), Mordtmann claimed that the town was likely to be hit by deportations very soon. That same day he had received a visit from two Mekhitarists (Benedictine monks of the Armenian Catholic Church), who begged the Imperial German Embassy to intercede on behalf of Baghtchedjik.

Dr. Dodd's account of September 8—just over a month later can, perhaps, be read as the next phase of that report. In it, he notes that "during the last four days the inhabitants of the villages above Baghtchedjik" have poured into Konya, in conditions that were insufferable for them. Coming from a cool and well-watered region, their agony in the burning heat, "without shelter and with a water supply so scanty that there is a constant struggle at the fountain to get their jars filled," was unmistakable. Once more, as a medical doctor Dodd's work was unceasing. His account is filled with tragic images of the weak, the sick, and the dying. For Dodd, the "saddest part" of what was happening was "our utter impotence to do anything to stay the awful deeds that are being perpetrated."

What he could not see from his vantage point was that the genocide was, at that time, still in the initial stages of a process that eventually wiped out the Armenian Evangelical movement within the Ottoman Empire, and destroyed most of the churches and their congregants. It was not until 1924 that the church was re-established, through the founding of the Lebanon-based Armenian Evangelical Union of the Near East.

Questions

1. Why do you think conditions at Konya were, in the words of Dr. Dodd, "so bewildering that it is hard to know how to present a general view of the situation"?
2. How does Dr. Dodd account for most of the deaths that took place at Konya, Eregli, and Baghtchedjik?

3. Does Dr. Dodd give an explanation for why the Turkish authorities engaged in the persecution and massacre of the Armenians? If so, what was it?

JOSEPH NAAYEM

One of the key witnesses to events surrounding the Ottoman destruction of the Assyrians was Joseph Naayem, an Assyro-Chaldean priest from Urfa in Turkey's southeast. In 1920, Fr. Naayem wrote a book on his experiences entitled Shall This Nation Die? *The book provides an account of Naayem's experiences, his observations of the genocide of the Armenians and the Greeks, and other firsthand accounts collected from Assyrians to whom Naayem spoke. Its preface was written by Lord James Bryce, a former British ambassador to the United States and the first British statesman to address the issue of genocide (in July 1915). Reverend Naayem's testimony, in turn, was one of the first major statements alerting an English-speaking audience to the horrors perpetrated against the Assyrians during the Great War.*

We received the news of my father's murder early in August 1915. That very evening one of my brothers, Djemil, who had come from Aleppo to Urfa some days before, fled on horseback with some companions back to Aleppo in fear. At Tell Abyadh he encountered Sallal, the son of an Arab Sheikh who was a friend of the family, whom he begged to return to Urfa with our horses and rescue the rest of the family.

Three days later some English civilian prisoners employed at the Ottoman Bank in the Administration of the Public Debt, obtained permission to leave the town, and despite the risk they ran, very kindly took with them in their carriage two of my brothers, George, aged thirteen, and Fattouh, who was two years older. Thus there remained in Urfa only my two youngest brothers and my mother. Soon after Saltal, accompanied by Aziz Djenjil, a very brave and devoted Christian employee of ours (dressed as a Bedouin) arrived, and took the rest of the family, excepting Emine and me, to Tel-Albiad. The stationmaster, another friend, put them in the train for Aleppo. . . .

My brother Emine and I remained at Urfa, where the arrests continued, several of my friends and acquaintances being taken and massacred.

On August the 19th a police agent with some soldiers went to the house of an unfortunate Armenian to take him into custody. Determined not to be trapped without making an effort to defend himself, the man knowing that arrest meant death, shot and killed the policeman and two soldiers. Armed Turks rushed through the markets and streets, killing all the Christians they encountered. Some managed to save themselves by hiding. Many took refuge in the presbytery. My brother Emine, who had been obliged to go to the bank, had the greatest difficulty in reaching me.

The streets were strewn with the bodies of the six hundred Christians killed that night, and their blood literally ran in the streets. The murderers steeped their hands in the steaming gore and made imprints on the walls that bordered the streets. In this frightful orgy English and French civilians, some of whom had been interned at Urfa a month previously, also perished. Several of them who happened to be in the streets at the moment of the outburst were taken back by soldiers to their homes, lest the populace should fall upon them by error. One of them, a Frenchman of Aleppo, M. Germain, had his throat cut by the ruffians. A Maltese who was pursued and stoned took refuge in the house of a Christian and was saved.

Two hours after the firing had ceased, I mounted to the roof to see what was happening in the streets, and noticed that the police, instead of calming the fanaticism of the Turks, were inciting them to renew the massacre. Not until all the Christians who were discovered in the shops or in the streets had been killed was an order issued to end the carnage.

In the evening, all was quiet, but no Christian dared show himself and the Armenians prepared to defend themselves, barricading their premises. But the cowardly murderers were afraid and attempted no further harm.

The next morning I heard cries in a little lane near our house where there was an oil press. A moment later I saw a Turk named Moutalib leave his house and make off in the direction of the cries. Half an hour later I saw him return with his dagger stained with blood, proud of his work, laughing and shouting: "Hiar Guibi Kestim" ("I chopped him up like a cucumber!"). The victims were two workmen who had hidden themselves in the oil press. The Turks, under pretence of saving them, had succeeded in making them come out into the streets, where they cut their throat, stamped on their heads and dragged their bodies along the ground.

It was the duty of the Jews to drive carts and pick up the dead bodies and throw them outside the town to the dogs and birds of prey. (This sinister duty had been imposed upon the Jews by the Turks during the massacre of the Christians.)

In the afternoon, a soldier, accompanied by the porter from the Bank, came by order of the Manager, M. Savoye, for my brother, Emine, who returned to the Bank, where he resided. There he was safe, the establishment being guarded by the police.

Towards ten o'clock I saw the Governor himself, Haidar Bey, passing through the streets with the Chief of Police, to show that he had no official cognizance of any disturbance, and to prove to the Christians that order had been restored, and that they could come out without fear.

M. Savoye, I should like to state, displayed the highest courage during these terrible days in the way he helped our family in our extremity. We owe him the warmest debt of gratitude.

Sallal, our Bedouin friend, had promised to return as soon as he had taken my mother and brother to a place of safety and the day after the massacre he came to see me at the Presbytery. Being now alone, I was in danger of arrest every moment, and decided to take to flight. It was a hazardous undertaking, but I was determined to make the attempt. Urfa had become a very hell! Muffling myself in Bedouin robes, I prepared to leave with Sallal.

The town was not yet quite calm, and Christians remained shut up in their houses, fearful of new out-bursts, although every one of prominence among them had already been executed. About five hundred Christian soldiers employed on the construction of roads near the town had also been put to death. One alone escaped. In giving me an account of his experiences, he declared that the officers were keeping in their tents young Christian girls, stolen from the convoys. He spoke in particular of one very beautiful Chaldean girl from Diarbekir, kept as a prostitute, and passed from one Turk to another. By a miracle the girl survived and is living today in Urfa.

At seven o'clock of the evening of August the 21st, 1915, Sallal came, and I bade farewell to my friends, including Father Emmanuel Kacha, who stayed behind with his family.

Hurrying through the almost deserted streets, we reached the house of one of my relatives, where I donned the costume of a Bedouin. This consisted of a long wide-sleeved shirt of white linen, an "aba" (a sleeveless cloak of camel hair) and on my head I wore a "tcheffie" (a headdress, square in shape, with long fringe, surmounted by an "agal," a kind of camelhair crown). As I spoke Bedouin a little, I was not likely to be recognized. Near the edge of the town we met a police agent and two soldiers, who seemed to be waiting for us. The valiant Sallal, who was armed with a large sword and a revolver and was a man of great height, advanced fearlessly. We both salaamed profoundly and passed on, our salute being returned. A hundred yards further on, my companion remarked that we had just had a very narrow escape.

At the house of a friend outside the town we found our two horses, and took the road to Tell Abyadh. . . .

[W]e rode at a gallop to Tell Abyadh. There I met several of my parishioners, who were in the service of the Baghdad Railway Company, and was taken to the house of one of them, M. Youssouf Cherchouba, who received me in a very friendly spirit. . . .

I knew the telegraph operator of the Railway Company, M. Dhiab, and on expressing a desire to see him, was taken to his office by George Khamis, one of my Chaldean parishioners. Circassian Guards, of whom the Railway employees were in deadly fear, were posted at the station. Had they suspected me, I should have found myself in considerable danger. The operator was very much astonished to see a Bedouin, and wondered what one could want with him. He was still more astonished when he found that the Bedouin spoke and understood French. He was the friend who had assisted to smuggle my mother and brothers through, and it might be compromising for me to remain in his office dressed as a Bedouin [who] was unable to change, as Sallal had left my clerical dress on the road, so I hid until the evening train left.

An Arab had been notified, and for baksheesh (a bribe) hid me in a neighboring village. . . . When night came the Arab took me back to the station, where I hid in a building until the arrival of the Aleppo train. My friend, the telegraph operator, came to an understanding with the conductor, receiving a guarantee that I should be taken safe and sound to Aleppo for a stipulated sum of money, which I readily paid. I was put aboard a cattle truck, which had not been cleaned since its prior load had been unshipped, so gave off a very disagreeable odor.

The train stopped and through the crack in the doors I saw a guard approach my truck. It was the conductor to offer me a place in a first-class carriage. Because of my dress, I asked him to let me travel third-class, but a brakesman, who noticed us conversing and who suspected our agreement, at Arab Punar forcibly put me into an open truck, during the absence of the conductor.

At this place we took on deported families of English and French civilians, going from Urfa to Aleppo. At the next stop, the first guard returned me to my compartment in the coach, which was shared with some invalid soldiers and some Turks from Urfa. The latter commenced to make fun of me, as is their custom with Bedouins, but I pretended to be asleep. We arrived in Aleppo at ten o'clock the next morning.

Source: Reverend Joseph Naayem, *Shall this Nation Die?* (New York: Chaldean Rescue, 1920). Republished by the Assyrian International News Agency, http://www.aina.org/books/stnd.htm.

Commentary

Perhaps up to three million Christians of Syriac, Armenian, or Greek Orthodox denominations were murdered by the Young Turk regime and their Kurdish collaborators. The Assyrian Genocide, or *Seyfo,* took place alongside those of the Armenians and the Pontic and Anatolian Greeks, during and after World War I.

The Assyrians, an ancient people inhabiting modern-day southeastern Iraq and northwestern Iran, refer to their experience as having taken place between 1915 and 1918. At the start of the twentieth century, the Assyrian population in the Ottoman Empire numbered about one million, and was concentrated largely in what are now Iran, Iraq, and Turkey.

As with the Armenian Genocide, a large proportion of the Assyrian deaths occurred as a result of death marches into the Syrian Desert. Most of those who died were the victims of heat, starvation and thirst, exposure, and incessant brutality.

Some scholars have referred to the Turkish campaign against the three subject peoples more broadly, calling it genocide against the Christian population of the Ottoman Empire. According to such analyses, the preference is not to divide the three national experiences into their constituent parts, but, rather, to categorize all of the deaths and atrocities as being of a single cloth. There is, certainly, a remarkable similarity between them, at least on the surface. The Assyrian population throughout the Empire was subjected to massacre, deportation, dismemberment, torture, and other atrocities. Whole cities were depopulated, and, when not killed outright, the inhabitants were sent on the aforementioned death marches.

The testimony of Fr. Joseph Naayem, an Assyro-Chaldean priest, is based on his own experiences as well as his observations and conversations with others. He was both an eyewitness to and a participant (as victim) in the events he describes. First published in New York in 1920 as *Shall This Nation Die?*, his account narrates the horrors experienced by the Assyrians prior to and during World War I. Fr. Naayem came from the southeastern Turkish city of Urfa, about 50 miles east of the Euphrates River. At the start of World War I, Urfa was home to about 75,000 inhabitants: 45,000 Muslims, 25,000 Armenians, and 5,000 Assyrians. In 1915 and 1916, the Young Turks hit the city's Armenians and Assyrians, resulting in an estimated loss to Urfa's population of some 40 percent of the pre-war total.

As a victim of the genocide, Fr. Naayem's aim in publishing his account was to inform readers overseas, particularly in the United Kingdom and the United States, of events that had been overshadowed by the more general horrors of the war. As we read his testimony, it is difficult to distinguish his experiences from those of the Armenian survivors, reflecting the very close parallels between the two genocides. His very personal account is far from dispassionate, but there is enough here to indicate just how horrific the sufferings of his people were.

The account begins with recognition of the willingness of others to put their well-being at risk in order to help Naayem's family. This is a recurrent theme throughout the testimony, reminding readers that, even during these terrible and uncertain times, there were good people who overlooked government directives.

One of the major factors contributing to the Turkish campaign against Christian minorities was the pre-war commitment to the "Turkification" of the Empire. Accompanying this was an Islamic incentive, whereby the Turkish national dimension could be wedded to an Islamic revival for the caliphate. Accordingly, on October 11, 1914, Sultan Mehmet V (1844–1918; reigned 1909–1918) declared jihad against all the Christians living in the Empire. The call to holy war was reaffirmed on November 14, 1914, by the Sheikh al-Islam, the most senior Islamic cleric in the Ottoman Empire. It was directed toward all Christians, hitting particularly hard for those of Armenian, Assyrian, and Greek descent; it is interesting that this did not apply to the Empire's Jewish population.

Fr. Naayem alludes to this anomaly in his account. He refers to the Jews who were assigned the detestable duty of removing the dead bodies from the town. They were not, however, the subjects of genocidal action. This is not to say that Jews in the Empire were left completely alone—just as it was for the Armenians in advance of the Russian offensive in 1915, so it was also that the entire civilian populations of Tel Aviv and Jaffa were forcibly deported on April 6, 1917, as British and ANZAC troops pressed forward during their own attack on Palestine. Although Muslim evacuees were soon permitted to return, Jewish evacuees were not allowed to go back until after the British conquest of Palestine in the summer of 1918.

Fr. Naayem managed to arrange his escape with the assistance of others. His disguise as a Bedouin enabled him to pass relatively undetected through Turkish society and among Turkish soldiers and gendarmes, even though, on the train that would ultimately take him to Aleppo, Syria, he was singled out and harassed as an Arab. The significance of this speaks for itself. While it was obvious that the Ottomans were genocidal in their policies toward Christians and discriminatory toward Jews, the Turks of the time were also aware of ethnic and racial differences among their fellow Muslims, and categorized them in a thoroughly negative light as a result.

Fr. Naayem's account is important in another respect as well: it shows us how neither the architects of the genocide, nor the perpetrators at ground level, made any distinction between Christians, regardless of whether they were Assyrians, Armenians, or Greeks. For the Turks, all were "infidels" deserving of their fate. In this lies an important clue as to why they behaved as they did. By combining all groups together without apparent distinction, the Turks were showing their true colors as the destroyers of a specific religious group, notwithstanding the fact that members of that group were from three distinct (and unrelated) ethnicities.

Questions

1. Per Fr. Naayem's account, in what way(s) did the persecution of the Assyrians differ from that of the Armenians?
2. Fr. Naayem notes that the Turks invested a lot of effort in identifying differences between ethnic and religious groups within the Ottoman Empire. Why do you think they found this to be an issue of importance?
3. Why do you think the Jews of the Empire, although also deported, were not massacred by the Turkish authorities?

"PAPAYIANNIS"

In chronicling the story of Tamama, a Greek girl lost to her family and raised as a Turk in the aftermath of the Pontic Greek genocide, author George Andreanis (b. 1936) uncovered an account of Tamama's father, a priest named

Yiannis (from the Kontanton family). As Papayiannis, or Father John, he was one of the leaders of the community of Espye. In this extract, we learn the fate of Papayiannis's brother Kostas, and of the Pontic community of Espye as it was being forcibly deported to an unknown destination.

When you deliberately deport a whole population in the depths of winter, you drive them to annihilation through starvation, cold and illness. When on top of this, the fifty kilometres, become two hundred, then the object of the plan is obvious. And the plan is proved to be even more despicable when in places every 20 kilometers along the expected route along which the procession of the deportees is travelling, hidden *tsetses* [militias] are waiting in ambush, as if by chance and fall on hapless Christians to slaughter them. Ten such deportations took place at different times from Samsun towards the south. They were waiting for them at Seytan Deresi (Devil's Valley). Screams and shouts rent the air. Very few escaped and these were the seriously injured, who were assumed to be dead, or some who succeeded in escaping into the mountains around there. Human wrecks, eye witnesses to the crime, arrived in Mersin on the south coast of Turkey and made their way from there to Greece after having crossed the whole of Turkey, after months of wandering. The villages of Kavak and Havza outside Samsun were burnt to the ground. Houses with people in them were burnt and the two villages were wiped out. In total 350,000 people lost their lives prematurely, due to various causes, before the exchange of populations. That is half the Greeks of the Black Sea.

The news reached Espye on the morning of Sunday 16th November. The town crier went around the Greek houses and summoned all the Greeks to gather shortly in front of the church, bringing with them only what they could carry. Turkish drovers with beasts of burden would undertake the transportation of more belongings, for those who could pay. The Christians gathered a short time later. Papayiannis arrived last, because his brother Kostas had been ill for two days with a fever and wanted his help. Grim looking *zapties* [Turkish police] who were strangers stood on the steps of Saint George's church and they were to accompany the deportees for a distance of 50 kilometers south of Espye, according to the plan. The Turkish drovers bargained with those who had money to pay their demands for the carriage. Papayiannis went directly to a mounted officer, who seemed to be in charge of the whole affair. He told him, that his brother Kostis was ill with a fever and asked if he could stay at home with his wife, Eleni. The officer did not even look him in the eye but said grimly that Kostis must come at the double, so that they could set off before noon to be in time to get to their first stop, before nightfall, for their first overnight stay. The days had already shortened and it went dark early.

With his head down, Papayiannis went to his brother's house, lifted his sick brother out of bed and with his sister in law Eleni, arrived in the church yard. All Christian Espye was there. 480 souls who set off at 11 o'clock on Sunday 16th November 1916 on the way to Golgotha. The road they followed, ironically, was the road they used to follow on their journey to the summer huts, every June. The road of joy and pleasure was to become the road of martyrdom. Bent under the weight of the burdens they were carrying, old people, sick people, children, all together and next to them the beasts of burden and the gendarmes. The latter had come along to ensure safety in case they should pass through Muslim villages, where the enraged Muslims might commit acts of vengeance for the evil that the Christians had done to Turkey. In all this tragedy, things looked innocent enough. As he left Espye Papayiannis was weeping. He did not know where they were being taken and they all expected him to keep them informed. As they went up the southern slopes nobody looked around at Espye and the sea.

They had not even gone half an hour's journey from Espye when the sound of a shot in the village was heard. Then silence. They stopped momentarily and then carried on with their march. It was 4 o'clock in the afternoon. They had already walked for more than 20 kilometers. Then, they stopped at a lovely spring. This was the spring at which they always stopped on their way to the summer huts. Cheerfully and to the sound of the *kementze* [a Pontic Greek musical instrument], they would drink water, freshen their faces and carry on. But now, neither cheers, nor kementzes. It was cold and nobody was in the mood. From this spot you could see Espye for the last time. After this the mountain sloped away and then one mountain followed the other and nobody could see the sea any more. They all turned their eyes towards Espye, instinctively. They were seized by a vague fear, that perhaps they were never to see Espye again. For the ones who were old, or ill, this fear was certain. The sun had already gone down and set in the Black Sea. And what did they see? The whole of their neighbourhood had gone up in smoke. Their Espye was on fire. Their world was on fire. Papayiannis wept, turned his head forward and never looked back again.

What had happened? The Christians had taken whatever they could carry with them and then double locked their doors and windows. The officer had reassured them, that there was no reason why they should be anxious about their property. Only they should take with them what they needed. The state would look after their houses and their property. Besides they would not be going very far. Only fifty kilometers and just for the short period till the war was finished with the drunken Russians. He did not tell them that they would be going more than 200 kilometers over the mountains to Sivas, the old Sevasteia, that their belongings would be stolen and their houses burnt. God knows if he even knew these things himself. Anyway, he reassured them about everything and so they set off from Espye. . . .

The road they had taken was a road without return. The adults understood a lot, but the children could not understand anything. Without care they followed the crowd. The road they were on, was their familiar road for the summer huts, they knew it was a road of joy and feast every summer. Why is nobody celebrating now, why are the adults crying and with tears in their eyes they look back at Espye now that we are at the spring? These things are inexplicable to the young children. But fear had entered their young souls, because on this occasion something strange was happening. The gendarmes, who accompanied them had become fierce and pushed the villagers with their guns to make them hurry up and set off, so that they would arrive in time at their destination for that day. Their destination was an inn, a short distance from the road to the summer huts, about seven hours' travelling distance from Espye.

When they arrived at the inn, they were all exhausted, hungry and frozen. They built rough fires to get warmer while outside the sleet continued to fall. They spread out their wet clothes round the fires. They ate dry pieces of bread and whatever they had ready with them and bundled up they lay down to sleep on the floor inside the inn. First they settled Uncle Kostis, who was exhausted from his fever and only wanted to drink some water. Because of their great exhaustion, they fell deeply asleep at once. Not even two hours had passed when a loud noise awakened them. The children did not wake even with the noise. The adults went outside the inn to see what the noise was. Papayiannis went outside with them. Kostas did not even open his eyes in his exhaustion. His wife moistened his lips with a little water. It was chaos outside the inn. Christian deportees from the villages around Tripolis had arrived in convoys from their exile. Where could so many people be accommodated and outside the cold and sleet continued.

Fortunately tiredness cut short the noise and quarrelling. Everybody lay down wherever they could and in a short time a deadly hush prevailed.

The morning of 17th November dawned with clear skies and shining sun. Every body knew that they were exiled 50 kilometers. Courageously, they faced the sun, which would help them a great deal on the remaining fifty kilometers of their journey of exile. The zapties shouted to wake the children until the march of the exiles started again. Suddenly screams were heard inside the inn. It was Aunt Eleni, the wife of Kostas. When she had gone to waken her husband, it was too late. Kostis was not alive, that same night he departed for ever breathing his last in the inn. He was the first victim from Espye on the Golgotha of exile. Papayiannis wept for his only brother. The zapties allowed a short delay for the burial of luckless Kostis. Fifty metres away from the inn, on the slope of the mountain, where the soil was softer, they opened a makeshift grave and Papayiannis read the funeral service in tears and then they covered him with earth. As they were leaving the inn Papayiannis, with tears in his eyes, looked back, once more at the grave of his beloved brother.

Source: George Andreadis, *Tamama, the Missing Girl of Pontos* (Athens: Gordios, 1993), 78–86.

Commentary

An ethnically Greek population traditionally living in the Pontus region of northeastern Turkey, on the southern shore of the Black Sea, the Pontic (or Pontian) Greeks have maintained a continuous presence in the area for the past three millennia. Between 1914 and 1923, in a campaign reminiscent of the Armenian and Assyrian genocides that were taking place at the same time, the Pontic Greeks suffered innumerable cruelties at the hands of the Turks. An estimated 353,000 died, many on forced marches through Anatolia and the Syrian Desert.

When the Armenian Genocide began in 1915, persecutions of Pontic Greeks, which had already started in 1914, increased dramatically. Greek businesses were boycotted at government order, and, based on the justification that the southern Black Sea coast was vulnerable to Russian attack, the government ordered mass deportations of Pontic Greeks to the south, far away from their ancestral lands. (Vulnerability was also the excuse that led to the Armenian deportations in the Caucasus.)

Trebizond (Trabzon), a city on the Black Sea coast of northeastern Turkey, was the site of one of the key battles between the Ottoman and Russian armies during the Caucasus Campaign of World War I. In April 1916, Russians captured the city. They permitted the area to be governed by local Greek religious and civic leaders. Many Pontic Greeks believed that the Russian presence would last, and that the area of the Pontus would become an autonomous state within the Russian Empire—perhaps even a Republic of Trebizond.

When the province was restored to Turkish control in early 1918 following the Russian Revolution, many Pontic Greeks left Trebizond as the Russians departed. It was then that the whole region became a major killing ground of Armenians.

Not too far from Trebizond is the coastal village of Espye (Espiye), where the family of Tamama, headed by Papayiannis, had lived for as long as people could remember. The inhabitants clearly had a strong identification with their village, and the sense of loss they had when they were deported from it, then saw it burning, reflects the importance of place to victims of genocide. We can understand why it was that the villagers—and, by extension, all such victims—found themselves disoriented when forced to move so far and so fast from their homes.

The account of Papayiannis's fate states that "the object of the plan" to deport the Greeks was "obvious." Deportation of the entire population in the depths of winter, in circumstances of starvation, cold, and illness, with the journey continually lengthening when it was expected to be over, was debilitating to those on what rapidly became a death march. Added to this were continual attacks from the feared "Tsetses," not regular Turkish troops but unsupervised guerrillas.

Behind Espye, the land rises sharply to the south up into the Giresun Mountains. There was to be no chance of escaping in that direction. On the morning of Sunday, November 16, 1916, "on the way to Golgotha," the town crier "went around the Greek houses and summoned all the Greeks to gather shortly in front of the church, bringing with them only what they could carry." At 11 o'clock that morning, the entire population of 480 began the trek out of the village.

Once they were over the first mountain, then the next, the sea disappeared. As they turned toward where their village had been, some felt the end had come, the more so when they saw smoke billowing from the direction of Espye. They looked at their village for the last time.

Papayiannis took up the rear, as he had waited behind to stay with his sick brother, Kostas. Zaptieh policemen guarded the caravan as they headed south of Espye. Before they had progressed too far Papayiannis showed his leadership abilities by attempting to negotiate with an officer over the fate of Kostas. This was to no avail— everyone from the village was forced to leave, including his sick brother who, we learn through the testimony, soon died as a result of his treatment on the march.

The account notes, "The road they had taken was a road without return." For the children, these events were largely inexplicable. The vulnerability of children in circumstances such as war and genocide has always made their situation especially touching. Throughout history they have been the victims of genocide and crimes against humanity, during times of peace and armed conflict. All too often they have been deliberately targeted, in order to destroy the next generation. The confusion of children with regard to genocidal violence only serves to enhance their wretched status. On the road out of Espye, "the children could not understand anything." All they knew was that the road on which they were traveling was where they usually went for their holidays; for them "it was a road of joy and feast every summer."

The destruction of the Pontic Greeks, and the forcible deportation that followed, had but a single planned outcome: the removal of all Greeks from Turkey. The case of Papayiannis, his family, and his village, is but a cameo in a much bigger drama (or is it a horror story?), but it is illustrative of thousands of similar cases that made up the whole throughout the Greek areas of the Ottoman Empire.

Ultimately, the Turkish campaign was "successful," in that it destroyed forever the ancient Anatolian Greek community. Those who survived were exiled. The largest surviving Greek community, centered in the city of Smyrna (Izmir), was literally pushed into the sea in 1922, when the advancing Turkish Nationalist army razed the city, resulting in thousands being killed. By then, though, Papayiannis and most of the villagers of Espye were already long dead.

Questions

1. The story of Papayiannis is the story of one who was both a community leader and a family man. In what way(s) do you see him filling each role?

2. In the description of the fate of the people of Espye, what is meant by the phrase "on the road to Golgotha"?
3. Do you think the experiences of the people of Espye differed from those of other victims of the Turks during and after World War I?

EFTHIMIOS N. COUZINOS

A member of Ottoman Turkey's ill-fated Greek minority group, Efthimios N. Couzinos (1899–1974) provided a memoir of his happy youth and the subsequent horrors he experienced and witnessed at the hands of the Ottoman Turks before, during, and after World War I. In the account produced here, Couzinos, while in hiding in a hospital, overhears a story related by Michael, a small boy who had observed the depopulation of his village.

There were several hospital beds on the second floor of the infirmary for seriously ill children of the orphanage. One of these was occupied by an Armenian boy about fourteen years old. During the three days' massacre of Greeks and Armenians, a Turk had hit him on the back of the neck with an ax, and though the cut was not very deep, the blow had stunned him and he had been left for dead. This had happened on the second night of the massacre. This boy, after becoming conscious, had crawled for several hours in the dark and had been admitted to the campus and the orphanage, and hence to a bed in the infirmary. There was hope for his recovery. But the poor boy was partly paralyzed and could not turn from one side to the other.

During one of my early trips from my hole under the kitchen on the first floor to the second-story storage room, my sister had gone ahead of me to unlock the storage room. It was about 11:00 P.M. As I reached the last steps to the second floor, I heard this boy pleading: "Let me kiss the bottom of your feet; will someone turn me, please?" It was a plea no human being could avoid. It was pitch dark. I instinctively went into his room and turned him. I don't think he saw me, but he said, "May God preserve you." It was good to hear an expression like that from a helpless victim of the Turk.

My sister understood the delay and said, "I hope he did not see you; but even if he did, he is O.K."

There were at this time a few people that actually knew of my hiding. You could trust everybody on the campus grounds, but it was not advisable that more than two or three individuals knew that I was alive. To be known as dead was the best, and to be missing was the next best. Those few that knew the secret never pronounced my name.

The months of August and September 1921 were months of deportation of women and children from the coast towns of the Black Sea to the interior. We had some news that the men of Alacham had been wiped out, but we wanted some definite news from my mother and two sisters.

One day in August my sister Anthe came with the news that a ten-year-old boy, Michael, the son of a tailor in Alacham, had escaped from the convoy in Tokat and had found his way to the orphanage. I wanted to interview the boy and hear all about the last days of Alacham. This direct questioning, however, was not advisable. So, one night, I entered the big clothes closet in the storage room, after I had opened a sizable hole for air and listening. Before the boy arrived, I asked my sister to interview him on six or seven points, to draw as much definite information as possible. Were the people of Alacham treated differently from those in other coastal towns? The information that my sister ingeniously extracted from this ten-year-old was somewhat sketchy, childish, and incomplete, but sincere. It was horrid and devastatingly cruel. This is what Michael said:

> Yes, it was about seven or eight weeks ago that the *zaptiehs* and gendarmes gathered all the men and locked them in the Rezi warehouse. On the third day after this, a few of the poor were sent to Vizir Kioprou and, really, the relatives in Alacham received letters from them. Then, on the fourth day, very early, all the rich men were taken out of Alacham and there were no letters from them. (Later on it was confirmed that all this convoy of men was machine-gunned.) After the men were gone, the women and children were told that now they are safe!
>
> But, you know, Miss Anthe, about two weeks ago they told us that there was a new order from Ankara. No one can change that—that we have to get ready and leave Alacham in two hours!
>
> There were a few horses in the convoy. Almost all of us walked. It was almost fun in the beginning, but in the afternoon, going uphill, there was a big wind and also heavy rain. In the wind I lost my cap. You know, Miss Anthe, my daddy had made that special for me. After the rain, we started again. Then, soon after that, the gendarmes said that this is an extra rest period.
>
> You know, Miss Anthe, your cousin Vasiliki was on horseback, and then she said she was very sick. The ladies held blankets around her, just like a little tent, and then they said she had a baby boy! All the ladies said they never saw such a pretty baby boy before. Then, after about one hour, the gendarmes said that we have to reach the next village before dark. So they put Vasiliki on the horse again, and a lady carried the little baby.
>
> No, no, Vasiliki did not fall from the horse, because four strong ladies were holding her, two on each side. Oh, yes, she was crying, but just the same she wanted to look at her little boy from time to time.
>
> Then, after about five or six days, from there we reached Tokat, and they told us we can't go to town. They said we have to sleep in the field. That night, there was big shouting and crying. . . . Then, some of the ladies said, "Where is my daughter?" In the morning, some of the girls came back.
>
> When we started going again, they said our convoy would go to Malatia. You know, Miss Anthe, that is very, very far away. So, someone said that morning that

Merzifon in only three days' walking distance. I knew you were the chief nurse here; so here I am.

Oh, yes, the day before we left Alacham, the government doctor from Kérze, Dr. Savvas, came to Alacham, and they said that your mother and two sisters will go with him to Kérze in a few days. The mayor of Alacham was moving into your house! He said it is much bigger and better than his own house!

On, yes, I forgot to tell you that before the rich men were sent away to be machine-gunned your cousin Cuzu and a few other rich young men were separated and sent for hiding in the mill village. I think there were three of them. You know, Miss Anthe, the mothers of these rich young merchants received letters from them, asking that they dig all the gold in the basements so that they can give it to the bad men and then be allowed to come to their houses safely.

Here, little Michael stopped short of the kidnappings and was changing the subject. I was sweating in the clothes closet, anxious to find out what had happened after the Turks received the gold. I should have known the inevitable. I must have moved in the clothes closet; in fact, I was almost ready to come out of it and ask the boy the outcome of this outrageous kidnapping. These three were very close and dear friends. Suddenly, I realized in what condition I was, with a long beard and disheveled hair and other transformations. I decided not to frighten poor little Michael with my apparition.

My sister kept on with the questioning, and Michael in an almost nonchalant manner said, "Miss Anthe, I guess you don't know these bad people (the kidnappers). After they got all the gold they could get from the rich young merchants' mothers they killed them just the same."

As he was leaving the room, little Michael asked, "Miss Anthe, excuse me for asking, but what happened to your brother Eftim?" Her answer was that, after the war was over, she hoped to see him again.

This was the ugliest interview of my life, but the last part at least gave us some consolation. We were so thankful to Dr. Savvas, who had come from Kérze to take along my mother and sisters and save them from the horrors and humiliations of deportation.

Source: Efthimios N. Couzinos, *Twenty-Three Years in Asia Minor (1899–1922)* (New York: Vantage Press, 1969), 115–119. Used by permission of the Asia Minor and Pontos Hellenic Research Center.

Commentary

Alacham (modern-day Alaçam) is located in Samsun Province, Turkey. It is a coastal town on the Black Sea, some 48 miles from the city of Samsun, with a long history dating back to ancient times. Michael, the boy overheard by Efthimios Couzinos, was a native of Alacham who, as Couzinos relates, escaped from a forced-march convoy and made his way to the orphanage/hospital where Couzinos had taken refuge and where his sister was also staying. Couzinos, keen to "hear all about the last days of Alacham" through a direct interview, thought better of asking Michael to describe what he had witnessed. Instead, he allowed his sister, Anthe, to speak to the boy while he remained in hiding, listening to what Michael had to say.

The aftermath of the Great War saw momentous changes in the Near East, among them the break-up of the Ottoman Empire, the establishment of new states, the expansion of British and French influence, and the founding of a new Turkey under Mustafa Kemal (1881–1938), named Atatürk. These changes took place as the wartime Allies, Britain, France, and Italy, reconsidered their relationship in light of promises made and hopes held during the war.

The peace accord agreed to by the Allies and Turkey, the Treaty of Sèvres, was signed on August 10, 1920. As their share in the spoils of war, the Greeks had landed at Smyrna, a Greek-speaking city in western Anatolia, on May 15, 1919. Kemal arrived in Samsun, on the other side of the country, on May 19. Within a month he had gathered around him the nucleus of an army with which to challenge the Greek invasion. By the end of July a revolutionary council, the National Congress, had been convened and was meeting at Erzerum, in eastern Turkey.

What this was to portend for those members of the Greek population of the Pontos region who had not yet been removed, was nothing short of yet another disaster. They had watched as neighboring Greek towns and villages had been depopulated up and down the coastal belt since 1915, but the Greeks of the Samsun region had, until this time, remained relatively unharmed.

A number of atrocities were now being committed against those same Greeks. Alarmed at the possibility that Greek warships could endanger Samsun, troops under the command of General Nureddin Pasha (1873–1932) executed an action in which all males between ages 16 and 50 years would be deported to Amasya, Tokat, and other places. The Nationalist government in Ankara authorized this action on June 16, 1921, and Nureddin's Central Army accordingly deported nearly 21,000 people.

This is the context in which Couzinos heard Michael's story. As Michael described his experiences, it became apparent that an obvious case of what would later be termed "ethnic cleansing" was taking place. Couzinos was already aware that the men of Alacham "had been wiped out," but he now learned that "the months of August and September 1921 were months of deportation of women and children from the coast towns of the Black Sea to the interior." This aligned well with Michael's recollection that "it was about seven or eight weeks ago that the *zaptiehs* [that is, Turkish policemen] and gendarmes gathered all the men and locked them in the Rezi warehouse," after which the murders began to take place.

The main issue Couzinos sought to resolve was whether or not the people of Alacham were treated any differently from those in other coastal towns. He was particularly interested in the fate of his own mother and other two sisters. While the information related by Michael was, in Couzinos's words, "sketchy, childish, and incomplete," Couzinos was nonetheless able to glean much of what had happened in Alacham. "It was," he wrote, "horrid and devastatingly cruel."

The degree to which such cruelty was a response to the Greek military offensive in Turkey is difficult to tell, as it was conducted almost simultaneously with (albeit a little later than) the overall genocidal program against the Christians of the Ottoman Empire. What makes the account from Michael so telling is that he reduced things down to a level that is both local and personal. Owing to his young age, he was not aware of any grander schemes on the part of the Ottoman (and now, Nationalist) state. All he could go on was what he saw with his own eyes.

It is this deeply intimate description that gives credibility to the bigger picture. Western newspaper articles reported widespread atrocities committed by Turkish forces against the Greek populations of Anatolia at the time, all of which built toward the inevitable conclusion that annihilation was the ultimate objective.

Although the scenes related in this account occurred in 1921, the horrors continued into the following year as well. During the winter of 1921–1922, several Greek villages in the affected region were destroyed by fire, the inhabitants having already been moved out in events reminiscent of what happened to "Papayiannis's" village of Espye. Also in the early months of 1922, many thousands of Greeks were killed by advancing Kemalist forces.

The observations recounted by both Efthemios Couzinos and little Michael are important pieces of testimony regarding the later phase of the anti-Christian measures that had been undertaken by three different regimes—Imperial, Young Turk, and Nationalist—since the 1890s. This was the last chapter in a period of intense and deliberate killing of civilians, before even worse horrors committed against other populations were to return within two decades. As Turkish successor regimes have constantly denied culpability ever since, it is clear that the writing of this history is still not yet complete.

Questions

1. Given his age and the circumstances of his interview with Anthe, to what degree do you think Michael's story is credible?
2. What drawbacks do you think there were in the way Couzinos tried to obtain news about his family?
3. Explain in your own words the significance of the story relating to Couzinos and the young boy who was wounded and in pain in the hospital.

3. The Holocaust

"The Holocaust" is the term in English most closely identified with the attempt by Germany's National Socialist regime, together with its European allies, to exterminate the Jews of Europe during World War II—particularly during the war's most destructive phase between 1941 and 1944. While an exact number of those murdered is impossible to determine, the best estimates settle at a figure approximating 6 million Jews, one million of whom were children under the age of 12 and half a million of whom were between 12 and 18 years old.

The term "Holocaust" has increasingly entered common parlance in order to describe the event, but two other terms are also employed, particularly within the Jewish world. The Hebrew word *Churban,* or "catastrophe," which historically has been employed to describe the destruction of the two Temples in Jerusalem, is one of these; the other, used increasingly by Jews, is the Hebrew term *Shoah* ("calamity," or, sometimes, "destruction").

The first step on the road to the Holocaust can be said to have taken place on the night of February 27, 1933, when the Reichstag building in Berlin, the home of the German parliament, was set ablaze. The day after the fire, on the pretext that it had been set by communists and that a left-wing revolution was imminent, newly-appointed chancellor Adolf Hitler (1889–1945) persuaded President Paul von Hindenburg (1847–1934) to sign a Decree for the Protection of the People and the State, suspending all the basic civil and individual liberties guaranteed under the constitution. It empowered the government to take such steps as were necessary to ensure that the current threat to German society was removed. In a mass crackdown, hundreds were detained in the first few days, followed by tens of thousands in succeeding weeks.

Then, on March 20, 1933, *Reichsführer-SS* Heinrich Himmler (1900–1945) announced the establishment of the first compound for political prisoners, about fifteen kilometers northwest of Munich on the outskirts of the town of Dachau. Other camps soon followed at Oranienburg, Papenburg, Esterwegen, Kemna, Lichtenburg, and Börgermoor, among others. These camps were originally places of political imprisonment. In their most basic sense they removed political opposition from the midst of the community and intimidated the population into accepting the Nazi regime.

Jews had often been arrested previously for transgressing within the framework of existing political classifications, but from 1935 onward they were frequently victimized for their Jewishness alone. This was due largely to the effects of the so-called Nuremberg Laws on Citizenship and Race, in which the formal status of Jews in the Nazi state was defined. Jewish businesses were boycotted; Jewish doctors were excluded from public hospitals and only permitted to practice on other Jews. Jewish judicial figures were dismissed and disbarred, and Jewish students were expelled from universities. Jews were increasingly excluded from participation in all forms of German life. The Nuremberg Laws also withdrew from Jews the privilege of German citizenship. It became illegal for a Jew and a non-Jew to marry or engage in sexual relationships. Life was to be made so intolerable for Jews that many sought to emigrate. Those who did not often found themselves arbitrarily arrested and sent to concentration camps. Arrests did not become widespread until 1938, and in most cases the victims were only held for a short time. The emphasis was on terrorizing them into leaving the country.

The first large-scale arrests of Jews were made after November 9, 1938, as "reprisals" for the assassination of consular official Ernst vom Rath (1909–1938) by Jewish student Herschel Grynszpan (1921–1945?) in Paris. The event precipitating these arrests has gone down in history as the *Kristallnacht,* the "Night of Broken Glass." The resultant pogrom was portrayed as a righteous and spontaneous outpouring of anger by ordinary German people against all Jews, even though it was Nazis in plainclothes who whipped up most of the action in the streets. The *Kristallnacht* resulted in greater concentrated destruction than any previous anti-Jewish measure under the Nazis, and spelled out to those Jews who had, until then, thought the regime was a passing phenomenon that this was not the case.

Henceforth, Jews were targeted for the sole reason of their Jewishness. Prior to the *Kristallnacht,* Nazi persecution of Jews was not premised on acts of wanton destruction or murder. The November pogrom had the effect of transforming earlier legislative measures against Jews into physical harassment on a broader and more indiscriminate scale. From that point on, physical acts of an anti-Semitic nature became state policy.

At the same time that Germany's Jews began frantically seeking havens to which they could immigrate in order to save their lives, the Free World began to close its doors to Jewish immigration. And with Hitler's foreign policy appetite growing and new areas being annexed to the Third Reich, the number of Jews coming under Nazi control increased to grave proportions.

Following the outbreak of war on September 1, 1939, a system of ghettos was established in occupied Poland from October 1939 onward, in order to confine Poland's Jewish population. There, Jews were persecuted and terrorized, starved and deprived of all medical care. During the summer of 1942, the ghettos began to be liquidated, with their occupants sent to one of six death camps located throughout Poland.

Prior to this, mobile killing squads known as *Einsatzgruppen* ("Special Action Groups"), which accompanied the German military during the Nazi assault on the Soviet Union beginning in June 1941, had been at work murdering all Jews found within their areas of control. The initial means by which the *Einsatzgruppen* operated involved rounding up captive Jewish populations—men, women, and children—taking them outside of village and town areas, forcing the victims to dig their own mass graves, then shooting them to death. When the repetition of that activity proved psychologically troublesome, mobile gas vans using carbon monoxide poisoning were brought in, both to remove the intimacy of contact and to sanitize the process. While at times this process was technologically inefficient, from an economic perspective it was cost-effective regarding the use of men and material.

It is estimated that between 1941 and 1943, the *Einsatzgruppen* were responsible for the deaths of more than one million Jews. It is not known when, precisely, the decision to exterminate the Jews of Europe was made, though best estimates settle on some time in the early fall of 1941. At a conference convened by SS General Reinhard Heydrich (1904–1942), held at Wannsee, Berlin, on January 20, 1942, the process was systematized and coordinated among Nazi Germany's relevant government departments; in the months following, the Nazis established six camps in Poland for the express purpose of killing large numbers of Jews. These camps—Auschwitz-Birkenau, Bełzec, Chełmno, Majdanek, Sobibór, and Treblinka—were a departure from anything previously visualized, in both their design and character. With the exception of Auschwitz, the camps did not perform any of the political, industrial, agricultural, or penal functions attributed to those farther west or north. These were the *Vernichtungslager,* the death (or extermination) camps.

The death camps were institutions designed to methodically and efficiently murder millions of people, specifically Jews. These mass murders took place in specially designed gas chambers, employing either carbon monoxide from diesel engines (in fixed installations or mobile vans) or crystallized hydrogen cyanide that, on contact with air, oxidized to become hydrocyanic (or prussic) acid gas.

As the Nazi armies on the Eastern Front began to retreat before advancing Soviet forces (and as they later retreated from American and British troops in the west), renewed efforts were made to annihilate Jews while there was still time. Then, in March 1944, a shock of cataclysmic proportions hit the Jews of Hungary, the last great center of Jewish population still untouched by the killing. Four hundred thousand Jews were annihilated in the space of four months, with the murder facilities working nonstop, day and night. This was the fastest killing operation of any of the Nazi campaigns against Jewish populations in occupied Europe.

Bełzec, Treblinka, Sobibór, and Chełmno had by this time already been evacuated. Only Auschwitz remained to carry out the massive undertaking of the spring of 1944, as April had already seen the start of the evacuation of Majdanek. With the Soviet armies continuing their advances toward Germany throughout the latter half of 1944, the position of Auschwitz itself seemed uncertain, and the complete evacuation of the complex was ordered for January 17, 1945. The earliest date of free contact with Soviet forces was January 22, 1945; when the site was formally occupied two days later, there were only 2,819 survivors left.

The Nazis evacuated any prisoners still alive in the eastern camps at the end of the war, so they would not fall into the hands of the advancing Russians. These evacuations have properly been called death marches, as vast numbers of prisoners died or were killed en route. Evidence that the Nazis tried to keep their prisoners alive is scant; any prisoners who did not make it to their final destination were treated with the same contempt as they would have been had they remained in the camps. Evacuated in the winter and early spring of 1944–1945, they had to contend with bitter cold, fatigue, hunger, and the SS guards, as well as their own debilitated conditions. For those who had already reached the limits of their endurance, the death marches could have only one result. For others, the experience represented yet another challenge to be overcome. Often, the Russians were so close while the prisoners marched away that the sounds of battle could be clearly distinguished, further adding to the prisoners' distress. When they arrived at their new destination, their trials were hardly eased, as they faced massive overcrowding in the camps to which they had been removed.

The prisoners, dropped into horrific camps such as Bergen-Belsen to await liberation through death or an Allied victory, had little time to wait in real terms, though each day dragged by unendingly. Painfully slowly, as German units both west and east surrendered, the camps were liberated. On April 12, 1945, Westerbork, in Holland, was set free. The day before, Buchenwald's inmates rose against their SS guards and took over the camp, handing it to the Americans on April 13. Belsen was liberated by the British Army on April 15, and on April 23 the SS transferred Mauthausen to the International Committee of the Red Cross. The next day, the U.S. army overran Dachau. Five days later, on April 29, the women's camp at Ravensbrück was liberated. The Nazis handed over Terezín, in Czechoslovakia, to the Red Cross on May 2, and on May 8 American troops occupied the main Austrian camp at Mauthausen—the last major camp to be liberated.

MARTHA DODD

Martha Dodd (1908–1990) was the daughter of William E. Dodd (1869–1940), the United States ambassador to Germany between 1933 and 1937. Initially she found the enthusiasm of Nazism appealing, but the violent purges of June 30 and July 2, 1934, known as "The Night of the Long Knives," forced her to change her views. In this extract from her 1939 memoir of the period, My Years in Germany *(the American title of which is* Through Embassy Eyes*),*

Dodd offers her perspective on the persecution of Germany's Jews. At the same time, she also attempts to find reasons for the Nazis' actions.

Among my own and my parents' circles of friends in Germany I had ample opportunity to experience the immediate impact of innumerable personal tragedies. I knew sons and daughters, fathers and mothers who broke their hearts with grief and despair. I knew a mother who told her daughter to become sterilized rather than bring another victim of Nazi fury into the world. I knew a Jewish woman of middle age, in the trying years of physical change, who was pronounced insane and whose son was forcibly sterilized to prevent procreation of a perfectly healthy line. . . .

When I have gone out at night with young Jewish men I have felt the sneers of the crowds, the mutterings and under-the-breath insults. At night clubs and restaurants we have been given the worst tables, the most abominable service and sometimes been refused admission. Some former so-called Christian friends through fear avoid their Jewish friends, cross the street rather than speak or chat with them. The son and daughter of one of Germany's wealthiest industrialists were dear friends of mine but they had few others except among Jews. However, many non-Jewish people in Germany have maintained a heroic stand against Nazi prejudice, defended publicly and privately their Jewish friends and their own humanitarian principles. At diplomatic parties to which we always invited our friends, no matter what their race, creed or politics, we would notice how the Nazi Germans refused to mingle with them even on foreign soil and in a mixed gathering.

When I first came to Germany there were still open incidents throughout the country of persecution of the Jews. . . . Since that time one hears of very few such cases in Franconia, the region where Streicher rules, for the simple reason that the Jewish people have either migrated from this section or have been exterminated.

When I came back to Berlin from this first trip I was told that Jews were forbidden to bathe in Wannsee, a popular lake near Berlin. I was shocked and disgusted and could scarcely believe that it was a government edict—as it was. For two years my favourite lake was Gross Glienicke, a beautiful, serene and quiet spot among hills and trees near Berlin. In 1935 I saw the inhuman black notice posted on the edge of the bathing beach: *Jews Not Admitted.* (I never went there again.)

These were minor and comparatively gentle methods—obvious to any stranger visiting Germany—of showing the Jews contempt. Other and more effective ways of eliminating the Jews from German social and economic life were the concentration camps, ostracism, killing and pillaging. . . .

[W]hen I first came to Germany I was no more and no less anti-Semitic than most gentiles of my background and education. I didn't like many of what were described to me as their people's characteristics (I fell into that common category of people who said, "Some of my best friends are Jews, but. . ."), I thought they were "pushy" and over-intellectual. I had the average gentile's envy of their brilliance and accomplishment, which was developed into a vague prejudice. Because their social and campus activities were circumscribed, I faintly deplored and yet did not understand their segregation. In Germany for the first year I was subjected to the most violent and transparent barrage of propaganda I had ever faced—this propaganda was an attempt to make me anti-Semitic as well as anti-socialist, anti-democratic, and anti-intellectual, to force me into emotional attitudes of hate and anger. I was asked to consider the Jewish people both subversive and sub-human. As factual and thoughtful literature began to seep in, against the Nazis' will, and replace the reams of Nazi propaganda, I began to see the German Jew in his historical role, in his good as well as his bad light.

There is no question that the Jews had prominent places in finance, the professions, and the arts. That they dominated these fields to the exclusion of the Aryans is ridiculous and untruthful. The Jewish population produced an incredible number of talented and productive men in proportion to their population. And one can only consider it creditable to their people. Being an American, I never had been trained in the prejudice that only the privileged, those of the moneyed or familied upper crust, should get to the top. So it did not seem abnormal to me that there were brilliant scientists, professors, artists, lawyers, and doctors who were Jewish. After all, the best man wins, or should win according to American mythology, and I saw no valid reason to excluding talent and constructive work because of religion or minority groups.

What came as a deep and unforgettable shock to me was the fact that many of the wealthy Jews among financial and industrial interests had actually supported Hitler financially and otherwise. They certainly knew what Hitler had in store for them and their people—he made no secret of it from the earliest days. What then could make them, with open eyes, commit their peoples' suicide? What was more important to them than the fact that they were Jews, in danger of imminent destruction by Hitler? The only answer that made any sense was that their class and their fortunes meant more to them than their own lives and freedom and the human birthright of their children. They would agree smilingly to the extinction of their people and glibly accept a temporary economic amnesty from Adolf Hitler.

These pitiable creatures in the throes of financial ambition and class power paid their penalty in due time. For a year or so Hitler left the wealthiest Jews alone, though he taxed them heavily and in many cases summarily confiscated their financial and agricultural holdings. Now Hitler's constant economic duress has led him to the logical conclusions—he is brazenly taking Jewish property of all types, and the rich Jew who thought he was safe by identifying himself with the capitalist class is under the Nazi axe. . . .

The ultimate effect of Hitler's anti-Semitic propaganda is as yet immeasurable. He does not intend his attitudes, his world theory and practice to be effective only in one country, or only in his Germanic world. He expects that other nations—far and near—and other peoples will become acutely conscious of the Jewish problem. He wants to influence the attitudes and actions of governments and citizens in every part of the world still not under his partial or complete domination. . . . In America, South America, England's Imperial holdings, as well as in countries that have no Jewish populations to speak of, Hitler intends to put "racial" consciousness on the map and incite Jewish prejudice everywhere.

For five years the Jewish people has been receiving daily publicity, such as it has never had before in its history, in the press and on the radio all over the world. No matter what had been the point of view expressed, whether sympathetic or not, the Jews have been prominent in the thoughts and conscience of mankind. The intelligent, wise and foreseeing gentiles are horrified and indignant—they act militantly in many ways to remedy the situation in every country. But this enlightened minority is not large enough, though during Hitler's horrible persecution in November, 1938, we had a stirring proof, in America, of outraged public opinion and a well-timed official challenge. Other gentiles, among society's upper brackets, knowing unconsciously that they are partially responsible for the plight of the Jew, resent the object of their cruel discrimination and want to be rid of the burden. They do not want to be continually faced with the serious economic and moral challenge involved. These gentiles, in all countries, are ready and ripe for the seeds of the anti-Semitism Hitler so viciously plants. They resent Jewish refugees coming in large numbers from Germany and further complicating economic problems. Hitler tells them that the Jews dominate economic and cultural life, that they are responsible for many of the world's evils. They look around them and see Jews prominent in financial and artistic life and they try to convince themselves, though they know better, that the Jews are running the country. As a solution they begin half heartedly to wonder if Hitler's policy of extermination isn't the most effective one. When a political crisis or economic emergency arises many of these gentiles are ready to believe the self-appointed prophets of their particular national brand of Fascism who point their finger at "destructive international Jewry."

Source: Martha Dodd, *My Years in Germany* (London: Victor Gollancz, 1939), 265–266, 268–269, 271–272. Published in the United States as *Through Embassy Eyes*. Copyright 1939 by Martha Dodd. Reprinted by permission of Houghton Mifflin Harcourt Publishing Company. All rights reserved.

Commentary

As the outspoken daughter of the American ambassador to Berlin, Martha Dodd was in an ideal position both to observe Nazi anti-Semitic policies firsthand, and to comment on them—not in any official capacity, but, rather, to her friends and confidantes. The source of her free-thinking and open-minded attitudes can be traced to her Democratic Party father, Dr. William E. Dodd, who had a stellar career as a cutting-edge and innovative professor of history before being nominated by President Franklin Delano Roosevelt (1882–1945) to represent the United States in Nazi Germany. Dodd's ambassadorship came to an end in December 1937, and his family returned to the United States. In 1939, Martha Dodd published her memoir of the years she spent in Berlin, from which this account is taken.

In her own career, before joining her family in Berlin, Martha had studied at the University of Chicago and in Washington, D.C., and Paris. For a short period she worked as an assistant literary editor at the *Chicago Tribune*, with an eye on a possible career in journalism.

Her testimony is distinguished by its willingness to observe a range of attitudes toward Jews from the non-Jewish populations of both Germany and the United States. Its honesty, from one who had little to gain or lose from guarded language, is refreshing. Not only does she evince disgust at the "innumerable personal tragedies" of "grief and despair" she witnessed; she also describes the many humiliations directed against Jews that happened within her own relationships, in nightclubs and restaurants.

At first, however, Martha actually found the Nazi movement attractive. Her outlook was conditioned by her feelings for Germany's unemployed, who, under the Nazis, were finding work at a rapid rate. She saw positive signs everywhere, and witnessed a feeling of national self-confidence that began to re-emerge after several years of despair.

Because of her contacts through the Embassy, she managed to acquaint herself with a number of well-placed Nazis, such as Ernst "Putzi" Hanfstaengl (1887–1975), a Harvard-educated, German businessman. Hanfstaengl was an intimate of Hitler during the days leading up to the Nazis' accession to power in January 1933. Martha Dodd's access to the leading figures of the Reich was hampered by internal political issues among the Nazis, however. Over time, a number of territorial disputes arose between Hanfstaengl and Hitler's minister of propaganda, Joseph Goebbels (1897–1945). Hanfstaengl was removed from Hitler's staff in 1933.

Between June 30 and July 2, 1934, the Nazi purge known as the "Night of the Long Knives"—during which a series of political murders was carried out—took place. Following this, Martha's views on the Nazis changed. Friends in her social circle began pleading for American assistance to leave Germany. Martha found that she could no longer go out without feeling revulsion for the regime, as she witnessed constant Jewish marginalization—not only in broad policies and sweeping actions, but also in the humdrum of everyday life.

Further, as her comments indicate, many propaganda efforts were directed toward the Jews. Not only did the Nazis fill a deep well with anti-Semitic literature, but they also poured out antisocialist, antidemocratic, and anti-intellectual materials in unceasing quantities.

What all this signified for Martha Dodd was that the position of those such as herself in the new Germany was totally untenable. At one point, when discussing the fate of the Jews in Franconia, the Bavarian region (with the iconic Nazi city of Nuremberg) that was dominated by Hitler's chief Jew-baiter Julius Streicher (1885–1946), Martha refers to the Jews as having either already emigrated or "been exterminated." While this was not an allusion to the Holocaust of later years, it is, nonetheless, a telling statement indicating severe anti-Semitic treatment from an early date.

Elsewhere, Martha notes that where anti-Semitism was concerned, Hitler had an agenda far greater than one intended for Germany alone. She observes, "He does not intend his attitudes, his world theory and practice to be effective only in one country, or only in his Germanic world. He expects that other nations—far and near—and other peoples will become acutely conscious of the Jewish problem." How is he to do this? "He wants to influence the attitudes and actions of governments and citizens in every part of the world still not under his partial or complete domination." Throughout the world, therefore, even "in countries that have no Jewish populations to speak of," Hitler's aim was to foment a racial agenda and thereby "incite Jewish prejudice everywhere."

Some of her comments regarding the Jews' acquiescence to their fate are open, and perhaps unexpected. She could not get over the fact that at the beginning of the Third Reich, many of Germany's wealthy Jews had actually given their support to Hitler. Why was it that, despite Hitler's often-quoted statements regarding his desire to eradicate the Jews from German life, many wealthy Jewish leaders were prepared to throw in their lot with Hitler's nationalist revival agenda? "What then could make them, with open eyes, commit their peoples' suicide? What was more important to them than the fact that they were Jews, in danger of imminent destruction by Hitler?" Martha's only possible answer was that "their class and their fortunes meant more to them than their own lives and freedom and the human birthright of their children." It was surely an exaggeration—and a wrong assumption to make—that the Jews about whom she writes "would agree smilingly to the extinction of their people," but it is true that before 1938 there were many who would have drawn confusing conclusions about Hitler's ultimate ambitions for the Jews and Germany. After November of that year, following the event that came to be known as the *Kristallnacht,* no one was under any illusions as to what was intended.

Questions

1. In what way(s) can it be argued that Martha's testimony is an eyewitness account?
2. How does Martha describe her change in attitude from one of apathy toward Jews to one of outrage at the Nazi policies against them?
3. Do you think Martha's criticism of German Jews, with regard to their own fate, is justifiable?

VALENTIN SENGER

Valentin Senger (1918–1997) was the child of a left-wing Russian Jewish family that fled to Britain and then Germany as a result of the Russian Revolution. His mother Olga, a member of the German Communist Party (KPD), raised her children to be active in various Party youth organizations. When the Nazis came to power in Germany in 1933, the Senger family was placed in danger on two levels, because of both their political views and their Jewish origin. Through a remarkable set of stratagems, they remained hidden throughout the duration of the Third Reich; they were the only Jewish family to survive the Nazi period in Frankfurt. Watching the Holocaust in real time, yet unable either to stop it or to declare themselves, the family remained "invisible" (as the title of Senger's memoir put it). Here, we read Senger's observations of the Kristallnacht *pogrom of November 9–10, 1938.*

I really did my level best to keep out of sight—until November 1938. Then came Crystal Night.

"*Oy vay,* what will be now!" cried Mama, when the news came over the radio that a certain Herschel Grynszpan had shot Ernst vom Rath, secretary of the German legation in Paris. The murdered man came of an old Frankfurt family. Mama held her head in her hands and her eyes were big with terror. "It's all they were waiting for," she gasped. And then, dwelling on every word, "What the Hitlers have done to us so far is nothing compared to what's coming now."

As usual Mama was right. Next morning as I was crossing the iron footbridge on my way to Sachsenhausen, one of the typists overtook me. "Heard the news? The synagogue on Börneplatz is on fire. They're smashing the windows of all the Jewish stores on Sandweg and throwing everything out in the street."

The office was in an uproar, all talking at once, everybody with something different to report. The new synagogue on Börneplatz wasn't the only one, all the synagogues were on fire. All over the East End and North End, Jews were being driven from their homes, all the Jewish shops were being smashed up. . . .

I was awfully stirred up, but I had to be careful not to arouse suspicion, not to show more curiosity than the others. Finally, I couldn't stand it any more, I put on my coat and ran to Börneplatz. When I was still far away, I saw a big cloud of smoke in the sky.

Then I stood in the crowd on the square, watching the flames rise from the big dome. About a hundred yards from the burning building, the SA and auxiliary police formed a cordon to keep the crowd from getting any closer. Up ahead of me, just beyond the barrier, a group of Hitler Youth were laughing and cracking jokes.

The people behind the barrier seemed subdued; I didn't hear one word of approval. A woman beside me said she'd been at the Stadtwald and seen Jews being hauled away in trucks. A man said he'd just come from Friedberger Anlage; there, too, the synagogue was burning, and so was the synagogue on Alkerheiligenstrasse.

The round synagogue building was burning like a torch. There were two fire engines right next to it. One had a big ladder but it hadn't been extended. The other carried equipment. Some firemen were standing around with hoses, but they weren't fighting the blaze, only spraying the pieces of burning wreckage that fell to the street. Obviously they had orders to let the synagogue burn and just to stop the fire from spreading to the buildings around it.

I don't remember how long I stood there, staring at the flames. I had a feeling I'd never known before. I felt that I was one of these humiliated and tormented people. I'd never realized so fully how much I was one of them. These people, whose windows were being smashed, whose homes were being ransacked, their shops demolished, their synagogues destroyed, their scrolls of the Torah desecrated, these people who were being tortured and killed were my brothers and sisters. Their fate was my fate; I, too, was one of the chosen people, certainly not among the bravest and noblest, or most pious, but one of them all the same, no matter how many lies we told. Nor at that moment did I want to lie my way out of it.

I knew that most of the people around me felt no horror at the sight of the burning synagogue, but I didn't hate them. To them it was a big show—the kind of thing that gives you gooseflesh for a while. I was very sad; it seemed to me that someone ought to say the *Shema Yisroel* aloud, a last profession of faith before the end. . . .

There were hundreds of people, but all I could see was flames and smoke. . . . The tears ran down my cheeks, and I didn't care if anyone were watching me or not.

Slowly I went back to the office. No one asked me where I'd been. Half an hour later the Hitler Youth member came in. His face and hands were covered with grime.

"What's new?" the others asked him.

"What's new? Do I have to tell you?"

No. But he told us all the same. His platoon leader had alerted him the previous afternoon; an action was being planned for the night and his unit should stand by. They'd woken him at three in the morning, and half an hour later he was at the meeting place in the North End. Hundreds of Hitler Youth members had been present. They'd been broken down into groups and then they had set out for the inner city by different routes. Each group had systematically smashed the windows of the Jewish stores in the street assigned to it, broken and gutted the interiors. They then had burst into the homes of Jews, forced them to leave, smashed the windows, and thrown the furniture out into the street.

The streets were strewn with glass; that's why that pogrom came to be known as Crystal Night.

The people who'd been driven out of the houses were rounded up by storm troopers and led away.

The Hitler Youth member was coming to the end of his story. "We caught one kike and clipped his beard and ear locks. He looked like a beet when we got through with him. You'd have died laughing. His eyes were popping out of his head like a frog."

An older man asked, "I suppose they beat them too?"

"What do you mean by that?" the squad leader asked.

"Nothing at all. You know how people talk."

"I guess you feel sorry for them?"

The man didn't answer. The Hitler Youth member turned away, offended at the lack of applause. . . .

The day of horror wasn't over yet. Late that evening Dr. Zely Hirschmann's sister Erika, who worked as a secretary for the Israelite community brought us bad news. The Jewish Welfare Agency on Königswarterstrasse had been raided by the SA. They had ransacked all the rooms, arrested the staff, and made off with a card file containing the names of all the people who had ever received assistance. Anyone who perused that file would be sure to come across our name. And the records of the Israelite community on Fahrgasse, including the membership file, had also been confiscated. There too our name was listed, though we had withdrawn from the Jewish community years before.

Our whole family agreed that this was the end when we discussed it later among ourselves. We only worried about what would happen to Sergeant Kaspar if someone studied the card file of inhabitants at the Hochstrasse police station and discovered that the religious affiliation on our card had been changed.

That some day we would come to the end of this road was something we'd accepted long since. But the uncertainty about when the time would come had grown to an almost intolerable burden. So we waited calmly, almost serenely, for the fatal knock on the door. We waited two, three, four days. Mama was having her heart seizures, and I was plagued by stomach cramps. We waited for weeks and months. But nothing happened.

Source: Valentin Senger, *The Invisible Jew: The Story of One Man's Survival in Nazi Germany* (London: Sidgwick and Jackson, 1980), 106–112. Used by permission.

Commentary

The night known as the *Kristallnacht,* or "Night of the Broken Glass," refers to the falsely advertised "spontaneous" German pogrom of November 9–10, 1938, against Jewish stores and synagogues. The event was supposedly in retaliation for the fatal wounding of Ernst vom Rath (1909–1938), the third secretary of the German Embassy in Paris, by sixteen-year-old Hershel Grynszpan (1921–1945?).

Grynszpan's parents and sister, originally from Poland, had been forcibly deported across the German-Polish border with several thousand others, and were living in destitute and squalid conditions, when Grynszpan decided to make a statement of protest by murdering a senior German official, thus drawing world attention to the Jewish plight.

Joseph Goebbels (1897–1945) carefully orchestrated the attacks of November 9–10 with Hitler's apparent consent, and with the collusion of local police forces throughout Germany. The SS report of November 11 listed 815 shops, 29 department stores, 171 dwellings, and 267 synagogues either vandalized or totally destroyed. Ninety-one Jews were officially listed as killed, and 36 were injured. More than 30,000 Jews were arrested. Many were imprisoned and sent to the concentration camps at Dachau, Sachsenhausen, and Buchenwald, where they were subjected to inhuman treatment.

The actual cost of the damage inflicted was more than 25 million Reichmarks, for which the Jews themselves were held liable. To add to the Jewish community's trauma, the Nazis levied a fine of one billion Reichsmarks to pay for the clean-up, disguised as "reparations" for vom Rath's murder.

Valentin Senger, who was "passing" as a non-Jew in Germany throughout this time, watched developments with a mixture of fascination and revulsion—and no small amount of fear. He provides a first-person account of the *Kristallnacht* from the perspective of one who still found himself emotionally attached to the fate of the Jewish people—*his* people—in a way that he had not anticipated.

Upon hearing the news, his mother's first words included the comment that the death of vom Rath was "all they [the Nazis] were waiting for." In other words, here was a signal, as she saw it, that the Nazis could use in order to make some sort of reckoning with Germany's Jews. "What the Hitlers have done to us so far," she said, "is nothing compared to what's coming now." Such prescient words, it might be felt, are too good to be true. The fact is, however, that for many Jews, it was felt that the various Nazi acts leading up to November 9 were, if not the worst, then at least the last such anti-Semitic acts that would be committed. Now, with the assassination of vom Rath, came the very real fear that even worse days were to come.

Hearing that the synagogue was on fire, Senger made his way to the Börneplatz in order to see for himself what was happening, though he knew he could not attract attention to himself. As he watched the flames, he observed both the mirth of the Hitler Youth and the quiet manner of the German people at the scene. He uses the term "subdued" to describe them, noting their comments about other anti-Semitic measures elsewhere in the city.

While his attention keeps being drawn back to the fire, he notes that he "never realized" until now just how strongly he feels his Jewishness. It dawns on him that the fate of these people is now going to be his fate also, and that, as a result, he is going to have to be even more careful than before not to disclose his true identity. He feels, nonetheless, as though "someone" ought to recite the *Shema,* one of the most sacred Jewish prayers ("Hear, O Israel/The Lord Our God/The Lord is One")—an affirmation of belief often said at the bedside of a dying person, or by that person as his or her final words.

An important part of Senger's account deals with the reactions to the anti-Semitic violence back at his workplace, particularly those evinced in exchanges with the Hitler Youth member who was one of his coworkers. What is obvious here seems to be the relative lack of enthusiasm of those around him regarding what was happening, particularly when measured alongside the obvious glee of the Hitler Youth. This young man is totally indifferent to the fate or feelings of the targets of the Nazis' victimization, seeing the whole thing as something of a lark. He seems personally offended when the others do not join him in his sadistic pleasure.

Senger's testimony concludes with an expression of worry as to what the event portends for his family's future. While no one could foresee precisely what the *Kristallnacht* would lead to, there was enough foreboding in the air to suggest that soon, the family's hiding would come to an end. It is almost with relief, therefore, that we read Senger's final words, "But nothing happened."

Of course, the reality was to be much worse. The *Kristallnacht* was the most extensive act of Nazi persecution against the Jews prior to the outbreak of World War II. The possibility that an accommodation could ever be reached with Nazism—a hope long held by many—now vanished for Germany's Jews. The painful truth, which they had for so long tried to avoid, broke through: they were being forced to quit the country, and they would have to leave Germany for other lands. Prior to the *Kristallnacht,* many could not face that awful reality, which was, perhaps, one of the reasons that Senger's family sought salvation by "hiding in plain sight."

Senger's observations of the awful destruction of that horrible night are clear, measured, and readable. In just a few words, he shows us what it was like for one young man, as a secret participant and witness, to experience what some have termed "the first day of the Holocaust."

Questions

1. In your view, should Senger have gone out to see for himself the destruction caused by the *Kristallnacht*? Did he expose himself to danger by doing so?
2. The Hitler Youth member in the factory where Senger worked was very proud of the destruction caused by the *Kristallnacht.* How did those around him take this?
3. Why do you think the Senger family felt that the events of November 9–10 signaled the end of their opportunities to avoid the Nazis?

SIDNEY SIMON

When war came to Belarus in July 1941, Sidney Simon (b. 1926) and his family were taken by the Nazis to a ghetto. One of five children, Simon was then fourteen years old. After a period of terror at the hands of the Nazis, the family escaped the ghetto and sought sanctuary in the woods. Simon joined the partisans and fought alongside them, before joining the Soviet army. His memoir, which recounts his experiences both as a partisan and as a soldier with the Soviets, provides an account of how and when Jewish opposition could take place, through the lens of what has become known as "forest resistance."

My brother Mojshe belonged to a group of about twenty or twenty-two men. When Mojshe heard about the liquidation, he went to the woods with this group of men to meet up with the partisans.

After a short time as a partisan Mojshe was killed by the Germans and the police. The Germans had surrounded a clearing. As the partisan group went through this clearing that they had thought was safe, the Germans opened fire from all four sides. The partisans didn't have a chance. One partisan, Jankel Orzhechowski, survived by jumping into the bushes when he wasn't noticed.

After our family escaped the ghetto, we met Jankel. Jankel told us that my brother had escaped; Jankel said he had seen Mojshe running, running. My father and I didn't believe Jankel, but he insisted this was the truth. Out of pain and concern to make Jankel tell us the truth, as if to stab himself, my father grabbed a knife, which I immediately took away from him. Jankel continued lying. He lied to protect my parents from pain.

A few days later—this was after Mojshe had left—my family escaped the ghetto because we were warned that, on April 28, 1942, all the Jews in the Żetel Ghetto were to be taken outside the ghetto, massacred, and buried. We went into a hiding place under a small stable—8' by 12'. My brother, Richard, sisters Katie and Ida, my parents, and three more people—neighbours—hid there. We made a shallow, square box and filled this with manure. Under this we made a hole. We would get in the hole and pull the box over the hole to cover our hiding place. The Germans would open the door and look around, but they didn't see anything but manure. We stayed there until night on the day the ghetto was liquidated. We heard a lot of explosions.

My father looked through the hole of the pipe we used for air and said, "They just got your mother's sister Bashe Malke, her husband Shimen, and the baby (two or three months old)." They had hidden in another place under the floor of a house.

My father continued, "They took them outside; she is holding the baby. Oh G-d, a German is choking the baby to death in his mother's arms. Now he is killing Bashe! And her husband is watching. The German beast killed Bashe's husband." Can you imagine the brutality of this!

Then we found that my cousin, Hirshe Leizer, the Hebrew teacher, who had been with us and was married to Civia, and now with a little baby, was hiding too. The baby started to cry. The others said, "Smother the baby or they'll find us." Hirshe said, "I am not killing my baby. I'll go out." He went out, and they killed him; they threw in hand grenades and everybody was murdered, including Civia and the baby. . . .

This horror was our life every day. I never dreamed we would ever get out. This goes for the ghetto, the partisans, and whatever else I went through.

Night came. Father said, "I am going to walk out first. If you hear shooting, don't come out." He left. There were no shots. We did not wait. Without hesitation, my mother, then the children, and then the neighbors followed my father and so we left the hiding place. It was dark but flames flared occasionally. My father took a stick and held it over his shoulder so if anybody saw this they would think he had a rifle.

We made it to the woods and slept there. We saw no partisans. We had no food, except wild berries. At night my mother went to the village from house to house asking for a slice of bread. She would not let us go because it was too dangerous. I saw my mother leaving and I didn't know if she would ever come back. Life was treacherous.

We were looking for a place to settle. We saw a place close to houses. But could the occupants be trusted? Would they betray us? This place was not far from a house occupied by a family named Shavel. We felt safe even though we were not close to him. He could give us news about the Germans. He couldn't give us much food, however, because he was poor.

Finally the Germans decided to go into the woods and kill the "Stalin dogs," what the Germans called the partisans. Everybody heard the news and abandoned their hiding places. We ran deeper into the forest. We had to run through creeks. My boots got wet. It had been rainy and the ground was deep with mud; then it turned cold and the ground froze. My feet were frostbitten. They swelled so much that they had to cut my boots off.

The Germans were still searching in the woods; we were short of places to hide. To be safe we dug an underground shelter that we shored up with saplings so that it wouldn't cave in. There were steps going up to the door. Inside there were bunks. We made torches from moss and sticks, lighting these with a flint stone. Sometimes we would inhale soot, the residue of these torches. Eight or nine people, including my family, lived in this bunker—Majewski, his wife, and a baby, Sanford. The baby caused us anxiety because if the baby cried our bunker could have been discovered. The father said, "if you want my baby killed, *you* kill him." So one of them put pillows over the baby's face. When they lifted the pillows, the baby was still breathing. They say that this baby was meant to live. After this, they agreed not to kill the baby, no matter what happened. The parents wanted to give their baby to a non-Jew; however, this man saw that the mother was having a hard time giving the baby away, so he said no. *That baby, Sanford, is alive today with a family of his own. We were invited to his wedding.*

When the Germans were in the woods looking for Jews, all the others from the bunker, except me, would leave the bunker and go deeper into the woods to flee. I could not leave; because of my frostbitten feet, I could not walk. When they left they would cover the opening of the shelter with wood to which they had attached moss and pieces of branches to camouflage the opening. I would be in the bunker hiding. I would hear the Germans calling to each other. I often would hear horses trotting and whinnying. Once a horse stepped right near me. If his hoof had been any closer, he and his rider would have been in the hole with me and I would have been killed. I had to wait in the bunker until the rest returned.

When the Germans were not searching for Jews and we were all in the bunker, I would sometimes climb out and put my feet in the sun. That seemed to help with the sores and cracks in my feet. During the night my feet would crack again. The next day I would start over again with my feet in the sun. I could feel the reforming during the day and then at night it would crack again. I would wrap my feet in burlap potato bags—these were dirty—full of mud and sand, but they were all I had. It was a wonder my feet did not become infected. In my old age, my feet are numb from the frostbite and I have trouble walking.

I tried to keep clean, using the snow to wash and rinse myself. We had to wear the same clothes all the time. In the spring when it was warmer, I would bathe and wash my clothes in a creek.

We had to move deeper into the woods to hide from the Germans who continued searching for Jews. I had to walk, leaning on two sticks, like crutches. I was in pain and very thirsty. One day I was so thirsty that when I saw a spot where a horse had urinated and the snow had melted, I knelt down and sucked the melted snow.

With me I had a hand grenade without the lever and a gun without ammunition. They were of no use to me but I kept them, hoping, I guess, that I would run into ammunition for the gun and a lever to arm the grenade. Eventually my feet were somewhat better. We continued hiding in the woods. We would still go to the villagers to ask for some food. We would go out and get potatoes and bread and bring these back. Sometimes the partisans would drop off some food.

That was our life for a while until one day a group of partisans came along to see us and give us information, dropping off some potatoes. They had heard that someone had buried a gun in the vicinity, so they had come along and dug up the gun. It had been buried in the woods, wrapped in an oiled cloth. While they were visiting with us, they asked me if I wanted to be a partisan. I said, "Yes, but I don't have a good gun nor any ammunition." To be allowed to join the partisans a person would usually need to bring a gun and ammunition or they didn't want him. But they said they had an extra rifle. They gave me the rifle—the buried one.

The partisans also received weapons from Russian planes that dropped ammunition and dynamite attached to parachutes. At the same time, they would also drop a Russian officer who made sure the partisans received the ammunition. For the time being, he became part of the partisans' group.

The partisans would then make signal fires for the planes—in different designs at different times—so that they not only would know where to drop the supplies but also so that the Germans would not anticipate where they would be dropping the supplies. On rare occasions the planes circled but did not drop any supplies, as if they had intelligence that the drop was unsafe. This was disturbing to us, waiting for supplies that were desperately needed.

The partisans told me to ask my father if I could join them. I walked up to my father and said, "I would like to become a partisan. They have a rifle for me." He said, "my son, do what you think is right and G-d should watch over you." Thus, I joined the partisans.

Source: Sidney Simon with Maryann McLoughlin, *In the Birch Woods of Belarus: A Partisan's Revenge,* ed. Rosalie Simon and Maryann McLoughlin (Galloway, NJ: Richard Stockton College of New Jersey, 2009), 34–38. Used by permission.

Commentary

Instances of what might be termed "forest resistance" saw persecuted Jews living under conditions that called for more than was required of regular soldiers in organized armies. In the forest, uncertainty as to the duration of the crisis that had led to the Jews being there in the first place was ever-present. Often the circumstances leading to their partisan existence were sudden and unexpected, meaning that there was little time or opportunity to plan an effective resistance. For the most part, forest partisans were initially civilians who either joined those possessing military training, or who learned about combat *in situ*. Not all of those who made it into the forest were armed or trained to fight, while many were not prepared or psychologically disposed to do so. Again, this could reduce their effectiveness—all too often leading to massive casualties and/or defeats.

An important predicament facing all partisan commanders concerned the dilemma of whether or not to try to save civilian lives or engage the enemy. Historically, doing so could have disastrous ramifications. Enemy reprisals against civilians, either with the intention of turning civilians against the resistance groups or causing the resisters to curb their activities, were often extensive and bloody. However, many forest fighters saw that the only reason for their existence in that role was to cause damage to the enemy's war effort.

It is estimated that between 20,000 and 30,000 Jewish partisans fought the Nazis and their allies. Their military operations were essentially sabotage and guerrilla tactics rather than direct confrontations, because of their relatively small numbers in any given location and their limited supplies of arms. An already-hostile anti-Semitic environment and a lack of supplies such as food and medicine provided further complications.

Sidney Simon's account brings several aspects of the Holocaust to the fore. In addition to showing that not all Jews who went into the ghettos died—indeed, some, like Simon and his family, managed to escape and survive in the woods—the account also provides important evidence of the role of Jewish partisans in resisting the Nazis. A necessary part of that role inevitably involved an interrelationship between Jewish and Russian partisans, which, unfortunately, did not always run smoothly. The historical record shows, in fact, that protection for Jews in the forest was never guaranteed, though on an individual level male Jews in good health (such as Simon) could be welcomed into Soviet partisan units. Jewish women, children, and the elderly were not usually made welcome, as they were considered to be "useless mouths" that could make no worthwhile contribution to the war effort.

As a general rule, most of those who went to the forest left with little more than the clothes they were wearing and whatever possessions they could carry. Constant wear in a harsh environment quickly reduced clothes to rags, while shoes wore out quickly. In the forest, replacements were sought constantly; often, the only way to replace items was by stealing from local farms or pilfering from the bodies of dead Germans on the battlefield.

Simon's story relates the manner in which he and his family managed to avoid capture just before the liquidation of the Žetel Ghetto on April 28, 1942. From their hiding place in a carefully constructed wooden bunker concealed by a pile of manure, the family watched the unfolding horror "that was our life every day." While the camouflage saved their lives, the ordeal of witnessing exacted a heavy price on the family emotionally, leaving Simon with a legacy of inner distress that comes through clearly in the account.

Simon also describes how, under some circumstances, there were good people who knew about the families hiding in the woods. Contrary to often-expressed recollections from many survivors, those people not only did not report those in hiding, but they also gave them whatever food they were able to spare. It is important to recall that there were those who committed good in the face of Nazi terror, as they were exceptions to otherwise generalized stereotypes about Eastern European civilians.

The accounts conveyed by survivors are often characterized by elements of physical subjectivity. Hence, we can be confronted by a survivor's recollections not only of sights and impressions, but also of smells, sounds, and, above all, of pain.

Simon provides us with these in his description of the injury caused to his feet by frostbite, after he was forced to live on freezing cold terrain. We read how vulnerable his disability made him when he writes that while everyone else would leave the bunker to go deeper into the woods during Nazi round-ups, Simon had to remain where he was because of his inability to walk.

Within the testimony, we are provided with examples of the role luck played in survival. This is something that many survivors discuss when recounting their experiences in concentration or death camps, but it was equally a feature of forest life or life in hiding. The story Simon tells of the German horse that almost stood on him while, incapacitated, he hid in his hole in the ground, illustrates this "luck" factor.

It was while living a forest existence that Simon made the transition from forest dweller to forest fighter. In a matter-of-fact statement, he introduces the latter part of his account by saying simply that, "One day a group of partisans came along to see us." When he asked them if he could join their group, they replied that they felt he was obviously old enough to join them, but first he had to ask permission from his father. In a context in which children were forced to mature faster than in peacetime, his father told his son, "Do what you think is right." And thus, Simon concludes, "I joined the partisans."

Questions

1. Can it be said that Sidney Simon is a Holocaust survivor? Why or why not?
2. Describe Sidney's perspective regarding luck and survival during the Holocaust.
3. What were some of the drawbacks of trying to survive in the forest during the war years?

FRED SPIEGEL

Whereas the story of Anne Frank is well known, that of Fred Spiegel has barely surfaced except in very few instances. Born in Dinslaken, Germany, in 1932, Spiegel was sent with his sister, Edith, to live with relatives in Holland after the Kristallnacht *(the "Night of Broken Glass"), the anti-Jewish pogrom of November 9–10, 1938, when the Nazis destroyed Jewish homes, shops, and villages in Germany and Austria. The Spiegel children were subjected to persecution after the German army invaded and occupied the Netherlands in May 1940. Fred Spiegel was sent to concentration camps at Vught, Westerbork, and Bergen-Belsen, and was only liberated on April 13, 1945. Later, in the fall of 1945, he and his sister were reunited with their mother in England.*

Spiegel's memoir deepens our understanding of the Holocaust as seen through the eyes of a child.

We were assembled early on the morning of May 23, 1943, and put on a train—destination Transit Camp Westerbork. I had just turned eleven. I was with my sister Edith, fifteen years old, Uncle Max, Aunt Paula, and cousin Alfred, twelve years old.

Westerbork had been established in 1939 by the Dutch, as a camp for German Jewish refugees who had crossed the border illegally after *Kristallnacht* and had nowhere to go. It was taken over by the Germans in 1942; they considered it a perfect place for a transit camp because of its location in northeastern Holland in the middle of nowhere, near the German border, and with good railroad connections east. It had previously been well organized by the Jews themselves when the camp was under Dutch control. The Germans took over on July 1, 1942.

Westerbork was very crowded because nearly everybody had a deferment, or exemption from being transported east to the so-called resettlement or work camps. These deferments were given for various reasons: for "essential" workers at the camp and for foreign or enemy nationals. Sometimes, with enough money, deferments could be bought. Because of this, it became difficult to fill the trains heading east every Tuesday. However, it was a transit camp, not a concentration camp, and very much better than Vught.

The problem was the weekly transports east to the "resettlement or work camps." We had noticed a very long train, consisting of cattle wagons standing on a siding. Inmates of Westerbork told us newcomers, "This is the train that takes Jews east to resettlement and work camps—every Tuesday."

The lists of those to be deported were prepared by the Jewish Council within the camp and submitted by the head of the council, Kurt Schlesinger, to the German commander, Albert Konrad Gemmeker. In order to make things easier for themselves, the *Judenrat,* or Jewish Council (Jewish leaders selected by the Nazis) often put all the people arriving the previous few days on the lists before they knew them and often before the new arrivals had the opportunity to obtain an exemption or deferment.

Soon after my arrival in Westerbork, I narrowly escaped being deported on one of these transports. . . .

We had arrived in Westerbork late Monday afternoon after about a six hour train ride, and we were immediately separated, my cousin and I in one huge barrack, my sister elsewhere, and my uncle and aunt also in different barracks. Most people in our barrack had arrived together with us. Yet our first night in Westerbork was uncomfortable. Nobody was able to sleep much that night. The barracks were huge, noisy, and very crowded; each barrack held about 500 to 1000 people. Bunks were stacked three high.

Very early in the morning, the barrack leader started to read out the names of the people to be put on the train that day. As my name and my cousin Alfred's name was called, we walked towards the train, carrying the few belongings we were allowed to take with us. It was dawn and the walk to the train was very scary. Nearly everybody was crying, especially the little children. The people not going on that train were under total curfew and could neither leave their barracks nor look out of the few windows. The only people we saw were the German SS guards with their dogs, Dutch policemen, and the Jewish camp police, or *Ordnungsdienst* (OD). I saw nobody I knew, nor anyone from my family, except Alfred.

When the OD started to push us on the train, I panicked. Everything was so crowded. Some people cried, but most went quietly onto the train. I screamed loudly, "I don't want to go onto this train." When Alfred heard me screaming, he also started to scream. This caught the attention of an SS guard who asked a Dutch policeman what the screaming was all about. He apparently answered, "I think the children are afraid and do not want to go on the train." The SS guard then immediately gave the order to take my cousin and me off that train. The same OD, who had been pushing us on, took us off, and we were put in a small room isolated from everybody else until after the train departed—without us. I did not realize at the time that I had narrowly escaped death.

As I found out years later, this was very unusual. There was always commotion when these trains left because nobody wanted to be crammed on the trains going to an unknown destination eastwards. However, it was indeed a rare occasion when a German guard ordered a Jew to be taken off a train destined for the gas chambers. The Germans preferred that the Jews went quietly and orderly. Apparently my screaming did not fit in with their plans.

Years later, I also found out that nearly everybody who had arrived from Vught the day before was on this train and sent to the death camp at Sobibor in Poland. There were no survivors. Between March and August 1943, about 35,000 Jews were transported from Westerbork to Sobibor. Only nineteen people are known to have survived.

Uncle Max and Aunt Paula had not been aware that we were almost deported. Immediately upon arrival in Westerbork, Uncle Max had applied for an exemption, not to be sent on one of those trains east. He had been a soldier in the German army in World War I and for this, for the time being, he had received an exemption. He thought this would keep all of us safe from being deported.

However, he soon realized, especially after what nearly happened to us, that his deferment would not apply to my sister and me because we were not his children. He felt it was his responsibility to try and save us. My uncle consulted with Kurt Schlesinger, the head of the Jewish council. Schlesinger suggested that my uncle put us on the so-called Weinreb deferment list. For a large amount of money paid to Weinreb, a German Jew living in Holland, people were put on a special list of people who would not be put on those transports east. My uncle was ready to do this, even though it meant that it would cost him almost all the money he still had hidden with non-Jewish friends.

Weinreb had been highly recommended because he was able to pay off the Nazis to save himself, his family, and other people who were willing to pay. My uncle decided to go ahead, but somehow at the last moment changed his mind. He then decided to go to see the German SS Camp *Kommandant,* Albert Gemmeker, even though everybody, including Kurt Schlesinger, strongly advised him against it, as this was considered very dangerous and might cost him his life. But he saw Gemmeker and tried to convince him that my sister and I were British citizens and as proof he brought with him the Red Cross letters we had received from my mother who was living in England at that time. We were foreign nationals. We had those Red Cross letters to prove it. I was never quite sure what transpired, whether we now had deferments as British citizens or if we were still on the Weinreb list.

About six weeks after this incident, my Uncle Max's exemption expired, as all exemptions and deferments eventually did in Westerbork. My uncle, aunt, and Alfred's names were on the list to be sent east to one of those "work or resettlement" camps. I spoke to my cousin before he left and I said to him, "I will see you soon." I believed that my sister and I would probably follow them, being sent on a later transport. Alfred seemed to have a premonition that this would not happen. He was crying and said, "I don't think so." Unfortunately he was right; as I found out after the war, they were deported to Sobibor and killed in the gas chambers on July 2, 1943.

Even though he would never know, my uncle's maneuvering had succeeded in keeping us off those trains to Sobibor and Auschwitz and allowed us to stay in Westerbork.

We could remain in Westerbork for the time being as we apparently were considered "Foreign Nationals" because our mother was living in Leeds, England, as an *au pair,* a foreign maid. We would now live in the orphanage of Transit Camp Westerbork, which was still under the jurisdiction of *Kommandant* Gemmeker.

Source: Fred Spiegel, *Once the Acacias Bloomed: Memories of a Childhood Lost,* ed. Maryann McLoughlin O'Donnell (Galloway, NJ: Richard Stockton College of New Jersey, 2004), 74–79. Used by permission.

Commentary

The Dutch "transit camp" of Westerbork, located in northeastern Holland just outside the town of the same name, was established on October 9, 1939, by the Dutch government as a camp to intern illegal refugee Jews from Nazi Germany. Earlier, on December 15, 1938, the government had closed the border to refugees.

When Germany invaded Holland on May 10, 1940, there were some 750 refugees in the camp. The Nazis permitted it to continue operating, and by 1941 its refugee population had grown to 1,100. Of these, most had originally come from Germany.

In early 1942, German occupation authorities enlarged the camp, and on July 1, 1942, the Nazis assumed direct control, turning it into a "transit camp" from which Jews would be deported to Auschwitz. On July 14 of that year, the Nazis made their initial "selection" of who would remain in the camp and who would be sent away. Two days later, the first train left with 1,135 deportees on board. By the end of July, nearly 6,000 Dutch Jews had been sent from Westerbork to Auschwitz, where most were gassed. Henceforth, deportation trains left every Tuesday.

Between July 1942 and September 3, 1944 (when the transports stopped), Westerbork was the transit point for about 101,000 Dutch and 5,000 German Jews, sent to their deaths at the Auschwitz and Sobibór death camps. Some 750 Jews also died at Westerbork itself during the German occupation. When Canadian troops liberated the camp on April 12, 1945, about 900 prisoners, most of whom were Dutch Jews, remained.

Fred Spiegel's testimony provides us with a glimpse into the complexity of the Nazi concentration camp system. Here, we see the categories of transit camp, concentration camp, and extermination camp, with a spread throughout Nazi-occupied Europe from the Netherlands to Poland. By 1943 the concentration camp system in fact functioned in a number of ways: as a means of removing real or potential opposition from German political life; as penal institutions for German criminals; as unofficial prisoner of war camps, generally for Soviet soldiers; as huge reservoirs of slave labor; as centers of agriculture, mining, and industry; as collection and transit points for so-called racial prisoners; and as extermination installations.

Westerbork was a different variety again. Because it was a "transit camp," most prisoners did not remain in the camp for long, but there was a permanent population retained in order to run the enterprise. A Jewish Council (*Joodse Raad*) was appointed to run the camp and make the deportation selections, and a Jewish police force managed the transfer process and kept order in the camp. Spiegel's account discusses the difficulties the Jewish Council faced in making decisions, which were often literally of a life-or-death urgency. The Jewish policemen's tasks resulted in a number of anomalies, not the least of which was Spiegel's salvation from a deportation transport.

Spiegel escaped being put on one of the transports because of an intervention by one of the SS guards supervising the Jewish camp police. When it appeared that Spiegel would be put on the train leaving Westerbork, he screamed, "I don't want to go onto this train." Alerted to the commotion, the SS guard ordered that Spiegel not be deported. Pure luck, and the unpredictable behavior of the SS guard, rendered this a highly unusual occurrence that could only be put down to a singular case of chance. Spiegel learned later that the train's destination was the death camp at Sobibór, and that all on board were murdered upon arrival.

Westerbork had cultural activities, workshops, a school for unaccompanied child refugees, and an orchestra (the latter not being uncommon in the death camps in the east). Such infrastructure gave a semblance of routine to those living in the camp, providing the SS with a means of compelling passive acquiescence from inmates. It also provided opportunities for the prisoners to engage in acts of corruption, to try to buy more time. There was a system in place allowing for deferments and exemptions that would—for a time—delay deportation for certain individuals. Once they were deported, many of the prisoners went quietly with the thought that the camps to which they were going in Poland would be the same as or similar to those they were leaving behind in Holland.

Spiegel remained at Westerbork for about eight months. His mother was at that time living in Britain as an au pair, a live-in domestic assistant. Through the Red Cross, she was able to send her son letters. Although the letters were each only 25 words long (including the address), their existence proved to be Spiegel's salvation. His Uncle Max, who was with him in the camp, decided to try to find a way to safeguard the boy's life by seeing the Nazi commandant of Westerbork, Albert Gemmeker (1907–1982). His aim was to convince Gemmeker that Spiegel and his sister were in fact British citizens rather than Dutch Jews or German refugees, and that, as such, they should be kept on the lists of those not to be transported. As proof of the children's "British" status, Uncle Max took with him the letters sent by Spiegel's mother, marked with both Red Cross and British stamps. On the basis of this, Gemmeker considered the children to be foreign nationals, and arranged for them to have deportation deferments from then on.

Though Spiegel's uncle, aunt, and cousin remained in Westerbork during this ruse, they were ultimately not so fortunate. About six weeks later, Uncle Max's exemption expired, and the family was sent "to the east." After the war, Spiegel learned that they had been deported to Sobibór and gassed on July 2, 1943.

Fred Spiegel's account highlights a child's resilience in the face of confused and incomprehensible events. Throughout their experience, he and his sister were frequently alone and terrified, the more so after their later evacuation from Westerbork and deportation to their final camp at Bergen-Belsen, where they would remain from January 1944 until their liberation in April 1945.

Questions

1. Was Westerbork a concentration camp in the sense that you understand the term?
2. In what way(s) was Fred Spiegel's life at risk while he was at Westerbork?
3. Describe briefly the anomaly that allowed Spiegel to avoid deportation.

SHIRLEY BERGER GOTTESMAN

Shirley Berger Gottesman's memoir of Kanada II *(the part of the camp to which she was assigned) in Auschwitz, and of various other slave labor camps in Germany, is an astonishing testimony that both horrifies and inspires. Originally from Záluž in Transcarpathian Poland/Ukraine, Shirley lived with her parents and four siblings in a community that included her grandmother, aunts, and uncles. In April 1944 the family was deported to a ghetto in nearby Munkács, and a short time later they were sent to Auschwitz. Shirley, then 16, was assigned to* Kanada II, *given a uniform (the red polka-dotted dress of her memoir's title), and told to sort the possessions brought from the cattle cars. Her barrack block was only 10 feet away from Crematorium IV. In her memoir, she describes the horror of what she witnessed and lived through on a daily basis.*

In the morning the *Kapos* (prisoners in charge of a group of inmates) took us to the big camp in Birkenau where *Lagers* A, B, and C were located. . . . They directed us to a barrack full of bunk beds.

Each morning we had to awake early and go outside for *Appell* (roll call) for a few hours, during which time we were counted. After *Appell,* they gave us food or something to drink. The food was unbelievably disgusting. We had one bowl for coffee and soup. We had no spoon; therefore we had to drink everything. We always had to share with the women in our row.

Because I had just arrived, I could not grasp what was happening. I was not even hungry. I was in shock.

At *Appell* we had to stand in alphabetical order. They counted us off—there were so many of us! They wrote down names: our parents' names and our names. They gave us numbers with the Star of David insignia. My number was A5812. They painted a red line on the back of our grey dresses with enamel paint, so it would not come off. They were very professional and efficient.

The Aryans had green triangles; they worked in the offices. There were other colors as well. Some Russians wore red triangles because they were Communists, political prisoners.

I was assigned to the *Effektenlager II* (camp of belongings), called *Kanada II Kommando* (work group). It was called *Kanada* because many considered Canada a wealthy country and a desired emigration destination.

They took us to *Kanada II,* or Section BIIg, where the thirty barracks for workers assigned to *Kanada II* were located—between Crematoria III and IV. . . . At first, they took us every day from the Birkenau women's camp to *Kanada II*—back and forth. Then they emptied two barracks for *Kanada II* women, so we did not have to go back and forth to the camp. My barrack was ten feet away from Crematorium IV that had a disrobing area, a large gas chamber, and crematorium ovens. Across the street were barracks for "Aryans," for SS and office workers.

Each barrack had a Kapo, a foreman (*Führerarbeiter*), and a few helpers. The Kapos watched over us all; the SS over everything. The Kapos were on good terms with the Germans—not a friendship, certainly; however, they would schmooze around a lot of the time. I remember an Austrian from Vienna, an elderly gentleman, an office worker. He was sitting on a windowsill across from our barracks, playing a song on his harmonica: "Vienna. Vienna. You alone, You will always be in my dreams." I suppose he was homesick for Vienna. I was homesick and lonely. I wanted my mother and aunts.

There were fifteen barracks in the compound. These were for different commodities that we were sorting as well as for the bathhouse and the mechanics and carpenters. Shoes, dishes, and pans were sorted outside in huge piles.

We could go to Barracks 5, 6, 7; that is, we could go where we worked and to the bathhouse. We could go to these as we pleased. If we had to go farther, however, we had to have guards with us.

Very few people in comparison to the numbers in the camp worked in *Kanada*. There were a lot of Slovaks who had been there a long time. They spoke perfect German because Slovakia was so close to the border. Jewish people tended to learn a number of languages. I remember we were with people from Poland. I spoke Yiddish and Czech, so I learned Polish quickly. The women I worked with were older: I remember Guta, Genya, and Mikla; we worked in groups. I was like a child to them because I was younger.

One had had a child. At the selection, she was told, "Give the girl to her grandfather. That will be easier. You will work and her grandfather will take care of her."

Both the child and her grandfather were murdered.

We talked about our past and our future hopes. We tried to make the best of our present. Of the future we were frightened, at times.

We were lucky in that we could have showers there. Thousands in Auschwitz-Birkenau did not have that chance; instead, they were murdered in the so-called showers. We also could have all the clean clothes that we wanted. At first we wore grey dresses. However, they decided that they wanted to know who was who. Therefore, each barrack was assigned a different colored dress: the women in my barrack wore red dresses with white polka dots; another barrack had blue dresses with the white polka dots. To me this seemed incongruous—bizarre! To be wearing cheerily colored uniforms, and ten feet away people were being gassed and burned. They still painted the red stripe on the back of our dresses.

In early June 1944, I began working in *Kanada II*. From the cattle cars everything was brought to *Kanada* I or II. We were isolated in our section of *Kanada,* sorting.

I saw only what happened near my section. I worked sorting what people had brought in. I sorted these into different piles. Then the trucks came and hauled the bundles away.

When I went to the barracks to work, I looked at what was happening in Crematoria III and IV. Long lines went into the building but never came out. Girls who had already been there for years told us, the more recent arrivals, that everybody not selected for work was gassed and burned.

They said, "It is only a matter of time; we will all go there."

When later I found my two aunts, Helen and Pepe, still alive in the camp, they said to me: "Imagine, the *Blockova* (Polish barrack leader) said, 'You will never see your parents again.' Imagine how mean she is."

I said, "No. She is correct. Look over there."

Helen said, "No!"

I said, "Yes. Believe it."

Two crematoria were on one side; two on the other side. When we went to work, we had to go between the crematoria. We could see inside. Near the crematoria the grass was nicely kept—green. I saw chimneys. The fumes were terrible, especially in the summer. The odor of burning flesh! *Years after, when I smelled burning, I would scream. For example, when my husband was burning trash.*

Once I saw a bunch of men with black faces marching from the crematoria; they looked like chimney sweeps. As they marched past me, I offered one a hankie. We could say a word or two, always we mentioned the town where we were from. If the *Kapos* saw us talking longer, we were beaten. These men, I learned, were the *Sonderkommandos,* who emptied the gas chambers, pulled the gold teeth of the victims and cut their hair; they also searched the bodies for valuables that they may have hidden. Then they burnt the bodies in the ovens, and when the bodies were consumed by the flames, they removed the ashes. They said that the *Sonderkommando* who worked inside prayed. I also heard that every three months, they changed the *Sonderkommandos.* The work was very hard on them; they rapidly deteriorated. Then the older ones were themselves put in the gas chambers. They selected new strong *Sonderkommandos* from incoming groups.

Daily and nightly I saw lines and lines, ten or fifteen feet away, all marching in a line. They motioned to us. We couldn't tell them. We motioned back, rubbing our cheeks—we meant by this to wash or to shower. . . .

I never saw anyone I knew in line for the gas chambers and crematorium. Our group had come in one transport. When I went home, people my age, as well as those younger and older, had not come back. Only a dozen or so returned. . . .

The people were usually quiet, walking slowly; rarely did they talk—they were too exhausted. The people had usually traveled for days. They didn't resist. They had been made to give up life before they were even in the gas chambers. The whole set up, traveling for days and everything! They were debilitated and despondent.

The transports usually arrived at night. People didn't know where they were going or where they had arrived. The SS sent them through quickly. Once they were inside the building we didn't hear anything. I heard that they prayed. . . .

It was unbelievable. No one could have imagined that they would do to people what they did. They were so systematic and so organized. Everything was planned to the T. Scientists must have worked on the plan. It was so unbelievable. I can't even conceive of what they did. Impossible! We were ready for work. We were even ready not to have enough food. We were *not* ready to be gassed. It is unbelievable to think that some of us could live through this and not lose our sanity.

Source: Shirley Berger Gottesman and Maryann McLoughlin, *A Red Polka-Dotted Dress: A Memoir of Kanada II* (Galloway, NJ: Richard Stockton College of New Jersey, 2011), 20–25. Used by permission.

Commentary

Just a few hundred yards from the gas chambers and crematoria at Birkenau, northwest of the Auschwitz main camp, was an area of the camp the inmates called *Kanada*. Comprised of 30 barrack blocks transformed into storehouses, *Kanada* was given its nickname because the Poles in the camp saw the country of Canada as a land of great plenty and riches. In the barracks, inmates sorted and packaged new arrivals' belongings. These were deposited into huge warehouses according to their type, after which they were baled or boxed, then sent back to Germany.

Between 1942 and 1943, there were two shifts of up to 1,600 inmates each employed at *Kanada*. Corruption among the SS was widespread, and many of the guards could be suborned to provide services or turn a blind eye, provided the prisoner in question could offer a worthwhile bribe and was known personally by the guard. Alcohol, great quantities of which were procured illegally by the *Kanadakommando,* became a major item of trade. Many of the SS at the camp enriched themselves by pilfering confiscated Jewish property.

For the most part, it was women who worked in *Kanada*. Because conditions were better than elsewhere and there existed the possibility of obtaining goods for trade, work in the *Kanadakommando*—the prisoner detachments stationed in Kanada—was one of the few jobs inmates actually sought at Auschwitz. Over time, the killing process intensified and the capacities of *Kanada* stopped being satisfactory, so a new complex was built in December 1943. The prisoners of the *Kanadakommando* were housed there, as were the SS offices. These new barracks were also used for sorting and storing the possessions of murdered Jews. The possessions of many non-Jewish prisoners were sent to *Kanada* as well.

By July 1944, the number of prisoner-workers at *Kanada* was about 600. As tens of thousands of Hungarian Jews were deported to Auschwitz, the

Kanadakommando grew by another thousand prisoners. As of early October 1944, there were 815 women and several hundred men employed at *Kanada*.

In April 1944, after Passover, the family of 16-year-old Shirley Berger Gottesman was deported to a ghetto in nearby Munkács, Hungary. A short time later they were sent to Auschwitz-Birkenau. Shirley was assigned to *Kanada II* and told to sort the possessions brought from the freight cars (termed "cattle cars" by the inmates). Describing the horror of what she witnessed, she states toward the end of her account: "It was so unbelievable. I can't even conceive of what they did. Impossible! We were ready for work. We were even ready not to have enough food. We were not ready to be gassed."

Shirley outlines the administrative arrangements that made it relatively simple for the Nazis to control so many prisoners. Within what was effectively a structure of terror, SS officers were able to recognize at a glance which classification a prisoner belonged to by means of a series of identification badges that explained exactly why each detainee had been arrested. The badges took the form of an inverted triangle and were sewn on both the prisoner's jacket and on a woman's dress or the right leg of a man's trousers. The distinguishing features of these triangles were their colors. A political prisoner, for example, wore a red triangle, while a common criminal had a green one.

Shirley also describes how camp regulations were administered. The system of discipline and punishment could not have operated without the compliance (sometimes willing, sometimes not) of prisoners, known as Kapos, who acted in correctional roles. Kapos were inmates appointed by the SS to serve as the foremen of labor detachments. They are mainly remembered as fearsome and harsh, infamous for their brutality, frequent sadism, and familiarity with the SS. As Shirley notes, "The Kapos watched over us all; the SS over everything." The relationship was not a simple one: just because a Kapo held authority over the other prisoners, in no sense did he have a guarantee of survival. The overwhelmingly powerful dominance of the SS saw the Kapos utterly dependent on the SS for everything. They, like any other prisoners, could be punished for the slightest infraction of the rules. They had to do exactly as they were told, nothing more or less. They were sandwiched in the middle of camp society—while enforcing SS structures and discipline on those below them, they could never forget that they, too, were prisoners. Kapos could be (and often were) killed by the common prisoners as traitors; they could equally by killed by the SS on a whim.

What Shirley shows us, therefore, is that even within the crematoria there were various social strata, notwithstanding the fact that this was a most unusual form of society. Her account also makes it clear that there were better and worse work assignments, with *Kanada* being among the best.

Perhaps most important, Shirley's narrative offers eyewitness testimony of the gas chambers and crematoria, from one who was only yards away from both for an extended period of time. It also records the passive, resigned, almost stupefied sense with which the victims of the gassings approached their fate, seemingly without any comprehension of what was about to befall them. The pain felt by Shirley and those around her must, at times, have been more than they thought they could bear, the more so as many of the personal items they were forced to sort had come from their fellow Hungarian Jews during the Nazis' final major action of the Holocaust.

Shirley Berger Gottesman's memoir is a crucial statement from a witness and survivor who, in innumerable ways, suffered brutal psychological torture while working in a horrific environment, day after day, for months on end.

Questions

1. What was the nature of the work in which Shirley was engaged while she was at *Kanada II*?
2. Can you identify from Shirley's account how she responded emotionally to the events she witnessed and experienced?
3. Assignment to *Kanada* was considered by some to be a way to enhance the prospects of survival. Do you see anything in Shirley's account that could authenticate that position?

JADZIA ALTMAN GREENBAUM

Bergen-Belsen was perhaps the supreme example of the chaos, overcrowding, and general horror that struck all the Nazi concentration camps. The image of the camp at the time of its liberation by the British in April 1945 has left just as indelible an impression of the Nazi system on the Western mind as Auschwitz has. Born in the Polish city of Będzin, Jadzia Altman Greenbaum survived a series of labor camps and a death march before arriving at Belsen. She was barely alive. Then she contracted typhus as well. The account here describes her recollections of that awful time in Belsen, and of the liberation of the camp, which saved her life.

_____

From Flossenbürg, they took us on a cattle train. We were on this train for one week with little food. They gave us black, clay-like bread and told us to save it for a few days. There was no water unless it rained. Then we would stick our hands out and get a little rainwater. There was only a bucket for a toilet. But who needed to go! We didn't eat. We didn't have water except for a little rainwater.

While we were traveling, we thought that they were taking us north. But then they took us south. Then the train stopped and we stayed a half-day on the tracks not moving. After this they brought us to Bergen-Belsen. By this time there were a lot of dead people on our train.

When we stopped we saw a little gully with big frogs in the water. The water was clear so we ran over and drank the water in that gully. What did we care about being sick! We needed water.

One German soldier said to us, "You are going to a paradise, to Hotel Paradise." We could not believe him. An older German soldier passing by said, "*Kinder,* you won't get out from here." . . .

Then they began to march us into the camp. At the entrance to Bergen-Belsen we saw little bungalows with little ribboned curtains on the windows and flower gardens around the bungalows. Initially we thought these were for us. (Actually, the SS lived in them.) However, once past the bungalows, we started to see barracks, then we saw dead bodies, and we saw skeletal people barely walking—*musselman.* As we were walking down the road, we saw a wheeled wagon that people were pushing. The wagon was loaded with dead bodies. We started to smell something dreadful. We could not understand what the smell was. Then we realized that dead people were piled up behind the barracks and the bodies were being burned. We let that wagon through and then we saw the barrack-section where we would be staying.

I saw that Bergen-Belsen had two main sections with a road running through the middle; one section on one side of the road and the other section on the other side. They took us into one section where we saw a huge tent and a big barrack. There were three rooms in this long barrack. In the first room were non-Jewish Polish women from the Warsaw Uprising (not the Warsaw Ghetto Uprising in which Jewish Poles fought). In the second room, more Polish women. In the third we went in to take a look and dead people were lying there. We looked in the tent—dead people there too. Next they took the dead bodies from the third room, putting these in the big tent. We were given the third room.

We went into the big room. Then we looked down at the cement floor. The floor seemed to be writhing. We looked closer and saw white crawling things—maggots from the dead bodies that had been in the room or big lice from their bodies. We wanted to leave immediately. The guard said, "No one leaves." We started to stamp on the maggots or lice. They told us to sit down on the floor. There was only one straw bed; this Mitzi and her two sisters took.

Next day when we woke up we were covered in lice. Mitzi came out and she and both sisters were also full of lice. She said, "Don't be shy." Each one took the back of the other girl. "Lice each other." She said, "You are full of lice. This is how you kill them." Then she showed us to how to crush them with our nails. From then until the end of the war, I had lice. A lot of girls became ill from typhus that the lice carried. But I didn't have typhus then.

We had no water not even to drink, and no toilet. Sometimes we needed to use the toilet. We had to go outside to an open pit that had a few seats. Running water was on the other side to clean away the waste. I went over one time.

Because we were so crowded the non-Jewish Polish women figured they could take a few Jewish women in their barracks. They took in forty of us. I was one. That was a little, teeny bit better. At least I was not on cement but on plywood on top of cement. But I still had the lice. Polish women had lice too. The whole place was full of lice.

Behind us was a road and barbed wire. On one side they were burning the dead. On the other side were foreigners, civilians—English, American, South American, and Chinese, wearing their own belongings—dressed nicely. The Germans had taken them as hostages, I suppose.

One night the Polish priest, a prisoner, came into the Polish barrack. He told them to pray. He said, "The war will soon be over." I said, "We're Jewish." He said to us, "You pray in your way. We'll pray in ours." So we prayed. . . .

Suddenly we heard little tanks approaching and stopping. We ran to the wires, screaming, and sticking our hands out the wire. We ran so hard that the dust from the ground came up in clouds. We saw a star on the tanks. I thought, "O my God! We're liberated." Then the tank turned around and went away. We were so disappointed that some girls began to cry and sob.

Later that day a jeep with four speakers drove in, broadcasting in many languages. "The war is not over, but you are liberated. However, we cannot open the gate and let you out because of the typhus in the camp. We still have to fight the Germans; we cannot let our soldiers become ill with typhus. We are bringing you food." We never got this food for two or three days. . . .

At last we knew we had been liberated. No one was on the watchtowers anymore. The Germans had run away before the British had arrived. The Germans had told the Hungarian POWs to watch us. Some girls got out and went over the ditches and the Hungarian guards shot them just before the end. Two girls tried to escape and one was shot. This was heartbreaking!

When the Germans left they had taken the foreign citizens with them. They left only the sick foreigners and a lot of clothing. We didn't have clothing, just rags. We went over, opened the wire between the barracks, and took some clothing. I took myself a fur coat. At least I was warm. But I was still hungry!

When we came back, the English started to give us food. We sent girls to the kitchen with a clean garbage can and they brought us back the food. At first they fed us a hearty soup with big pieces of meat and fat. They meant well, but this was not good for people who had not eaten for days and who were not used to a rich diet. People became very sick and some died.

Source: Jadzia (Jeanette) Altman Greenbaum and Maryann McLoughlin, *2 More Weeks, Deutschland Kaput!,* ed. Maryann McLoughlin (Galloway, NJ: Richard Stockton College of New Jersey, 2008), 40–45. Used by permission.

Commentary

Born in the southern Polish city of Będzin, Jadzia Altman Greenbaum survived a series of labor camps and a death march to the Bergen-Belsen concentration camp in 1945. Belsen, established during the second half of 1943, is best remembered for the images brought to the world at the time of its April 1945 liberation by British troops. It was strewn with corpses, while thousands of emaciated and desperately sick people crowded into miserable barracks. Pictures of these horrors circulated throughout the world. Bergen-Belsen provided the first evidence of the inhuman barbarity embedded within the National Socialist concentration camp system.

On April 15, the day of liberation, the British found 60,985 survivors. About 10,000 unburied dead lay where they had fallen in the compound, and another 15,000 succumbed to disease and starvation after the British arrived.

Following the dislocation of the north German rail network caused by constant Allied bombing, the Nazis could not transport food to Belsen. Medical science, in the form of both doctors and equipment, was completely lacking. By the end of the war, the camp had become nothing but a dumping ground for enfeebled prisoners who had been sent to Germany from camps in the east. After the liberation, the British set the captured Nazi guards to work helping to gather the dead together for mass burial. Most of those who had died were simply piled up in what became mountains of putrescent flesh, then shoved unceremoniously into giant pits dug by British army bulldozers.

Jadzia's account gives us a riveting picture of the inhuman conditions of the train transport from the Flossenbürg concentration camp, then of her initial impressions of Bergen-Belsen upon arrival: "We started to see barracks, then we saw dead bodies, and we saw skeletal people barely walking—*musselman*. As we were walking down the road, we saw a wheeled wagon that people were pushing. The wagon was loaded with dead bodies."

One of the topics not often depicted in regular memoir literature is the sense of smell, but survivors refer to it frequently. In Jadzia's case, it was the smell of Belsen that hit her immediately: "We started to smell something dreadful. We could not understand what the smell was. Then we realized that dead people were piled up behind the barracks and the bodies were being burned."

Another feature of Jadzia's account is the open manner in which she discusses non-Jewish Polish women in the camp. Referring to them as having been sent as prisoners from the Warsaw Uprising (August 1 to October 2, 1944), she is pointed in distinguishing them from the Jews who perished in the Warsaw Ghetto Uprising a year earlier. She does not condemn them, however. Her observation is a useful reminder that Poles also suffered under the Nazis, and that they too were prisoners at Belsen. This reminder of common suffering is reinforced during another episode in Jadzia's account, when a Polish priest, also a prisoner, visits the barrack block containing the Polish women. Telling them to pray, he buoys their spirits with the words that the war will soon be over. Jadzia comments to him that she is Jewish and not Christian, but in a spirit of fellow feeling he replies: "You pray in your way. We'll pray in ours." This was, to say the least, probably an unexpected outcome.

The conditions were awful in the barrack block housing these women. In the third room, where Jadzia was put, the cement floor "seemed to be writhing." The source was "white crawling things—maggots from the dead bodies that had been in the room or big lice from their bodies."

In this context, there was little opportunity to reflect upon the future. Given what they were up against, few would have seen themselves staying in that state for long, as death was omnipresent and there seemed to be little hope for liberation. The priest had sounded a positive note, but until the very moment of release it seemed as though "freedom" was nothing but a state that existed in a previous life. Then, suddenly, "We heard little tanks approaching." This could have been the start of the liberation process, so Jadzia was bitterly disappointed when the tank she saw "turned around and went away." It was, of course, a combat unit, not equipped to liberate a camp. Soon, however, other units arrived.

When the camp was finally liberated, the military side of the war was not yet over, but a British officer announced, "You are liberated." Belsen would have to be quarantined, however, because of the typhus epidemic. In an arranged truce with the Nazis, British troops negotiated for an exclusion zone to be placed around the camp, as SS chief Heinrich Himmler (1900–1945) had earlier agreed to have the camp handed over without a fight. In honor of the truce arrangements, most of the SS were permitted to leave, while a small number of SS men and women, including the camp commandant, Josef Kramer (1906–1945), remained. The outside was guarded by Hungarian and regular German troops. When the British arrived, they took control and arrested the remaining Nazis. Kramer and several others were eventually tried and executed for crimes against humanity.

Jadzia's account notes that when she looked up, "No one was on the watchtowers anymore," and "the Germans had run away before the British had arrived." It might well have been the case that in her debilitated state, she had not noticed that some Germans still remained, though she did notice the Hungarians (whom she identified as prisoners of war). The overcrowding, the lice, the maggots, the lack of food, and the prevalence of those already diseased eventually infected Jadzia herself, and it was not long before she contracted typhus—which she had when she was found at the time of liberation. Barely alive, she was placed in the hospital, where she lingered near death for weeks.

What now remained? Reconstructing a new life from the ashes and ruins of the old was a task that would prove as daunting as it was heart-rending. Jadzia's powerful account relates the story of how she overcame the deaths of her family members in this, the most horrible of genocidal environments, at the end of World War II.

Questions

1. What was the relationship between Poles and Jews in Bergen-Belsen, as seen by Jadzia?
2. Bergen-Belsen was not a labor camp, meaning that there was little for the prisoners to do once they arrived. Can you identify Jadzia's main concerns as she tried to live through the camp experience?
3. Describe the liberation of Belsen. In your view, was there anything unusual about it?

IDA WEISBAUM FEINBERG

The Nazis established a ghetto at Vilna after their occupation of Lithuania on June 25, 1941. The Vilna Ghetto was known for its brutality and high mortality rate, as starvation, disease, shootings, and deportations to concentration camps and extermination camps steadily took a horrendous toll on the population. In 1943 Ida Weisbaum Feinberg, her husband Sender, and her father were deported from the ghetto to the Vaivara concentration camp, the largest Nazi camp in Estonia. Ida survived despite typhus, malnourishment, hard labor, and a death march. Her memoir is one of the few we have of Holocaust survivors sent to Vaivara. Here, she describes what life was like there, up to and including her liberation in 1944.

Upon arrival in Estonia, I discovered the destination of the train that had deported us. We were sent, as were tens of thousands of Jews from other countries, to forced labor camps in Estonia as part of the Nazi resettlement plan. The main holding camp was Vaivara, a concentration and transit camp in northeast Estonia, located near the Soviet/Estonian border. . . .

In 1943, I arrived in Estonia and was sent to Vaivara. . . . My father and Sender had also been deported, but they were not deported in the same cattle car as I. We had arrived from Vilna after a journey of several days, a journey that seemed much longer because of the over-crowded cars, the stench, and the lack of water.

At Vaivara, the cattle cars were unloaded, and we lined up. I saw that the camp was surrounded by barbed wire as well as by a kind of moat—a ditch full of water encircled the camp. I looked for Sender and my father among the others. However, I did not see them. I felt very much alone.

After selection in Vaivara, the women who had been selected for work were taken to a building, stripped, and put on tables. They shaved us all over. Some young girls cried and cried. I said to them, in Yiddish, "Don't cry! As long as you have a head, you'll have hair. Don't give them the satisfaction of seeing you crying." At this time they gave me a striped uniform and my number, 1055 or 1059, on a *shmatteh*. . . that I pinned to my clothing.

They then put us in wooden huts with thin walls that were not insulated against the heat and cold. These huts, the so-called barracks, were divided into three sections with seventy or eighty prisoners in each section—each hut was very over-crowded. In my barrack, there was a small stove but it didn't heat well; therefore I was very cold—freezing. We slept in three-tiered bunk beds, ten in a row. I wore a blanket in the morning to wrap around me when I went to roll call in the brutally cold early morning air.

Each day we had roll call at 5:00 AM. We waited a long time while they counted us before we could go to work. In the morning we had a watery drink they called coffee. In the afternoon we were given watery soup to drink and a small piece of moldy bread to eat. I was desperately hungry. I "organized" potatoes from the fields so I wouldn't starve. I hid them in my clothing when I returned to the camp. I used to roast them in the small stove in our barrack.

Water was scarce. There were no washing facilities. In the beginning there were just holes to be used as toilets. Later there were boards with holes in them—inadequate because there were many prisoners. I washed in snow or with a little of the drinking water they gave us. I tried to keep myself clean because I was afraid that I would catch diseases if I didn't.

Despite my efforts at cleanliness, I caught typhus. Many people in Vaivara died from typhus carried by lice. These were big lice—all over everyone, thousands of them. I was very ill, but some kind person in my barrack helped me, giving me warm water to drink. Therefore, somehow I survived this deadly disease. I also survived a big selection in which three hundred people who had typhus were taken away to be murdered.

Later there were selections every two weeks, when about 500 prisoners were murdered—often taken to the forest and shot by the German or Estonian SS.

Their bodies were carried away and burned by Jewish men, *Sonderkommandos* (special *Kommando* or work duty, dealing with corpses). They were forced to do this. Most *Sonderkommando* only lasted three or four months, and then they were killed, so they would not tell about what they had seen.

The Germans forced me to do many different kinds of work: I worked in the woods, chopping wood; I cleaned police stations for the Germans; and I worked on the railroad, laying down new railroad ties. All of this was back-breaking work, especially to malnourished people; the SS wanted to work us to death.

We were guarded by a few older German civilians, who could speak Polish. They were good to us, sometimes giving us salt or whatever food they could hide for us.

In July and August of 1944 the Soviet Army advanced north through Nazi-occupied Estonia toward Vaivara.

I saw neither my father nor my husband in Vaivara Concentration Camp. However, over a year after my arrival in Vaivara, when I was sent to a sub camp to work, I saw my father. He was working at different jobs, in the woods or on the railroad. I was so happy to see him and to know that he was still alive. I had hoped to see that Sender may also have survived. Then, I heard, they had taken my father away to the woods and murdered him. They gave me his shoes to hurt me so that I would know he was dead. I was terribly upset. . . .

Ahead of the advancing Soviet army, the SS began to evacuate Vaivara Concentration Camp and its sub-camps in late August 1944. In Western Europe, the Allied armies began liberating other concentration camps in April of 1945. . . . Many prisoners from Vaivara were sent west by the sea to Stutthof Concentration Camp, a camp about 22 miles east of Danzig. Others were sent on death marches along the Baltic coast.

I was sent on a death march to the south, wearing wooden clogs, which were almost impossible to walk in. The weather was already quite frigid. I was freezing. I said to the Germans walking with us, "Kill me here." But they didn't. Other women on the death march encouraged me, coaxing me, "Come with us. We'll help each other." So they *shlepped* me with them.

One night we stopped at a cement factory to rest. People from the village came to look at us. They didn't know what was going on. In Polish I said to them, "I am a Jew." They may already have known this because the SS had painted a red cross on the back of my coat—to mark me as a Jew. In addition, I wore my number on a *shmatteh* pinned to my coat. One Pole said to me, "I live across the road. I'll walk across. You follow me because, otherwise, they will kill you tomorrow." Four of us escaped like that. (*Two of us are still alive.*)

I stayed with these Poles for six weeks. They were refugees from other areas of Poland, sent by the Germans to do slave labor. These kind Poles gave me food. In the daytime they hid me and watched for the Germans. At night I slept in a bed with pillows! Other places in the village were hiding the other girls.

When the Germans left the area, the Russians, advancing from the east, arrived near the cement factory. So I was liberated and had to then think what I would do. I decided to go back to Vilna to try to find Sender. I met a Polish woman, also a refugee, who helped me because I was weak and malnourished. She took me on a train. I got off at a small train station, at a suburb to the west of Vilna. When I got off the train and walked into the station, I met this Holocaust survivor group there. I knew some of the people in this group. They were trying to decide where they would go.

I stayed in this village with the other survivors for a while. Then I began walking east towards Vilna to see if I could find anyone alive. I still had a little hope that Sender had survived—but only a glimmer of hope.

Source: Ida Weisbaum Feinberg and Maryann McLoughlin, *If the Dawn is Late in Coming: Surviving Vilna and Vaivara* (Galloway, NJ: Richard Stockton College of New Jersey, 2008), 30–39. Used by permission.

Commentary

Vaivara, a concentration camp in northeastern Estonia, was the largest camp established in that country by the Nazi regime after Estonia was invaded on June 22, 1941. It acted as the headquarters of 20 forced labor camps located throughout Estonia. Most of the 20,000 Jewish prisoners deported to Vaivara arrived from the Vilna and Kovno ghettos and were eventually sent on to forced labor camps, and in that sense Vaivara was a transit camp as well as a concentration camp. It existed from August 1943 until its liquidation on February 4 and 5, 1944. Hans Aumeier (1906–1948), the former deputy commandant of Auschwitz, was in charge. The camp was unusual in that only 15 Germans were present there, the guard company being made up mostly of Estonian and Russian collaborators.

The main purpose of Vaivara was the exploitation of Jewish labor, but as a concentration camp it also housed around 1,300 prisoners on a permanent basis. The prisoners worked from morning to night at different types of hard labor, including felling trees in forests, working in a nearby quarry, doing railroad construction and repair, and, in an intensive and taxing process, extracting oil from shale. Prisoners unable to meet the work demands were considered expendable.

Inadequate food rations and hard work took their toll. Hygiene was always an implausible prospect owing to insufficient water supplies; consequently, lice outbreaks were frequent and disease was common. This resulted in periodic "selections," in which prisoners who were sick or weak, or who were too old or too young to work, were murdered. The first such selection, numbering well over a hundred victims, took place in the fall of 1943. Over 20 additional selections took place before the camp was finally evacuated.

Ida Weisbaum Feinberg's (1920–2011) memoir, *If the Dawn Is Late in Coming: Surviving Vilna and Vaivara,* provides one of the few accounts we have of the Holocaust as witnessed from Vaivara. Born in Vilna (at the time still part of Poland), Ida lived happily with her mother, father, younger brother Peter, and grandmother Bubbe until the German army arrived on June 25, 1941. By July 1941, SS mobile killing squads were already murdering the Jews of Vilna in the Ponary Forest outside the town. By September of that year, two ghettos had been established in Vilna. Ida's family, including her new husband Sender, was forced to move into Ghetto 1, where they lived until they were deported to Vaivara.

Upon arrival, they were subjected to the camp registration process in the usual manner: they were stripped, shaved, provided with striped uniforms, and numbered. Roll call was at 5:00 a.m. As the purpose of keeping the prisoners alive was so that they could work, their hours were long. And their food was poor—as Ida recalls it, the prisoners were always "desperately hungry," so their food sources had somehow to be augmented from external sources. Here, we learn about the practice of "organizing" in the camp.

To improve living conditions, "organizing"—the practice of stealing or procuring items in other than strictly legal ways—became one of the main forms of clandestine activity. This word has no ready equivalent in English, but the verb "to scrounge" may come close. In the camp it meant obtaining anything through any means, honest or dishonest, honorable or dishonorable. Thus, in order to improve her chances of staying alive and to suppress the pangs of hunger, Ida "organized" potatoes from the fields: "I hid them in my clothing when I returned to the camp," after which she would roast them in the small stove in the barrack block.

As the Soviets approached Estonia, the SS began to evacuate Vaivara in late August 1944. The Soviet offensives to retake Estonia took place in August and September. Because it seemed as though the Germans would be pushed out of the country and Estonia would be reoccupied by the Soviet army, 80,000 people fled by sea to Finland and Sweden. An additional 25,000 Estonians went to Sweden, 42,000 to Germany.

Ida survived Vaivara, but additional trials were still to come. The Nazis organized several of the departures by sea—traveling across the Baltic to Stutthof, near Danzig—but other departures (including the one Ida was a part of) took the form of death marches along the coast. The reasoning behind the evacuations was simple: they would maintain secrecy. The Nazis, who had been practicing deception throughout the Holocaust, kept information as restricted as possible for as long as possible. In many cases, they not only abandoned the camps, but they also removed the remaining inmates to other locations or killed them in large numbers even before the marches commenced.

Ida's testimony describes how the Nazis were obviously committed to killing as many victims as possible before they had to lay down their arms.

During a break in the march one night, local Polish villagers approached the convoy to try to find out who its members were and what they were doing there. Defying the very real prospect that they might have turned on her, Ida addressed them in Polish with the words, "I am a Jew." By way of response, some of the Poles came to the aid of the Jewish prisoners, showing great kindness by hiding and protecting them at what would have been considerable risk. In a remarkable show of fellow feeling, the Poles provided the Jews with food and kept watch during daylight hours, in case any Germans might appear.

The risks these people took were immense. Of all the countries occupied by the Nazis during World War II, it was only Poland in which help given to Jews was punishable by death. This applied not only to the rescuer but also to his or her family, a fact publicized widely by the Germans. Poles were under no obligation to risk their lives—and their families' lives—for Jews. And yet Ida and the other women in the convoy remained safe because of the goodwill of a few Poles in a small village witnessing a death march.

Ida's testimony ends with her liberation by the Soviets. She made her way back to the vicinity of Vilna and was eventually reunited with her husband Sender, who had, unbeknownst to Ida, managed to escape from Vaivara.

Questions

1. Ida's account of her experiences at the Vaivara concentration camp in Estonia is one of the few we have available. Do you think it is a representative example? Why or why not?
2. Do you think that the practice of "organizing" in the camp, a form of theft, could be justified?
3. Why do you think the Nazis decided to evacuate Vaivara as Soviet troops neared the camp?

RUDOLF HOESS

In May 1940, SS-Obersturmbannführer *Rudolf Hoess (1901–1947) received his first senior posting when he was appointed to be the* Kommandant *of a new camp, which he would establish, at Auschwitz. His initial orders were to build a transit camp capable of accommodating 10,000 prisoners, but he later became responsible for carrying out the Nazi "Final Solution of the Jewish Question" at Auschwitz, through the industrial mass murder of Jews sent from across Europe. In 1945 he was arrested by the Americans and transferred to Polish jurisdiction. While awaiting trial in 1946, he wrote his autobiography, in which he showed himself to be a devoted husband and father, dedicated employee, diligent administrator, and sensitive individual— as well as a first-rank mass murderer. The Polish court sentenced him to death on March 29, 1947. He was hanged on April 16 of that year.*

Where did the Jews on the Special Detachment derive the strength to carry on night and day with their grisly work? Did they hope that some whim of fortune might at the last moment snatch them from the jaws of death? Or had they become so dulled by the accumulation of horror that they were no longer capable even of ending their own lives and thus escaping from this "existence"?

I have certainly watched them closely enough, but I have never really been able to get to the bottom of their behaviour.

The Jew's way of living and of dying was a true riddle that I never managed to solve.

All these experiences and incidents which I have described could be multiplied many times over. They are excerpts only, taken from the whole vast business of the extermination, sidelights as it were.

This mass extermination, with all its attendant circumstances, did not, as I know, fail to affect all those who took a part in it. With very few exceptions, nearly all of those detailed to do this monstrous "work," this "service," and who, like myself, have given sufficient thought to the matter, have been deeply marked by these events.

Many of the men involved approached me as I went my rounds through the extermination buildings, and poured out their anxieties and impressions on me, in the hope that I could allay them.

Again and again during these confidential conversations I was asked: is it necessary that we do all this? Is it necessary that hundreds of thousands of women and children be destroyed? And I, who in my innermost being had on countless occasions asked myself exactly this question, could only fob them off and attempt to console them by repeating that it was done on Hitler's order. I had to tell them that this extermination of Jewry had to be, so that Germany and our posterity might be freed for ever from their relentless adversaries.

There was no doubt in the mind of any of us that Hitler's order had to be obeyed regardless, and that it was the duty of the SS to carry it out. Nevertheless we were all tormented by secret doubts.

I myself dared not admit to such doubts. In order to make my subordinates carry on with their task, it was psychologically essential that I myself appear convinced of the necessity for this gruesomely harsh order.

Everyone watched me. They observed the impression produced upon me by the kind of scenes that I have described above, and my reactions. Every word I said on the subject was discussed. I had to exercise intense self-control in order to prevent my innermost doubts and feelings of oppression from becoming apparent.

I had to appear cold and indifferent to events that must have wrung the heart of anyone possessed of human feelings. I might not even look away when afraid lest my natural emotions got the upper hand. I had to watch coldly, while the mothers with laughing or crying children went into the gas-chambers.

On one occasion two small children were so absorbed in some game that they quite refused to let their mother tear them away from it. Even the Jews of the Special Detachment were reluctant to pick the children up. The imploring look in the eyes of the mother, who certainly knew what was happening, is something I shall never forget. The people were already in the gas-chamber and becoming restive, and I had to act. Everyone was looking at me. I nodded to the junior non-commissioned officer on duty and he picked up the screaming, struggling children in his arms and carried them into the gas-chamber, accompanied by their mother who was weeping in the most heart-rending fashion. My pity was so great that I longed to vanish from the scene: yet I might not show the slightest trace of emotion.

I had to see everything. I had to watch hour after hour, by day and by night, the removal of the bodies, the extraction of the teeth, the cutting of the hair, the whole grisly, interminable business. I had to stand for hours on end in the ghastly stench, while the mass graves were being opened and the bodies dragged out and burned.

I had to look through the peephole of the gas-chambers and watch the process of death itself, because the doctors wanted me to see it.

I had to do all this because I was the one to whom everyone looked, because I had to show them all that I did not merely issue the orders and make the regulations but was also prepared myself to be present at whatever task I had assigned to my subordinates. . . .

I had many detailed discussions with Eichmann concerning all matters connected with the "final solution of the Jewish problem," but without ever disclosing my inner anxieties. . . . I was forced to bury all my human considerations as deeply as possible. . . . There was no escape for me from this dilemma. . . .

I had to go on with this process of extermination. I had to continue this mass murder and coldly to watch it, without regard for the doubts that were seething deep inside me.

I had to observe every happening with a cold indifference. Even those petty incidents that others might not notice I found hard to forget. In Auschwitz I truly had no reason to complain that I was bored.

If I was deeply affected by some incident, I found it impossible to go back to my home and family. I would mount my horse and ride, until I had chased the terrible picture away. Often, at night, I would walk through the stables and seek relief among my beloved animals.

It would often happen, when at home, that my thoughts suddenly turned to incidents that had occurred during the extermination. I then had to go out. I could no longer bear to be in my homely family circle. When I saw my children happily playing, or observed my wife's delight over our youngest, the thought would often come to me: how long will our happiness last? My wife could never understand these gloomy moods of mine, and ascribed them to some annoyance connected with my work.

When at night I stood out there beside the transports, or by the gas-chambers or the fires, I was often compelled to think of my wife and children, without, however, allowing myself to connect them closely with all that was happening.

It was the same with the married men who worked in the crematoria or at the fire-pits.

When they saw the women and children going into the gas-chambers, their thoughts instinctively turned to their own families. . . .

Yet everyone in Auschwitz believed that the commandant lived a wonderful life.

My family, to be sure, were well provided for in Auschwitz. Every wish that my wife or children expressed was granted them. The children could live a free and untrammelled life. My wife's garden was a paradise of flowers. The prisoners never missed an opportunity for doing some little act of kindness to my wife or children, and thus attracting their attention.

No former prisoner can ever say that he was in any way or at any time badly treated in our house. My wife's greatest pleasure would have been to give a present to every prisoner who was in any way connected with our household.

The children were perpetually begging me for cigarettes for the prisoners. They were particularly fond of the ones who worked in the garden.

My whole family displayed an intense love of agriculture and particularly for animals of all sorts. Every Sunday I had to walk them all across the fields, and visit the stables, and we might never miss out the kennels where the dogs were kept. Our two horses and the foal were especially beloved.

The children always kept animals in the garden, creatures the prisoners were forever bringing them. Tortoises, martens, cats, lizards: there was always something new and interesting to be seen there. In summer they splashed in the paddling pool in the garden, or in the Sola. But their greatest joy was when Daddy bathed with them. He had, however, so little time for all these childish pleasures. Today I deeply regret that I did not devote more time to my family. I always felt that I had to be on duty the whole time. This exaggerated sense of duty has always made life more difficult for me than it actually need have been. Again and again my wife reproached me and said: "You must think not only of the service always, but of your family too."

Yet what did my wife know about all that lay so heavily on my mind? She has never been told.

Source: Rudolf Hoess, *Commandant of Auschwitz: The Autobiography of Rudolf Hoess* (Cleveland, OH: World Publishing, 1960), 169–174. Used by permission.

Commentary

The testimony presented in Rudolf Hoess's memoir is, in the view of many, entirely self-serving. He wrote his autobiography while awaiting execution, after having been sentenced to death by Poland's Supreme National Tribunal on April 2, 1947. Some have argued that he had nothing to lose by painting himself in the best light possible. He writes of himself as a caring (even compassionate) family man who loved his children, was considerate toward his wife, and was beloved by his servants—notwithstanding the fact that they were Jewish inmates of the Auschwitz concentration camp.

Hoess joined the SS on April 1, 1934. That year he became a member of the *SS-Totenkopfverbände* ("Death's Head Units"), and in December he was transferred to the concentration camp at Dachau. There, he fell under the sway of Theodor Eicke (1892–1943), commander of the *Totenkopf* and the prime mover behind the development of the Nazi concentration camp system in Germany from 1933 on. During four years at Dachau, Hoess rose through the ranks; by 1938 he had been promoted to *SS-Hauptsturmführer* (captain). He was moved to the camp at Sachsenhausen for additional experience. In 1939 he joined the Waffen-SS, the military wing of the SS.

On May 1, 1940, Hoess was appointed commandant of a new camp in western Poland, near the town of Oświęcim, or, in German, Auschwitz. He would serve as commandant there for the next three and a half years. During that time, in his own words, he oversaw the murder of at least two and a half million victims by gassing, and at least another half million by starvation or disease. As Hoess estimated it, those figure represented about 70 or 80 percent of all persons sent to Auschwitz as prisoners.

The account presented here shows a man who, at first glance, would not seem to be the monster reviled by history. Expressing his "innermost doubts and feelings" about the killings he oversaw, Hoess explains the steeliness with which he went about directing those killings as a requirement of command. He seems convinced that Hitler had to be obeyed no matter what, and thus, in an austere and grossly simplified explanation, he manages to justify (at least in his own mind) the horrors that took place on his watch and at his command.

Where, he asks, did the Jews in what he refers to as the "Special Detachment"—which the world has come to know as the *Sonderkommando* (work units comprised of inmates who were forced to aid in the disposal of gas chamber victims)—manage to find the strength necessary to carry out their gruesome tasks? For Hoess, this was an unsolvable riddle. He was unable to see that the value of life transcended even the ghastliness of where the inmates worked. We have to ask what this suggests about his sense of right and wrong—indeed, what it says about the direction in which his moral compass pointed.

Further, while he speaks glowingly about the need to follow orders; of the difficulty of maintaining his men's morale in spite of the grimness of their daily tasks; and of the equal difficulty of keeping his doubts to himself, he shows that he really has no remorse for his victims. Their extermination, he says, "had to be, so Germany and our posterity might be freed for ever from their relentless adversaries."

He also mentions the coping mechanism of compartmentalizing, the effect which American psychiatrist Robert Jay Lifton (b. 1926) has referred to as "doubling," or the division of the self into two functioning wholes so that a part-self acts as an entire self. In Auschwitz, some Nazi officials, through doubling, could not only kill and contribute to killing, but they could also live fully and comfortably, with seeming obliviousness to the mass human destruction for which they were responsible. In the case of Hoess, this enabled him to kill during the day and go home to his family at night.

One of the issues likely to generate distaste for readers today relates to Hoess's expressions of anxiety over the times when, at home, his thoughts "suddenly turned to incidents that had occurred during the extermination." In such situations, he writes, he would have to get out of the house, as he "could no longer bear to be in my homely family circle." This is a horrid indictment of the man's moral code. When thousands of people were being murdered every day on his orders, his major concern appeared to be the upset this caused in his happy family life. Moreover, he actually complained that he was having a difficult time in his relationship with his wife, who did not know "about all that lay so heavily on my mind" and kept telling him not to let his thoughts of work intrude into his domestic bliss. "My wife," he writes, "could never understand these gloomy moods of mine." We have to ask: under such circumstances, in which Hoess regrets only that he did not spend more time with his family, is he asking us to feel sorry for him?

Taking things further, Hoess continually portrays himself as an able administrator concerned with the larger issues of running the camp. By intimating that he was a good soldier who received orders and obeyed them unquestioningly, he is in effect absolving himself of responsibility for his actions and, just as important, of his conscience. As one of the key perpetrators of the Holocaust, he shows himself to be a man with no emotional depth and no imagination. Hoess's account provides us with insights into how a man with limited human empathy can rise to a position of authority and power in an antihuman, totalitarian regime such as that of Nazi Germany. His example sends a warning to all who value the principles of human empathy, meritocracy, and common decency.

Questions

1. Why do you think Hoess found it so difficult to understand Jewish passivity, in view of the horrors to which the Jews were exposed?
2. Is there any ground for sympathizing with Hoess over the personal problems he says he faced as *Kommandant*?
3. Do you think Hoess is sincere when recounting his feelings about his role?

FILIP MÜLLER

Filip Müller (b. 1922) was a Czech Jew from the city of Sered. In April 1942, at the age of 20, he was deported to Auschwitz, where he became prisoner number 29236. Placed into a work group responsible for the construction and maintenance of the crematoria, Müller was destined to be one of the very few Sonderkommandos to survive Auschwitz. In subsequent years his story was told in a piecemeal fashion, until a full account was published in English in 1979. In Auschwitz Inferno: The Testimony of a Sonderkommando *(U.S. title:* Eyewitness Auschwitz: Three Years in the Gas Chambers*), Müller gives one of the most detailed accounts of how the gas chambers and crematoria operated, from one who was there as a witness-participant.*

In the first Republic of Czechoslovakia, Theresienstadt, now Terezin, remained a garrison town. But after the occupation of Bohemia and Moravia by the Germans, all inhabitants were compulsorily resettled, while the town which is surrounded by wide ramparts became a ghetto for Jews from Bohemia, Moravia, Germany, Austria, and later also from Holland. From the autumn of 1941 an increasing number of Jews were quartered in the depopulated residential districts as well as in the roomy barracks of Theresienstadt. They provided a reservoir for the places of extermination which had been established further east, and very few of them survived the Third Reich. The little fortress, on the other hand, was used as a prison for political prisoners.

In September 1943 a few thousand Jews were deported from Theresienstadt to Auschwitz and put in the camp without the usual selection on the ramp. To us older prisoners this seemed almost unbelievable. Still more unbelievable was the fact that behind the barbed wire of their camp the detainees did not wear prison garb but were allowed civilian clothes. They did not even have their hair shaved off. Compared to the rest of the camp inmates their physical and mental condition was relatively good.

Nobody could find a valid reason why it was these Jews from Theresienstadt had been spared the walk to the gas chamber, or why their living conditions were incomparably better that those of the other prisoners. They were made to do the work of building their own camp, but they were never used as forced labour. Every month they were allowed to write one post-card and receive one parcel from outside. Pregnant women were given small quantities of milk, butter and even white bread. Children under six went to a nursery school, while the older children were taught by Jewish teachers. In the Family Camp there existed an excellent orchestra among whose members were well-known artists, and which on occasions had to perform before the SS. There was even a hospital where noted university professors and doctors worked, and all this in a place where, not 100 metres away, a human life was worth nothing. It was, therefore, not surprising that these unusual conditions led us to assume that the Family Camp was under the special protection of the International Red Cross. However, the secret order which I had read that night showed me that this was not so. It was more likely that the Jews in the Family Camp were used to provide an alibi for the Nazis, to demonstrate to the world how well they treated the Jews in concentration camps, and that this was the reason why they had been given special status.

Voss was still sitting at the table, thoughtfully drumming the table top with his pencil and consulting his wrist-watch; then he began scribbling figures on a scrap of paper. After a while he turned to the *Kapos* and said: "To get the stiffs burnt by tomorrow morning is no problem. All you have to do is see that every other load consists of two men and one woman from the transport, together with a *Musselman* and a child. For every other load use only good material from the transport, two men, one woman and a child. After every two loadings empty out the ashes to prevent the channels from getting blocked." Then he continued menacingly: "I hold you responsible for seeing to it that every twelve minutes the loads are stoked, and don't forget to switch on the fans. Today it's working flat out, understood?"

"Yes, *Herr Oberscharführer,*" cried the two *Kapos.*

"And another thing," Voss snapped, "when you've finished, clean up everything, you know, hosing down, chlorinating, and all that sort of thing. And to finish up, lime-wash the walls! Everything clear? By 8 tomorrow morning everything's got to be shipshape! Off you go!"

About 500 dead bodies were still lying in heaps in the changing room. They must now be sorted according to their combustibility: for the corpses of the well-nourished were to help burn the emaciated. Under the direction of the *Kapos,* the bearers began sorting the dead into four stacks. The largest consisted mainly of strong men, the next in size of women, then came children, and lastly a stack of dead *Musselmans,* emaciated and nothing but skin and bones. This technique was called "express work," a designation thought up by the *Kommandoführers* and originating from experiments carried out in crematorium 5 in the autumn of 1943. The purpose of these experiments was to find a way of saving coke. On a few occasions groups of SS men and civilians visited the crematorium to watch the experiments. From conversations between Voss and Gorges we gathered that the civilians were technicians employed by the firm of Topf and Sons of Erfurt who had manufactured and installed the cremation ovens.

In the course of these experiments corpses were selected according to different criteria and then cremated. Thus the corpses of two *Musselmans* were cremated together with those of two children or the bodies of two well-nourished men together with that of an emaciated woman, each load consisting of three, or sometimes four, bodies. Members of these groups were especially interested in the amount of coke required to burn corpses of any particular category, and in the time it took to cremate them. During these macabre experiments different kinds of coke were used and the results carefully recorded.

Afterwards, all corpses were divided into the above-mentioned four categories, the criterion being the amount of coke required to reduce them to ashes. Thus it was decreed that the most economical and fuel-saving procedure would be to burn the bodies of a well-nourished man and an emaciated woman, or vice versa, together with that of a child, because, as the experiments had established, in this combination, once they had caught fire, the dead would continue to burn without any further coke being required.

As the number of people being gassed grew apace, the four crematoria in Birkenau, even though they were working round the clock with two shifts, could no longer cope with their workload. According to the makers' instructions the ovens required cooling down at regular intervals, repairs needed to be done and the channels leading to the chimneys to be cleaned out. These unavoidable interruptions resulted in the "quota" of no more than three corpses to each oven load being kept to only very rarely.

The decision as to whether it was to be "express" or "normal" work was taken by the *Kommandoführers*. If outsiders or perhaps even the *Lagerkommandant* arrived at the crematorium for an inspection we switched over to normal work immediately. On such occasions Voss and his *Kommandoführers* would put on a grand performance. They pretended to pay meticulous attention to the strict observing of instructions, bustling about in a show of efficiency, ordering us around, hustling us along and generally creating the impression that the smooth running of the crematorium was their sole purpose in life. And if a stoker dared to push his iron fork against the fire-brick lining, if the fans were not switched off in time, or if anything else unforeseen occurred there would be much shouting on the part of the SS. "Can't you watch what you're doing, you bloody Jewish bastard," they would yell. "Watch it, or you'll end up inside the oven too!" Once the visitors had gone, "express work" continued at the usual pace, significantly raising the output of the ovens.

In crematorium 5 the most floor space was taken up by the changing room, about 300 square metres. With its exposed rafters it looked just like a spacious barn. The changing room was on the same level as the two gas chambers and the cremation room. As in the other crematoria its scanty furnishings consisted of two wooden benches, numbered clothes-hooks and signboards along the walls. However, there was in crematoria 4 and 5 one signboard whose inscription was actually correct. It was the one which referred to return "after the bath." For in these two crematoria the changing rooms served also as mortuaries: after each gassing the corpses had to be dragged back there from the gas chamber. Nowhere were the omnipresence and inexorability of death more obvious than in this place. Because of our constant handling of the dead we seemed to forget they were corpses. We would talk to them as if they were still alive, and even though there was no reply it appeared to worry no one, for we supplied our own answers.

Source: Filip Müller, *Auschwitz Inferno: The Testimony of a Sonderkommando* (London: Routledge and Kegan Paul, 1979), 97–100. Used by permission of Ivan R. Dee and Taylor & Francis Books (UK).

Commentary

Originally an SS term for units assigned to special tasks—primarily the killing of Jews—the word *Sonderkommando* later came to mean Jewish prisoners in the death camps who worked in the gas chambers and crematoria. These prisoners would help the victims remove their clothing and shave their hair. Later, after the victims had been murdered, they would inspect the bodies for hidden coins and jewels, remove any gold teeth, and take the bodies from the gas chambers to the crematoria. Their job also entailed stoking the crematoria and doing the "heavy work" involved in such operations.

The lives of the *Sonderkommando* prisoners were short, as they themselves would be murdered after approximately three months. After all, they were witnesses to the most ghastly expressions of the Nazi campaign—that is, industrialized mass murder—so the Nazis had no other way to ensure secrecy. The knowledge possessed by the *Sonderkommando* men was far too sensitive for anyone in the outside world to know about. The Nazis would regularly gas the men of a *Sonderkommando* unit and replace them with a new team. The first task of the incoming group would be to dispose of their predecessors' corpses.

Filip Müller was a member of Birkenau's Twelfth *Sonderkommando.* Featured in his account is an SS-*Oberscharführer,* Peter Voss (1897–1976). Others to whom Müller refers include SS-*Oberscharführer* Eric Muhsfeldt (1913–1948) and SS-*Hauptscharführer* Otto Moll (1915–1946). During the spring and early summer of 1943, when the four crematoria became operational, Voss became their overall commander. Müller discusses Voss throughout his memoir, and in a section of his book after the extract herein he describes Voss as an "uncritical and willing tool [of the Nazis] rather than a fanatically cruel exterminator." Voss's command of the crematoria came to an end on May 9, 1944, when he was replaced by Moll. Moll, in turn, was given command of Crematoria IV and V, where he remained throughout both the period leading up to, and during, the only major revolt of the *Sonderkommandos,* in October of that year.

On October 7, 1944, the men working at Crematorium IV rose in revolt. Setting fire to the crematorium, they attacked the SS guards with hammers, axes, and stones. Upon learning that a revolt had begun, the men working at Crematorium II joined in, killing a Kapo and several SS men. Then the Hungarian prisoners working in Crematoria III also entered what by now had become a full-scale rebellion. The revolt was successful in damaging Crematorium IV beyond repair; it was never used again. During the chaos, several hundred prisoners escaped from Birkenau, though most were caught and killed by the SS. Later that day, an additional 200 prisoners who had taken part in the revolt were executed.

One month later, on November 7, the Nazis destroyed the entire gas chamber-crematorium complex, closing down the operation altogether.

Müller's testimony is remarkable in that it is one of very few *Sonderkommando* accounts from any of the Nazi camps. What makes it even more extraordinary is that he survived the revolt.

The account he provides deals directly with the efforts made by the Nazis to fool the outside world into believing that concentration camps provided decent living standards, and even a certain level of luxury. In his discussion of how the Jews from Theresienstadt were duped, he shows just how complete the Nazi deception was, right down to the children's nursery school, the orchestra, and the hospital.

Lest there be any doubt as to the nature of the deception, however, Müller offers clear evidence regarding the Nazi extermination process. He describes in detail how the cremations were reduced to mathematical equations, whereby certain combinations of dead bodies—some still with fat, some, reduced by starvation, with little or none—were found to produce more efficient cremation processes. These "experiments," he tells us, were undertaken in order to "find a way of saving coke." Compounding the criminality of the Nazis' actions was the deliberation accompanying them—they were observed by civilian technicians employed by Topf and Sons, the firm that had manufactured and installed the cremation ovens. Müller believed they were there to ensure a measure of quality control and to look for any improvements that might be introduced.

Müller's testimony depicts the numbing effect that working with bodies had on the Jewish prisoners of the *Sonderkommando*. His descriptions leave readers wondering how the human mind could cope with such horrors as a matter of daily routine, without completely losing its reason.

Perhaps one way prisoners could achieve some sense of normality in this most bizarre of environments was by speaking to the corpses as though they were still alive. Although this might sound sick in a healthy society, the world of the *Sonderkommando* was different from others, and even from that of the concentration camp outside of the crematoria. This was a world in which prisoners would undertake "express work," significantly raising the output of the ovens, until outsiders—such as *Oberscharführer* Voss—came on an inspection tour. Then, the senior prisoners would switch over to "normal" work, pretending to be super-efficient, paying careful attention to a strict observation of instructions, "and generally creating the impression that the smooth running of the crematorium was their sole purpose in life." Once the visitors had gone, "express work" continued at the usual pace. With fewer bodies to load, less physical labor was expended.

Filip Müller did not choose to be, or remain, a member of the *Sonderkommando*. The grisly work was forced upon him, and he had no alternative but to continue to perform it. At one point, feeling unable to go on, he tried to take his own life by joining a group of Czech Jews entering the gas chamber, but he was talked out of it by one of those condemned—he had a responsibility, she told him, to try to stay alive in order to bear witness. The drive to expose the truth of the murderous Nazi program ultimately became Müller's sole *raison d'être,* resulting, decades after the event, in the appearance of his astonishing memoir.

Questions

1. Müller was working as a *Sonderkommando* in the gas chamber complex at Auschwitz. Do you see this as presenting a moral dilemma, if it gave him an opportunity to stay alive?
2. How did Müller react emotionally to the horror he had to work amidst on a daily basis?
3. Can you account for Müller's survival during the revolt of the Twelfth *Sonderkommando* in October 1944? What might be some possible explanations?

4. The Cambodian Genocide

Genocide took place in Cambodia between April 17, 1975 and January 6, 1979, during the rule of communist dictator Pol Pot (1925–1998). His military forces, the Khmer Rouge, carried out a policy that aimed to totally erase all signs of French colonial rule and restore Cambodia to the pristine condition that prevailed before foreigners stamped their cultural traits on the land and its people.

For nearly four years, Cambodia was brutally eradicated of any evidence of "alien" ways. The primary targets were the cities, in particular the capital, Phnom Penh. Buildings and institutions were torn down, and the city's population of nearly two million was uprooted and resettled in the countryside in order to purge citizens of their so-called bourgeois ways. This move would indoctrinate them, in turn, in rural, traditional Khmer (or Cambodian) culture, ostensibly unspoiled by colonialism and capitalism—the twin enemies of the anticolonialist, communist, and mono-ethnic nationalist Khmer Rouge. Millions were forced to undergo "re-education," including public confessions, during which hundreds of thousands perished from exposure and lethal violence.

The Khmer Rouge's fanaticism led to executions of "enemies" who covered the full spectrum of society. Intellectuals, artists, professionals, those who had traveled abroad, and those who spoke a foreign language were all targets. In short, all who embodied foreign—that is, anticommunist or non-Khmer ideals were systematically killed, as they were deemed too "contaminated" to participate in building the new society under Pol Pot's rule. The Khmer Rouge was so committed to destroying the old society and creating a new one that it completely obliterated even the most fundamental of social forms, namely, the family; this is to say nothing of such expressions of modernity as transportation, education, technology, administration, and governance. Under Khmer Rouge rule, all citizens were compelled to be dedicated to serving *Angka,* "the Organization," from which everything was to emanate in the new Democratic Republic of Kampuchea.

Up to 40 percent of the deaths in this new regime were caused by starvation and disease, as Cambodia's traditional agricultural systems, markets, and family plots were all eliminated and replaced by inadequately directed and viciously applied policies from the Party Center.

By the time the carnage was over, stopped by an invasion from Vietnam in January 1979, it is estimated that at least 1.7 million (and perhaps up to 2 million) people had been killed, the equivalent of one in four Cambodians. The number of deaths caused by Pol Pot's brutal regime renders this one of the greatest tragedies of the twentieth century. Among the dead, deliberately targeted for extinction, were Buddhist monks and non-Khmer minorities, including the Muslim Chams, ethnic Chinese, and Vietnamese.

By way of illustration, we can consider one group, the Muslim Chams. Under communism, they were viewed as separatist nationalists with a different identity from that of other Cambodians. Because of this, it was held, they had to be integrated forcefully into the Cambodian mainstream. The fact that they were Muslims only served to aggravate relations between the state and the Cham minority, as Islam was seen as an alien, foreign culture that had no place in the new communist order. Whereas ethnic nationalism was considered a bourgeois aberration, Islam was seen as an alien import that must be excised, along with other foreign elements, if Cambodia was to become the healthy nation it was remembered to be from mythological, precolonial times.

The Khmer Rouge became determined to expunge the Cham presence from revolutionary Cambodia. The government's plan was to dislodge the Chams from their villages and scatter them across the country, in the hope that this would force assimilation by thinning their ranks. As the Chams resisted, Pol Pot tried intimidation. Village elders and prominent families were murdered. Finally, the regime opted for mass killing, which, in the end, led to the massacres of entire Cham village populations. Had it not been for the end of the Khmer Rouge regime in January 1979, the Chams may very well have been annihilated except for those few who collaborated with the government. As it was, at least half of the Cham population was killed during the Pol Pot years, the victims of a mentality that would not tolerate pluralism and instead actively sought to eliminate difference through violence and mass slaughter.

All minorities were reviled, banned from speaking their own languages or carrying out their own religious or cultural practices, dispersed across the country and separated from each other. The Cambodian population was divided into those referred to as the "new people" and the "old people." The latter, those who had lived in territories controlled by the Khmer Rouge prior to April 17, 1975, were treated better than the "new people," who were effectively given the status of a captured, subject people. All of Cambodia, in fact, became one large labor camp, as the regime sought to turn the clock back and eradicate modernity in pursuit of an idealistic pipe dream.

Quite simply, nothing was allowed to stand in the way of the Khmer Rouge's overarching project of social engineering, in what was perhaps the most radical expression of restructuring that any society has ever undergone.

It should be made clear, though, that the vast majority of those whose lives were lost under the Khmer Rouge regime were mainstream Cambodians, and not members of any of the minority populations. This brings up some difficulties relating to the United Nations Convention on Genocide (UNCG) definition of genocide, primarily regarding whether or not it can be called genocide when a regime targets members of its own majority group on the grounds of social background or political belief—which was why most of the victims in Cambodia perished.

Many of the crimes committed by the Khmer Rouge may not easily be termed genocide in its strict legal sense. If the overwhelming majority of the deaths were those of Cambodia's Khmer people—thus leading some to term what happened as "autogenocide"—then, it has been argued, the experience of the Khmer people under Pol Pot does not fall within the legal definition of genocide. Moreover, the UNCG requires proof of a specific intent to destroy the group being targeted, presenting further difficulties of definition. Because of the destruction of ethnic minorities, however, and because of Pol Pot's deliberate targeting of Cambodians living in the country's Eastern Zone toward the end of the regime, there should be little hesitation in applying the term genocide, to these crimes at least.

With the Vietnamese invasion in January 1979, the Pol Pot government fell, and the Khmer Rouge fled into the jungles of western Cambodia. Since the end of the genocide, the country has struggled to re-establish itself as a stable political and economic entity, founded on democracy and the rule of law. Especially disturbing, in this context, is that in all this time the principal actors of the Cambodian genocide were not brought to justice until very recently. Even then, any form of accounting and redress at the Extraordinary Chambers in the Courts of Cambodia has been painfully slow in coming, and extremely limited.

TEEDA BUTT MAM

Teeda Butt Mam was a 15-year-old schoolgirl when the Khmer Rouge came to power in 1975. This account relates her impressions of the class-based nature of the Khmer Rouge campaign, viewed from the perspective of one who was categorized as a major enemy of the new society.

I was fifteen years old when the Khmer Rouge came to power in April 1975. I can still remember how overwhelmed with joy I was that the war had finally ended.

It did not matter who won. I and many Cambodians wanted peace at any price. The civil war had tired us out, and we could not make much sense out of killing our own brothers and sisters for a cause that was not ours. We were ready to support our new government to rebuild our country. We wanted to bring back that slow-paced, simple life we grew up with and loved dearly. At the time we didn't realize how high the price was that we had to pay for the Khmer Rouge's peace.

The Khmer Rouge were very clever and brutal. Their tactics were effective because most of us refused to believe their malicious intentions. Their goal was to liberate us. They risked their own lives and gave up their families for "justice" and "equality." How could these worms have come out of our own skin?

Even after our warmest welcome, the first word from the Khmer Rouge was a lie wrapped around a deep anger and hatred of the kind of society they felt Cambodia was becoming. They told us that Americans were going to bomb the cities. They forced millions of residents of Phnom Penh and other cities out of their homes. They separated us from our friends and neighbors to keep us off balance, to prevent us from forming any alliance to stand up and win back our rights. They ripped off our homes and our possessions. They did this intentionally, without mercy.

They were willing to pay any cost, any lost lives for their mission. Innocent children, old women, and sick patients from hospital beds were included. Along the way, many innocent Cambodians were dying of starvation, disease, loss of loved ones, confusion, and execution.

We were seduced into returning to our hometowns in the villages so they could reveal our true identities. Then the genocide began. First, it was the men.

They took my father. They told my family that my father needed to be reeducated. Brainwashed. But my father's fate is unknown to this day. We can only imagine what happened to him. This is true for almost all Cambodian widows and orphans. We live in fear of finding out what atrocities were committed against our fathers, husbands, brothers. What could they have done that deserved a tortured death?

Later the Khmer Rouge killed the wives and children of the executed men in order to avoid revenge. They encouraged children to find fault with their own parents and spy on them. They openly showed their intention to destroy the family structure that once held love, faith, comfort, happiness, and companionship. They took young children from their homes to live in a commune so that they could indoctrinate them.

Parents lost their children. Families were separated. We were not allowed to cry or show any grief when they took away our loved ones. A man would be killed if he lost an ox he was assigned to tend. A woman would be killed if she was too tired to work. Human life wasn't even worth a bullet. They clubbed the back of our necks and pushed us down to smother us and let us die in a deep hole with hundreds of other bodies.

They told us we were VOID. We were less than a grain of rice in a large pile. The Khmer Rouge said that the Communist revolution could be successful with only two people. Our lives had no significance to their great Communist nation, and they told us, "To keep you is no benefit, to destroy you is no loss." . . .

The people on the Khmer Rouge death list were the group called the city people. They were the "new" people. These were any Cambodian men, women, girls, boys, and babies who did not live in their "liberated zones" before they won the war in 1975. Their crime was that they lived in the enemy's zone, helping and supporting the enemy.

The city people were the enemy, and the list was long. Former soldiers, the police, the CIA, and the KGB. Their crime was fighting in the civil war. The merchants, the capitalists, and the businessmen. Their crime was exploiting the poor. The rich farmers and the landlords. Their crime was exploiting the peasants. The intellectuals, the doctors, the lawyers, the monks, the teachers, and the civil servants. These people thought, and their memories were tainted by the evil Westerners. Students were getting education to exploit the poor. Former celebrities, the poets. These people carried bad memories of the old, corrupted Cambodia.

The list goes on and on. The rebellious, the kind-hearted, the brave, the clever, the individualists, the people who wore glasses, the literate, the popular, the complainers, the lazy, those with talent, those with trouble getting along with others, and those with soft hands. These people were corrupted and lived off the blood and sweat of the farmers and the poor.

Very few of us escaped these categories. My family were not villagers. We were from Phnom Penh. I was afraid of who I was. I was an educated girl from a middle-class family. I could read, write, and think. I was proud of my family and my roots. I was scared that they would hear my thoughts and prayers, that they could see my dreams and feel my anger and disapproval of their regime.

I was always hungry. I woke up hungry before sunrise and walked many kilometers to the worksite with no breakfast. I worked until noon. My lunch was either rice porridge with a few grains or boiled young bananas or boiled corn. I continued working until sunset. My dinner was the same as lunch. I couldn't protest to Angka, but my stomach protested to me that it needed more food. Every night I went to sleep dirty and hungry. I was sad because I missed my mom. I was fearful that this might be the night I'd be taken away, tortured, raped, and killed.

I wanted to commit suicide but I couldn't. If I did, I would be labeled "the enemy" because I dared to show my unhappiness with their regime. My death would be followed by my family's death because they were the family of the enemy. My greatest fear was not my death, but how much suffering I had to go through before they killed me.

They kept moving us around, from the fields into the woods. They purposely did this to disorient us so they could have complete control. They did it to get rid of the "useless people." Those who were too old or too weak to work. Those who did not produce their quota. We were cold because we had so few clothes and blankets. We had no shoes. We were sick and had little or no medical care. They told us that we "volunteered" to work fifteen hours or more a day in the rain or in the moonlight with no holidays. We were timid and lost. We had to be silent. We not only lost our identities, but we lost our pride, our senses, our religion, our loved ones, our souls, ourselves. . . .

Near my hut there was a woman named Chamroeun. She watched her three children die of starvation, one at a time. She would have been able to save their lives had she had gold or silk or perfume to trade for food and medicine on the black market. The Khmer Rouge veterans and village leaders had control of the black market. They traded rice that Chamroeun toiled over for fancy possessions. The Khmer Rouge gave a new meaning to corruption.

The female soldiers were jealous of my lighter skin and feminine figure. While they were enjoying their nice black pajamas, silk scarves, jewelry, new shoes, and perfume, they stared at me, seeing if I had anything better than they did. I tried to appear timid with my ragged clothes, but it was hard to hide the pride in my eyes.

In January 1979 I was called to join a district meeting. The district leader told us that it was time to get rid of "all the wheat that grows among the rice plants." The city people were the wheat. The city people were to be eliminated. My life was saved because the Vietnamese invasion came just two weeks later. . . .

In April 1979, the Buddhist New Year, exactly four years after the Khmer Rouge came to power, I joined a group of corpselike bodies dancing freely to the sound of clapping and songs of folk music that defined who we were. We danced under the moonlight around the bonfire. We were celebrating the miracles that saved our lives. At that moment, I felt that my spirit and my soul had returned to my weak body. Once again, I was human.

Source: Teeda Butt Mam, "Worms from Our Skin," in Dith Pran (compiler) and Kim DePaul (ed.), *Children of Cambodia's Killing Fields: Memoirs by Survivors* (New Haven, CT: Yale University Press, 1999), 11–17. Used by permission of Yale University Press.

Commentary

When the Khmer Rouge entered Phnom Penh on April 17, 1975, there were wild scenes of celebration across the country. With an end to the destructive civil war that had raged since 1970 and resulted in the deaths of an estimated 156,000 people (half of them civilians), there now came a momentary respite. Cambodians greeted the victory of the Khmer Rouge with joy—not having any sense of what was to come. But within a very short space of time, the Khmer Rouge began what was perhaps the most radical attempt to reorder a society ever seen. They destroyed the fabric of precommunist Cambodian life at every level, right down to the family unit, which they abolished. Towns and cities were evacuated, and the fruits of modernity were abandoned for a return to a premodern, primitive, communist lifestyle.

The Khmer Rouge's stance was that a total re-alignment was needed in every sector of society. Millions were forced to undergo public confessions, in the course of which hundreds of thousands perished from exposure and lethal violence.

Teeda Butt Mam provides us with the Khmer Rouge mantra, "To keep you is no benefit, to destroy you is no loss." Such was the thinking behind the drive to bring the revolution to a successful outcome. Transforming Cambodia into a rural, class-less society meant eliminating money, free markets, regular schooling, private property, religion, and modern Khmer culture. Public schools, pagodas, mosques, churches, universities, shops, and government buildings were shut or turned into prisons, stables, re-education camps, and granaries.

The Khmer Rouge used deceit and, where they deemed it necessary, brutal force in order to create their new society as quickly as possible. They moved speedily and efficiently to uproot and disorient city dwellers. This was done to return Cambodian society to its premodern agrarian roots; along the way, citizens were deprived of their basic rights. Henceforth, the Khmer Rouge demanded that all Cambodians believe, obey, and respect only "*Angkar*," (the Organization), which, in the new society, would act on everyone's behalf and to which everyone would be required to pay ultimate fealty.

In such an environment it was not, for example, wise for someone like Teeda to express any form of discontent—even to articulate, as she does in her account, that "I was always hungry," "I woke up hungry before sunrise," or, "Every night I went to sleep dirty and hungry." Such expressions were an indictment of the munificence of Angka and the glory of the revolution, in which she was being asked to play her part through sacrifice. In like manner, it was no use for her to say that she was "sad because I missed my mom." In the new Cambodia, Angka was to assume the parental role, as the traditional family was no longer deemed to have any useful purpose.

Even the ultimate form of dissent—suicide—could not be permitted, notwithstanding the fact that in the new society, "Human life wasn't even worth a bullet." Even death had to be controlled by the Khmer Rouge. If Teeda were to commit suicide, she recognized, she "would be labeled 'the enemy' because I dared to show my unhappiness with their regime." Moreover, "My death would be followed by my family's death because they were the family of the enemy."

Teeda's memoir is also valuable in that it describes the fate of one who came from an upper-middle-class background. Repeatedly she describes the differences, real or perceived, between herself and those around her. "My family were not villagers," she writes, and "I was an educated girl from a middle-class family" who could "read, write, and think." She was "proud of my family and my roots." By contrast, "The female soldiers were jealous of my lighter skin and feminine figure. While they were enjoying their nice black pajamas, silk scarves, jewelry, new shoes, and perfume, they stared at me, seeing if I had anything better than they did." A definite class dimension was introduced into Teeda's perception of her persecution, mixed with an understanding on her part that much of the dynamic of that persecution was based on jealousy.

Of note in her account is also the observation that, from the beginning, before the Khmer Rouge destroyed the family structure, it was the men who were seized—and who then disappeared. Over time, this has become a recurring motif in the study of genocide. We can recall the experience of the Armenians in April 1915, when 250 of the most important civic community leaders were taken into custody on the first night; most were murdered, after which men serving in the armed forces were disarmed, then killed. In Teeda's case, the Khmer Rouge took her father, telling the family that he had to be "re-educated." (Teeda adds the word "brainwashed.") At the time that she was writing, nearly a quarter-century later, her father's fate was still unknown. In despair, she writes: "We can only imagine what happened to him." The truth might be more than many could bear, were they to learn of that fate: "We live in fear of finding out what atrocities were committed against our fathers, husbands, brothers. What could they have done that deserved a tortured death?"

Overall, we see Teeda's account as one filled with anger at what happened, and with despair over what was lost. It is simultaneously incensed, despondent, and resentful, but along the way it also offers us an insight into the heart of a survivor. We find ourselves drawn to Teeda's reflections on the inhuman conditions in which people worked and died under this most cruel of regimes, during a time of intense social trauma and mass murder.

Questions

1. What was the relationship between Teeda and the girls of the Khmer Rouge, and why did it take that form?
2. In what way(s) did Teeda experience the Khmer Rouge attempt to transform Cambodian society?
3. Why do you think the Khmer Rouge intended to destroy the family unit? How did this destruction become manifest in Teeda's case?

SAMNANG SHAWN VANN

When the Khmer Rouge took power in April 1975, Samnang Shawn Vann was five years old. While just a young boy, he became part of the regime's vast slave labor force. His account of life as a child is highly evocative—and an indictment of the brutality of the Khmer Rouge. The account provided here retains the original syntax and spellings, the better to appreciate the words and emotions that have seemingly been wrenched from Samnang's very soul.

I was about five year old when the Khmer Rough took over the Khmer Empire in 1975. . . .

At that time, they did not start to do their killing yet. However, they make all my family work for them every single days and nights without giving us a chance to rest. When I was a little bouy [boy] at the age of five, I use to get up one o'clock mid-night to go to the barn and herd the cows, to the rice field and pick up losen crop after harvest, to the barns and take out the cow manuever [manure] to the gardens, to the barns and feeds the cows, to the barns and grine [grind] the rice, digged the pitt to make a water run way, to the garden and plant the flowers and fruits, to the forest and fetch fire woods, to the rice field and cut out the grass that grow in the rice fields and harvest the rice, and digged dirt to build the road. These are part of the work that I have to performed for them. At that time, I worked and work, and I never had enough sleep. Each day, I slept at least one or one hour and a half which is the most. I always work from one or twelves mid-night until eleven mid-night depending on their time. I remember those time, my healthy is as worst as a dying human whom partly alive and partly dead. I suffered from mousquito and other insects bits every single day because I was forced to work without any break. There is never a single day or time that I have to rest in peace. I always slept with horror and a terrible nightmare everyday. I never get to eat a full meal eventhough I work hard for them. My healthy was so bad that I always suffered from all kind of maleria, diarrea, malnutrition, and more. Almost all the time, I never get to eat a full meal which I sometimes, have to eat plants and dirt to stopped my hunger.

Sometimes, when I refused to work, they would torture me by wipping me and making me worked over time without rest of drink. I work like an animal during a hot sunny day which the temperature sometimes reached up to 120 degree. Sometimes, I never got to eat because they told us that they ran out of food for us to eat. I remember, I use to sneak out and when into the forest to hunt for lizard and birds and animals to kill for food. Then when we sneak out, and they caught me, they took me back and over work me without letting me eat anything for that whole day or sometimes up to two days and a half. I used to eat all kinds of insects and animal like grass hopper, cricket, scorpion, tarantula, rats, snake, porcupine, wild baor [boar], rain deer, water beetle, and more. Like I mentioned before, these are just part of the kind of food that I ate to try to survived. I used to eat all of these things just to keep myself alive so that I can survive and maybe lives another day hopping the war was over. Because my life, and not just me, but my whole family's life was complicated, we wish that would find our freedom soon. Sometimes, I wish I wake up and open my eyes and pretend that my suffering life was just a dream, but when I actually look at it carefully, it's not a dreams at all, it's become real. There is never one day during those year that I had to celebrate any ceremony. I always prayed to Lord Buddha that my nightmare will end soon, but my called to him never been answered because my people continued to suffered until this day.

At that same time, I am not the only person in my family who suffered, my parents and brother also suffered this pain. My father and mother used to eat leaf and roots as well as my big brother and me. At one time, my mother went out to the rice field and work, and she caught one big fish. My mother took the fish back home to cook for the family, especially for my brother and I, one of the Khmer Rough leader whom lived in the same Poumm as us almost took my parents away to execute. At that time, they find out from their fellows group that my mother had caught a fish and used it as a personal property and did not share with everyoen in the groups, and that my mother was greedy, therefore, they threatening my mother and father that the next time they catched my family cheating on them, they will execute our whole family. I remember my mother and father never get to sleep too, especially my mother because she always sit a cry through out every night worried about her family. At the same time, she always pray to my ancester and grandfathers and grandmothers who had passed away for so long to look after us.

At that time, we really wanted to get away from that area, but we cannot escaped because we try to do so, they will try to killed us and called us trator whom does not care about our country or care about others. I remember one of the leader who lived next door to us have two son whom always causes trouble and beat my brother and I up for pleasure. The two kids always come under my straw house which made out of palm leaf and used the area under my house as their restroom area. They would do it under my house and my brother and I always be the one who picked it up after they leave. We can't never do anything to them because if we did, they will killed us all. One of the Khmer Rough leader which I don't remember the name, always get to eat good foods and never work that at all, while my family worked to death and ate only roots and leaves. Since the Khmer Rough ruled, we never get to eat rice, we only get to eat liquid rice [bor-bor] which hardly any rice in it mostly water.

Then, at the end of 1975, after we worked so hard for them and they decide that they have enough of my family and other nine family in the area, they decided to forced us out of the areas which in their mind was to execute us all. We gather about ten family together and forced us out and told us that we will go to other area which called Thaa-genh, in the Battambong Province. And when we arrive there, they plan to execute us all, but luckily, the non-communist allies arrived and the two forces fought each other there. While they were at war, my family and five other family got a chance to escaped the tragedy. Eventhough we escape the execution, however, that's only the beginning of our escape, the nightmare has not end yet. From then, my parents decide to take us back to Kondall Province. There in Kondall Province, we decide to settled in Chbaa Ompov near Phnom Penh. We lived there a while and again still live in fear. I remember each evening I went to use the bathroom, . . . I use to when I'm in an emergeny and the bullet would flew above my head tenths or fifteen, but unfortunately, I was so lucky that the bullet never struct me.

Soon, after a while, my parents figured that it is not going to be safe to live there because soon, the large groups of Khmer Rough going to marched into Phnom Penh and took over the capital. So, we decide to travel across from Phnom Penh back to Battambong so that we can stay in Thailand for a while until this raged war over. Between 1976–79 we travel across many Provinces. At the same time, we incounter many other problems because when we get to a place called Srok Baa-runk Tlaegg, we ran into another Khmer Rough allies. . . . Many people still die because those unthinkable animal Khmer Rough killed them. At the same time, my family and I suffered from malnutition and lagged of food. I, on the other hand, suffered from many kind of diseases. When we travel, we traveled with about twelves family, four family die from starvations, and disease, and executions at the same time. We're not only lagged of food, but also lagged of water. My family and I as well as other family used to drink water from a pond where the water buffalow laid in and at the same time, used the same water to cooked rice or roots or what-ever food we can find to stay alive. I also use to used a water in a pond where the Khmer Rough killed the innocent and throw their body into the pond. We drink all kind water because sometimes, we can hardly find water to drink beside drinking whatever water we can find. We also drink water where people shower in it and body hang on top of a tree by the Khmer Rough above that water. We use to eat left over rice after a week and more; also eat roots and leave which we sometimes don't even know what's we're eating. We ate leaves and roots and insects or whatever we can find because it is the only resources that keep us alive. I saw many body dies and float over the river floor and body dies in a huts, or palm leave cottage. I've seen people dies with their body swallon and rotten. I seen people dies in a pitt with sharp bamboo stick cut through their body and from mine explosions. I seen baby, men, women, elder people left behind in places without any helped. I seen people fought over food and other sources of nutrition to keep themselves alive.

One of the shockest thing of all is when we travel across each provinces to Thai-land and faces river full of blood. The Khmer Rough killed not just scholars, farmers, teachers, monks, men, elder, women, but they're also killed babies and animals. These rudeless and man eating man never choose it's victims, just like the wild animals, they killed anyone, anythings that they can get their hand on. They don't choose faces or think whether you are human, cat, or dog, they killed every-things. I remember on time late evening around four or five evening, my parents and brother get together to eat our dinner when all of a sudden, a loud voice flew across the groups of people and said, "Old man, go to hell and die. We'll blow your head off." . . . I didn't even know the reason why they killed him, because I didn't dare to asked any question and beside I was too little to asked question. Beside this reason, I was too scare to open my mouth and speak. I was eight when this happened. The old man was about his seventy when they took him away. . . . They took him away into the forest about 500 meter away from where we reside and shot him away with his hands tied behind his back. . . . The only niose I heard was the niose that come from the gun that they used. I heard two shot and that's was all I hear. My family and I still shocked after they return, escpecially me, because I never faced anyone that killed an old man before. I have seen dead body along the way, young, and old from all kind of suffering. But at that time, I saw the old man got killed with my own eyes. I saw an AK pointed at his head as they took him away.

If I have a chance, I will try to finished this painful memory more for you. You probably think that it's pocus focus because I still haven't forgetten about the past. But it's true because the past still haunt me until today. I still have some nightmare about it and it's not easy to talk about something like this after what I have been through. Many of my relative die because the Khmer Rough.

Source: Samnang Shawn Vann, "Samnang," *The Digital Archive of Cambodian Holocaust Survivors,* http://www.cybercambodia.com/dachs/stories/samnang.html. Used by permission.

Commentary

Samnang Shawn Vann learned English later in life, once he had moved to the United States from a refugee camp in Thailand. His account is very powerful, made more so because of his vernacular syntax, informal language, and use of colloquialisms. Surprisingly, it is not always understood that people who have suffered the savagery of genocide carry deep scars. As Samnang's testimony shows, the nightmare does not disappear once the killing stops.

When the Khmer Rouge took power in April 1975, Samnang was five years old. His family home was in Kampong Speu Province in south-central Cambodia. Although still a very young child, he was forced to become part of the regime's vast compulsory work force, an important part of the Khmer Rouge's vision for how its new society would be built. The purpose behind the resettlement of urban dwellers in the countryside was to build a new Cambodia founded on principles of agrarian communism.

In order to achieve this, the Khmer Rouge developed strictly enforced policies requiring workers to labor in the fields for up to 14 hours a day, on minimal rations and with little in the way of rest breaks. Hunger became the main obsession of these people's lives; under such circumstances, sickness soon developed as well. As it was in the Nazi concentration camps, those unable to work were considered "useless eaters," and they frequently vanished into what became known as the "killing fields." After being removed from the worksite, they would be forced to dig their own graves, before Khmer Rouge soldiers would bash them on the back of the head with shovels or hoes or shoot them, execution style, from behind.

As Samnang shows, even the most minor infraction provided enough reason to attract severe punishments: "Sometimes, when I refused to work, they would torture me by wipping me and making me worked over time without rest of drink." On days of extreme temperatures—up to 120 degrees, on occasion—he would still be required to work. With hunger ever-present, he would "sneak out and when into the forest to hunt for lizard and birds and animals to kill for food," despite the fact that scavenging for extra food was an offense punishable by death. Samnang was perhaps luckier than many, for at least he was not killed when caught: "When we sneak out, and they caught me, they took me back and over work me without letting me eat anything for that whole day or sometimes up to two days and a half." Samnang and his friends would eat anything to try to satisfy their gnawing emptiness, including "all kinds of insects and animal like grass hopper, cricket, scorpion, tarantula, rats, snake, porcupine, wild baor, rain deer, water beetle, and more." For these children the desperate quest to survive, and to stop the horrible pain of hunger, surmounted all scruples.

In Democratic Kampuchea, as Cambodia was henceforth to be known under the Khmer Rouge, family relationships not approved by Angka were banned. The "ideal" community that was forming had a communal structure in which the family unit was not an approved institution; family members could even be put to death for communicating with each other. For children, this was a vital reform in the new state structure. The Khmer Rouge saw adults as "tainted" by religion, capitalist democracy, Western ideas, and consumerism, whereas children, not having grown up with such notions, could still be "saved," their purity intact. The younger a child, the better he or she could properly be indoctrinated, and consequently it was not uncommon for very young children to be given positions of authority (extending even to life and death) over older people. In situations where any semblance of family life managed to prevail, children were coached to spy on their elders, and were told to report suspicious conversations to the nearest Khmer Rouge soldier.

In Samnang's account, we see numerous instances of the communist assault against the family structure. Many of his recollections are those a child would remember: being bullied by the children next door, who could get away with it because their father was a "Khmer Rough" leader; seeing his mother ritually humiliated because she dared to try to find some fish to supplement her children's diet; or finding that his parents had been threatened with death for the same infraction. Still, Samnang's account provides a glimpse into how families did try to stay together in spite of the Khmer Rouge's policies regarding the family unit. This is one of the prevailing insights of his testimony. It is important for us to learn here that families did their best to remain intact, as much of the secondary literature glosses over this, considering it so unlikely that it could not have happened.

Clearly, options for survival in this environment were extremely limited. Khmer Rouge cadres would look for any excuse to kill those seen as "contaminated" by the former ways, one of which was religious observance. In the new Cambodia, observing the tenets of Buddhism could be a death sentence. Samnang, possibly unaware of this but eager to find a way to alleviate his desperate condition, "always prayed to Lord Buddha that my nightmare will end soon, but my called to him never been answered because my people continued to suffered until this day."

Despite this, the family did manage to stay together and reach sanctuary in Thailand, after a grueling and nightmarish trip that took years. As they proceeded, evidence of Khmer Rouge savagery was everywhere: "One of the shockest thing of all is when we travel across each provinces to Thailand and faces river full of blood. The Khmer Rough killed not just scholars, farmers, teachers, monks, men, elder, women, but they're also killed babies and animals."

To an eight-year-old boy, the trauma this generated must have been intense, the psychological wounds slow to heal. About those dark days, Samnang concludes his account with poignant words: "The past still haunt me until today. I still have some nightmare about it and it's not easy to talk about something like this after what I have been through." Nor could it be, we might venture, for most other survivors of this cruel regime.

Questions

1. Do you think it is useful to read Samnang's account as it was originally produced, without grammatical correction?
2. How does Samnang characterize daily life in Democratic Kampuchea?
3. Samnang was a child during the events he describes. Do you think his views would have been any different if he had been an adult, recounting the same experiences?

LENG HOUTH

Everyday life in Khmer Rouge Cambodia was upended completely from what it had been before the takeover in April 1975. Just before the end of the civil war that month, Leng Houth and her husband, Houth Lach, arrived in Phnom Penh, where they meant to ensure their survival in what was certain to be a time of upheaval. Events overtook them, however, and they were separated by subsequent developments. Later, Leng learned that her husband had died. In this account, she describes what it was like trying to survive the Khmer Rouge period without him. In just a few words, her account of survival reads as an extraordinary example of opportunity and luck in the face of adversity.

I was [born in 1951 in Svay Rieng], the second from the oldest child, but the oldest daughter so I took care of my younger brothers and sisters. I went to primary school for six years and came home at noon to take care of the younger kids. Our family lived as traders. My mother opened shop, like a supermarket on our front door step and her and my father ran the business. My mother was illiterate and she wanted me to study and go to school and get a high [school] education. She also had me learn Vietnamese, because our home was so near the Khmer-Vietnamese border, she felt it would benefit me. I went to high school and later went on to two years of college and I went for teacher qualification tests in Phnom Penh when I was 18.

While I was in school I met my husband, Houth Lach. We had gone to high school together and were interested in each other since then. But he left to serve in the *Police Militaire* for a year and left Svay Rieng to work in Phnom Penh. He visited my family daily that year and finally we were engaged in November of 1971. We married soon after and settled in Svay Rieng in a house of our own near my mother's home. By that time the war was escalating but everything was so uncertain, we weren't in a rush to do anything just yet.

I had my first child in November of 1972. Maranet, my daughter, stayed with her grandmother for a month as it is tradition to have the grandmother be a caretaker for the first child. Meanwhile, I never got into teaching, so I opened my own fabric company. Marital life was full of joys for me. My husband was very caring and an easy-going man. He helped with everything in the house and loved his daughter very much. He was gentle and careful with her always. Maranet was born in our home. I was in labor for only two hours and he had helped with the childbirth.

The roads turned in 1975. On April 12, 1975 my husband knew it was time for us to leave Svay Rieng and find shelter in the city. Maranet was 3-years-old now and I was six-months pregnant with my second child. I remember the day very clearly. It was the last time I saw my husband. He sent me on a plane and promised that we would meet up again in the city when he could get out. I saw him waving and he had tears in his eyes. It was just like that movie, *The Killing Fields*. I knew how much he loved his children and never doubted that he would not come for us. When we got to Pochetong Airport in Phnom Penh bombs were falling like pebbles from the sky. I rushed to hear the news reports over the radio. Four hours after I touched down in the city, Svay Rieng was surrendered to the Khmer Rouge. I hoped my husband would be spared.

Five days after I arrived in Phnom Penh, the Khmer Rouge arrived and "liberated" the city. We were all told to go back to our hometowns. There was ten people in my group and I was pregnant still. We walked along for a month and a half before we reached Svay Rieng. The killings were already starting. As [we] walked along the road we stepped over corpses which had either been people who could not make the trip or were killed and left on the roadside. I drank from ponds that had dead bodies floating in them.

Before we left on our journey, the Khmer Rouge had given us two-day's worth of rice and salt. They set up stations along the roadside and handed us more rice every five-six kilometers we walked. It was just enough rice to get us by. We fished in nearby ponds and picked vegetables that grew along the road. I was with my family and my brothers did all the fishing.

We finally got to a village on the outskirts of Svay Rieng and settled beneath a hut where the "old people" lived. The old people were the Khmer Rouge peasant families who were like village keepers in the commune. The first thing they asked for were volunteers who had been former students, teachers, soldiers, doctors or anyone with an education to help them on special assignments. My brother, who had worked for the Red Cross with Americans and was in his second year of university studies, volunteered. My mother later discovered that they had sent him to a big labor camp down the road. They were ordered to dig up huge ditches and they were fed nothing. My mother—she's a courageous woman—she, went up into the camp and asked the camp leader, she pleaded with him to see her son. They let her see him and when she did, she found his head was full of lice and he had been starving for days. She snuck grains into his hands. They couldn't say anything to each other. He worked at gunpoint. They just looked at each other.

While I was living in this village, I was surprised by a visit from my husband's uncle. It was May 1976 and he had come with news that my husband was still alive. All along I knew my hope was not left for vain. But strangely I had a bad premonition. My mother warned me not to go and I decided to stay with my mother instead of be reunited with my husband. I let my chance pass by.

I remember one day in 1977. Thirty people—all teachers, soldiers, doctors and nurses—were gathered together for a big feast. They took all their utensils and burning wood and had a huge meal with the best foods, like lemongrass fish soup and roasted beef and fried fish. It [was] all the foods I hadn't seen in two years. The Khmer Rouge fed them very well that night, but I knew they were to disappear the next day. And sure enough, the next day, when I went to the water well to fetch water, I found it full with floating bodies. I ran away full of fear, running in silence, afraid someone would hear me and punish me for seeing what I wasn't supposed to.

Thinking of food, I remember the things we lived on. We all ate at a community kitchen where we'd get our daily share of rice porridge which had more water than rice. I worked in the kitchen, chopping vegetables and roots. They fed us potatoes and roots on occasion. One day as I was chopping roots and I was so hungry my stomach churned. As I chopped I thought of stowing away the scraps of the roots, the tips that weren't being used for the group soup. I slipped them in my pocket, hoping no one would notice. Then I felt a hard thump on my back. I don't remember anything from that experience, but my mother told me I was unconscious for three days. My mother told me she prayed everyday for my life and for my sanity. She said I would sit up and make strange noises then faint back again. I was stiff as a rock, my muscles were tight when I regained my consciousness. My poor children thought I was crazy. That was my first brush with death.

In that same year, I was almost killed again. You see, my family was one of two Chinese-Cambodian families and there was only four families who were pure Chinese, full-blooded Chinese. One night I saw a young group of Khmer Rouge soldiers, they must have been around 13 or 14 years old. These boys were holding ropes and knives in their hands and they took the four Chinese families and killed them. I know they killed them because the next day, I saw the same boys wearing the Chinese families' clothes.

Two weeks after that night, rumor circulated that our families were to be the next victims. The "old people" who lived above us came to us with the news. The old grandma whispered it to us, that there was plans to take away all the Chinese-Cambodians in the village. After she told us, she asked for our clothes. I gave them to her, thinking we'd have no use for them since we'd be dead soon anyway. That night at around seven in the evening, we heard horses coming toward our village. It was three men on horseback. But just as they entered our village, two men ran to them and told them to [go] away. They told the men on horses that "Angkar Leou" had declared a decree to stop all killing! The whole village knew they had come for us and that they left without us. Oh, I can't tell you how relieved I was.

But it is August 20, 1978 when I celebrated my new life. I've celebrated it every year ever since. Early that morning, the Khmer Rouge woke me up at 4 a.m. and told me to bring my two daughters. We were scheduled for a meeting with "Angkar Thom," they told me. They took us to the kitchen area, where we meet with some 240 families who had come from four different villages. There must have been about 400 women and children there, who were all wives and children of former soldiers. Many of the women were dressed in their best clothes, because they knew they were going to die. They fed us with the best foods, just like they fed that group of people I had seen. I ate as I had never eaten before and I fed my kids until they were stuffed. The Khmer Rouge asked me what my husband used to do and I told him that he sold ice at the market. Even though, I knew I was going to die, I felt this urge to save myself from the situation. I went to talk to the Khmer Rouge village leaders and said smilingly, "This is a very nice meal you've planned, but why can't my whole family come with me?" The leader smiled and said nothing. Just then, my little brother came running into my arms, sobbing like a baby. It surprised me so much, I nearly yelled at him for risking his life just to come after me. But on seeing this, the leader told me to take him and my daughters back to the village. I was saved. I was so elated and joyous that as I ran back to the village, I felt like I was flying. I have never felt so grateful in my life. That day all 240 wives died with their children, I was the only one to survive from that massacre.

Source: Interview by Elizabeth Chey with Leng Houth, *Three Women: Oral Histories,* compiled and translated by Elizabeth Chey. Part of the *Beauty and Darkness Project: Cambodia in Modern History,* 1995, http://www.mekong.net/cambodia/3women3.htm. Used by permission of Elizabeth Chey.

Commentary

Leng Houth's testimony describes an idyllic prewar life. She enjoyed strong family relationships, among them a bond with a mother who sought an education for her children (including the development of the ability to speak a foreign language), and a happy marriage to her high school sweetheart, which resulted in a daughter. Leng went into business for herself. Her life seemed content.

The arrival of the Khmer Rouge in April 1975 soon brought this life to an end, as it did for all members of the Cambodian middle class. Khmer Rouge ideology saw Cambodian society divided into several classes: the royal family and aristocracy, who embodied the remnants of feudalism; large capitalists; professionals, small business owners, and intellectuals; peasants; urban workers; and "revolutionary workers."

Although the leaders of the Communist Party were themselves almost exclusively of middle-class backgrounds originally, the Cambodian middle class was completely devastated over the next three and a half years. It could have had the insight and expertise to be a modernizing force for the country, but it was destroyed in the communist quest to create a new, "perfect" society. No opposition from those labeled "class enemies" was tolerated. Currency was abolished. Property became collective. Markets, schools, newspapers, religious practices, and private property were outlawed. The family unit was broken up. Those who were now prisoners of the regime in their own country were subjected to ceaseless rounds of political indoctrination. Anyone with ties to the old way of life was targeted. This included city dwellers; members of the former government; public servants; police; military officers; teachers; ethnic Vietnamese, Chinese, and Thais; Christian clergy; Buddhist monks; members of the Cham Muslim minority; and members of the middle and educated classes (who could be anyone with a high school education or above). Those with "soft" hands were not considered to be workers but "bourgeois," and they were therefore meant only for slave labor or death. All were ruthlessly cut out of Cambodian society.

Leng's experience in this environment saw her cast among those who were now called "New People," the term given to recently conquered urban dwellers. They comprised both city folk and peasant refugees who had earlier fled to the cities trying to avoid the Khmer Rouge takeover in the countryside. Upon being transferred out of the cities in a mass movement of forced relocation, the "New People" suffered innumerable hardships at the hands of the Khmer Rouge. Their treatment was conditioned by two basic motives. First, they had been "corrupted" by urban living in the Western style, and thus had to be "re-educated" in pure Khmer communist ideals, or die. Second, their status as the last group to be brought under Khmer Rouge rule meant that this transformation had to occur much more rapidly than the transformations of other groups. "New People" were systematically discriminated against within the Khmer Rouge state, frequently receiving less food (of poorer quality) than others, and possessing fewer rights than those who had already been living under Khmer Rouge rule. Because of this, "New People" were even more vulnerable than others. Many hundreds of thousands were killed because of their social and class origins.

Leng was aware of this immediately after the Khmer Rouge took over Phnom Penh. When orders came for all of the city's recent arrivals to return to their hometowns as part of the urban evacuation program, Leng and a small group of others walked for a month and a half in order to reach the Svay Rieng Province in southeast Cambodia. Even then, there was abundant evidence of mass killing—as the group "walked along the road we stepped over corpses which had either been people who could not make the trip or were killed and left on the roadside." The horror was then compounded, as Leng "drank from ponds that had dead bodies floating in them." This was a clear and early statement of the Khmer Rouge's total disregard for basic humanity.

Another example of Khmer Rouge brutality came "one day in 1977." Having assembled a group of some 30 people who were despised "New People," the Khmer Rouge permitted them to partake of a last meal in high style, with "the best foods, like lemongrass fish soup and roasted beef and fried fish." With hunger prevailing throughout the country, this was simple cruelty for those remaining—as Leng writes, "I knew they were to disappear the next day." And so it was. The next day, "when I went to the water well to fetch water, I found it full with floating bodies."

Hunger was one of the innumerable sufferings brought on by the Khmer Rouge, and it was ubiquitous. As it was forbidden to supplement the food sources being rationed out by the authorities, the agony of starvation was evident everywhere. Given that it dominates the very nature of existence, survivors speak of hunger frequently. On one occasion, Leng was working on a detail preparing the communal meal, such as it was. She recalls, "We all ate at a community kitchen where we'd get our daily share of rice porridge which had more water than rice." Often, the Khmer Rouge would give their consent for a meal that consisted of whatever the local neighborhood had at hand. Leng remembers that one day she was chopping roots that were to go into a communal stew or soup. "I was so hungry," she states, that "my stomach churned." The thought occurred to her "of stowing away the scraps of the roots, the tips that weren't being used." Hoping no one would notice, she hid some in her pocket, but, as though the guards had been reading her mind, she received such a severe beating that she was unconscious for three days.

This was the first of a number of lucky escapes for Leng. It was thought that she would die from the beating, but she survived that assault and at least two other close encounters with death. Leng's fall from a pleasant and happy existence prior to the Khmer Rouge takeover was matched only by her good fortune in being able to survive in order to bear witness. She endured the most horrible privations, lost her husband to the genocide, and saw cruel and hideous death up close. Yet her testimony reminds us of the role luck plays in the survival of victims, and of her determination to resist despair, even during the darkest moments.

Questions

1. How does Leng articulate her thoughts regarding food and hunger during the Khmer Rouge years?
2. Leng was designated one of the "New People." What does that term mean, and what did it signify for Leng's future in Democratic Kampuchea?
3. In what ways did Leng's life change after April 1975?

SAMBO THOUCH

Sambo Thouch was born on June 6, 1938, in Phnom Penh. Her husband, a general in the Cambodian regular army, was murdered as a result of the Khmer Rouge takeover in 1975. In the aftermath of the genocide and the Vietnamese invasion of the country in 1979, Sambo tried to rebuild her life as an educator, but, finding communist Vietnamese rule as oppressive in many ways as the Khmer Rouge regime had been, she sought an escape for herself and her family. She sent four of her children to a cousin in Connecticut, then made a run for the Thai border with her two remaining sons and an orphan boy she had adopted. It took several years before she managed to arrive in the United States, where she found ultimate sanctuary and a new life. This account is based on an interview she gave in 1995.

[I was born on] June 6, 1938 in Phnom Penh. I taught grammar for 17 years. I was the Vice Principal, second in charge, at the grammar school for two years—until the war began. I was the oldest of 11 siblings and only 2 younger sisters survived during the Pol Pot regime. Well, my story is quite long.

They took my husband on May 28, 1975. He was a four-and-half star general, but he wasn't a war general. He never went to battle. During Sihanouk's reign, he served as a police chief in the Police Royale, as they called it. The Police Royale solely served and assisted the king. But when Lon Nol came to power, the police security force was dissolved and my husband and I traveled from province to province in his new position in the military. I was teaching in Kampong Speu when I was promoted to the position of vice principal. But life was interrupted by the Khmer Rouge. Since we feared the encroachment of the communist forces, my husband asked to be transferred back to Phnom Penh. We took our children and went back to live deep inside the city, in a Buddhist hospital right on Monivong Blvd.

We did not stay in the city for long. When the Khmer Rouge entered the city, they commanded everyone to evacuate their homes. We were directed by the Khmer Rouge to walk along National Road No. 1. As we were walking we'd stop along the side to spend the night. My whole family, my husband and six kids and my sisters and mother went along the road with our car. We moved along until we got to Kheann Svay. When we arrived in Kheann Svay, I saw a tall gateway leading into a temple. We walked toward it and some of my husband's underlings came to greet him. He stood silently. All this time he had tried to conceal his rank and identity by wearing layman clothes and rubber sandals, but he was still recognized. He nodded, but we tried to hide ourselves from those few workers.

At that place, there was a big gateway they had built. Yes, they built it to attract people. They extended the gateway by attaching leaves over it to make a roof. Under that roof there was a desk and some civilians sat at the desk recruiting people up to "help rebuild the country." They didn't have Khmer Rouge soldiers sit there, they forced other city people to sit there, so people would trust them. You see, my husband's workers had run to him near the desk. It was hard to conceal his status from them.

My husband wasn't the head honcho at his bureau. He held the second most important job. He held all the bureaucratic and accounting responsibilities under a major war general who was a figure-head office holder. But now we were dressed in rags. Seeing the desk, I thought things were normal and I told my husband to sign up. I didn't know what was to come. I just thought it would help us. They offered a cup of rice for each individual in our family, including the children. At the time, we thought only of food and where we could get it next. At this part of the road, there was no where to grow rice, not water to transplant the stalks. I had never farmed before either. I could never separate the rice from the stalks; that always bothered me. Anyhow, they said he would teach new soldiers for the government. They said he would be educating soldiers on military tactics. They lied. They had taken him for a week and they didn't give us a grain of rice. But the mission was supposed to be three months, as I was later told.

On the day my husband left, I packed his clothes. I asked him if he wanted a blanket and towels. He said, no. He told me not to pack anything. He knew what they were going to do to him, but he said nothing to me. I asked again, thinking it was strange that he should be gone for three months and not want a blanket to keep himself warm. He just took off his wedding band and said, "Save this. Save this so you can feed the children." He left with only the clothes on his body and rubber sandals.

Three months passed and all the wives were getting suspicious as to where their husbands had been sent. We asked them when our husbands would return, and because so many had inquired about their husbands' well-being, the Khmer Rouge leaders held a big meeting for all the wives; about 11 families were there. At the meeting, they said the teaching program was extended to six months. All the wives staying at the temple had been workers; women who held jobs as nurses, teachers and secretaries before the Khmer Rouge disrupted their daily lives. They said in their lingo, "Don't fret. We will all meet each other at that other plain." We'd all be reunited in hell was what they really meant. When they ordered us to leave the temple, to go back to our hometowns, I realized my husband had been killed. Me and all the wives cried at the announcement. We used to see truckloads of men dressed in black being driven away, but we could barely make out the faces and could not recognize that their faces were the faces of our husbands. Until then, I hadn't realized I was being held prisoner. They had a 24-hour surveillance on us and when we left to do work in the fields, they kept tabs.

I don't understand my karma. At the same time we were relieved from the temple, my three youngest kids were suffering from terrible fevers. They were drenched in sweat. Good thing, I knew what to do or else they would have died then and there. I care very much about my children and am very cautious about their health and hygiene. But I was thin and weak then. We headed toward Phnom Penh in the car, but discovered that the gasoline was stolen out of the tank. Not only that the car was stripped that night by Khmer Rouge hoodlums. Our nice clothes, that we had saved to trade for food were also taken. It was so rude when we were burglarized. They stole our belongings while we were asleep and they knocked on the window and woke us up to tell us that someone had just run away with the tires.

When we finally got to the town which was the station to go to Phnom Penh, the Khmer Rouge leaders told me that we would take a boat to Phnom Penh. Who'd ever heard of taking a boat to Phnom Penh when it was so near people could drive!? I knew we were going to be settled somewhere else on the other side of Tonle Sap. When we crossed the lake and docked on December 1975 and I gave birth to another child. After three months of traveling with little to eat, I gave birth to a baby, but it died of tetanus nine days after birth. . . .

Later on, I was transferred to Kompong Thom district and in that village a former employee of my husband settled there too. I recognized him and his family, but they pretended not to recognize me, which kept us both safe and mute. I sewed dresses while I was there.

I stayed there until the Vietnamese invaded. Immediately after the invasion, the Khmer Rouge leaders all fled and people from within the village took on leadership roles under the Vietnamese. . . .

Within a year, schools were reopened. The Vietnamese know how to treat the people they use. They gave us a lot to keep us happy. Even though I was working for the Vietnamese, I told myself that this was for the benefit of the Cambodian people. I was helping the people, not the government of Vietnam.

Source: Interview by Elizabeth Chey with Sambo Thouch, *Three Women: Oral Histories,* compiled and translated by Elizabeth Chey. Part of the *Beauty and Darkness Project: Cambodia in Modern History,* 1995, http://www.mekong.net/cambodia/3women1.htm. Used by permission of Elizabeth Chey.

Commentary

Soon after seizing power on April 17, 1975, the Khmer Rouge arrested and killed thousands of soldiers, military officers, and civil servants from the previous dictatorial regime of General Lon Nol (1913–1985). The military forces, by this time, were a demoralized multitude with thousands of young urban Cambodians. The army had inflated its numbers through conscription during the civil war from 1970 onward, but, desperate to defeat the Khmer Rouge guerrillas, it had expanded beyond its capacity to absorb the new recruits. As a result, it was poorly trained and badly equipped. Significant military assistance from the United States did not help to stop the rot. As combat casualties mounted, there was insufficient time for continued training, which remained a major problem right through to 1975.

Additionally, the officer corps was known to be corrupt. Payroll rosters were inflated; officers often skimmed off allowances for rations; and arms sales on the black market were frequent. Soldiers in the field were hampered by low pay and ammunition shortages. Morale plummeted. Over time, things only got worse.

By contrast, the Khmer Rouge army, which in 1970 was small, had grown to over 700,000 men. It was highly motivated, and was kept in check by Communist Party cadres who accompanied the soldiers everywhere. Lon Nol's army was forced to confront not only the country's domestic threat of a communist insurgency, but also North Vietnamese communists who continually infiltrated Cambodian territory. The effort, overall, proved to be too great, resulting in the government's ultimate collapse in April 1975—and in victory for the Khmer Rouge.

Sambo Thouch's story differs from many other accounts of the Khmer Rouge years in Cambodia. She was a highly educated adult woman with a senior role as the vice principal of a grammar school, where she had taught for 17 years before the war began. Sambo was a member of the Cambodian elite, married to a general in the military forces of the republic under Lon Nol and with a family of six children.

All were victims of the forced evacuation of Phnom Penh after April 17, 1975, but because of their status, Sambo's family members, including some extended family, were permitted to travel in their car. This alone marked their situation as an unusual one. While Sambo's husband attempted to conceal his rank, he was, nonetheless, recognized and impressed into service as a trainer, supposedly to help train new soldiers for the revolution. As Sambo writes, "They said he would be educating soldiers on military tactics. They lied. . . . The mission was supposed to be three months." Her husband seemed to know instinctively that this was a ruse to kill him, as he told Sambo not to pack anything for him, and he gave her his wedding band "so you can feed the children." At this time the women were sent to perform manual labor in the fields.

Sambo's worst fears about her husband were realized only three months later, when the Khmer Rouge informed her, and the wives of other officers, that the teaching assignment that had sent their husbands away had been extended to six months. The women and children were ordered to return to their hometowns from the temple where they had been staying. It was at that time that "I realized my husband had been killed."

Sambo and her family moved back to Phnom Penh, again, remarkably, in the car. Her testimony provides an example of how the so-called "pure" Khmer Rouge was in actuality often corrupt. The car's gasoline was stolen out of the tank, the car was stripped, and their clothes were taken. In an action that no one could possibly misunderstand, the little group was raided while they slept. To add insult to injury, the Khmer Rouge miscreants then woke up the victims in order to tell them that they had been robbed, and that "someone" had run off with their goods.

Because of her age, in her account issues relating to social status and education interest Sambo, in contrast to many other survivors. Hunger is a constant, but concerns we do not often see in other testimonies are present here: concern for the fate of her husband; for the illnesses that befall her children; over the places to which they are being sent; over the theft of personal goods; and, finally, concerns regarding the manner in which the Khmer Rouge regime will come to an end.

Toward the end of the Khmer Rouge period, Sambo was transferred to Kampong Thom, Cambodia's second largest province by area, located in the center of the country. She remained there until soon after the Vietnamese invasion of Cambodia on January 2, 1979, when the Vietnamese launched a swift armored campaign that raced across Cambodia along the main highways. The force captured Kampong Thom and Angkor Wat, the symbol of traditional Cambodian nationalism.

Sambo notes in her account that upon the Vietnamese invasion, the Khmer Rouge leaders fled, leaving the local villagers in her area in charge of their own fate "under the Vietnamese." As "people from within the village took on leadership roles," some sense of normality began to resurface. Within a year, schools were reopened, meaning that Sambo was able to resume her career as a teacher and exercise her skills as a senior administrator. There was traditionally little love lost between the Cambodians and the Vietnamese, but Sambo did not have much difficulty working within the newly imposed regime. As she was able to rationalize it, "I told myself that this was for the benefit of the Cambodian people," and that "I was helping the people, not the government of Vietnam." The task was made easier by virtue of the fact that the Vietnamese "know how to treat the people they use," giving the local people "a lot to keep us happy." This was a marked difference from the Cambodian experience under the Khmer Rouge. A path had been opened, however slightly, for a resumption of the better times that survivors craved—and that the country needed so desperately.

Questions

1. Sambo Thouch's husband had been a high-ranking member of the Cambodian armed forces under Lon Nol, before the Khmer Rouge takeover. Why do you think he was targeted for persecution after May 1975?
2. Do you think that Sambo's social status helped her survive, or did it make her more vulnerable?
3. Describe how Sambo's leadership skills were shown in her transactions with the Khmer Rouge.

JON SWAIN

Award-winning British journalist Jon Swain (b. 1948), who recorded his experiences during the war in Indochina between 1970 and 1975 in a book entitled River of Time *(1995), gives an insightful depiction of the last days of Phnom Penh, before and during the Khmer Rouge takeover. It accords closely with the events portrayed in the 1984 Oscar-winning film* The Killing Fields *(directed by Roland Joffe), and refers to several other leading journalist/ observers of the time, including Sydney Schanberg (b. 1934), Dith Pran (1942–2008), and Al Rockoff (b. 1948). The account is remarkable for its level of detail and the degree to which it evokes the drama and fears of the time.*

It was 12:30 p.m. We now felt secure enough to drive around the northern part of the city. A few of us went to the Preah Ket Meala Hospital, a gloomy set of buildings five minutes from Le Phnom on the banks of the Mekong, where hundreds of people were being subjected to a hideous death. The doctors had not reported for work for two days. There was no one to treat the 2000 wounded and the plasma bottles and saline drips were emptying one by one.

People were bleeding to death by the dozen in the corridors. The floors of the wards were caked with blood. The hot, fetid air was thick with flies—the sight of these swarming over the living and the dead, over the anguished faces of those who knew they were doomed to die, churned my stomach and made my mind reel. I asked a distraught nurse for an explanation. She said she had phoned the doctors. "They say they are coming in a short time, but they are not here yet. Maybe they are afraid."

These scenes of horror wiped out the work of the Scottish team who had filled a downstairs ward with sophisticated equipment and brightened it with children's pictures.

Upstairs was worse. The dead and the dying lay in pools of their own blood. The long corridor outside the operating theatre was literally awash with it. A man and his wife had died in each other's arms. A few feet away, an old man was pushed hard up against the wall, his intestines tumbling out like laundry. Further down the corridor was a soldier with arm, head and stomach wounds—a Khmer Rouge who had somehow been brought in for treatment.

A single harassed doctor fussed about impotently, stethoscope around his neck. It was easy to see that, but for our presence, he would already have gone home. Through fly-blown lips, the Khmer Rouge croaked: "Water, water, please get me some water." We could not give him any because of his stomach wound.

Hospital workers with scrubbing-brushes and bowls of soapy water started to wash the blood off the floor. They brushed between the legs of the corpses and sent the red mixture splashing down the open lift shaft. With one accord, Sydney, Al, Pran and I sloshed our way through the blood to the exit and left.

It was one o'clock, the hottest time of the day. We emerged into the oven-like heat to find people edging inside the buildings and running away from the front gate. There was a distinct mood of danger. We drove cautiously through the hospital grounds towards the street, but before we could reach it, there came a rush of foot-steps. Half a dozen Khmer Rouge soldiers, bristling with guns, stopped the car, dragged us out and shook their rifles at us. They were boys, some perhaps twelve years old, hardly taller than their tightly held AK47 rifles. Their ignorance and fanaticism made them super-deadly.

Their leader's eyes were coals of hate. He was screaming and ranting, foaming at the mouth. He held his pistol against my head, finger firm on the trigger. My hands were high in the air and I was paralysed with fear. My camera, notebooks and other belongings littered the ground where the Khmer Rouge had thrown them. The seconds ticked by. Pran uttered some soothing words in Khmer. Then I was able to rejoin the others on their side of the car. A chastened, terrified group, we moved under escort to a captured APC in the street outside.

Sydney, Al and I were forced at gunpoint into the back of the APC. . . . We rode through the streets and stopped to pick up two more prisoners, Cambodians in civilian clothes. The big one with a moustache and a crew-cut wore a white T-shirt and jeans. The smaller man was wearing a sports shirt and slacks. Both were officers and quite as frightened as we were.

The big man was second-in-command of the government navy. He tried to pass us his wallet with his ID card. We whispered that it was no use. Finally he hid it in the back of the APC among some oily rags. The small man put an ivory Buddha in his mouth as a talisman. . . .

I was still young enough to believe that death, even in Cambodia, happens mostly to others. Now I was faced with death myself. I had coped with it a number of times on the battlefield, but this was different. To have my head blown off by a teenage soldier at close range when the war was over seemed a ridiculous, ineffectual and unfair ending to life. I longed to be told it was all make-believe. I cursed myself for ever having left the security of the hotel to see the casualties in the hospital and wished the clock could be turned back a couple of hours. The same emotions must have run through the minds of all those other journalists in the minutes before they were murdered by the Khmer Rouge.

We were prisoners inside the APC for about twenty-five minutes, sweating like pigs in the heat. But time no longer existed; I was already beginning to feel remote from the world outside. I thought of the wastefulness of my life, the people I loved and would never see again. I prayed softly. I know that I wanted desperately to live but I am struck by our lack of protests or resistance. Of course, they would have done no good. The young Khmer Rouge had eyes as cold as stone and were determined to kill us. We were condemned men. Our deaths would be squalid. But surely we should not have gone like lambs to slaughter.

The top hatch unfolded with a clang and a man pointing a gun at me screamed, "We are not Vietnamese. We don't like Vietnamese." It was an odd thing to say. I had been speaking in French only to establish that I was not American. Perhaps he thought I had been talking in Vietnamese. Evidently he harboured the traditional Cambodian hatred for their Vietnamese neighbours.

The wretched minutes ticked by. At 1:40 p.m., the APC shuddered to a halt. Bolts slid back. The rear door was opened. I saw water and a pair of Khmer Rouge soldiers, pointing rifles, beckoning us out. We stared at one another. We were sure this was journey's end; we would be executed and our bodies tossed into the Mekong.

Eyes blinking, we stepped into the sunlight. Immediately Pran began to talk. He talked and talked. He spoke softly and firmly, telling the Khmer Rouge that we were neutral journalists, there to witness their historic "liberation" of Phnom Penh and Cambodia. By and by, the tension went out of the air. We were ordered to stand across the street from the river and wait. We drank water from a bucket and watched people stream out of the city up Route Five.

We assumed they were refugees from the war returning to their homes now the fighting was over. In fact, the Khmer Rouge had issued orders for the entire city to be evacuated. They had also started to loot, a process that continued for days. As we stood there, guerrillas drove past in cars heaped high with cigarettes, soft drinks and wines. Few knew how to drive: the crash of gearboxes was the prevailing sound. In other circumstances, their efforts would have been hilarious; now they were grotesque: the peasant boys with death at the tips of their fingers were behaving like spoilt brats. They seemed every bit as irresponsible as the Cambodian army they had defeated.

At 3:30 a man of authority ordered us to be released, and most of our belongings were returned. The Khmer Rouge kept the car, my notebooks, films and hotel key. We were too tired to argue. Hitching a ride with two Frenchmen, we drove straight to the Ministry of Information, where we understood there was to be a news conference. We left behind the two Cambodian prisoners. I remember them standing limply on the riverbank, beseeching looks in their eyes. They knew they were condemned to die, and there was nothing we could do. We made a feeble sign of pity and abandoned them to their fate.

Source: Jon Swain, *River of Time* (London: William Heinemann, 1995), 138–143. Used by permission of Random House and St. Martin's Press.

Commentary

Jon Swain went to Indochina in March 1970 to cover the war for *Agence France-Presse.* By the time of the Khmer Rouge takeover in April 1975, he was working as a journalist for *The Sunday Times.* He was the only British journalist in Phnom Penh when the city fell on April 17 of that year, and his reporting of the event won him the prestigious British Press Awards' Journalist of the Year distinction. At the age of 27, he was the youngest recipient of the award at that time.

Although Swain had been a correspondent in Southeast Asia for five years, it was only at the last minute—on April 12, 1975—that he decided to go back to Phnom Penh to witness the final collapse of the government forces. Ironically, this was the same day that U.S. Embassy personnel, led by Ambassador John Gunther Dean (b. 1926), were evacuated from the capital by helicopter. After this, together with several other journalists, Swain witnessed the first weeks of the Khmer Rouge assault against the Cambodian people.

In this account, taken from his award-winning memoir *River of Time,* Swain begins with a description of the absolutely terrible conditions in one of the Phnom Penh hospitals at the time the city fell. The description he gives of the gore, the horror, and the hopelessness of the scant and severely overworked medical staff is graphic and gut-wrenching. While many of those who had come to the hospital seeking treatment were wounded soldiers, the majority appeared to be innocent civilians—especially children—who had been caught in the crossfire or in mortar attacks while the city was in its final collapse.

Leaving the hospital, Swain and the other journalists were captured in a Khmer Rouge advance. There was substantial confusion as to what their fate would be. Swain's account is useful in reminding us that the Khmer Rouge force comprised many young people—really boys and adolescent teenagers—who, in this new society, were viewed by the Communist Party of Kampuchea (CPK) as "untainted" by corruption or Western education (which, in the Party's view, amounted to the same thing). Child soldiers younger than 10 years of age were often drafted into the Khmer Rouge for the purpose of planting landmines and identifying city dwellers, professionals, educated individuals, and, indeed, anyone whose values conflicted with those of the Khmer Rouge. Swain and the other journalists were held up by "boys, some perhaps twelve years old, hardly taller than their tightly held AK47 rifles." Given their brainwashed state, "their ignorance and fanaticism made them super-deadly." This was compounded by what appeared to be an unthinking hatred of all things Western, which totally consumed them. Elsewhere, Swain referred to one of the boys as having "eyes as cold as stone."

Swain shows us the fate of members of the old regime, as two of them, both military officers in the former government forces, were caught up in the same action as he and the other journalists. The former officers were arrested and incarcerated along with the Westerners; there could be little doubt as to what their fates would be, just as, in Swain's words, "we were condemned men," and "our deaths would be squalid."

The youthful Khmer Rouge soldiers were irresponsible because of their indoctrination. They were also thoroughly destructive. Swain's account shows the extent to which they engaged in wholesale looting during the evacuation of Phnom Penh, in the days after the fall of the city. The Khmer Rouge had ordered that the entire population of Phnom Penh, swelled by refugees from the fighting, leave in order to build the agrarian communist utopia that was the CPK ideal. During the evacuation, the roads became clogged, and conditions for those being forced out were appalling. Even the sick in their hospital beds—together with the beds themselves—were forced onto the roads.

Accompanying this removal was terrible looting of the property the people left behind. As Swain shows, "They had also started to loot, a process that continued for days," with "cars heaped high with cigarettes, soft drinks and wines." The city, quite simply, was left a remnant of what it had been, and a tragic example of revolutionary fervor gone mad.

Upon their eventual release, the journalists managed to find refuge with the rest of the foreign community in the compound of the French Embassy. At its height, the expatriate population numbered some 800 people who had little in the way of food, water, or communication with the outside world. Not all were foreign journalists. Innumerable personal dramas played out in that small space, particularly after an order came from the Khmer Rouge that indigenous Cambodians would have to leave. Cambodian women who were married to foreigners could stay, but Cambodian men were forced out of the compound and, in all likelihood, murdered by the Khmer Rouge.

After three weeks, by the beginning of May 1975, the journalists and others at the embassy were evacuated in trucks to the Thai border. Swain and all other foreigners were expelled from Cambodia, leaving Phnom Penh a ghost town.

When placed alongside accounts written by American journalist Sydney Schanberg and others from the time, Jon Swain's is one of the key testimonies of the fall of Phnom Penh from a Western perspective. It is also a deeply personal and sensitive memoir, in which he holds back little of his own emotional turmoil at leaving Cambodia at a time when so much human destruction was taking place.

Questions

1. What was Swain's attitude toward the youthful Khmer Rouge soldiers?
2. Do you think Swain and the other journalists could have done anything to help the two Cambodian prisoners?
3. When Swain and his colleagues were captured by the Khmer Rouge, did it seem as though they were in danger? Can you see any evidence of this?

5. The Guatemalan Genocide

Throughout the late 1970s, the 1980s, and into the early 1990s, Guatemalan government death squads and government-supported militias killed up to 200,000 people, most of whom were impoverished Maya residing in tiny countryside villages. They were the victims of terror, extrajudicial killings, hundreds of massacres, and, ultimately, genocide.

During the 1960s and 1970s, Guatemala experienced a period of almost unbroken military rule. By way of response, political activism, in the form of Catholic "Liberation Theology," emerged. This emphasized solidarity with the poor, employed Marxist analysis to critique capitalist exploitation, and organized local development projects. The movement spread throughout the Guatemalan highlands, involving tens of thousands of village-level Mayan leaders as catechists and cooperative members. At the same time, new guerrilla organizations extended their reach into the Mayan regions.

On March 23, 1982, following a disputed presidential election, General José Efraín Ríos Montt (b. 1926) seized power in a coup d'état. Nine years earlier, in 1973, Ríos Montt had run in the presidential election of Guatemala, but he had been unsuccessful in the run-off. Accusations of electoral inconsistencies were made, and a decision was called for from the National Congress, which elected Ríos Montt's rival, General Kjell Eugenio Laugerud García (1930–2009). The experience seared Ríos Montt, who saw in his defeat a conspiracy from the Catholic Church and the Mayan minority.

Following Ríos Montt's coup in March 1982, a military junta immediately suspended the constitution, shut down the legislature, and began a campaign against political dissidents that included kidnapping, torture, and extrajudicial assassinations. He introduced a "National Plan of Security and Development" under which martial law was declared; special secret tribunals were established to try a variety of crimes; and Congress, together with all political parties, was shut down indefinitely.

At first, many welcomed Ríos Montt's tough approach, as it portended an end to corruption. Moreover, he appeared to have a vision for Guatemala that included education, nationalism, a stop to want and hunger, and a sense of civic pride that previously seemed to have been lacking.

149

A number of guerrilla factions that predated Ríos Montt's ascent to power united as a group called the Guatemalan National Revolutionary Unity organization (*Unidad Revolucionaria Nacional Guatemalteca,* or URNG). They denounced the junta and began to intensify their attacks against the central government.

Beginning in 1981, before Ríos Montt's coup, the Guatemalan army launched a scorched-earth counterinsurgency offensive in the Mayan highlands. This targeted not only insurgents but also the Mayan communities the government believed were supporting the guerrillas. On April 20, 1982, after the coup, the junta and military high command officially launched operation *Victoria 82* ("Victory 82"), a campaign designed to destroy the support base of the guerrillas. The slaughter by government forces was in one sense indiscriminate in that civilian villages and civilians themselves were attacked; in another sense, however, it was not indiscriminate, as the campaign appeared to be aimed directly at those of Mayan descent who eked out an impoverished existence in the highlands where the insurgency was being carried out.

To be sure, the campaign made little or no distinction between guerrilla combatants and the mainly Mayan civilian population in the targeted areas, inducing widespread terror. Ríos Montt's time in charge became the bloodiest single period in Guatemala's independent history. Maya suspected of sympathizing with the leftist antigovernment guerrillas were killed en masse and subjected to atrocities that included mutilation, torture, and rape. Hundreds of villages were destroyed by government troops, and up to a million Maya were displaced from their homes. It is estimated that more than 600 individual massacres took place in the Mayan highlands; these included the widespread killing of women, children, and the elderly.

The massacres followed a predetermined pattern. Soldiers would surround a village, usually during a market day or on some other occasion when the population would have gathered. Often, they would separate the men and women. Rape of Mayan women by troops was a systematic practice during the massacres. Mayan children who were not killed were sometimes kidnapped and "sold" as indentured labor. Houses and public buildings were burned to the ground. Aerial bombing was used to hunt down people who fled into the mountains and jungles to escape the army. In one five-year period that began before Ríos Montt's campaign, in 1978, it is estimated that almost one-third of Guatemala's 85,000 Ixil Mayan Indians were wiped out. Overall, an estimated 150,000 Maya fled across the border into Mexico as refugees. Forty-six thousand of these refugees settled in camps run by the United Nations.

Internally displaced Maya were rounded up and forcibly resettled into army-run "model villages" or "strategic hamlets," where the military controlled every facet of daily life. Mayan men were conscripted into army-run civil patrols and sometimes made to attack neighboring villages.

An Amnesty International report estimated that up to 10,000 Maya and others were killed between March and July 1982, with another 100,000 internally displaced. Other estimates provide figures of up to 70,000 killed or "disappeared" during Ríos Montt's 14-month tenure as president. This was but part of a much larger civil war that plagued Guatemala between 1960 and 1996, during which at least 200,000 people were killed.

A United Nations–sanctioned inquiry, the Historical Clarification Commission, concluded that Ríos Montt's regime conducted a campaign of genocide against the Mayan population. On January 28, 2013, Guatemalan judge Miguel Ángel Gálvez commenced pretrial proceedings against Ríos Montt and retired general José Mauricio Rodríguez Sánchez (b. 1945) for genocide and crimes against humanity. After a short trial, Ríos Montt was convicted of genocide and crimes against humanity on May 10, 2013, and, at the age of almost 87, sentenced to 80 years' imprisonment. It was the first time a former head of state had been convicted of genocide in the country in which the crimes had taken place, in accord with the domestic legal system over which he previously presided.

Then, on May 20, 2013, Guatemala's Constitutional Court overturned the conviction, subject to a reopening of the trial at a later time, to be determined.

RICARDO FALLA

The Spanish National Court (Audiencia Nacional) *is a leader in applying the international legal concept of universal jurisdiction, which has its roots in the United Nations Convention on Genocide. In 1999, Nobel Laureate Rigoberta Menchú (b. 1959) filed a lawsuit in the Spanish Supreme Court against six Guatemalan military leaders and two police officials linked to killings during the country's civil war. The case was referred to the Spanish National Court. In 2006, Judge Santiago Pedraz invited witnesses to come to Spain. Pursuant to this, in 2008 the Center for Justice and Accountability, a nonprofit international human rights organization based in San Francisco, brought some forty indigenous Guatemalans to Madrid to testify in three separate groups, marking the first time a national court heard evidence from Mayan survivors. Guatemalan anthropologist, author, and Jesuit priest Ricardo Falla presented testimony before Judge Pedraz. His account was based on years of interviewing massacre survivors; part of that testimony is presented here.*

The first massacre that I documented was the massacre at the Finca San Francisco. I met the principal witness in La Gloria refugee camp in Mexico, on the border with Guatemala, at the beginning of September 1982—two months after the massacre. He told us what happened and I taped his testimony. We also taped Monsignor Samuel Ruiz, the bishop of San Cristobal de las Casas, who described seeing the Guatemalans arrive in Mexico after fleeing the massacre. They were in a complete panic, carrying their children with them, their bundles, their chickens, and anything else they could take out of Guatemala.

The witness told me how the military arrived in the village on Saturday, July 17, 1982. They came in helicopters, so the witness knew they were not guerrillas. The men were working in the fields and the women were inside their houses. There were hundreds of soldiers. They gathered the men and brought them to the courthouse, where they locked them inside. The women and children were locked inside a church. The men could hear the rattle of machine gun fire and the screams of the women. The women were being raped. (I asked him, "How did you know?" He said because he and other survivors went to see later and found the women's bodies with their skirts pushed up.) The soldiers took the children and smashed their heads against the ground.

Then the soldiers rested. The massacre was a lot of work. The soldiers closed the door on the building and chatted, played guitar. Later they would kill everyone inside. The eyewitness escaped out of a window while the soldiers were resting.

The hamlet was razed. It was never reconstructed. I realized that this testimony was precious—and a responsibility. I wanted to understand, how did this happen? How did this come about?

In 1983, I went into the jungles of the Ixcán to speak with the people fleeing the massacres. I stayed with a group of people and moved around with them while they hid. We talked—I filled 5 notebooks with the interviews. Bit by bit, each interview gave me more until I was able to create a map of how the massacres took place. It was difficult work; we were in the mountain, and there were soldiers, guerrillas, there was a war going on. Later I went to [a] refugee camp that was nearby, maybe three or four hours walking from where we were hiding. To be in the camp was like being in a Hilton hotel. There was milk, cheese. You didn't have to worry about being chased by the army. I had the opportunity to take many declarations. And the people talked and talked. They told me what they had suffered. They told me their life stories.

I never stopped being a priest. And the people were glad to be able to tell me their stories.

In the map I made, I documented what had happened between the Rio Ixcán y Rio Xalbal—those were the best documented massacres, because there were more people there. But I also heard about massacres in Santa María Tzejá and other places. I interviewed survivors of the massacre of Cuarto Pueblos, which happened in two different places. Then the soldiers went to Los Angeles. They didn't massacre. Why not? I think it was the day that Ríos Montt took over in a coup. So they didn't massacre because there was no high command to give the orders. Then the Xalbal massacre took place. In June came the amnesty, and there were no massacres. There was only one massacre then, and it was by the guerrillas, one of the few by them. All of these massacres were part of a plan and followed the same pattern: the soldiers would surround a town, divide the men and women, rape the women, kill the women and children and then the men, and burn the town. One witness told me how the officers had to encourage the soldiers to keep working, that they were fighting communism. They thought these villages were supporting the guerrilla and so had to be destroyed "down to the last seed." According to some news reports at the time, the army had in their headquarters a map with little red flags marking the villages. They had a plan to destroy the people because of their belief that they were behind the guerrilla. Of course most of the villagers didn't have anything to do with guerrillas. I am not an eyewitness to the massacres. But I am a witness of the persecution that the soldiers carried out against the people: the people who were resisting. At first we didn't know or use this word, "resisting." We were holding on. We would be in little groups of 7 or 8 households, maybe 50 people. And a group of soldiers would surprise us in the mountain. What would we do? We would flee: running, running through streams so we wouldn't leave footprints. We would have already agreed a place to meet later. And so we would scatter, running, and then meet later in the place. And God, it would rain—such tremendous rain. There were at one point about 450 people hiding up there in tiny groups. Because there was food at that time—it was hard to find, but it was there. Sometimes you had to go for a day or two without eating, but then you could eat, because there were hidden crops and other sources of food that we would forage.

Later I went to Mexico. I shut myself up in a room and wrote for two years. I wrote—and I cried. You know when there is something fresh and you are motivated? I wrote down everything I could—1,400 pages. It was two volumes, too much.

In 1984, Mexico took everyone gathered in the refugee camps by the border, and dispersed them in Campeche and Quintana Roo. Many people refused to go to the new camps and resettle away from the border, so some of them decided to return and resist. They joined the organized people in the mountain. We always talk about people as victims, but not about all the amazing things they did to resist and survive. The people were much more organized by then. They could stay for up to three months in one place without moving. The army was bombing them with huge bombs that would leave gigantic craters. But they didn't actually kill that many people. The people just hid from the bombs. So, they were victims, but in resistance—a resistance that began with the massacres.

Source: "Testimony from a Spanish Court: Guatemalan Genocide Hearings," Guatemala Human Rights Commission/USA, http://www.ghrc-usa.org/AboutGuatemala/Spanish-CourtTestimony.htm.

Commentary

General José Efraín Ríos Montt was president of a military junta in Guatemala established by coup d'état on March 23, 1982. His regime presided over the genocide of well over 70,000 people, chiefly Maya, during 1982–1983. Many of the killings took place during assaults against small villages, when mass murder, rape, kidnappings, and torture were the order of the day.

The annihilation of victims in a localized massacre (for example, during the wiping out of a whole village of men, women, and children) contains some of the elements of genocide, even though such events do not always, *by themselves,* constitute genocide. In Guatemala, the motives that underlay these massacres were, in their temporal and geographic circumstances, directed by a genocidal intent. Although the attacks were ostensibly conducted in order to discipline what was viewed as a rebellious population, the fact that they targeted Maya specifically introduces a clear racial dimension to the persecution.

Jesuit anthropologist (and Guatemalan exile) Fr. Ricardo Falla's account depicts the Finca San Francisco massacre of 1982, when the army slaughtered some 300 people. Fr. Falla provides an excellent synopsis of the massacre. Not only were victims killed in the hundreds, but the rest of the population fled for their lives, mainly to refugee camps in Mexico. In Fr. Falla's account, we see heavily armed airborne military forces pitted against men working in fields and women inside their homes. We see that the perpetrators—the military arm of the government—were acting on behalf of that same government, while the victims were civilians engaged in the routines of everyday life.

In 1983, Fr. Falla went to the jungles of the Ixcán municipality, near the Mexican border. There, he spoke confidentially with those who were fleeing the massacres. The refugees, perhaps partially influenced by his priestly office, confided to him their thoughts and fears, and as they walked together they talked about their experiences. When the group Fr. Falla was accompanying eventually reached the safety of a refugee camp, he was able to conduct many more interviews. In his own idiom, "the people talked and talked," telling him "what they had suffered," along with their life stories.

The people described the massacres as appearing to be part of a plan with a set pattern: "[T]he soldiers would surround a town, divide the men and women, rape the women, kill the women and children and then the men, and burn the town." This closely resembles a textbook pattern of genocidal destruction, characteristic of many cases in other similar situations.

Of particular interest in this case is that, as one witness related to Fr. Falla, the officers had to encourage the soldiers to continue their grisly tasks, reminding them that what they were doing was necessary to fight communism. It was believed that the villages supported leftist guerrillas, so they had to be destroyed "down to the last seed."

Another feature of Fr. Falla's account pertains to a very special form of resistance: flight. When the people were ambushed by a group of soldiers, the only form of defense they had was departure, "running, running through streams so we wouldn't leave footprints." As a strategy, the refugees had already predetermined a place where they would reassemble, and so "we would scatter, running, and then meet later."

Since 1980, it is estimated that 150,000 refugees, most of them Indian, have fled Guatemala for Mexico, most often through the region discussed by Fr. Falla. Most left Guatemala in 1982, at the height of the violence. In response, between 1982 and 1984 Ríos Montt's army crossed into Mexico over 40 times to attack the refugee camps. Many in the camps were killed by these incursions, prompting the idea that rebels were not returning to Guatemala because they were needed to protect the camps. Mexico's response was to pull back its troop presence along its southern border and mute any response to the Guatemalan incursions. Its cautious attitude was rooted in a preference not to engage in a possible war with militaristic, Ríos Montt–directed Guatemala.

Mexico's main response, in fact, was to resettle refugees in large camps in Campeche, in the area bordering northern Guatemala—also a Mayan region, but one that was more secure from Guatemalan military incursions than Ixcán.

At one point in the account, conscious of the fact that he was collecting testimonies rather than witnessing atrocities, Fr. Falla states, "I am not an eyewitness to the massacres." That said, he is quick to qualify his position by writing, "I am a witness of the persecution that the soldiers carried out against the people." This persecution was something Falla shared, and it left a mark. After walking and talking with the refugees for a considerable period, he, too, went to Mexico, where "I shut myself up in a room and wrote for two years." Thinking back to his own experiences and the experiences of those with whom he had shared so much, he notes, "I wrote—and I cried."

In January 1994, Fr. Falla published his memoir of the Guatemalan Genocide, *Massacres in the Jungle: Ixcán, Guatemala, 1975–1982.* He describes how the Guatemalan military systematically and sadistically punished the Mayan peasant population for the activities of antiregime guerrillas in their region. The book shows how the victims and their communities were destroyed, and provides a detailed record of assassinations and disappearances. In addition, it commemorates the work of Catholic priests who opposed the Ríos Montt regime, a large number of whom fell in with their Mayan parishioners on the grounds of social justice and resistance to persecution.

Questions

1. Do you see any difficulties in the nature of the material gathered by Fr. Falla and presented before the Spanish National Court?

2. As one who collected testimonies from survivors, could it be said that Fr. Falla was himself a witness to the genocide in Guatemala?

3. As a priest, what advantages, if any, did Fr. Falla have when seeking out accounts from survivors?

BEATRIZ MANZ

Beatriz Manz, a professor of geography and ethnic studies at the University of California, Berkeley, was, like Fr. Falla, trained as an anthropologist. Her research has focused on Mayan communities in rural Guatemala. Manz has written extensively on the human rights abuses committed by the military against indigenous rural communities in Guatemala, at both the national and local levels. In her testimony before Judge Pedraz at the Audiencia Nacional, *she recounted both her own experiences in Guatemala and those of refugees living in Mexico.*

I am here to speak about my work as an anthropologist in Guatemala and in the refugee camps in Mexico.

The army's counterinsurgency campaign caused massacres. According to the Catholic Church, some one and a half million people were displaced. The army pursued and persecuted the displaced people, capturing or killing them, destroying their fields, their trees, and fruits. The constant persecution created insupportable conditions that caused the deaths of many more people, especially children. The constant surveillance of the displaced people by airplane also created terrible conditions for them. They had to cook in the middle of night. They had to wear wet clothes because they couldn't wait for them to dry after a rain; they had to kill their dogs so they wouldn't bark, and silence their own children. When they couldn't bear it any more, they crossed into Mexico.

The first time I learned about the massacres was when I was in Mexican camps. I had read something about them in the press in 1981, but it wasn't until I was conducting interviews in the camps in 1982 that I realized the immensity of these massacres. In the 1970s the government had carried out selective persecution targeting certain sectors, such as activist Catholics, teachers, union leaders. But the people did not flee the areas where they lived, they stayed in their villages.

In 1982, what the refugees described was a much higher level of persecution. It was something completely different. I carried out about 100 interviews with them. When I got to the Puerto Rico refugee camp, people were pouring over the border—in one day some 600–800 came in. It's difficult to describe the conditions in which these people arrived. To get to the camp you had to walk through the dense jungle. Their physical condition when they arrived was very poor: some had no shoes, they arrived in a state of malnutrition, sick, cold, etc. They had only herbs in the forest to eat, with very little water. Several women gave birth in the forest.

Already in 1982 we were hearing about many deaths. Those who left were the ones who were able to escape the army's attacks. It was hard to get from the Altiplano to Mexico. They left from all over that area: from Huehuetenango, the Petén, Ixcán. They told similar stories. The army surrounded an aldea. If they found people there, they killed them and then they destroyed the village: burned the houses, killed the animals, and destroyed the crops. The people who managed to hide fled to the jungle and lived in horrible conditions, and those that survived displacement fled to Mexico. The people would hide deep, deep in the jungle and the patrollers would chase them. They would find their little milpas inside the jungle, small and dispersed so they couldn't be found by air. When the soldiers destroyed those, the people would lose hope.

Sometimes 6 or 7 families would hide together, sometimes huge groups of 700 people. It was much more difficult to survive that way. They couldn't walk on the paths together. They had to move toward the border in the north by cutting a path through the dense jungle in the middle of the night. During the day they had to stop and be silent. If they were a big group it was even more complicated—hundreds of people trying to walk through the dense jungle.

The army's goal was to clean the region. The soldiers were responding to orders to control everything and everyone in the zone of Ixcán. "Plan Victoria 82" was focused on total victory—which meant control by the military of the area—not only about control of the guerrillas or of persecution of certain activist Catholics. The army took over the churches, the schools. Never before did the Catholic Church have to shut down an entire diocese, as they did in El Quiché. But that wasn't sufficient. That wasn't enough. The army had to continue with their campaign to control everything and everyone, alive or dead.

In Mexico, the government created COMAR (the Mexican Commission for Refugees). The UN agency to aid refugees, ACNUR, opened offices in Mexico also—it was a recognition of the disaster of refugees from Guatemala. These new institutions helped address the crisis. Nevertheless, the incursions of the Guatemalan army into Mexico created panic among the refugees in the camp. The incursions had to be very small; the Guatemalans knew they were violating the sovereignty of the Mexican government. I remember one incident in particular when seven people were killed by Guatemalan soldiers. So they were able to get in and attack people. Before all this happened, the people of Ixcán were well organized by the Maryknolls and the diocese of El Quiche to settle in the area. They belonged to cooperatives, took classes, it was a democratic organization of the aldeas. When the villages were destroyed and people displaced, the villagers maintained this level of organization. And it was an important form of survival. In the refugee camps, the leaders of communities would go from house to house and make sure everyone had a tarp over their family's head, that they knew where to get food, how to build a place to cook, and so on. Of course, the conditions in the camp were terrible. These people were already poor campesinos. Now they had to live in awful conditions, and many people died as a result.

In 1983, I went into Guatemala to see what was happening in the Altiplano. I went into the model villages, where the population that had been captured or turned over to the army now lived. The way the army talked about the civilians was to turn them into prisoners, criminals. They "captured" them, they "detained" them, they "interrogated" them, and they talked of "pardoning" them. They tortured them so that the people had to say something, "accuse" others. They had to turn others in, give names; it was not possible to be silent. The Army would take groups of people, prisoners they had interrogated, away from the large army base in Playa Grande in trucks. The trucks would leave the base, and would come back empty. Everyone left in the army base was apprehensive that they would be put in those trucks and also be taken away to be killed. You didn't have to tell the interrogators the names of guerrilla collaborators— they knew. They knew which person's brother was involved in the guerrilla. But they interrogated everyone anyhow to see if they would be willing to cooperate with the army and accuse others. It was a way of involving the population psychologically in a very difficult situation. They created a terrible feeling of guilt among the people.

In the first phase of army counterinsurgency sweeps, they would kill everyone. Later the tactics changed, and they would kill those who fled but the ones who stayed would be rounded up and taken to the military base. They were interrogated there and eventually taken to model villages.

The village I knew best, since 1973, was Santa María Tzejá, which became a model village. The model villages represented a new organization of space, so the army could control the people better. New residents who had been brought in by the army changed the village as well. Originally, the people who came to Ixcán were Catholics, and in Santa María Tzejá they were all from El Quiche and K'iche' speakers. But when Santa María Tzejá became a "model village" the army brought in evangelicals and people from different parts of the country. So in Sta. María Tzejá, for example, there were 116 families and they spoke seven languages. The army's strategic plan was to mix the people that way so that it would be impossible for the people to unify themselves.

In the villages, the army carried out re-education programs. After the horrors these people had seen, the people were more vulnerable to psychological pressure from the army. The army would say: "this is the Guatemalan flag! You have to honor it! You are manipulated by foreigners!" So the ideological re-education was intense. "You are bad people, with bad ideas, but we pardon you."

International groups would send food to be distributed (presumably by civilians) to the people. But the army would always distribute the food and the medical assistance. The community leaders would be named by the army. How many tortillas you were allowed to carry, how much salt, it was all controlled by the army. You couldn't just come and go as you pleased, all movements were controlled by the army. If a man wanted to leave and miss his patrol service, he had to pay a replacement. You had to show your cédula (ID card) everywhere. The military took down all of this in their notebooks by hand. If you lost your cédula, you were in trouble.

The Army is very hierarchal and very disciplined. The officers were well trained, often in the United States. The idea that a group of low-ranking soldiers would arrive in a village and commit a massacre based on their own decision was not sustainable, not possible. They always had lists of suspects by names when they arrived. Their level of control and the organization of their campaign were such that it was clearly designed by superiors.

The consequences of the massacres are very long term: first, many people were left with deep psychological problems and social problems. Second, the deep fear caused by the military violence, the mayhem, and the destruction of the economy has produced waves of illegal immigrants over [the] US border. Third, the economic setback in the rural areas, already dismally poor, is and will continue to have deep consequences. No one has reimbursed the campesino families for the land they lost, for their houses, their animals. So if they were poor to begin with, imagine their condition now. Fourth, in the past farmers in the Ixcán for example, were well organized in cooperatives. Now everyone is isolated—you plant your little plot of cardamom or whatever you are growing and sell it on your own. Finally Guatemala is faced with the legacy of the brutal violence, the lynching—adults and young people alike only know violence. There were and are no laws. There is chaos. The people are very apathetic. Why should they act? They know the consequences. This combination of malaise is not a recipe for success, for social and economic development. How can you have social progress when you have a society that is pessimistic about the future because of what they experienced in the past, and have no reason or assurance that what happened will not reoccur again?

We realize that the dead will not come back to us. The disappeared will never return. I will not see my colleague Myrna Mack, who was killed by the army for her work, again. But the world needs to render a judgment. To judge those responsible! In the 21st century we cannot continue to keep these horrors hidden, we cannot continue being silent about what happened in Guatemala. At least through this case, the world will hear, the world will know, and the Guatemalan society, especially the survivors, will know that it was judged to have been a crime against humanity. So that this damaged society can become a dignified society again.

Source: "Testimony from a Spanish Court: Guatemalan Genocide Hearings," Guatemala Human Rights Commission/USA, http://www.ghrc-usa.org/AboutGuatemala/SpanishCourtTestimony.htm.

Commentary

Similarly to the account of Fr. Falla, that of Beatriz Manz was written by someone not directly involved in the Guatemalan Genocide. An anthropologist, Dr. Manz was in this case interviewing survivors after the events being described, when they had found some measure of safety in refugee camps in Mexico.

During the government's campaigns of repression against the Maya, the Guatemalan army worked methodically. Using its own forces alongside locally raised "civil patrols"—in reality, forcibly conscripted men who had to join or they would be labeled antigovernment rebels—the army moved through the Mayan areas, eventually striking no fewer that 626 villages. Guatemalan counterinsurgency forces were known to define themselves as killing machines, whose task it was to root out all forms of perceived left-wing opposition through terror and murder.

Communities were often attacked, then occupied, on occasions when the citizens were already gathered together, such as on market days or during a fiesta. The villagers might then simply be murdered. Sometimes, members were forced to watch while killings took place; from time to time, they were actually compelled to participate in the murders. After the killings, buildings might be destroyed, while outside the troops would wipe out crops, butcher livestock, and desecrate local icons. Because the army viewed Mayan communities as natural allies of the leftist opposition, it was those communities that they targeted directly. What this meant was that the political dimension of the army's campaign of oppression was overlaid with obvious racist characteristics, leading to the wholesale extermination of Mayan districts without regard for children, women, and the elderly.

It has been estimated that more than 200,000 Maya fled as refugees to Mexico, Honduras, Belize, the United States, and elsewhere, while as many as 500,000 became internal refugees within Guatemala, fleeing what had become a war zone. The overall impact on the Mayan population saw the devastation of whole localities, in what was clearly the most sustained attempt to destroy the Maya as a people and a culture since the Spanish conquest during the sixteenth century.

It was in the refugee camps that Beatriz Manz (b. 1945), a native Spanish speaker born in rural southern Chile, investigated the circumstances of the refugees: why they were displaced, what their experiences were, and the consequences of the massacres they had suffered. Later, in 1983, she went to Guatemala, where she visited a jungle village called Santa María Tzejá. The tragedy of that remote village was, in some respects, a paradigm of the wider tragedy of Guatemala as a whole. In 1982 it was completely destroyed by the military and burned to the ground. Villagers who could not escape fell into the hands of the army, after which they were killed. The destruction was total—even the animals in the village were slaughtered. The survivors fled into the rainforest, from which many managed to make it into Mexico.

Dr. Manz first visited Santa María Tzejá in 1973. By the time of her visit ten years later, the village had been reconstituted into a "model village" by the military, representing "a new organization of space, so that the army could control the people better." The army altered the composition of the village by bringing new residents into the area—including people from different parts of the country and evangelical Christians—who transformed the region's linguistic and Catholic character. As Dr. Manz writes, the army's strategic plan "was to mix the people that way so that it would be impossible for the people to unify themselves."

Then, throughout broader areas of the country, the army carried out so-called "ideological re-education" programs, in which the army emphasized Guatemalan patriotism in a particularly draconian fashion: either the people acquiesced to the nationalistic fervor brought by the army, or they would suffer further punishment.

Dr. Manz sets forth five long-term consequences of the massacres. In the first place, she notes, many people were left with deep psychological and social problems. Second—in a statement of note for all democratic states that consider genocidal outbreaks to be internal matters only—she writes that the fear, mayhem, and economic destruction of the country have resulted in waves of illegal immigration, affecting bordering countries such as the United States. Third, the economic dislocation in rural areas has set these regions back irretrievably. Fourth, farming life and folkways have been disrupted, again irretrievably. Finally, she writes, "Guatemala is faced with the legacy of the brutal violence," translating into a society that is largely lawless, and in which both adults and children know violence as the only means of living. Overall, the combination of all of these consequences offers a very poor prognosis for recovery or future development.

What Dr. Manz's account does not mention is the fact that in 1983, she herself became a victim of the army. Kidnapped in the streets of a highland town by two plainclothes soldiers, she was dragged to a cell at a military base. She was eventually released, but her experience at the hands of the Guatemalan military provided her with a firsthand example of the nature of the regime.

Dr. Manz's account describes the army's ultimate aim of gaining control of "everything and everyone, alive or dead" in Guatemala. In an analysis of the campaign, which sought total domination over all elements of society, we see an explanation of why the military also sought to take over churches and schools, in addition to executing massive killing actions. This account, in short, is a description of major social and physical displacement in the face of genocidal destruction, and of the betrayal of citizens by the army and regime that should have defended them.

Questions

1. Describe the manner in which the Guatemalan army attempted to transform society.

2. As reported by Beatriz Manz, was there anything genocidal to be found in the "model villages" established in Guatemala?
3. In Dr. Manz's view, what were the consequences of the massacres committed by the Guatemalan army against the Mayan population?

JESÚS TECÚ OSORIO

Born in 1971 in Río Negro, Baja Verapaz, Jesús Tecú witnessed the deaths of most of his immediate family members in a major massacre on March 13, 1982. He spent two years as a household slave to one of the perpetrators before being remanded to the custody of his older sister, who had also survived. In 1993, Tecú began legal proceedings to have the mass grave of Río Negro exhumed. Evidence collected there resulted in the prosecution of three of those responsible for the massacre. In 1998 they were sentenced to death for crimes against humanity; a year later their sentences were commuted to 60 years' imprisonment. It is from Tecú's memoir, The Río Negro Massacres, *that this extract has been taken. Here, he relates in graphic detail how the massacre unfolded.*

On the 13th of March 1982, at around six in the morning the military and the patrollers, who were dressed in uniforms and armed, entered the village and forced all the people out of their homes. There were boys, girls and pregnant women.

They took me from our house together with my brothers Marcelo, Anastasio and Jaime, who were seven, five and two years old. My sister Juana Tecú Osorio, who was 25 years old, was forced from her house together with her sons Juan and Catharine who were five and two years old. They lived by the road to Chitucán.

One day before, on the 12th of March 1982, in the evening, my sister Juana asked me to get up early the next morning to collect firewood from the hillside with another boy. At nine in the morning on the 13th of March we were in the hills collecting firewood when a man came running past. He was fleeing from the military and the patrollers. We were yelling and joking between us when the man scolded us and said: "Kids, stop yelling. The military and patrollers are in the village and they are taking all the women." I was very worried and I went straight back to our house. When I got back to the house I realized that the soldiers and patrollers were taking all the women and children. So I said to my sister Juana: "Let's leave the house before they get here."

She didn't want to. They were about two hundred meters from our house. She said to me: "If the patrollers find us hiding in the hills, they will accuse us of being guerrillas." I wanted to take my younger brother Jaime. My sister insisted on not fleeing. We entered the house and closed ourselves in.

A few minutes passed and then a soldier with his face covered by a red bandana came by. He had the look of an assassin. He walked in front of the women of the village. He began beating down the door of the house. The soldiers and patrollers surrounded the house so that no one could escape. The house was made of wood with a thatched roof. We had a wooden door.

They entered and said: "Where are the weapons that you took from the officers? If you don't give them back everyone will die. Where are all the men? Where have they gone?"

My sister said that we didn't know anything about the weapons and that the men had been killed in Xococ.

The patrollers and the military said that the men had gone with the guerrillas and that they were not dead. After searching the house they made us leave. They took us and put us under the concaste tree that was in front of the house. There we saw a group of patrollers who were rounding up the women.

The assassins, who were in our house, began to cook and eat our food. Now there would be no breakfast for us. Having stolen our food, they then began to mistreat the women and asked them the same question. "Where are the weapons that you took from the officers? If you don't hand them over you will all die. Where have the men gone?" The women gave the same reply: "All the men were assassinated in Xococ." The patrollers and the military wanted to convince the women that the men were not dead, that instead they had joined the guerrillas.

After the interrogation they started raping the fifteen- and fourteen-year-old girls. They took them to the bushes and laughed after they had been raped. I saw the patroller Ambrosio Pérez Lauj from Xococ taking Justa Osorio Sic into the forest. She came back very frightened. He yelled obscenities at her. He said that she wasn't a virgin and that her body was weak.

After that they forced us to walk to Pak'oxom. This place is on the hill Portezuelo e Monterredondo. The soldiers and the patrollers mistreated us and said that we were children of guerrilla fighters.

They cut branches with thorns and beat us. No one could bear the pain. Women and children cried. At this time of year it's very hot. We asked for water and the patrollers said to us: "We are almost there. Once we are there we will rest and have some water."

It was an ironic response. They already knew what they were going to do with us. The children and women were exhausted when we arrived at Pak'oxom. The soldiers and patrollers brought us together in the flat area where we waited for the women who had not yet arrived. While they waited for them to arrive, the soldiers began to cut tree branches and one meter lengths of rope. They were preparing materials to use to massacre the people.

The military official threatened the women with a grenade that he carried on his chest. He pulled the pin and pretended to throw it into the women and children. Everyone screamed. They thought the official had let the grenade off. He made fun of them and said: "OK, you wanted some water, now we'll give you water. We will pardon your lives if you hand over the weapons that you took from the officers."

The women insisted that they did not know anything. The official threatened them in Spanish and the patrollers translated into Achi. While this was happening soldiers and patrollers took women into the bushes and raped them. If any of them resisted rape, the assassins threatened to kill them. The whole group from Río Negro was surrounded by military and patrollers.

Once all the material was prepared, they began to kill the women and children. They took them one by one to a ravine that was about twenty meters from where we were. We heard shots, screams and crying. The patrollers killed the women out of sight. They did not want us to see their cruelty. They made us lie face down on the sacred ground. I did not want to suffer or die like the other children and women. I searched for a way to escape. My younger brother, who was two years old, and I were right in front of the patrollers. Every second I could feel death encroaching on me.

When a patroller came close to us I thought he would take me next. I thought of two things: die or escape with my brother. I began to move towards the last line of women.

I told one of the patrollers that my brother needed to go to the bathroom. He gave me permission to leave. I walked towards a low ridge looking for a place where my brother and I could escape, but I realized that the whole place was surrounded by soldiers. I wanted to run but the weight of my brother prevented me from running. I came across a soldier raping a woman and he scolded me and sent me to where the group of women was.

When I arrived, I saw the patroller Pedro González Gómez trying to murder Vicenta Iboy Chen. Even though this woman had a baby on her back, she fought back trying to defend herself from the rapist. She picked up a rock and threw it at Pedro. The patroller took his machete from its sheath that was on his belt and gave her two blows. The patroller not only wounded the woman badly, but he cut in half the baby around her back. Vicenta fell down heavily at the edge of the ravine. Pedro immediately came up to her and gave her two machete blows in the neck.

I remember other bitter moments of the slaughter. The patroller Pablo Ruiz Alvarado had Tomasa López Ixpatá face down. He had tied a rope around her neck forming a noose. The assassin removed the rope from her neck thinking that he had already killed her, however her body still trembled. The patroller took a club and beat her to death. He treated her like an animal. When she was dead he took her by the feet and dragged her to the ravine.

Margarita Sánchez did not want to die like the other women. She wanted to escape but the official saw her. He took her by the hair, threw her to the ground and kicked her. She apologized and said: "Don't kill me, my father lives in Pacux." The patrollers said: "We'll send you to your father in Pacux."

She sat down beside me, weeping a sea of tears. Then I realized she was vomiting blood. She no longer had any teeth. The rest of the women cried and asked to be pardoned. They offered their cattle in exchange for their lives but the assassins had already decided to kill them.

They no longer took them to the ravine, instead they killed them right there in the same place. They killed them in front of the other women and children.

Around two in the afternoon the patrollers took Petronila Sánchez and Paula Chen, who were about fifty-five years old. They forced them to lie face down and placed ropes around their necks, forming a noose. I was two meters away. I heard it when they could no longer breathe. They buried their fingers in the holy ground as if they were asking for help.

Their necks cracked. When they were dead they dragged them to the ravine. The bodies were swollen and the faces were bruised. All of the children we were crying.

We were sitting on the ground. The children were the easiest victims to kill. When they came for a child, they just put the rope around its neck and took the child away hanging by the rope. The child began to kick. Once they got to the ravine they let them go. They grabbed the child by their feet and then smashed them against rocks and trees that are still found at that place. Other children were killed with machete blows or from blows to the ears. This is the way the assassins took the life of defenseless children.

Seventeen boys and girls remained. The patrollers came closer to the older ones. At this point Mrs. Juana Tum asked the patroller Macariao Alvarado Toj to take her daughter Silveria Lajuj Tum to Xococ, asking him to care for her as his own daughter. When there were only twenty women remaining the patroller Pedro González called me and said: "I'm not going to kill you but you have to come with me to Xococ and help me with my work. I am only taking you because I have no children."

I said yes immediately to save my life. He separated me from the group and told me to go above the ravine. I took my younger brother Jaime. The rest of the soldiers came closer to the children and chose the ones they would take with them to Xococ.

After killing the twenty women who remained they brought us all together. They prepared us for the walk to Xococ. The assassin Pedro González came to where my brother and I were and said: "OK, let's go to Xococ."

Then he realized that I had my little brother Jaime with me. He told me that he could not take him as he was tired and we had to walk all night from Río Negro to Xococ. I told him that I could carry my brother and that I would take all responsibility for him. Enraged he said to me: "No because my wife is not used to caring for a child as small as your brother."

I insisted on taking my brother with me. He became angry and said that if I insisted he would kill us both. I was sitting on the trunk of a fallen tree. I had my brother in my arms and he took him from me by force. He wrapped a rope around his neck and took him hanging from one of his hands. Jaime was kicking his feet. I followed behind him crying. I asked him a million times to spare my brother's life but it didn't matter.

I wished for someone to help me but no one appeared. We arrived at the ravine where the bodies of the victims were dumped. He threw my brother on the ground. He took him by the feet and smashed him against the rocks. Seeing that he was dead he threw him down the ravine.

There, I saw the women who had been raped, hung, shot and stabbed with machetes. Some of the bodies were still trembling. . . .

I was alone, sad, without my parents and there was no one to care for me. . . . I can't forget the moment in which they killed all the women and the children. I can still remember the screams and the gunshots in the ravine.

Source: Jesús Tecú Osorio, *The Río Negro Massacres,* translated into English and published by Rights Action (info@rightsaction.org) (Washington, D.C., 2003). Accessed at http://www.pbs.org/pov/discoveringdominga/special_witnessjt.php. Used by permission of Jesus Tecú Osorio with the assistance of Rights Action.

Commentary

Between 1980 and 1982, during what the government officially declared to be counterinsurgency activities, a series of massacres took place in the vicinity of Baja Verapaz in central Guatemala. The community of Río Negro, on the banks of the Chixoy River, lived on agriculture, fishing, and the exchange of goods with the neighboring community of Xococ. In the 1970s, Río Negro had a population of about 800 people, all indigenous Achís.

On March 13, 1982, twelve members of an army patrol, accompanied by fifteen civilian patrollers from Xococ, entered the village of Río Negro. They went to every house searching for men they considered to be rebel guerrillas. Finding none, they demanded that the villagers leave their homes to participate in a town meeting. Amidst much violence, the soldiers and patrollers looted the village, taking what they wanted. Several of the young women and girls were raped.

They then evacuated the village, forcing the inhabitants to walk three miles up the mountain behind Río Negro. When they got to the top, they proceeded to torture and kill many of the villagers. Some were hung from trees, others were killed with machetes, and yet others were shot. At around five in the afternoon, the slaughter ended, and the survivors, with their captors, headed toward Xococ. The attackers took away 18 surviving children. Reports concur that 177 people, of whom 70 were women and 107 were children, were murdered in the Río Negro massacre.

The key feature of Tecú's testimony relates to the invasion by the military of his village. The account conveys much of the terror and chaos of the action, during which rape and torture were commonplace and committed casually by the soldiers. It is important to realize that Tecú is describing a slaughter, not a random or systematized killing. We are left in no doubt as to the inhuman cruelty of the army. Very few were permitted to remain alive.

Tecú's description of the murder of two women, Petronila Sánchez and Paula Chen, makes for disturbing reading. The killers "forced them to lie face down and placed ropes around their necks, forming a noose." Tecú, who was "two meters away," could barely stand what he was witnessing: "I heard it when they could no longer breathe. They buried their fingers in the holy ground as if they were asking for help." At this point, he writes, "Their necks cracked." He saw that their bodies were swollen and their faces bruised, clear indications of the intensity of the beatings they must have received prior to their brutal execution.

Tecú's style is simultaneously evocative and highly personal. Thus, when we read in short, staccato sentences that "Once all the material was prepared, they began to kill the women and children," or, "We heard shots, screams and crying. The patrollers killed the women out of sight," we see that Tecú's understanding of the situation is not being recounted by a practiced writer. Rather, he is an observer—in this case, a participant-observer. He continues: "They did not want us to see their cruelty. They made us lie face down on the sacred ground. I did not want to suffer or die like the other children and women." This is Tecú giving us his testimony from a purely singular and intimate perspective.

The final scene, in which Tecú relates the killing of his younger brother and the bodies lying in the ravine, is as gripping as any description of mass killing can be: "I wished for someone to help me but no one appeared. We arrived at the ravine where the bodies of the victims were dumped. He threw my brother on the ground. He took him by the feet and smashed him against the rocks. Seeing that he was dead he threw him down the ravine." Passages such as this remind readers that what happened in Guatemala deserves far more attention than it is generally accorded.

Tecú describes how, at Río Negro, he saw "women who had been raped, hung, shot and stabbed with machetes." As he was being taken away, he noticed, "Some of the bodies were still trembling."

One of the most crucial points to keep in mind about testimonies of this nature is that they are torn from a victim's innermost thoughts and reflections—and from his pain. This should not be forgotten when considering genocide survivor testimony, as the very appearance of that testimony all too frequently has been accompanied by tears and sorrow. As Tecú tells us, when it was over, "I was alone, sad, without my parents and there was no one to care for me. . . . I can't forget the moment in which they killed all the women and the children. I can still remember the screams and the gunshots in the ravine."

Tecú's testimony was a major contributing factor in the assignment of responsibility to José Efraín Ríos Montt and his men for their base actions. Tecú worked to transcend the pain of his ordeal for the greater good. For this—and for all such survivor accounts—we should be grateful.

Questions

1. What was Tecú's emotional response to the murders taking place before his eyes?
2. Can you explain why Tecú's life was spared by the soldiers?
3. What, in your view, was the most shocking aspect of the Río Negro massacre? Why?

6. The East Timor Genocide

East Timor is an island nation located in the Indonesian archipelago, between Indonesia and Australia. For three centuries, the territory had been part of the Portuguese overseas empire, but in 1974 a coup took place in Portugal, leading to a sudden withdrawal from its imperial presence. East Timor's governor, Mário Lemos Pires (1930–2009), announced immediate plans to grant the colony independence, a premature move—little had been done to prepare the territory for decolonization.

In short time, a number of hastily formed political parties surfaced. Among these was a local Marxist group, the *Frente Revolucionária do Timor-Leste Independente* (Revolutionary Front for East Timor's Independence, or FRETILIN), founded on May 20, 1974.

FRETILIN was established for the purpose of securing independence. It grew out of an earlier body, the *Associação Social Democratica Timorense* (ASDT), a broad-based, anticolonial association with nationalist leanings. FRETILIN had a strong socialist foundation, and it differed from the ASDT in that it sought immediate independence and claimed to speak on behalf of all East Timorese people. By December 1974, it had developed nationwide programs in education, social welfare, health, agriculture, literacy, and the like. FRETILIN ran into opposition from a rival party, the UDT (*União Democratica Timorense,* the Timorese Democratic Union). The UDT was less radical and called for a more progressive and multistage timeline for independence, which would be slanted toward some sort of federal model with Portugal. On August 11, 1975, the UDT staged a coup, and for the next three weeks civil war raged throughout East Timor as forces of the UDT battled with a hastily formed armed wing of FRETILIN, called FALINTIL (*Forças Armadas de Libertação Nacional de Timor-Leste,* National Liberation Forces of an Independent East Timor). Somewhere between 1,500 and 3,000 people died during this time.

As FRETILIN became more influential, Cold War politics intervened. East Timor's huge neighbor Indonesia, which had for a long time coveted the territory, began expressing concern that a socialist movement could attain power so close to home. By September 1975, with FRETILIN's victory, Indonesia's policy on East Timor had hardened into outright opposition.

As Portuguese administrators began to leave, FRETILIN troops seized the bulk of the colonial armory. On November 28, 1975, it proclaimed the Democratic Republic of East Timor. FALINTIL was organized into the state army.

Nine days later, on December 7, Indonesian military forces responded by invading the newly proclaimed republic. In the first few days of the invasion, 2,000 citizens of the capital, Dili, were killed, and a systematic campaign of human rights abuses commenced. It was clear from the outset that this campaign had the singular intention of intimidating the population and crushing the prospect of any resistance before it could get organized. What the Indonesians had not sufficiently considered, however, was the extent of difference between the two peoples. The East Timorese had a different ethnic identity from the Indonesians; spoke Tetum or Portuguese (or more likely, a localized Creole form of Tetum, Tetun Dili, heavily influenced by Portuguese syntax and grammar) rather than Bahasa Indonesia; were almost exclusively Roman Catholic rather than Muslim; and historically had never been interested in aligning themselves with Indonesia. As the Indonesians saw it, therefore, the only way they could absorb the territory as Indonesia's twenty-seventh state (which did eventually take place, officially on July 17, 1976) was through terror and military occupation.

The result was a series of campaigns resulting in mass murder, starvation, and death by torture. Within two months of the invasion, 60,000 people, or 10 percent of the pre-invasion population, had been killed. Over the next three years, up to 200,000 people—that is, one-third of East Timor's pre-invasion population—lost their lives.

Much of the destruction was brought about because of the Jakarta government's policy of "Indonesianizing" East Timor. To do so, it planned to transform the territory from a Portuguese colony with aspirations to independence, to a full-fledged (and loyal) state of Indonesia. This was to be achieved in several ways: through the complete disruption (then elimination) of regular East Timorese life, and its replacement with Javanese ways; through the forcible removal of the population from large rural areas, and its relocation to newly created "strategic hamlets" (which some would later equate with de facto internment camps); and through the effect the hamlets would have of dissolving traditional agriculture, village life, trade, and extended family life. These measures brought food shortages and diseases, and they created a culture of dependence in which the population was forced to rely on Indonesian handouts for health services and medicine.

"Indonesianization" also involved the repression of East Timorese culture, such that only Indonesian songs, dances, and other forms of cultural expression were permitted publicly. In education, a purely Indonesian school system was introduced. Many new schools were established, but the curriculum was Indonesian, the language of instruction was Bahasa Indonesia, history lessons focused on Indonesian history only, and the study of East Timorese language and culture was forbidden.

Finally, the Indonesian authorities imposed a harsh regime of physical repression on the territory; all attempts by the East Timorese people to embrace, encourage, or express their own art, music, and literature were physically suppressed. People were often killed on the spot, arrested and tortured, or they simply "disappeared."

Over the two decades (and more) of Indonesian rule, the international response was largely one of indifference. Indonesia's neighbor, Australia, was especially keen not to antagonize the populous nation to its north. It was the only country to recognize the de jure incorporation of East Timor into Indonesia. The Australians even went so far as to advocate Indonesia's case at the United Nations.

For its part, even though the United Nations passed numerous resolutions calling on Indonesia to withdraw, these were either ignored by Jakarta, or not pushed hard enough by the Security Council. Within the Cold War context there was never the possibility that the government of President Mohammed Suharto (1921–2008) would align with the Soviet Union or China in the face of Western opposition. Nonetheless, the United States, anxious lest a hard-line approach to the occupation be seen by the Indonesians as a reason to look elsewhere—for example, to the nonaligned nations—for friends with whom to side, trod very softly on the whole issue.

In 1998, President Suharto retired. His successor, B.J. Habibie (b. 1936), made it clear that East Timorese independence was out of the question (though he said he might consider giving East Timor special autonomy). Then, in January 1999—to everyone's surprise—he announced that a referendum would be held on East Timor's future status. Habibie's move made him extremely unpopular with ABRI, the Indonesian armed forces, and local pro-Indonesian militia groups were established to stop voter registration through a campaign of intimidation, in the hope that this would result in a low turnout on referendum day. The coercion and violence were unsuccessful: 451,792 voters registered, from a population that had crept back up to about 680,000. On Election Day, the turnout was estimated to be 95 percent. Those agreeing to remain part of Indonesia numbered 94,388 (21.5 percent), while 344,580 (78.5 percent) voted for independence.

In response, the pro-Indonesian militias went on a rampage. Approximately 1,500 East Timorese were killed and at least 300,000 were forcibly pushed into West Timor as refugees. Hundreds of women and girls were raped. At least 75 percent of the country's infrastructure, including homes, irrigation systems, water supply systems, and schools, was destroyed, as was nearly 100 percent of the country's electrical grid. The capital city, Dili, was effectively burned to the ground.

The killing and destruction only came to an end once international peacekeepers intervened to halt the violence and place East Timor under United Nations rule, which took place on September 20, 1999, some three weeks after the election. Ultimately, Indonesia relinquished its claim to the territory, and in 2002 the first parliament, elected by universal suffrage and guaranteed by the United Nations, met in the reconstructed capital. Under the name Timor Leste, the country was admitted to the United Nations on September 27, 2002.

CONSTÂNCIO PINTO

In September 1977, the situation in the mountains of northern East Timor deteriorated for those fighting Indonesian rule. A major military campaign was organized to encircle the fighters, leading to serious privation and suffering (and loss of lives) for civilians as well as fighters. Constâncio Pinto (b. 1963) was one such fighter. A teenager in 1977, he became one of the many victims of Indonesia's war against the East Timorese. This account describes the nature of the attacks of that September, and their aftermath. Pinto's subsequent history is one of success, despite his three years in the jungle, many years in the underground, and brutal beatings in Indonesian jails. Escaping from East Timor, he made his way to the United States, where he studied at Brown University. After East Timor's independence, in 2009, he was appointed ambassador to the United States.

While we were on the run, I couldn't take care of people on a regular basis because of the difficult circumstances. We couldn't even get enough medicine from the jungle; in many places it was not possible to find the right plants and trees for traditional medicines. We tried to use some of the Western medicine that we had, but thousands of people died of starvation and diseases. I saw this every day when we moved from one place to another. We walked among the dead bodies. Often people did not have time to bury their dead family members. I saw the bodies of a lot of children and parents and old people who died of starvation or disease as a result of the lack of food and medicine. I also saw a lot of children crying because their parents were killed by the Indonesians or because their parents had abandoned them. Parents abandoned their children because they were afraid that they would slow them down, because their crying would put everyone else's life in danger, or because there was no more food to feed them. The smell of rotting human corpses was everywhere. Some of the corpses seemed to have been there for days; others looked as if they just died a few hours before we arrived. As I say this, I can smell the dead bodies again.

We couldn't help anyone. How could we? We were also trying to escape from the Indonesians. There was no time for us to help each other. It was sad seeing the abandoned children. I still hear the crying of those children. I couldn't help those children or babies because I had to save my own life and those of my other family members. We left those abandoned children with the hope that someone else would take care of them, but I don't think anyone did. Everyone feared for his or her own life. In my own family we had three children to carry.

Death was not news for the East Timorese at this time, but we were all afraid of being killed. Everyone thought that he or she was going to be alive for only another one or two days. We didn't know what was going to happen. We just tried to survive.

My family was suffering. Some of my brothers and sisters and I were really sick from malaria and diarrhea. We were close to starving. Sometimes we had only a piece of manioc to eat for the whole day, and at other times we would go a whole day without eating anything. Luckily, my parents were physically strong enough to take care of us.

My parents always asked the children to pray, to pray to God and ask Him to save our lives and to bless the medicine that we were taking. My parents always said to the children, "*Tutua sei tulun o hanoin maromak*" (God will help you. Think of God). My parents always believed that our family's life was in God's hands. They believed that God would save our family in whatever circumstances of the war. My family was very lucky. God protected us. None of us was killed or injured during the war, though we did lose close relatives.

During the encirclement, all we could do was to stay hidden, looking for food at night and studying the possibilities to move around. By early 1978, the whole FRE-TILIN structure was broken down. We didn't see any political activists walking around to educate people. When the Indonesian army took over the villages there were no more coordinated guerrilla activities or communications. Even the guerrilla fighters were split up. Radio Maubere was no longer operating, either.

When we hid, we always hid in the forest. There were no more *aldeias* (villages) around; the Indonesian army had burned then all down. Each family hid by itself. We were more secure if we separated into many places in a given area, rather than all camping in a small, restricted area. There were a few hundred people with us altogether.

Several months after the encirclement had begun, we headed back towards Bereliurai because we couldn't get enough food. About one month after the Indonesians had captured Bereliurai, they abandoned it. They continued to chase people toward the east, so we tried to go around them. We were successful. While the Indonesian soldiers were moving east, we were going toward the west. We returned successfully to Bereliurai. By that time there were about 150 of us from the original group that had fled from Bereliurai. We were lucky: only 10 people from our group had died since we had left; unfortunately, we never had time to bury them.

Again, I saw many dead bodies on the way; some of them were already bones, skeletons. Seeing this made me think that this would also be the fate of us who were still alive, that no one could escape from death. One day, after the sun had set, everyone stopped for a while. I tried to find a place to rest. While I was looking for a spot, I found an old woman sleeping face down. The place was nice and I also tried to rest there. Around six the next morning I woke up because we had to continue our journey. I tried to wake her up and tell her that we had to move ahead. When I touched her body it felt like a stone. She was dead, but I felt nothing.

When we got back to Bereliurai it was empty. Everything had been destroyed. All the houses were burnt down, the gardens abandoned. We could only hear wild birds singing. There were no roosters, no cows, no human beings. The Indonesians burned the fields when they first occupied Bereliurai, but some manioc, sweet potatoes and other root crops, and banana trees survived the fire.

We had to be very conscious of everything we did in Bereliurai. We tried not to leave any evidence of human activity because the Indonesian military was close by. Almost every morning Indonesian soldiers did exercises along the trail to the village while we were hiding along a riverbank.

Unfortunately, a family that was hiding nearby made a big mistake. One day they found an abandoned cow and killed it. After they killed the cow, they tried to dry the meat as soon as possible. During the day they dried the meat in the sun; but when the evening came, they continued drying it by using a fire. Unfortunately, they didn't extinguish the fire and, early in the morning, it produced a lot of smoke. The smoke immediately attracted the Indonesian army to their shelter. Some Indonesians arrested them and took them to Remexio without anyone knowing. The big group was still hiding with us in the same area. The Indonesian army later used that family to find the rest of us hiding in Bereliurai, including me and my family. . . .

So the Indonesians took us to Remexio. We had to walk. Before we left, they searched everyone's clothes, baskets and packs. Some people were forced to take off their clothes so the Indonesians could see if they had guns or not. . . .

The Indonesians sent us to a house that we had to share with a family of five or six people. We didn't know them, but they recognized us because they had been our patients in the jungle. The house was one of many built by the Indonesians for East Timorese who came down from the mountains. The houses were very small and had two rooms. Each house had a zinc roof, bamboo walls, and a dirt floor. There was no land.

In many ways, life was worse in the village than in the jungle because so many people were there. The whole town had become a concentration camp. People were not allowed to look for food in the outlying areas of the town. People could grow food in the town, but there was not enough land for most people. We got some food from the military, but our family of 10 was given only 22 pounds of rice for a whole week. If we wanted vegetables, we had to buy them or find them ourselves. But how could we look for vegetables if we were not allowed to leave the town? There were also no places where we could buy food in Remexio. There were no shops. There was only the Indonesian military. The Indonesians grew a small amount of vegetables and brought food from Dili, but we couldn't afford to buy it from them because we didn't have any money and there was almost no work in Remexio. When we came back to Remexio, we still had some Portuguese *escudo,* but the money was worthless. We couldn't even exchange *escudos* with *rupiah,* the Indonesian currency.

At least in the jungle we lived in freedom and friendship. In the town, there was no freedom: we lived like fenced-in sheep. The town was like a prison. There were regulations against people leaving the town and there were soldiers everywhere. There were certain areas of the town that we were forbidden to go; if someone went to any of these places, he or she could be killed. The soldiers searched people's houses day and night, threatening people not to think about returning to the jungle, trying to persuade people to tell their families and friends who were still in the jungle to surrender, and forcing people to learn the Indonesian language and attend the flag-raising ceremony every Monday morning.

Source: Constâncio Pinto and Matthew Jardine, *Inside the East Timor Resistance* (Toronto: James Lorimer and Co., 1997), 64–66, 68–70. Used by permission of James Lorimer & Company Ltd., publishers.

Commentary

Constâncio Pinto's account reminds us that where genocide is concerned, starvation and disease are as fatal as bullets and gas, if not more so. A large part of the crisis originated in attempts by the invaders to "Indonesianize" East Timor. Indonesia's efforts first to gain military control of the country, then to enforce complete integration, were made through a number of actions aimed at the total disruption—and, ultimately, elimination—of normal East Timorese life, and its replacement by a Javanese lifestyle.

The first step was the forcible removal of the population from its traditional village life, and its relocation to newly created "strategic hamlets"—which some have called concentration camps. (Indeed, Pinto himself employs this term when describing what happened in his town of Remexio.) It was a vicious cycle that drew the East Timorese population further and further into the Indonesian trap.

As Pinto shows, the total destruction of villages and towns by the Indonesians made it even more difficult for survivors to find safety, which served to further destroy the concept of community among survivors. This was far from an unexpected development; in fact, it was part of the Indonesian goal. The drive to transform the East Timorese into willing Indonesians extended to areas such as culture and education.

Wherever Pinto went in this bleak environment, there seemed to be nothing but dead bodies and material destruction. He writes of the trail of death he encountered in many places: "We walked among the dead bodies. Often people did not have time to bury their dead family members. I saw the bodies of a lot of children and parents and old people." Elsewhere he notes, "The smell of rotting human corpses was everywhere"; "10 people from our group had died since we had left; unfortunately, we never had time to bury them"; and, "I saw many dead bodies on the way; some of them were already bones, skeletons." With death ever-present, Pinto concludes that "death was not news for the East Timorese at this time." Despite this,

"We were all afraid of being killed." "Everyone thought that he or she was going to be alive for only another one or two days," and "we didn't know what was going to happen," yet there was no surrender to abject fatalism. The most important thing was to keep going, or, as Pinto put it, "We just tried to survive."

Some, in their desperation, were less careful than Pinto and those around him. When he returned to his town of Bereliurai after the Indonesians had been through it, the town was empty. "Everything" had been destroyed. One family that had been in hiding came forward and, starving, found a stray cow and killed it. They attempted to dry the meat as quickly as they could, but the fires and smoke attracted Indonesian attention. The family was arrested and interrogated, leading, eventually, to Pinto's group being found and taken into custody.

In the account's earlier description of Pinto and his family on the run, we learn how vital Roman Catholicism—an important part of East Timorese life after four centuries of Portuguese rule—was to sustaining the human spirit during this ordeal. When Pinto references God (something that is relatively uncommon among survivor accounts), we are reminded that the horrors many victims encountered had an impact on their religious convictions. Sometimes, this confrontation brought them closer to God, as they sought comfort; other times, it drove them away from their beliefs. In Pinto's case, it was his parents who were the main initiators of prayer, but religious conviction was shared by the family, as Pinto writes: "My family was very lucky. God protected us."

When the Indonesians "resettled" groups and families in their newly created "strategic hamlets," life changed immensely. Not only were the people's living quarters more cramped than those to which they were accustomed, but there were also many more people than in the traditional village structure.

For Pinto, being forced to live there was a form of imprisonment. Government-supplied food was insufficient, but people were not permitted to supplement it from outside sources. If there had been opportunities to buy more food—and there were not—transactions had to be conducted in Indonesian *rupiah* rather than Portuguese colonial *escudos*. In every direction, it seemed, Indonesian rule was strangling the former East Timorese way of life, in a brutal occupation conducted in a climate of repression, torture, mass murder, and total disregard for fundamental human rights. The Indonesian program was a campaign of social transformation for the tiny territory, in which every effort was made to alter permanently the very identity of the people living there. This was done by destroying the concept of community that had kept the East Timorese together through 400 years of Portuguese colonial rule.

Questions

1. What was Pinto's attitude toward life and death in East Timor under Indonesian rule?

2. Pinto witnessed the deliberate destruction of village life under the Indonesians. What do you think was the strategy behind this destruction?
3. In his testimony, Pinto makes references to God and religion. What do you think prompted him to include these?

"LOURENCO"

An encirclement campaign, designed to concentrate and then flush out the East Timorese fighters, took place at Matebian Mountain in 1978. After hundreds of bombs rained down daily in air attacks, a large number of civilians were forced to march ahead of the Indonesian troops as they closed in. Many were killed in the air raids, while many others were murdered in nearby villages, either burned alive or shot. Lourenco was both a witness and a victim at Matebian. Here, he gives an account of his observations, in which his rage comes through clearly.

The Indonesians couldn't trust the Timorese they made join their army; often they'd turn and fire on the Indonesians or bring their weapons and join us in the bush. At first fighters or civilians could move freely between the bush and the towns, visit the markets—the Indonesians held only some towns. There were six FRETILIN zones and they controlled the countryside. Then the Indonesians started their encirclement campaigns.

I was in Matebian, where it's all mountain and rocks. We captured three Indonesian soldiers and found out that we were to be attacked soon. Everyone was very curious to see them. One was an extraordinary soldier and he was very stupid, didn't know anything. Another died from dysentery after a short time, but the third was a corporal who was married to the daughter of a colonel. He had a knee injury we helped to heal. He learned a bit of Tetun and started to be friendly. He was surprised to find us just ordinary people. He said he'd been told to come and fight communist enemies of Indonesia, not people wanting freedom in their own land. I don't know what happened to him later. I've heard Indonesians kill soldiers who become friendly with us to discourage others, but I don't know if he died.

Our section in the east was the last to be attacked. In 1978 they started to come against us. At first we didn't resist, just watched the enemy, let them feel confident. Matebian Mountain is a big area and there were 160,000 of us, fighters and civilians, divided into small groups.

On 17 October 1978 some Indonesians got right to the bottom of Matebian Mountain and that's when we started to fight back. For those first two months,

October and November, we were very successful and about 3000 Indonesians died. Then they got angry and scared to come close and started to bomb us from the air. They bombed twice a day, in the morning and afternoon with four black planes. Their name I know now is Broncos, but we called them scorpions because they had a tail that curves up at the back like that insect. Their bombs left a big hole about two metres deep. Then they got new supersonic planes. Our people were very frightened of those because you didn't even hear they were there until they were gone. Those supersonics would zoom along the valley so fast we couldn't shoot them.

The bombing became constant, in rotation. Three supersonics came to bomb for about forty-five minutes and then went back to reload. Half an hour later the black scorpions came, and this would go on all day. In Matebian there are a lot of caves and we hid there and only moved at night.

We knew by radio from the south that the Indonesians had dropped four napalm bombs there. Then they dropped two of these on us. I saw all the flames and heard people shouting and screaming. I was on another mountain but I could see well; there was a close view of it, straight across. Some of us set out straight away to help those people. By foot it took half an hour to go down and up again, and by the time we got there everything was completely burnt. We saw a whole area about fifty metres square all burnt, no grass, nothing except ash. On the rocks it was a brown reddish colour and on the ground ash too, not ordinary grey ash, a sort of yellow ash, like beach sand. You couldn't see where bodies had been. There was nothing except ash and burnt rocks on the whole area, but we had heard those people screaming.

We could find no bones or bodies, but people near said there were about a hundred people living there who were killed by this. Those people disappeared, they were not sheltering, we never saw them again. The population was large but people were in small groups in different places and knew where each group was. The whole population were very upset—no bodies of those people left to bury. My cousin said, "If this is what they can do there is no hope for the world."

We had no food because of all the bombing and we lost radio contact. FRETILIN decided they couldn't defend the people properly any more and the population should surrender, otherwise we would all be wiped out. When they announced this decision the people cried. FALINTIL said they couldn't force us, that they had sworn to defend the people, but this was the best thing for all. . . . Then FALINTIL gave up their responsibility for the people and everyone decided for themselves to stay or go. Also the fighters were free to do what they wanted. Most didn't surrender. FALINTIL broke up into small groups to fight as guerrillas.

About 2000 of us tried to stay in the mountains. We broke into three groups to escape and I was in one of these trying to get through the encirclement. In our group there were a few hundred, mostly fighters, only about a hundred ordinary people. We kept walking and walking. The Indonesians would drop some bombs, we would hide, then walk again. We were in a valley and the Indonesians were up higher. If they shot at us our fighters didn't shoot back so that the Indonesians would think we were just a normal group of people walking to surrender. We had no food, the area we were going through was mostly rocks. The enemy burnt the trees and any food growing; the animals were dead.

We tried to stay quiet, not attract attention. One day a woman carrying a metal pot dropped the lid and the echo went around and around loudly off the bare rock. Soon a plane flew over looking, but we all hid. We moved mostly at night.

A father carrying his baby, a few weeks old, and it started crying because the mother didn't have any breastmilk left—she was starving too. The baby's cries, echoing in the valley, could be heard by the enemy. The father hit the baby against a rock, just one hit and it died instantly, no cry. It was merciful. The people with our group felt very sad, that soon we would die too. The baby was just killed sooner, it had relief, it wouldn't have to wait to die. We thought our deaths may not be quick, that the baby was lucky to die fast and with love. We were very low. There was no time to bury the baby, we had to keep moving. Matebian by then anyway was full of dead, there were bodies everywhere.

I found out later that different things happened to people who surrendered. If they found a village they had some protection because the Indonesians then didn't want people there to see them kill civilians. Many were killed who surrendered on Mt Matebian where the enemy thought there was no one watching, especially if they were with somebody with long hair whom the Indonesians could tell was educated. Then they'd not only kill that one they thought was FRETILIN, but the whole group.

The Indonesians didn't kill many important ones who surrendered though; they could be useful. They didn't kill Alarico Fernandes for example. He operated FRE-TILIN radio to the outside world, so many knew of him. He co-operated and gave a lot of information and they thought of a clever plan for him. They landed a helicopter in the market where everyone could see and put Alarico and his family inside and went. Word was spread that they were thrown in the sea like is usually done if they take people by helicopter. After a while that story got outside. When a group of journalists was allowed into Dili they asked about Alarico, said they heard he was dropped into the sea. The Indonesians said, "Oh no, you should not believe these people and their propaganda against Indonesia, he is here and alive, you can talk to him." Then they bring Alarico from where they had hidden him and his family. It was all planned, so clever. We didn't think it could come from an Indonesian mind, it was too clever; we thought it must have been a plan from the Americans who were often in Dili talking to the Indonesians.

After many years I got to Dili and friends protected and relatives outside paid for me to escape. Now my mind is not good. I've tried but I can't study any more. I read something one day and the next day I can't remember it. Sometimes I want to remember things to tell about them and they're gone; my mind's lost them. The doctor says there's nothing I can do, it's from the war, maybe with time it will get better. When I talk about Timor and the war it's like I'm back there. If I talk to people I think I have betrayed Timor. I get so angry I can't find words, my mind sticks.

Source: Michele Turner (ed.), *Telling East Timor: Personal Testimonies, 1942–1992* (Sydney: University of New South Wales Press, 1992), 113–116.

Commentary

Matebian, the "Mountain of the Dead Souls," is a sacred site for the people of East Timor. During the Indonesian occupation, it was a refuge for both the East Timorese resistance movement and local people seeking sanctuary from the Indonesians. The population displacement that occurred between 1976 and 1979 led to ongoing "evacuations" organized by the leading East Timorese resistance movement, FRETILIN. Additional dislocation took place when individuals and family groups also moved toward Matebian. Sometimes people took shelter for only a few days in a particular area; sometimes, they stayed for several months.

In September 1978, the population of the eastern part of the country endured the long march to Matebian, which had long been seen as a place of refuge for the East Timorese. As they arrived, the Indonesians launched a major campaign to clear the area. By October 17, Indonesians had surrounded Matebian's foothills, where 160,000 fighters and civilians were trying to hide. During October and November fierce battles took place, resulting in some 3,000 Indonesian casualties. When the Indonesians realized that resistance was not going to dissipate, saturation bombardments of the area began. These included the use of napalm. By December 4, 1978, the various armed units of FALINTIL broke up into smaller units and were forced to operate in the forest independently of each other.

Much of this is described in Lourenco's account, along with his observations regarding the rapidly dwindling (because of the bombings) food supplies. It is interesting to learn that the active resistance movement, led by FRETILIN, commanded the civilians and villagers on the mountain to surrender. Lourenco shows us that FRETILIN had decided the people could no longer be protected, and therefore it would be better for them to put themselves at the mercy of the Indonesian occupiers. Individuals would have to decide for themselves whether or not to stay, at their own risk. FRETILIN could no longer defend its own population.

It was at this time that Lourenco and some 200 others decided to stay in the mountains and try to break through the Indonesian grip in order to reach safety. Lourenco observes that not only did his group not have any food, but the Indonesians introduced a campaign of deforestation intended to burn out anything that could be harvested for food. They also killed animals.

As people fled, looking for shelter from the aerial bombardments, conditions on Matebian grew traumatic. The East Timorese lived in a state of constant fear, taking shifts to sleep in cramped conditions with little food or water. Lourenco describes how "we tried to stay quiet, not attract attention," and to illustrate the danger he relates a story of how a woman carrying a metal pot dropped the lid. "The echo went around and around loudly off the bare rock," attracting an Indonesian military plane. With these constrictions, the people became creatures of the night, moving silently and hoping they would not be seen.

Living under such restricting conditions took an enormous toll. We learn of a father killing his baby, just a few weeks old, in order to prevent the child from crying and revealing the group's position to the Indonesians. As Lourenco relates, "The father hit the baby against a rock, just one hit and it died instantly, no cry. It was merciful." The problem of dealing with crying children is found in many testimonial accounts in all genocidal situations, and it is almost always resolved in the same way. It is another example of why genocide is regarded in international law as "the crime of crimes."

A sense of fatalism characterized the East Timorese people caught in the region. While the baby's death was quick, the people in Lourenco's group believed that "our deaths may not be quick." He notes that Matebian by that stage was "full of dead, there were bodies everywhere."

Near the end of his account, Lourenco tells of a clever ruse perpetrated by the Indonesians to make the East Timorese believe that one of their people, Alarico Fernandes, had been killed. Fernandes, the Minister of Information in the FRETILIN government, allegedly entered into negotiations with the Indonesians, and was later accused of denouncing FRETILIN positions to the Indonesian army. As it turned out, Fernandes was not killed, but was actually taken by the Indonesians to safety, then brought out before foreign journalists in Dili to show how benevolent the Indonesians were. Lourenco reports that the ruse was so clever that the East Timorese "thought it must have been a plan from the Americans who were often in Dili talking to the Indonesians." This final, throw-away line raises another issue: the very cloudy position of the United States relative to the East Timor situation from 1975 onward.

Lourenco, both a witness and a victim at Matebian, did not start out as a member of FRETILIN. At first he was a member of the UDT, the *União Democrática Timorense,* or Timorese Democratic Union, a conservative political party that originally advocated continued links with Portugal. Lourenco broke with the UDT and began working with FRETILIN, which is why he found himself at Matebian in 1978. He is forthright and detailed in describing the annihilation of his FALINTIL section. He also attempts to offer explanations. Despite his efforts at calmness, though, we can certainly detect anger at the destruction of human lives at the hands of the Indonesian invaders. He acknowledges this with his final words: "Now my mind is not good. . . .

When I talk about Timor and the war it's like I'm back there. If I talk to people I think I have betrayed Timor. I get so angry I can't find words, my mind sticks."

Questions

1. How does Lourenco assess the impact and effectiveness of the Indonesian bombing campaign at Matebian Mountain?
2. In your view, should Lourenco and his comrades have stayed in the mountains, or should they have surrendered in order to avoid the bombing?
3. What was the overall effect of Lourenco's experiences at Matebian on him psychologically?

RUSSELL ANDERSON

On November 12, 1991, a massacre took place at the Santa Cruz cemetery in East Timor's capital, Dili. The perpetrators of the massacre were members of the much-feared KOPASSUS, the special forces of the Indonesian military. The catalyst for the massacre was a funeral procession for an East Timorese student, Sebastião Gomes (1969–1991), who had been shot dead by Indonesian troops a few days earlier. As the procession approached the cemetery, banners were unfurled calling for independence, showing images of FRETILIN leader Jose Alexandre "Xanana" Gusmão (b. 1946). The protest was the final justification KOPASSUS needed. As the procession entered the cemetery, truckloads of troops appeared and fired on the unarmed crowd. While figures regarding the number of people killed and wounded in the ensuing violence vary, the most commonly accepted numbers are 271 killed, 382 wounded, and a further 250 missing. The massacre was witnessed and filmed by Western journalists, including an Australian, Russell Anderson. This account is his report submitted to Australia's Department of Foreign Affairs and Trade.

I attended the Catholic Mass held at the Motael Church on 12 November at 6 am in commemoration of Sebastiao Gomes Rangel's death. Due to the large crowd, approximately 4000, the Mass was moved outdoors, to the west of the church but still within the church grounds. All was quiet. Open jeeps with military sitting in the back drove by and observed the crowd.

A demonstration was planned to start after the Mass. I believe the demonstration was organised because of the expectations held by the visit of the Parliamentary Delegation and the frustration felt due to its cancellation.

With the Mass over, people moved to the entrance way of the churchyard and onto the street.

Concealed banners were unfurled and hidden T-shirts with slogans were displayed. No military were to be seen.

As more and more banners unfurled into a sea of waving slogans, the crowd became vocal, with shouts of "Viva Sebastiao, Viva Timor Leste, Independence, Viva Xanana." The age grouping of the demonstrators was again mixed, but younger people were more visible in the front. The faces of the East Timorese lit up with an expression of life and vigour. Pent-up frustrations seemed to be released with a feeling of at last being able to show openly their cries for independence in the hope that the world was watching. I felt a nervousness, a sense of fear swell within me as I remembered I was in an occupied country. I also saw a nervous fear on people's faces as their eyes scanned the streets.

From the beginning, organised demonstration marshals were in attendance. It seemed the marshals were a youth group, distinguished by similar clothing. A marshal tried to operate a megaphone but had problems with feedback, creating a siren sound. Eventually he spoke to the crowd, who were still unfurling banners and starting to move along the planned route.

The march was led by two women carrying traditional baskets of flowers draped with knitted colourful cloth. From the beginning, marshals joined arms to contain the lead by slowing down enthusiastic banner wavers who wanted to run (not in any direction—it never looked like a riotous situation—they jogged and ran along the route). The marshals had a hard time, shouting at people to slow down and having to continually regroup.

I stayed in front of the march and had a hard time keeping up. In the simmering heat I was sweating and panting. The march proceeded along the harbourside. Ironically a military ship was preparing to dock. The seafront was lined with Indonesian ships, and the soldiers standing in the confines of the harbour looked on with disgust and hatred on their faces. . . .

By the time I got to the cemetery entrance, demonstrators were still climbing the wall for photographers to take pictures of the banners and their hands held high in a V-sign.

I gave a quick count as the crowd swelled in front of the cemetery. I estimated between 5000 and 6000 people. I remembered that at Sebastiao Gomes' funeral many people joined the procession at the cemetery. I put this down to the area being more residential and a safe place for more afraid people to join in. . . .

As the photos were taken of the people standing on the front cemetery wall, others moved inside to say prayers and lay flowers on Sebastiao Gomes' grave. Again the demonstration was organised. A marshal announced the ceremony of prayers and laying of flowers through a megaphone. . . .

To the south of the demonstration the military were forming. The first truck was about 100 meters away. . . . These soldiers, in what I will call "the first truck," wore

a distinctive camouflaged uniform. These were the ones I saw methodically form
the frontal assembly of the military attack and they were the ones who created the
initial onslaught and deaths. . . .

Two trucks stopped behind the "first truck." I noticed military marching down
the road along the route the demonstration had just walked. The second truck, with
a roar of its engine, drove towards the crowd but turned left. The crowd yelled. I felt
there was excitement because the military were leaving. They, however, parked
around the corner and started filing out of the truck. . . . .

From the position I stood, I heard no warning to the crowd to disperse. Not that
I would have understood the language, but any shout or order through a megaphone
I would have heard and recognised. There was none. Not a single warning. . . .

Suddenly a few shots rang out, continued by an explosive volley of automatic
rifle fire that persisted for two to three minutes. It sounded like the whole fifteen in
the front row had their fingers pressed firmly on the trigger. They were firing directly into the crowd.

I ran, like everybody else. I took a quick glance around and saw people falling.
I realised that I would be shot in the back if a bullet lodged into my body. Most people,
especially in that initial burst of fire, would have been shot in the back, running away.

In my vicinity, most people ran around the south side of the cemetery to get out
of the line of fire. Once around the corner I scampered through barbed-wire fences,
frantically jumping over tin fences, following the rivers of people past houses and
trees and more fences. . . .

My body began to convulse from fear and I was out of breath. I felt very sick and
sat down, unable to run. There didn't seem to be as many shots being fired. Suddenly it started again from the direction of the cemetery, and some shots seemed
much closer. I was up and running again. The soldiers were chasing us. . . .

Back at the hotel there was no-one. I was terrified, pacing up and down. I waited.
I had a shower and changed my clothes, which had been ripped by the barbed-wire
fences.

After waiting half an hour, I decided to ride around town on a motorbike. Looking back now, this was madness, but I had to know what happened to the others.
I turned the bike up JI Belarmino Lobo, the street I had walked down. Noticing
there were no military I rode cautiously up the street. About three-quarters of the
way, twenty soldiers rounded the corner. Thinking I would look suspicious turning
the bike around, I continued.

The soldiers noticed me and glared. Some of them were looking in houses,
around corners and over fences. Some had their automatic weapons in a position to
fire and others had them strapped over their shoulders. I thought it would be safe:
I'd changed clothes, was wearing a helmet and had sunglasses on. I gave a warm
"good morning" and a smile. The glare on most of them changed to a smile and
I motored on.

Turning right, I saw soldiers all along the street. It looked like a mopping-up operation. They, too, were searching the area. I noticed but did not stare at three bodies in front of a house about 30 metres off the road.

Upon reaching the next corner, I gave way to two military trucks packed with soldiers. I again waved and smiled, but soldiers in the second truck started yelling and pointing at me. The driver didn't stop. Turning right again, I was close to the cemetery. There were three speeding trucks heading towards the cemetery so I diverted and went back to the hotel.

Bob Muntz was back. Bob had a wound on his arm. Blood seeped through his shirt. He told me that Kamal had been shot several times, and had been found bleeding profusely in the street. Kamal had been taken to the military hospital. There was no time for sadness. We had to think. We still feared for our lives. How do we get to the hospital to see him? What about the others? What about the East Timorese?

Source: Russell Anderson, "The Massacre of 12 November 1991," Jim Aubrey (ed.), *Free East Timor: Australia's Culpability in East Timor's Genocide* (Sydney: Random House, 1998), 145–152. Used by permission of Russell Anderson.

Commentary

In October 1991, a humanitarian and fact-finding delegation was scheduled to visit East Timor. The visit was to include Portuguese politicians and a number of foreign journalists, and was to coincide with an official visit from UN Special Rapporteur for Human Rights Pieter Kooijmans (1933–2013). The delegation was always going to be the focus of pro-East Timorese agitation. Once this became clear, Portuguese authorities cancelled the delegation's visit.

East Timorese independence activists, seeing that their opportunity to raise the profile of their cause was now lost, were severely disheartened by the cancellation, and several groups met to plan their next step. When student groups supporting FRETILIN threatened to turn the group's arrival—and then, non-arrival—into a protest demonstration against Indonesian rule, the authorities grew wary and stepped up the military presence in the capital.

On October 28, Indonesian troops found one such activist group in Dili's Motael Church. Violence ensued, resulting in the death of one of the East Timorese students, eighteen-year-old Sebastião Gomes (1969–1991). An activist for integration with Indonesia, Afonso Henriques (1962–1991), was killed accidentally. A large number of others were arrested, and in the days that followed other churches were attacked—not only in Dili, but also in areas such as Lospalos, Viqueque, Fatumaca, and Manatuto.

Tensions were thus at flashpoint by the middle of November. They culminated on November 12, 1991, when a massacre took place at the Santa Cruz cemetery in

Dili. The perpetrators were members of KOPASSUS, the special forces of the Indonesian military (the *Tentara Nasional Indonesia,* or TNI). The catalyst for the massacre was the funeral procession for Gomes. Several thousand men, women, and children walked from the Motael Church to the nearby Santa Cruz cemetery. As the procession approached its destination, some of the students took the opportunity to wave East Timorese flags and banners calling for independence. It was the largest (and certainly the loudest) demonstration against the Indonesian occupation since the invasion in December 1975.

In the incendiary environment, the protest was the final justification the KOPASSUS forces needed to clamp down on what they viewed as an unauthorized political demonstration. As the procession entered the cemetery, truckloads of troops appeared; shortly thereafter, they opened fire on the unarmed crowd. Those fleeing ran through the main entrance and deeper into the cemetery and they, in turn, were pursued by the soldiers. The most commonly accepted figures to come out of the massacre are 271 killed, 382 wounded, and 250 missing (those who ran away when the shooting began, or were taken into custody and never seen again).

The massacre was witnessed and filmed by Western journalists, including American journalists Amy Goodman (b. 1957) and Allan Nairn (b. 1956), British cameraman Max Stahl (b. 1954), and Australian Russell Anderson.

Film of the massacre was smuggled out of East Timor and broadcast around the world, to the universal condemnation of Indonesia. The facts that KOPASSUS forces were at the cemetery on the day of the funeral, were heavily armed, and did not hesitate to open fire at an opportune moment, indicated the likelihood that the action had been prepared in advance in order to suppress even the slightest expression of anti-integrationist agitation. The massacre at the Santa Cruz cemetery was a clear statement of the Indonesian government's determination to continue its repression of East Timor, and to maintain its ruthless control over the territory.

Russell Anderson's account of the Dili massacre describes his direct observations at the cemetery. One of his starkest comments states that no warning of any kind came from the Indonesian military before they commenced firing: "From the position I stood, I heard no warning to the crowd to disperse." Fully aware that he could not speak Bahasa, Tetum, or Portuguese, he knew, nonetheless, that "any shout or order through a megaphone I would have heard and recognised." There was none, "not a single warning."

Anderson's description of the actual shooting is equally frank. He observes that it seemed as though "the whole fifteen in the front row had their fingers pressed firmly on the trigger," as the "explosive volley of automatic rifle fire" was shooting "directly into the crowd." In such a situation, he had one option. He, like everyone else, ran away from the shooting, providing an important piece of evidence regarding Indonesian culpability in the massacre. Should there have been casualties, they would have occurred as a result of people being shot in the back while running away—and not as a result of acts of aggression or threats toward the troops.

Anderson's witness role did not end when the killing stopped. Having escaped the massacre, he took it upon himself to find out what was happening elsewhere. Riding around Dili on a motorcycle, he encountered soldiers in a number of places, all, it seemed, engaged in what "looked like a mopping-up operation." Many of the soldiers viewed Anderson as an unsavory witness and expressed concern about his presence. As he reconnected with others in the foreign community, he learned that someone he knew, Australian humanitarian aid worker Bob Muntz, had been wounded. Muntz's companion of the past few days had been Kamal Bamadhaj, a political science student and human rights activist of Malaysian and New Zealand parentage. Bamadhaj, Muntz told Anderson, "had been shot several times, and had been found bleeding profusely in the street." He died later that day, the only foreign national to have been killed in the massacre.

There had already been a number of massacres, killings, and tortures of the people of East Timor under the Indonesians. Few were chronicled. The major difference between what happened at the Santa Cruz cemetery and what happened elsewhere is that at the cemetery, foreign witnesses were not only present, but they were also able to film the event and smuggle footage of it overseas. Russell Anderson was one of those witnesses. He lived to fulfill that witness role upon his return to Australia.

Questions

1. What evidence is there in Russell Anderson's account that the massacre at the Santa Cruz cemetery was preplanned?
2. While Anderson was certainly a witness of the Santa Cruz massacre, could it be said that he was also a victim of Indonesian oppression?
3. In your opinion, was the Santa Cruz massacre an example of genocide?

7. The Kurdistan Genocide

The Kurds are the largest national entity in the world without a sovereign state of their own. There are anywhere between 25 and 35 million Kurds living primarily in four nation-states: Iran, Iraq, Syria, and Turkey. The Kurds are a Muslim people who do not see themselves as Arabs and are united by language, culture, and history. An ancient nation, their origins are somewhat shrouded in mystery, but they are believed to have been a group of tribal communities inhabiting the mountainous region of present-day northern Iraq and the surrounding areas.

Iraqi dictator Saddam Hussein (1937–2006) possessed what can only be described as an outright hatred of the Kurds, and was single-minded in his pursuit of their destruction. In 1963, well before the genocide of 1987–1988—known as the al-Anfal campaign—anti-Kurdish measures began with the forced Arabization of villages around Kirkuk. Further measures saw the deportations and disappearances of Faylee Kurds in the 1970s and early 1980s; the murder of 8,000 male Barzanis in 1983; the use of chemical weapons in the late 1980s, most notably against Halabja; and finally the Anfal campaign.

Ali Hassan al-Majid (1941–2010), commonly known as "Chemical Ali," was the minister of defense in Saddam's Ba'ath Party regime. Not coincidentally, al-Majid also happened to be Saddam's cousin, as well as one of his senior advisers and a brutally tough "enforcer" for the regime.

In March 1987, al-Majid was given the post of secretary-general of the administrative zone called the Northern Bureau, where Iraqi Kurdistan was located. In this role, he promised "to solve the Kurdish problem and slaughter the saboteurs." The Kurds were perceived to be a problem for Iraq because they desired their own autonomous area, were hard to control, often clashed with Iraqi military forces, and were known to have sided with Iran during the Iran-Iraq War of 1980–1988. Al-Majid issued orders for the Kurds to vacate their ancestral villages and homes and move into camps, where they could be scrutinized by the Iraqi government. Those who refused to move from the "prohibited zones" were deemed traitors and targeted for annihilation.

The Iraqi attacks, when they came, included the gassing of Kurds in their villages and the killing of others with machine guns after they had been captured and taken to remote locations. The campaign, which began in 1987, was code-named "al-Anfal." In Arabic, the word *Anfal* is used to describe plundering, or carting off the spoils of plunder. The term's origin is in *Al-Anfal,* the title of the eighth sura, *The Spoils,* in the Koran. It was an odd choice for a code name, as the Kurds, like the Iraqi Arabs, are Muslim. Iraq, moreover, is a secular state. The Iraqi government used the term to provide a religious rationale for its attack on the Kurds— whom the Iraqis perceived to be rabble-rousers, occupiers of Iraqi land, and, reportedly, collaborators with Iran against Iraq.

The campaign continued through 1988 and saw Iraqi troops, military police, and reserve forces of the National Defense Battalions destroy a thousand or more Iraqi Kurdish villages and kill nearly 200,000 Iraqi Kurds, most of whom were unarmed and many of whom were defenseless women and children. Those who survived were, generally, forced into areas bereft of water, food, housing, and medical care.

The genocide of Iraq's Kurds took place in the span of just six months. For international observers, there was little doubt that the Iraqi campaign was systematic, state-driven, and genocidal.

Al-Majid earned his nickname, "Chemical Ali," from the crime for which he was eventually convicted. During attacks, he ordered the indiscriminate use of chemical weapons such as mustard gas, sarin, tabun, and VX against Kurdish targets.

Among those killed were some 5,000 who died in one day when Halabja, a Kurdish town in Northern Iraq about 150 miles northeast of Baghdad (and only some 10 miles from the Iranian border), was saturated with chemical weapons. A genocidal massacre took place there on March 16, 1988, in the largest chemical weapons attack against a civilian-populated area in history. For many, the attack on Halabja is considered to be a separate event from the Anfal genocide, though the destruction took place simultaneously with the broader campaign.

Al-Majid's attitude toward the al-Anfal slaughter was captured on videotape when he told a group of party officials in the middle of the campaign: "Who will say anything? The international community? Fuck them." By 1988, up to 4,000 villages had been destroyed, at least 180,000 Kurds had been killed, and some 1.5 million Kurds had been deported to the south of Iraq. For these and other actions, Al-Majid also became known as "the Butcher of Kurdistan."

Al-Majid's willingness to use mustard and nerve gas against the Kurds led to international accusations of genocide leveled at Saddam Hussein's government, accusations that were subsequently verified by numerous independent organizations such as Human Rights Watch. After Iraq's defeat in the Gulf War of 1991, Kurds in the north and Shi'ites in the south (specifically, the Ma'dan people, or "Marsh Arabs"), encouraged by U.S. President George H. W. Bush (b. 1924), rebelled against Ba'ath Party rule. Again, al-Majid was at the forefront of the suppression of this resistance.

Following the spring 2003 final defeat of Saddam's government by the U.S.-led "Coalition of the Willing," al-Majid became one of the highest-profile alleged Iraqi war criminals. Along with Saddam and other leading members of the regime, al-Majid was placed on trial before the Iraq Special Tribunal for Crimes against Humanity (IST), an ad hoc court established by the Iraqi Governing Council in December 2003. He was charged with war crimes, crimes against humanity, and genocide, and convicted on all counts on June 24, 2007. Al-Majid received five death sentences for genocide, crimes against humanity (specifically willful killing, forced disappearances, and extermination), and war crimes (intentionally directing attacks against a civilian population). He was also sentenced to multiple prison terms ranging from seven years to life for other crimes. On December 2, 2008, he was again sentenced to death, this time for his role in the killing of between 20,000 and 100,000 Shi'ite Muslims during the revolt in southern Iraq that followed the 1991 Persian Gulf War. Then, on March 2, 2009, al-Majid was sentenced to death for the third time, for the 1999 assassination of Grand Ayatollah Mohammad Sadeq al-Sadr (1943–1999). Finally, on January 17, 2010, a fourth death penalty (in reality, his eighth if the initial five are considered separately) was issued in response to his acts of genocide against Kurds during the Anfal campaign. He was executed in Baghdad, by hanging, on January 25, 2010.

Like many peoples who have suffered the collective trauma of genocide, the Kurds have long memories of what was done to them in 1987 and 1988. Memorials have been erected throughout northern Iraqi Kurdistan, and evidence of the grisly toll of the genocide is everywhere, from uncovered mass graves to Saddam Hussein's torture prisons, which have been preserved. A memorial day for the Anfal is observed annually on April 14.

DANA HALABJAYI

Under the genocidal rule of Saddam Hussein, the Kurds of Iraq were targeted for various forms of persecution, which included genocide. Al-Anfal, the genocidal campaign against the Kurds conducted between February and September 1988, led to the murders of up to 200,000 Kurds, many through the use of chemical weapons. The devastation was particularly great in the town of Halabja. In this account, Dana Halabjayi recounts his experiences as a witness to some of the horrors inflicted on his people, including his own father. Dana's narrative gives a clear indication of how appalling the situation was for those who struggled to survive it.

The artillery were shelling non-stop. After spending two days and nights in the basement of our home, our family decided to move to the basement of my elder brother's home on March 14, 1988. We thought it was better to die all together, if we had to, or survive all together. But a barrage of missiles destroyed the neighborhood, including the courtyard of my brother's home. The missiles destroyed a tractor and a car. I saw a man named Hama Tal lose his leg and another man, Nasri Hama Karimi Chaychi, die in front of my eyes. We were feeling the approach of death every moment. We could neither get out of the basement nor run away from Halabja. We were trapped.

All of a sudden, Jalal Azabani, a young poet, stormed into the basement with his face gleaming and his eyes shining.

"Take this. I brought you cigarettes because I knew you were here. Get up. We will be free from the Baath's reign. Friends will reach town tomorrow morning," Jalal said. He then gave me a pack of Sumer cigarettes and we kissed on the cheeks.

"I will go to Bawa Kochak," Jalal said. It was as if he knew it would be our last meeting. After that, I never saw him again. I don't even know where he took his last breath. His body was never found. I am sure that, up to the last beat of his heart, he was confident "friends" would liberate the town. It is true greatness when one dies full of hope and longing for freedom.

In the afternoon that same day, my brother-in-law Kawa and I decided to take his pickup truck out of the garage and flee. Risking our lives, and running under the shelling, we finally made it to the Osmani Hama Pirajin garage. But there was a large bulldozer parked in front of the truck. We could not move the bulldozer or the truck and so returned home frustrated. One day after our unsuccessful effort, the family of Kawa's uncle was able to take the truck out of the garage, but they could not run away from death. The truck became their final home. The picture of the truck with the dead inside later became an iconic image. The plate number was 5814, Sulaimaniya, 1958 model. All 14 passengers in the truck went to their permanent rest. I can still remember the scene where I saw Mariwan, Mahabad and Uncle Ahmed in the basement of their home. Their eyes were full of waiting. It turned out they were waiting for the final farewell, just like Jalal.

It was a day of shortages. People were running out of bread, milk for their children and food. They had to do something about it. Death was pouring down on the town. Fear and darkness had taken over. People were distressed. After a while, we learned my brother had parked his mud-covered bus at the other end of the alley, waiting to save us just like an angel. He shouted, "Hurry up, get on the bus now that the shelling has weakened." He hadn't yet put his own children on the bus. There was no space in the bus. All the residents of the neighborhood and the basement were inside. While it could only hold 21 people, 64 passengers had squeezed in. My father and uncle decided to stay back and protect our home. They had a car and thought they could escape to the Iranian border if anything happened. We begged them to come along with us but to no avail.

"You are young. You should survive. We will take care of ourselves anyway," said my father.

It was the afternoon of March 15, 1988. It was raining lightly. I had never seen Halabja in such darkness amid smoke and anxiety. People were all out on the main road from Halabja to Sulaimani; some on foot, others in cars and tractors. Soldiers, just like the civilians, were trying to save their lives; all were exhausted. Our bus was the last vehicle that was able to pass a bridge that connected Sulaimani to Halabja. After we passed, it was blown up. There were many military trucks and armored vehicles going toward Halabja, clueless that the Zalm Bridge had been destroyed. When we reached the town of Sayid Sadiq, we found out people had been waiting to hear news from Halabja. They threw bread through the windows into our bus. They were crying for us, showing sympathy. They did not know that they would be forced to leave their homes shortly after.

When we reached Sulaimani, my brother stopped the bus in front of the Bardarki Sara Square so everybody could go to the homes of relatives from there. When I got off of the bus, the first thing that attracted my attention was the electricity. I hadn't seen any in Halabja for the last three days. Then I noticed I had no shoes on. I was wearing a shirt and a pair of Kurdish trousers covered with blood. I had brought the blood of the injured and dead to Sulaimani. We were divided into groups, each going to the home of a relative or an acquaintance. The next day when we went back to the downtown area to get some news, Bardarki Sara and the Ashapa Sepi area looked as though the ashes of death had rained down on them. You could not find a face that did not look sad or as if waiting for someone.

We were like children separated from our mothers. Soon, we learned about the chemical massacre. We learned that death had come to town. Back home, we were all overcome with sadness, silent and still. We were waiting for the situation to calm down so that we could get some news about our father and relatives back in Halabja. As if it was not enough that we had been struck by tragedy, the government forces started detaining and rounding up people from Halabja who were in Sulaimani.

There was no news of my father. After almost a month, a friend named Burhan Haji Mohammedi Bamoki told us that he had seen my father with his head against the truck's steering wheel and his hands on his eyes.

"His body was swollen. I think he was dead," said Burhan. I did not tell the family about the news and Burhan promised not to tell anyone about it. Unfortunately, that good friend of mine later died in an accident.

After a while, we got another piece of news.

"Your dad is alive but he is blind," they said. This news consoled us a bit because we knew he had been seen alive by people. Burhan was right. When my father had gone blind on the road to a village near Halabja called Anab, he could no longer drive. Later, someone took him and his car to the village of Balkha. There he had stayed with some acquaintances.

Iranian soldiers treated him there. They provided him with food and a blanket. He did not want to move to Iran, like many people from Halabja did after the attack. He wanted to stay and see us.

We were finally able to rent a house, despite the odds. The owner was a benevolent man from Sulaimani. He did not want Saddam Hussein's regime to find out about it and get into trouble. He did not take any rent from us. Up until this day, I am still looking for this man to offer my thanks. Unfortunately, he never introduced himself to us.

After the Iraq-Iran war came to an end on Aug. 8, 1988, the Iranian army withdrew from Halabja. We expected our father and people like him from the border areas to be allowed to return to their families. But that did not happen. They were all rounded up as part of the Anfal genocide campaign and taken to Sulaimani Stadium, the military intelligence's and the security forces' headquarters.

I finally managed to get a five-minute appointment with my father in prison. I took two packs of Sumer cigarettes and 25 Iraqi dinars to him. He looked tired and full of sorrow. Upon seeing me, his face cheered up, just a flower in spring. After kissing each other, he immediately said, "You take care of yourselves. You may never see me again."

After a pause, he continued, "I wish I had died and had not seen that massacre in Halabja. I don't know why God kept me alive." We were in the middle of the conversation when two guards came, blindfolded him and took him away. All I could hear him say was: "Don't worry about me."

After a week, they separated the women and children from the men and took them to Topzawa military base near Kirkuk. They apparently shot some of the men dead there. My father and other men were transferred from Topzawa to Nogra Salman camp in southern Iraq. It was in this camp that many were massacred.

Thereafter, nobody knew what happened to those people from Halabja. Where were they massacred or imprisoned? Or were they still alive? The Anfal operations had ended. We had given up all hope to see our father come back to us.

After two months, the Baath regime issued a general amnesty. We could move freely and start breathing again. We were allowed to visit Halabja to fetch the furniture we had left behind, only to find there was nothing left. Everything was in ruins. Not even a single one of my books was left for me to take back as a memory. Our home had been completely looted.

One day around noon, the doorbell rang. My younger sister told me, "There is a man at the door. He might be a beggar. See what he wants." When I opened the door, I saw a dirty, white-bearded man with a thin face. He was so thin and frail he looked as though he was about to fall over. He was wearing an old, worn-out pair of Kurdish trousers and a military jacket.

"How can I help you, uncle?" I asked politely. When I looked at his face more carefully, I saw tears had circled in his eyes.

"My son, it seems you don't recognize me," said the man. Upon saying that, tears ran down his cheeks. I knew only through his voice that it was my father.

Source: Dana Halabjayi, "My Father's Story: from Halabja to Nugra Salman," *Rudaw in English*, April 22, 2012, http://www.rudaw.net/english/science/op-ed-contributors/4663 .html. Used by permission of RUDAW.

Commentary

Within the context of the Iran-Iraq War (1980–1988), the position of Iraq's Kurdish population, always precarious, appeared to become untenable. A program in which the Kurdistan region was being transformed into something more "Arabized" had already been in progress for some time. Repressive measures against the Kurds led to clashes between the Iraqi army of Saddam Hussein and Kurdish guerrillas in 1977. In the years following, some 600 Kurdish villages were burned down and up to 200,000 Kurds were deported to other parts of the country. During the Iran-Iraq War, Saddam again implemented anti-Kurdish policies, this time on the grounds that the Kurds were disloyal. The war devastated the population of Iraqi Kurdistan, even before the so-called al-Anfal Campaign of 1987–1988.

When the Halabja poison gassing took place on March 16, 1988, thousands of people were killed. Military aircraft, said to include Iraqi Migs and Mirages, were seen dropping chemical bombs of various kinds: mustard gas; the nerve agents sarin, tabun and VX; and possibly cyanide. The Iraqi attack on Halabja—considered an important center for Kurdish resistance in their struggle for autonomy—came right at the end of the Iran-Iraq War.

The assault occurred after two days of shelling from nearby mountains by mortars, artillery, and rockets, and was far from spontaneous. Military aircraft flew several sorties in waves, concentrating their attacks on the city and all the roads leading out of it. Up to 75 percent of the victims were women and children, with most of the wounded suffering from mustard gas exposure, particularly its effects of skin lesions and breathing difficulties.

Most of the details of the Halabja killings only emerged a few days later, with first reports in the West suggesting that Iran was behind the attack. Evidence, however, indicated that the gas attack was an Iraqi assault against Iranian forces, pro-Iranian Kurdish forces, and Halabja's citizens. The attack on Halabja is thought to be the first documented assault on the Kurds in which chemicals were employed. The Iran-Iraq War itself is recognized as the first occasion since the Italian invasion of Abyssinia in 1935–1936 in which poison gas was used in warfare.

Dana Halabjayi's testimony tells the story of the al-Anfal campaign, as witnessed by an Iraqi Kurd from Halabja. It is very much the story of one family's experiences under oppression, as several of Halabjayi's relatives feature in his account. Starting on March 14, 1988, the account deals with missiles in his neighborhood; a truck destroyed, causing substantial loss of life; and "death pouring down on the town." All, it seemed, were "trying to save their lives," as people were attempting to flee to nearby Sulaimani, the so-called cultural capital of Kurdistan.

What Halabjayi really depicts is a population in the midst of war and genocide. As he sees it, "We were like children separated from our mothers," particularly after "we learned about the chemical massacre." To add insult to injury, Saddam's forces began rounding up and detaining people from Halabja who, by that stage, had made it to Sulaimani.

One of the biggest ongoing personal concerns Halabjayi faced was the fate of his father, who had gone missing in Halabja after the rest of the family had sought refuge in Sulaimani. Upon learning that "death had come to town," "we were all overcome with sadness, silent and still," "waiting for the situation to calm down so that we could get some news about our father and relatives back in Halabja." After almost a month with no news, word came that his father had been seen alive, but that he was now blind. He had been rescued by some acquaintances, then taken in by occupying Iranian forces, who treated him and provided him with essential comforts. Offered the chance to travel to safety in Iran, he refused, preferring to stay and possibly see his family once more.

Halabjayi's account mentions the end of the Iran-Iraq War on August 8, 1988, and the withdrawal of Iranian forces from Halabja. While the expectation was that this would lead to some sort of alleviation of the situation for the Kurds, instead the Iraqis began to unleash the Anfal genocide even more forcefully.

Those who had found refuge in the formerly Iranian-controlled border areas were rounded up and taken to the Sulaimani Sports Stadium, where Iraqi military intelligence had established their headquarters. Halabjayi was fortunate in that he managed to see his father, who was imprisoned there. His father's words were to the point: "I wish I had died and had not seen that massacre in Halabja." Immediately after this, the women and children were separated from the men, who were taken to Topzawa, a sprawling army base covering some two square miles on a highway leading southwest out of the oil-rich city of Kirkuk. At Topzawa, it became obvious that the al-Anfal was anything but a counterinsurgency campaign. Many of the men were shot; others were tortured.

There were further transfers from Topzawa to the desert camp of Nuqra Salman in southern Iraq. Many others were massacred, though Halabjayi's father survived and managed to return to what was left of his family at Halabja. In his account of the end of the Iran-Iraq War, the al-Anfal genocide, and the means of destruction employed by Saddam Hussein's regime—in which gas was employed for wholesale and purposeful killing—Dana Halabjayi provides important details of an attempted annihilation that was little recognized in the West while it was in progress.

Questions

1. In Dana Halabjayi's account, we read of a society that was a victim of war. Do we see any examples of genocide as well? What are they?
2. How was the condition of Halabjayi's father traced throughout the account? Did his circumstances change? How?
3. What were some of the horrors Halabjayi witnessed?

8. The Rwandan Genocide

Between April and July 1994, a genocide was committed against Tutsis and liberal democratic, or "moderate," Hutus by the extremist Hutu Power regime of the *Mouvement Révolutionnaire Nationale pour le Développement* (National Revolutionary Movement for Development, or MRND) in the tiny central African country of Rwanda.

Traditionally, Hutu life was founded on a clan system in which small kingdoms prevailed. After the arrival of the Tutsis sometime in the fifteenth century, a feudal system was established in which the Hutus were reduced to vassal status and ruled over by a Tutsi aristocracy headed by a king (*mwaami*). The fundamental division between Hutus and Tutsis was, therefore, based more on a form of class difference than on ethnicity, particularly as a great deal of intermarriage took place. The language spoken by both peoples is Kinyarwanda.

While the relationship between the Hutus and their neighbors prior to the 1950s had essentially been based on hierarchy and dominance—the Hutus, a farming people, were exploited by a tithe system and other feudal disadvantages by the Tutsis, a wealthier, cattle-raising community—Hutu-Tutsi relations were, for the most part, relatively peaceful. Hutu dissatisfaction, where it existed, was expressed nonviolently. After Rwanda's independence from Belgium in 1962, however, frequent Hutu persecutions of Tutsis began taking place. The genocide of 1994 was thus the most extreme expression of a relationship of violence between the two peoples in the second half of the twentieth century.

Though the actual genocide lasted a mere one hundred days, the background of those three murderous months dated back to the German and Belgian colonial periods (1890s to 1962), when Hutus and Tutsis were identified as different peoples. The Tutsis held a higher social status than most of the Hutus, who were perceived as belonging to a lower socioeconomic order. Under Belgian colonial rule in Rwanda, identity cards bearing an individual's ethnic group were introduced in 1933. Not only was his or her ethnic background stated, but the bearer's place of residence was also recorded on the card. The person in whose name the card was held could not relocate to another address without approval from the colonial authorities. After Rwanda's independence in 1962, the identity cards were retained as a means of discrimination in favor of the Hutu majority.

The end of colonial rule overturned this ranking of peoples, with the Hutus claiming majority rights politically. This triggered periodic outbursts of escalating violence in 1959, 1962, and 1973. By the early 1990s, extensive and somewhat transparent plans were established to carry out a campaign of extermination of the Tutsis and their Hutu political allies. The blueprint included an intense propaganda campaign broadcast over *Radio-Télévision Libre des Mille Collines* (RTLM); the organization of killing units, the *Interahamwe* and the *Impuzamugambi* militias; and the ethnic politicization of the Rwandan armed forces.

The proverbial last straw was the death of President Juvénal Habyarimana (1937–1994) on April 6, 1994, when a missile shot down an airplane he was traveling in as it approached Kigali International Airport. There has been intense debate regarding who was responsible for the attack. Some argue that the missiles were fired by radical Hutus enraged by Habyarimana's willingness to negotiate with rebels from the Tutsi-led Rwandan Patriotic Front (RPF), and by his agreement to forge ahead with the Arusha Peace Agreement. Others state that it was a direct RPF attack on the president. The truth may never be known.

What is certain is that the death of Habyarimana acted as a tocsin for radical Hutus across the country—now was the time to commence the long-planned operation meant to completely eliminate the Tutsi population of Rwanda. Within two hours of Habyarimana's assassination, roadblocks were erected in many parts of Kigali, stopping the traffic flow. Occupants of cars, trucks, and buses were required to present their identity cards to the Hutu militias. If the identity card showed the bearer to be a Tutsi, immediate and summary execution by machetes, clubs, or (less frequently) gunfire usually followed. The implementation of the roadblocks had been carefully planned and coordinated sometime beforehand, providing further evidence of the premeditated nature of the genocide. They were often of the most rudimentary kind: tires (burning or not); planks of timber laid between supports such as logs or oil drums; or rocks, stones, or bricks strewn across a specific point in the road. In fact, anything that could induce drivers to stop their vehicles counted as a roadblock.

Stopping all traffic also provided an opportunity for the Hutus—that is, the militias such as *Interahamwe* and *Impuzamugambi,* the Rwandan National Army (FAR), the police, and the Presidential Guard—to detain and concentrate Tutsis in particular areas in order to effectuate their murders at a later time. As the genocide spread, the use of roadblocks became a key element of the Hutu campaign of mass murder, and they were employed in cities and towns throughout the country.

The first to be targeted were Hutu officials identified with opposition parties (and therefore seen to hold pro-RPF sympathies). Opposition figures, both Hutu and Tutsi, were disposed of in a matter of hours. Doing away with hundreds of thousands of Tutsi civilians proved a more difficult undertaking, especially in the southern region, where mixed marriages were more common. Nonetheless, the scale and swiftness of the massacre leave no doubt about the determination of the machete-wielding militias.

A major feature of the killings was the manner in which they took place. Most victims were butchered with hand-held agricultural tools, particularly machetes, or with nail-studded clubs that had only one possible function. Moreover, the government exhorted *every* Hutu to kill Tutsis wherever they could be found. As mass murder thus became a civic virtue, family members killed each other and neighbors killed neighbors. What was striking was the efficiency of the *génocidaires*; there was little improvisation. Nor was there much room for doubt that this was a *bona fide* case of genocide, especially when it became clear that only outside intervention could stop the process of mass murder.

For weeks and months, across regions, hundreds and thousands of Tutsi civilians were shot, speared, clubbed, or hacked to pieces in their homes, church compounds, and courtyards. That carnage of this magnitude could have been going on day after day, week after week, without interference speaks volumes about the international community's lack of resolve in dealing with the atrocities.

Among the bystanders unwilling to intervene was the United Nations Security Council. It failed totally to prevent the genocide, or to stop the killing once it had begun. It even reduced by nine-tenths a small peacekeeping force, UNAMIR (United Nations Assistance Mission for Rwanda), under the command of Canadian general Roméo Dallaire (b. 1946). The UN also oversaw the evacuation of all whites across the country within days of the genocide's start. Were it not for the intervention of the RPF, led by Tutsi rebel leader General Paul Kagame (b. 1957), the genocide might have been total.

On July 18, 1994, the RPF took power in Kigali, ending the genocide. The international community promptly recognized the RPF victory and the new government. On July 19, Pasteur Bizimungu (b. 1950), a Hutu member of the RPF, was proclaimed to be Rwanda's new president, and Faustin Twagiramungu (b. 1945), also a Hutu, became prime minister of a national unity government. Kagame was named vice-president.

Only the return of Tutsi refugees from Uganda and elsewhere enabled a reconstituted Rwandan Tutsi population to be established, as up to 90 percent of the pregenocide Tutsi population within Rwanda—by some accounts, one million, by others, 800,000 to 900,000—was slaughtered.

By August 1994, the RPF was in complete control of the country, and six years later, in March 2000, Paul Kagame was installed as president. Once in power, the pressures of justice and national identity dominated the new government's agenda for reconstruction.

ELS DE TEMMERMAN

One of the few journalists who managed to remain in Rwanda for any length of time after the start of the genocide, Els de Temmerman (b. 1962), the Nairobi-based Africa correspondent for De Volkskrant *(The Netherlands) and BRT (Belgian Radio and Television), kept information coming out after many other news outlets had closed down. Soon after the genocide, she published her memoir of the experience, which was based in large part on a diary she kept during the period. It was later the inspiration for an important documentary film,* The Dead are Alive: Eyewitness in Rwanda *(directed by Anna van der Wee, 1999). The book has never been translated into English; the unnerving account here—which was also referenced in the film—has been specially translated for this volume by G. Jan Colijn.*

Only the stray dogs are victorious in Rwanda. They hunt through the abandoned villages in hordes, drag weeks-old corpses from the homes and tear the remains to pieces. It looks like a disgusting horror movie: the mountains of bodies stacked behind doors and houses, in churches and schools, among wheat fields and banana trees. You are driving on a road and suddenly you have to avoid a skull, a leg, a small human bundle. You push a door open and you gape into a mountain of corpses. You walk through a backyard and find whole families murdered: men, women and children with limbs chopped off, tied up or the arms spread in desperation. Only the smell is real. The all-penetrating smell of death and putrefaction hangs over the hills and the valleys. It follows us on our trip through the eastern province Kibungo and later through the outskirts of Kigali. Even Tony, our RPF-guide, comes asking for my eau de cologne. "We'll never get this published," grouse the photographers who have tied handkerchiefs across their noses. They photograph some ten corpses around a car in the verge of the road. A man has been thrown half-way through a windshield. "Nobody in Europe wants to see this. At most you can show a detail: an arm, or a Santana t-shirt with a kid's head sticking out."

The dazed survivors in Rubanda village walk with us from farm to farm: There is Kagambira's house, they point out: fifty corpses, there Shamukigas's: forty corpses, there Mushoza's: twenty corpses. And then we have not yet seen the lake: "Thousands and thousands of corpses!" Of the twelve thousand Tutsis in Rubanda only five hundred survived the slaughter.

"Can you still believe in God?" I ask merchant Emmanuel who, upon his return, found his wife, brothers, sisters and thirteen of his children dead. "Yes," he says pensively. "Because he saved me." Does he therefore believe that God punished the rest of his family? He gets confused, then says: "No, no, God forgives everybody." Even the killers? It gets too difficult for him. "I have to believe in God," he says defensively. "Taking revenge makes no sense. Then it will never stop. The killers have to be brought to justice by his authorities." By which authorities, I want to ask. But I keep my mouth shut.

The survivors of Rubanda have only emerged from their hiding places in the swamp last week, since the rebels seized their town from the governmental army. Some come out of the brushwood, when they see us, whites. They cry both because of relief about their rescue and because of sadness in the memory of their family members who have been killed.

"The murderers were neighbors, friends." The villagers shake their heads in incomprehension. "The majority of the Hutu-population joined in the killings here. Women and children roared and shouted 'Aoeaoe, there they are! Aoeaoe, there they are walking!'"

They tell that, already in the morning of the attack on the president, the local authorities distributed pamphlets, wherein the population was summoned to grab their machetes and to kill the Tutsis. I learn that the Interahamwe were youth movements of the former unity party MRND. "The Interahamwe were established in 1992, together with the introduction of the multiparty system," Viateur says. "They got military training in the woods of Gishwati, Nyungwe and Mutara and in the camps of the governmental army. Often, when they were drunk, they blabbered vulgarities and threatened to kill all Tutsis. But during the slaughter they were dead sober."

The puzzle becomes more and more clear. And more and more repulsive. It is clear that a carefully prepared holocaust-scenario has taken place here, that a group of people has very consciously drawn up the master plan, the definite solution to the Tutsi problem, and that this is the same people that now try to distort the reality, to deny the mass murders or to blame the other side.

More fresh corpses are lying along the road as we get closer to the front near Kigali. The road is covered with pieces of luggage left behind, school exercise books, shoes, blood drenched clothes and an occasional torn up bible. The local Tutsis have already been attacked by Interahamwe gangs in March 1992. Many were killed then. Nyamata itself, an outlying district of Kigali, has only been taken over by the rebels a few days ago. We can't get closer to the front: the bridge to Kigali has purportedly been blown up.

The surviving Tutsis of Nyamata, about a tenth of the surviving population, gather fearfully around the rebel camp in the former Italian orphanage. They only dare to move in a radius of a kilometer around that orphanage, out of fear of remaining Interahamwe. Hundreds of heavily wounded lie in the little hospital of the Italian sisters, now being run by a RPF doctor. Again I walk by rows of women and children with slash wounds on head, neck or shoulder. Again I listen to the horror stories about out-of-control militia gangs and neighbors who suddenly changed into murderers. I don't even take note any more when twenty-five year old Claudine tells me how Hutu gangs chopped off her left hand and ripped open her shoulder and neck. For three weeks she lay in the swamp without help. She has survived her wounds in miraculous fashion. But her mind is confused and she looks at me with frightened eyes when we ask her when she wants to return to her village. "Only if the Interahamwe are gone," she whispers.

The evening falls. A little boy in a much too large shirt slowly ambles through the ruins of the church in Nyamata. His name is Olivier, he is eleven and the only survivor of his family. Inside it smells like death. Wooden benches are lying criss-cross on the soot covered ground and the roof shows hundreds of holes from shell attacks. Two mountains of blood drenched clothes are lying in front of the entrance. "Thousands of people sought refuge in the church" an inhabitant says. "But the army and the Interahamwe threw grenades inside and massacred everyone with rifles and machetes. Then they took their clothes off and buried them with bulldozers."

Behind the church there is an enormous mass grave. A skull sticks out from the earth. Olivier brings me a destroyed crucifix. The Interahamwe threw it on the ground and stamped it flat, he gestures. The tattered face of Jesus looks like the head of a goat. We sit silently in the dark in front of a pile of clothes.

Softly Olivier tells how he climbed into the attic when the gangs came. From there he saw how his entire family got killed by the neighbors, Nkuriri, Munyentisari and Ngaruye. For three days he stayed in the attic, paralysed with fear. Until he got hungry and climbed down, in search of food. But the neighbors saw him and chased him with sticks and cleavers. Then the rebels came and shot his pursuers dead. "When I hear shots, I am afraid" he says, his hands drawn over his face. What he really would like is to go back to school. But the teachers are gone. And he does not know how many of his classmates are still alive.

We sleep in the orphanage, where the number of children increases every day. The director of the orphanage managed to protect the shelter by paying the army thirty million Rwanda francs. But later he himself escaped to Burundi. Even the smallest ones realize what is happening. "They kill the Tutsis because they think they are rebels," Jean says gravely. "But women and children can't be rebels, can they?" He thinks for a moment and then says: "They kill the women and children of the Tutsis because they think they are helping the rebels." Later the children tell how the rebels gathered all inhabitants upon arrival in the courtyard of the orphanage. "They asked to point out the killers. One Hutu man stepped forward, gave himself up and then nine others. They were beaten to death with sticks." They point to the raised sand hills behind the little Maria grotto where they are buried.

We are sitting with the rebels around the candle light. I have got the only bed. The men, ten of them, sleep on six mattresses. "After we take Kigali, I will give you a suite in the Meridien Hotel," our guide Tony laughs. The story of the children does not let go of me. Yes, there have been revenge actions, the RPF doctor later admits. "We cannot control the rage of the people."

The singing of the children rises from the dining room when we drive off the next day. It almost sounds heavenly across the little Maria grotto and the church of Nyamata, across the wheat field and the banana plantations where the corpses are rotting.

Olivier disappears as a small, waving dot on the horizon.

Source: Els de Temmerman, *De doden zijn niet dood: Rwanda, een ooggetuigenserslag* (Brussels: Globe, 1994), 64–68. Translated by G. Jan Colijn.

Commentary

Els de Temmerman's account is distinctive in that it is based on a diary written by one of the few Western journalists to have stayed in Rwanda for almost the entire duration of the genocide. Earlier, between 1987 and 1988, de Temmerman had served as an aid worker with *Médecins Sans Frontières* in Nyala, the capital of South Darfur, Sudan. Following that experience, she developed into an Africa specialist for a number of Belgian news outlets: from 1988 to 1990 she was a staff reporter with the daily *Het Volk,* from 1990 to 1992 she was with the magazine *Wereldwijd,* and during 1992–1995 (including the period of the genocide in 1994) she was the Africa correspondent for the Dutch newspaper *De Volkskrant* and BRT (Belgian Radio and Television). She was based in Nairobi, Kenya.

On April 6, 1994, when the aircraft of President Juvénal Habyarimana was shot down, de Temmerman was not in Rwanda. As the killings were beginning to develop momentum, she rushed to Kigali, where she witnessed the European air evacuation of expatriate nationals from the capital, as well as the abandonment of foreign embassies during the initial stages of the violence.

Throughout this time, until early September 1994, de Temmerman kept a diary of what she was witnessing, resulting, later in the year, in a book entitled *De doden zijn niet dood* ("The Dead are not Dead"). It presented a sensitive eyewitness account of the genocide, written with an immediacy and poignancy that could only have come from one who was actually there. De Temmerman has said that her primary motivation was to bear witness so that people could say they did not know about the genocide. Hers is a very personal journey exploring the nature of evil.

The excerpt from de Temmerman's diary focuses on the immediate aftermath of the killing. The accumulation of bodies, with their overwhelming stench, is the primary image of the account. The honesty of those around her, in light of what they were seeing, is refreshing, as the photo crew members proclaim: "We'll never get this published. . . . Nobody in Europe wants to see this." Seasoned photojournalists, they recognized what would be accepted and what would not be: "At most you can show a detail: an arm, or a Santana t-shirt with a kid's head sticking out." But the whole picture, they understood, would not be acceptable to sensitive Western audiences.

Another feature of de Temmerman's report is her awareness that the killings were frequently a local matter, in which close relationships from before the genocide were inverted and denied. At one point she spoke with survivors from Rubanda, in western Rwanda, who had managed to stay alive by hiding in nearby swamps. The part of their testimony de Temmerman highlights was that "the murderers were neighbors, friends," and that most of the local Hutu population joined in the killing. Even women and children participated, exposing hiding places to the *Interahamwe* and rejoicing in the deaths they caused.

One of the revelations in her testimony—though it was plain enough for all to see at the time—was that the tragedy in Rwanda was far from a spontaneous outburst of collective violence. Rather, it was a meticulously prepared and premeditated mass slaughter. De Temmerman notes that the Hutu population had already been prepared to attack the Tutsis well before April 6, and that they had been "summoned to grab their machetes" the moment the president's plane went down. As she reflects on the situation, the "puzzle becomes more and more clear." And as that realization takes place, the events become "more and more repulsive." She sees that this is no ordinary war, and that the fronts are everywhere at once. The premeditation is palpable: "It is clear that a carefully prepared holocaust-scenario has taken place here, that a group of people has very consciously drawn up the master plan, the definite solution to the Tutsi problem."

The Hutu attack against the Tutsis was a massacre resulting in the deaths of nearly one million Rwandans. De Temmerman's use of the word "holocaust" is not accidental. The English-language term, when capitalized, has been most closely identified with the Nazi genocide of the Jews of Europe during World War II. Often, today, the word is used in ways that cheapen, distort, or demean it. De Temmerman uses the word to describe what happened in Rwanda because there was no other word that would express what she had witnessed. The massacres, the looting, the flight of refugees, the huge outbreaks of disease accompanying that flight, the massive number of dead: All added up to a setting with all the hallmarks of a true genocide. In her understanding, there was only one possible description.

At the Catholic Parish Church in Nyamata, a town in southeastern Rwanda directly south of Kigali, de Temmerman became aware of the nature of the destruction as she approached the front line. As she writes, the road was "covered with pieces of luggage left behind, school exercise books, shoes, blood drenched clothes and an occasional torn up bible." With the immediacy of a diary writer, she then writes that she "can't get closer to the front" because "the bridge to Kigali has purportedly been blown up."

As evening falls, de Temmerman sees a small boy at the church. She learns that he is an 11-year-old named Olivier. He is the only survivor of his family. Inside the church, "it smells like death"; behind the church there is an enormous mass grave. The only scream de Temmerman can make amidst the complete devastation is a silent one: "We sit silently in the dark in front of a pile of clothes," the possessions of a multitude whose lives were taken in the most ghastly manner possible, under conditions that, for her, defy description.

Questions

1. Why do you think the photographers accompanying Els de Temmerman believed their images of the genocide would never be published?
2. In her account de Temmerman did not see any specific genocidal crimes, though she could, nonetheless, easily be described as a witness. Why?
3. In your view, was it appropriate for de Temmerman to use the word "holocaust" to describe the events she saw?

MARIE-LOUISE KAGOYIRE

Had it not been for the interviewing skills of French author and journalist Jean Hatzfeld (b. 1949), Marie-Louise Kagoyire's story would be lost to history. Raised among farmers and cattle breeders from Mugesera, Marie-Louise moved to Nyamata, a town in southeastern Rwanda about 30 miles from Kigali. She married a local man named Léonard, and the two settled down to a happy and comfortable domestic life. Then, over 10,000 Tutsis were massacred at Nyamata's local Parish Catholic Church (now the site of the Nyamata Genocide Memorial, which houses the remains of over 45,000 genocide victims). Her husband was among those murdered. Marie-Louise's survival, as her account shows, resulted from a remarkable set of circumstances.

On the day the plane crashed, the Tutsis who lived in the town centre could no longer go out. Many people came seeking protection behind the solid brick wall around our house. Léonard had known several massacres in his youth and understood that the situation this time was catastrophic and advised young people to make tracks to Kayumba. But he himself did not want to flee, he said that his legs had already done enough running.

On the morning of the 11th of April, the first day of the massacres, the *interahamwe* turned up in a great uproar right in front of our gate. Léonard took the keys and went to open up without delay, thinking that in this way he could save the women and children. A soldier shot him dead without uttering one word. A mass of *interahamwe* came into the courtyard, they caught all the children they could, they laid them in rows on the ground, they began to cut them. They even killed a Hutu boy, the son of a colonel who was there with his friends. As for me, I managed to skirt around the house with my mother-in-law and we lay down behind a pile of tyres. The killers stopped before the end, because they were in a great hurry to start looting. We could hear them. They got into our cars, our vans, they loaded them with crates of Primus, they argued over furniture and all sorts of things; they searched under the beds for money.

That evening, my mother-in-law came out of the hiding place and sat down in front of the tyres. Some young people noticed and asked her: "Maman, what are you doing here?" She answered: "I no longer do anything, because now I am alone." They took her, they chopped her, then they took what was left in the bedrooms and the living room. They lit a fire; this is how they forgot me.

In the courtyard there was a child who had not been killed. So I put a ladder up against the dividing wall, I climbed up with the child and jumped into our neighbour Florient's place. His courtyard was empty. I hid the child in the log storeroom and I huddled up in the dog's kennel. On the third morning, I heard the sound of footsteps and I spotted my neighbour, I came out. My neighbour exclaimed: "Marie-Louise, they are killing everyone in town, your house has been burned, but you are still here? Now, what can I do for you?" I said to him: "Florient, do this for me—kill me. But do not expose me to the *interahamwe* who will undress and chop me."

Monsieur Florient was a Hutu. He was head of military intelligence in the Bugesera, but had built his house on our plot and, before the war, we would speak to one another kindly, share good moments, our children ran around together in the courtyards. So he locked myself and the child up in his home, he gave us some food to eat and he went away. The next day he warned me: "Marie-Louise, they are checking corpses in town and have not found your face. They are looking for you. You must leave, because if they find you here in my home, then they will fine me with my life."

That night, he took us to a Hutu acquaintance of his who was hiding a small number of Tutsi acquaintances. One day, the *interahamwe* came knocking on the door to search the house. The lady of the house went out to talk to them, she returned, and she said: "Has anyone got any money on them?" I gave her a wad of notes I carried in my cloth. She kept a small amount for herself, she went back out to the *interahamwe,* who left. Every day, the bargaining began again, and the woman was becoming very nervous. One day, Monsieur Florient warned me: "Marie-Louise, the young men in town hold too great a grudge against you, you must leave." I repeated to him: "Florient, you have the materials, kill me. I want to die in a house. Do not abandon me in the hands of the *interahamwe.*" He said:

"I am not going to kill my wife's friend. If I found transport, would you have money to pay for it?" I gave him another wad of notes, he counted them out and said: "That is quite something, sure to be enough." He came back again and suggested: "We will put you in a sack and take you into the forest, then you will have to fend for yourself." At the same time he asked: "The *interahamwe* have looted your house, the soldiers will leave with money. Is it right that I who have saved you will have nothing to show for it?" So I said to him: "Florient, I have two villas in Kigali, take them. The shop in the high street, I leave it to you. I will sign a paper granting you the power of attorney over everything. But I want you to accompany me to Burundi."

We left—me lying down in an army van between the driver and Florient. I first stayed in his house at the military base at Gako. I was locked up in a bedroom. When everyone was asleep, someone brought me food. I only had a cloth on me. This lasted weeks, I do not know how long anymore. One night, a friend of Florient's came in. He explained: "The *inkotanyi* are coming at speed, we are going to evacuate the barracks. It's too awkward to keep you here. I have to take you away." He put me aboard a truck which delivered sacks to the front. We drove—all road blocks opened up for us—we entered a dark forest, the driver stopped beneath the trees. I shivered and said to him: "Alright, I have nothing left. It is my turn to die now. As long as it is fast." He answered: "Marie-Louise, I am not going to kill you here, because I work for Florient. Go straight as a die, and never stop. When the forest comes to an end, you will lay your hand on the Burundi frontier-post and on deliverance." I walked, I fell, I crawled on my hands and knees. When I came to the frontier-post, I heard voices calling out in the dark, I fell asleep.

Later, a Burundian associate of my husband came in a van to collect me from the refugee camp. When he looked at me, he did not recognise me. He did not even want to believe I was Léonard's wife. I had lost twenty kilos, I was wearing a cloth made out of sacking, I had swollen feet, a head full of lice. Monsieur Florient now awaits trial at the prison in Rilima. He was an officer. He left every morning and every evening came back with tales of the killings in town. In the corridor I saw piles of new axes and machetes. He spent my money, he looted my wares. Despite this, never will I go to court to accuse him, because, when all anyone could think of was killing, he saved one life.

I returned to Nyamata at the end of the genocide in July. Not a single member of my family in Mugesera had survived, not a single member of my family in Nyamata either, the neighbouring folk were dead, the warehouse looted, the trucks stolen. I had lost everything, I was indifferent to life. Nyamata was very desolate, since all the roofs, all the doors and windows, had been taken off. But it was above all time itself that seemed broken in the town. It seemed as though it had stopped forever or, on the contrary, had flown all too quickly in our absence. I mean that we no longer knew when it had all begun, the number of days and nights it had lasted, what season it was, and truly in the end we didn't care. The children went out to catch hens in the undergrowth; we started to eat meat, we began to fix things, we tried to get back into at least some of the old routines. We took one day at a time, which we spent seeking the company of friends with whom we could spend the night, so as to avoid running the risk of dying, forsaken in a nightmare.

> Source: Jean Hatzfeld (ed.), *Into the Quick of Life. The Rwandan Genocide: The Survivors Speak* (London: Serpent's Tail, 2005), 87–92. Used by permission of Other Press and Profile Books.

Commentary

Hutu antipathy toward Tutsis predated the Rwandan Genocide by several decades. Although the relationship between Tutsis and their Hutu neighbors prior to the 1950s had essentially been based on feudal hierarchy and dominance, Tutsi-Hutu connections were, for the most part, peaceful. The approach of the end of colonial rule, however, overturned the situation, with the Hutus claiming majority rights. After Rwanda's independence from Belgium, frequent Hutu persecutions of Tutsis took place. One such outburst had already taken place in 1959; major outbursts of escalating violence also occurred in 1962 and 1973.

In the first paragraph of Marie-Louise Kagoyire's story of survival, she refers to those past massacres and the fact that the love of her life, her husband Léonard, experienced them firsthand in his youth. Based on his experiences, Léonard knew that the situation in April 1994 was "catastrophic." But he refused to flee, declaring that "his legs had already done enough running."

Marie-Louise describes how on April 11, the first morning of the killings in her district, a large number of *Interahamwe* appeared "right in front of our gate." Hoping there might be a measure of negotiation that could save the lives of the women and children, Léonard complied immediately when the *Interahamwe* demanded that he open the gate. Doing so did not save his own life; he was shot immediately. The *Interahamwe* entered the courtyard en masse and slaughtered all the children. Before they began to kill the women, they went on a looting spree, enabling Marie-Louise and her mother-in-law to escape. The *Interahamwe* stole cars and vans, loaded them with crates of Primus beer and furniture, and pilfered whatever money they could find.

During the genocide, as we know, Tutsis sought sanctuary in churches, in schools, and with the United Nations. Many of those targeted who could not find sanctuary, when faced with the imminence of death by machete, sought release through other, less horrible, means. Marie-Louise was herself confronted with this when she encountered one of her Hutu neighbors, Florient, who was the head of military intelligence in Rwanda's eastern region of Bugesera. Terrified by the prospect of humiliation, rape, and murder, she begged him to kill her: "Do not expose me to the *interahamwe* who will undress and chop me." Florient refused to kill her (she repeated the request a second time), and instead offered to find a way to get her to safety if she could pay for her transport. His motives were far from altruistic— noting that the *Interahamwe* were leaving her home with loot and money, he asked her, "Is it right that I who have saved you will have nothing to show for it?" Marie-Louise transferred the title deeds of her two villas and a shop in Kigali to Florient, who then organized a truck to take her to safety.

While this is an example of a Hutu helping a Tutsi, that help was given with an eye to personal gain. It is doubtful that Florient operated from purely honorable motives. We must wonder how forthcoming his assistance would have been if Marie-Louise had not possessed property he coveted.

Still, the action did save her life. After leaving Nyamata in a truck Florient had arranged to take her through the roadblocks, Marie-Louise hid in Florient's house at the Rwanda Military Academy in Gako, about 30 miles southeast of Kigali.

Florient, a senior officer in the *Forces Armées Rwandaises,* the Rwandan regular army, was arrested after the victory of the RPF in July 1994. Marie-Louise recalls that during her enforced confinement in his house he "left every morning and every evening came back with tales of the killings in town." Within the camp compound, she saw "piles of new axes and machetes," over which, she suggests, he had control. He was, quite simply, a *génocidaire* and war criminal. Conscious that he robbed her, looted her house, and forced her to relinquish control over her properties, Marie-Louise did not, however, bring charges or testify against him. Her rationale was that, "When all anyone could think of was killing, he saved one life."

After Marie-Louise had spent weeks living in a locked bedroom in Florient's home, the barracks at Gako were hurriedly evacuated when it seemed as though units of the RPF—referred to in the testimony as the *inkotanyi* (rebels)—were about to overrun the area. One of Florient's friends, in this case someone with nothing to gain, helped Marie-Louise escape by taking her to an approach point that would eventually lead to safety at the Burundian border.

Marie-Louise found sanctuary in a refugee camp in Burundi. When, finally, she was repatriated after the genocide to Rwanda via a colleague of her late husband Léonard, she was unrecognizable. She had lost nearly 45 pounds, wore clothing made out of sacking, had swollen feet, and her head was full of lice. Her hometown of Mugesera, to which she returned, was a site of devastation. Not a single member of her family had survived. The same was true of the family of her in-laws in Nyamata. All her neighbors were dead, and the physical surroundings were destroyed utterly.

In an insightful comment, Marie-Louise notes, "It was above all time itself that seemed broken." It appeared as though time "had stopped forever or, on the contrary, had flown all too quickly in our absence." The period of the genocide had put her surroundings in a state of suspended animation, such that "we no longer knew when it had all begun, the number of days and nights it had lasted, what season it was." With their country in urgent need of rebuilding, Marie-Louise and the other survivors would have to get on with their lives. They would have to attempt to regain something of what had been, in the hope that they could create a future. They sought each other's company "so as to avoid running the risk of dying, forsaken in a nightmare."

Questions

1. Marie-Louise survived as a result of Monsieur Florient's greed. If he had not known that Marie-Louise had property he could steal, do you think he would have been so accommodating? Why or why not?
2. What evidence did Marie-Louise see of genocide while she was being hidden in the military camp?
3. Describe, in your own words, what you think Marie-Louise meant when she said time "stopped forever" during the genocide.

RÉVÉRIEN RURANGWA

Révérien Rurangwa's account of how he managed to cheat death at the hands of the Interahamwe *is both riveting and disturbing—and for many, highly confronting. Révérien was a 15-year-old boy at the time of the genocide. The experience he describes would seem astonishing even if it were fiction; that it really happened is borne out by his scars, which even today he is reluctant to have removed through surgery. They are, as he sees it, a living reminder of what the spirit of "never again" should mean. In his account, he relates his efforts to be put out of his misery by seeking death, after having been assaulted by the machetes of the same people who murdered all 43 members of his family before his very eyes.*

On the threshold of the hut, dazed and staggering, I sense the end is nigh. Finally. Behind me lies the inferno. Before me await the machetes. All my being yearns for the pain to be over. The exterminators can hardly believe their eyes when they see a survivor emerging from the flames. Thousands and thousands of corpses carpet the hillside, not counting those in the various buildings and in the church. Sibomana bursts out laughing as he comes towards me: "Look! It's the eldest Tutsi child sticking his nose out the door!" In an extremely swift arc, he slices my face at nose height. (Tutsis do not have the flattened nose of the Hutu—is this another reason for jealousy? During the genocide, they paid particular attention to correcting this natural difference.)

Another killer deals me a blow with a studded club. He misses my head and hits my shoulder. I topple to the ground. My nose, now attached by just the edge of my nostril, dangles in front of my mouth. Sibomana changes machete. He grabs a hooked blade which we normally use for cutting banana leaves. He lunges at my face again and the curved metal snags my left eye. Another blow to the head. Now one to my neck. They circle me, taking turns to strike. A lance is aimed at my chest, another at my groin. Their faces dance above my head. The branches of the great acacia tree begin to swirl round. I sink into the void. ...

They have killed me but I can't quite manage to die. At least, I think I'm still alive, which actually seems impossible to me. I can feel damp mist on my burning face. How long did I black out for? I've really no idea. The acacia branches protect me from rain. Our assassins have gone. The hut is no longer there. Even the bricks seem to have melted away. An arm juts out from the pile of ashes; it's probably my uncle Jean's. I crawl over to the pyre, which is smouldering, belching out an acrid, unbearable odour from the burned corpses. It's impossible to tell the charred bodies apart. Teeth are all that remain of my loved ones. Dozens of sets of teeth look at me and seem to smile.

I want to get away from this horror film. I want it all to stop. I want to sleep, to sink into oblivion, plunge into the abyss, into the shifting sands where consciousness fades away and with it, the procession of monstrous images, and the suffering. Sleep or die, what does it matter, so long as I never wake up again.

I am dead but not dead enough. I can't quite manage it alone. I need help. I need someone to finish me off. Quickly.

Some Hutu girls are roaming over the hillside, zigzagging among the bodies, offering water. It's a trap. As soon as one of the dying asks for a drink, they point him out to a militiaman who comes to finish him off. "Here's one, and another there!" It's a game that children can play. Of course, the girls don't actually waste their water by giving it to those condemned to death. But why do they not come when I call to them? Do I repulse them so much?

I try to haul myself up. My ankles have not been hacked nor my legs slashed. I manage to advance three paces; I collapse, then drag myself up. Just a few days ago, I was bounding around like a gazelle, and here I am struggling to make one step without panting and shivering. I approach the gang of killers. Crouched close to the other acacia tree, they divvy up their booty.

"Kill me! Please, kill me!" I beg them.

"What, Tutsi, you're still here?! You're a tough nut to crack!"

"Finish me off, kill me."

"Killing you would be too kind," one says.

"Why should we get our hands dirty?" adds another. "Have you seen how filthy you are?"

I can see nothing, I've only got one eye. And anyway, looking at myself is the last thing I want to do right now. I sense that I'm a walking crust of dried blood, one enormous wound, a brownish phantom with a staggering gait. Am I suffering? I can barely reply. My body hurts, my heart hurts, my soul hurts. Is it possible to be in any more pain? Since Sibomana does not want to end my suffering, I go to ask another Hutu. I begin to creep along the edge of the football field, amid the rotting bodies, the crows pecking their eyes out and the dogs worrying the pink flesh of dying babies, but not a single militiaman wants to put me out of my misery.

If my dried-up mouth could pronounce the words, it would say: "For pity's sake, just one swipe of the machete, please! Can't you just do that for me? Look, the job's been started, all you need is to finish it off. Just one little nick behind the ear, and there you are! It's nothing to you, one blow of the blade, you've swiped thousands these past few days, why not just one more?" But seeing a cockroach crawling through the mud is clearly much too amusing for them to want to put an end to it.

It takes a good couple of hours, sometimes creeping, sometimes shuffling on my buttocks, sometimes stumbling on my haunches, to cover the 300 metres of road that separates the church from the town hall. The main courtyard in front of it has been transformed into a canteen. Around one hundred Hutus are draining beer bottles and on improvised barbecues are grilling hunks of meat from our cows (which they killed by slicing the tendons of their hind legs in order to make them suffer as well). They cry out when they see me.

"Hey Tutsi, go die somewhere else, you're putting me off my food."

"You're going to croak anyway, Tutsi, so why should we help you?" yells another.

I think I can hear the noise of further debauchery in the dispensary, which is about a hundred metres from the town hall. Perhaps in there there's a chance someone will finish me off: it was there I was born fifteen years ago. The suffocating smell of burned meat fills the air and blots out the stench of the dead bodies. (I am still incapable of describing exactly what sort of mental state I was in during those hours. I only remember that I was obsessed by wanting to end the interminable suffering that devoured me, of which the physical pain was but a minor symptom.)

I progress on my buttocks, like a child on the beach sliding down towards the sea. My throat is on fire, my palate sticks, my mouth feels like clay. My nose bats at my lips, the skin from my sliced neck flaps and joggles about. The Hutus struggle to believe that I am still alive. They laugh and hurl abuse at me. "Hey, Dead-on-Legs, can't you go any faster?!" Another dubs me "the Walking Dead" and he's not wrong. But they do not want to finish me off. My torture becomes a game for them. Some take bets on how long I'll keep going. "Two primus stoves that he'll last till dawn!"

Since I can't seem to manage to die, I'm at least going to try to quench the thirst that is burning my throat. I creep off up towards the church. "Hi there, cockroach." "Faster, Tutsi cockroach!" I creep and I crawl. I have taken the *pange* wrap from a corpse because I'm frozen. It's not raining any more but a damp, greyish mist clothes the hillside. On my left is a banana plantation. I let myself slide into the ditch. More crawling, into the field, towards a tree-trunk. Two hundred metres away, I glimpse the church, and I wonder at the strange silence shrouding it. There are light silences and there are heavy silences. This one is heavier than a tomb. I have little difficulty imagining what must have happened.

Those bastards must have really got off on penetrating that jam-packed sanctuary. All that crowd to scythe through, and no emergency exit. The two entrance doors—one opening on to the Kigali road, the other on the right, giving on to the bottom of the football pitch—are both blocked off by the militias' side-kicks. They get down to work, slowly but surely, amid the screams and panic which just excite the pleasure of those cowards. Three weeks ago, most of the assassins had been praying in that church, alongside those they are now murdering, between the pews, on the steps of the chancel, in the sacristy.

Gratia Musabende was a beautiful woman with clear skin. The wife of our neighbor Sylvestre Nkingiye, son of old André Gakara, she just gave birth to twin boys the night before. These little innocents are lying on the church altar, in the chancel, with their mother, who has been hacked and laid out on the sacrificial stone. Survivors will later testify that the killers, after smashing the skulls of the two babies against the great pink wall of the building, rubbed the mother's face in the infants' blood, before sacrificing her.

After the genocide, this same church was completely scoured with copious amounts of bleach when the missionaries returned. People worship there now as they did before; yesterday's assassins are in the front rows and God's forgiveness—which incidentally they haven't asked for since it's not a sin to kill a Tutsi—seems a foregone conclusion, judging by their smug faces. Everyone carries on as if nothing had happened. This general hypocrisy pollutes the atmosphere.

Only a small octagonal memorial, comprising three symbolic coffins, erected on the old football pitch, reminds us that this parish was, like the hillside on which it is perched, the site of an enormous and methodical massacre.

There is not a church in Rwanda untouched by Tutsi blood. If, as Catholic faith demands it, we join here to celebrate the memory of Christ's sacrifice, there is another sacrifice mixed up in it: that of the innocents.

But for now, I'm not thinking mystical thoughts. Those reflections will come later, much later. For the moment, I want to drink; I want to dampen the blazing oven that is my mouth, put out the fire. Blood worsens thirst. Twenty hours have passed since, like an animal, I lapped up the few drops of milk at the bottom of my grandmother's pots (she would forbid me to drain them dry because, in her words,

"You should always leave a little for the gods at the bottom of the pot"). It was while I was trying to retrieve the hand that had flown behind me after a swipe of the machete that I found her bag and the remains of the precious liquid, which quite probably saved my life.

As a child, while we tended the cattle, we would enjoy pricking the banana trees with little hollow sticks in so we could suck up the sap. I gather up a branch and jab mine into the trunk of the tree. It splinters. A second attempt works. I greedily suck at the improvised straw. The sticky, sugary sap is not refreshing but it soothes the burning in my throat, and so gives me some strength. I fill up on banana plant juice and head back off. I want to die near my own kin, what is left of them. I want to lie down next to the funeral pyre and wait for the end to come.

On the way, lines of Hutus move slowly along, tired out, bearing reddened machetes, as if they are returning from a long day's labouring in the fields. I try to climb towards the church and the hut with the aid of a stick. Strangely, in the midst of the overriding pain radiating across my body, there is a more horrible feeling making itself felt: that of disgust. I walk over bloated, decomposing bodies, my feet sinking into burst stomachs, the stench billowing, the maggots squirming. My feet have swollen up from trampling over the dead. I hold up my injured arm to stop the bleeding and force myself to look at the sky. Crows whirl and caw above, stray dogs yelp between mouthfuls. For the Hutus and these other predators, it's party-time. They've had a food haul.

Source: Révérien Rurangwa, *Genocide: My Stolen Rwanda* (London: Reportage Press, 2009), 51–57.

Commentary

To say that this is a remarkable piece of testimony would be a gross understatement. While most of the accounts from genocide survivors in this book have been told at enormous emotional cost, none has been composed in the present tense, as though the horrendous events being described are taking place in real time. Moreover, none describes the agony or sense of fatalism of this account. This is a unique narrative of a most intimate—and truly heart-rending—nature.

Révérien Rurangwa was born in 1978 in the tiny village of Mugina, in the province of Gitarama. On April 20, 1994, 43 members of his family were murdered there. It was intended that he, too, should die. He was ultimately the only survivor in his entire family.

In the immediate aftermath of President Habyarimana's plane being shot down and the start of the genocide, Révérien Rurangwa and his family hid, in silence, in their small cabin on the hillside of Mugina. This precarious existence came to a sudden end on the afternoon of April 20, when their Hutu neighbors caught up with them. These were people who had been friends and workmates, but they closed in as if Rurangwa's family members were mortal enemies. Within minutes, the whole family had been massacred. Révérien was the only witness. The murderers then set fire to the building in which the killings had taken place, just as Rurangwa, with part of his hand cut off, managed to reach the door. This is where the present account begins.

The graphic nature of the account almost defies description, as we see a young man desperately seeking death. He says of his murderers, "They have killed me but I can't quite manage to die." Upon further reflection, in what must have been a swirling mass of confusion coupled with pain, anxiety, and extreme grief, he muses: "At least, I think I'm still alive, which actually seems impossible to me."

Following the murders, fire, and departure of the killers, Rurangwa manages to crawl back into the burned-out ruin of the hut, only to find that there is nothing left but the charred remains of dismembered bodies. He sees that "it's impossible to tell the charred bodies apart." Teeth, he notes, "are all that remain of my loved ones. Dozens of sets of teeth look at me and seem to smile."

A second attack on what is left of Rurangwa's mangled body, led by his Hutu neighbor Simon Sibomana, leaves him with part of an arm ripped off, an eye gone, his nose "now attached by just the edge of my nostril," and a horribly gashed face. Under such circumstances, survival no longer seemed worth the effort.

It would be superfluous—and inadequate—here simply to summarize Révérien Rurangwa's story. His words themselves are what matter, as it is these that provide the best illustration of what the reality of genocide is for those who experience it.

Consider, for example, a young man who has seen his whole family be wiped out before his very eyes, who has himself been sliced and hacked mercilessly by his own neighbor. That same young man, in excruciating physical and emotional pain, now begs his killer to take his life—but in vain. As Rurangwa's story unfolds, we see him hauling his broken body from place to place, and from killer to killer, beseeching them with the same request. All he is met with is mirth. This is an account that does not ask us to imagine; the details are there already. It is only the limitations of language that deny us the opportunity to achieve full understanding.

In many respects, Rurangwa's account can be seen as a complement to those of Els de Temmerman and Fergal Keane, both in this volume. In de Temmerman and Keane's accounts, in which we see the aftermath of the killing, Western journalists attempt to describe for their readers what they have witnessed. De Temmerman's camera crew announces that "we'll never get this published"; "nobody in Europe," they say, "wants to see this." Fergal Keane, in his diary entry about entering the murder site at Nyarubuye, records that he is asked by one of his companions, "Can you imagine what these poor bastards went through?" Keane responds, "No, I cannot imagine it because my powers of visualization cannot possibly imagine the magnitude of the terror."

In Révérien Rurangwa's description of his own torment, he provides a glimpse of what it was like to be one of those "poor bastards." This raises a question that must be asked: How representative is Rurangwa's account of what happened throughout Rwanda in the three months following April 6, 1994?

In many respects, what happened to the family of Révérien Rurangwa was typical in form, if not in detail. Across the country, the chosen method of killing was face-to-face, and the chosen device was a farming implement. (The weapons were mostly machetes, which were distributed by government authorities, but often the daily tools of an agricultural community, such as hoes, pruning hooks, and scythes, were also used. Sometimes a specially designed tool, the nail-studded club, was employed.) What this signifies is that Rurangwa's family met its tragic and grisly fate in a manner that was repeated, with variations, all over Rwanda during the hundred days of genocide.

What *is* unusual is Rurangwa's survival, as well as the spellbinding nature of his testimony, and the fact that he has been able to relate his story with such an even voice. His is an account with much to offer successive generations, particularly those with an eye to educating humanity.

Questions

1. Would you describe Révérien Rurangwa as a victim, a witness, or both? Give reasons for your answer.
2. Why do you think the Hutus Rurangwa encountered, when he begged them to kill him, only responded with sarcasm and laughter?
3. If you could ask one question of Rurangwa, what would it be? Explain the thinking behind your question.

"WITNESS JJ"

In 1997 the trial of Jean-Paul Akayesu (b. 1953), the former mayor of the village of Taba, commenced at the International Criminal Tribunal for Rwanda (ICTR). At one point during the trial, a so-called "secret witness," known only by the initials JJ, appeared. Her testimony was one of the accounts that led to Akayesu being sentenced to life imprisonment for genocide. A Tutsi from Taba, JJ lived with her husband, sister, and four children before the genocide. After April 1994, the farm on which she lived was attacked. Three of her children fled. Her sister was severely wounded by machete cuts and became lost. In the confusion, JJ managed to escape with her baby son. She fled to the bureau communale, *where she sought protection from Akayesu, but it had been taken over by the* Interahamwe. *During the days that followed,*

*she and other Tutsi women were subjected to repeated beatings and system-
atic rapes. Part of her shocking testimony before the ICTR is produced here.*

---

418. Following the amendment of the Indictment, Witness JJ, a Tutsi woman, testified about the events which took place in Taba after the plane crash. She [testified]
that she was driven away from her home, which was destroyed by her Hutu neighbours who attacked her and her family after a man came to the hill near where she
lived and said that the bourgmestre had sent him so that no Tutsi would remain on
the hill that night. Witness JJ saw her Tutsi neighbours killed and she fled, seeking
refuge in a nearby forest with her baby on her back and her younger sister, who had
been wounded in the attack by a blow with an axe and two machete cuts. As she
was being chased everywhere she went, Witness JJ said she went to the bureau
communal. There she found more than sixty refugees down the road and on the
field nearby. She testified that most of the refugees were women and children.

419. Witness JJ testified that the refugees at the bureau communal had been
beaten by the Interahamwe and were lying on the ground when she arrived. Witness
JJ encountered four Interahamwe outside the bureau communal, armed with knives,
clubs, small axes and small hoes. That afternoon, she said, approximately forty
more Interahamwe came and beat the refugees, including Witness JJ. At this time
she said she saw the Accused, standing in the courtyard of the communal office,
with two communal police officers who were armed with guns, one of whom was
called Mushumba. Witness JJ said she was beaten on the head, the ribs and the
right leg, which left her disabled. That evening, she said, the Accused came with a
policeman to look for refugees and ordered the Interahamwe to beat them up, calling them "wicked, wicked people" and saying they "no longer had a right to
shelter." The refugees were then beaten and chased away. Witness JJ said she was
beaten by the policeman Mushumna, who hit her with the butt of his gun just behind her ear.

420. Witness JJ testified that she spent the night in the rain in a field. The next
day she said she returned to the bureau communal and went to the Accused, in a
group of ten people representing the refugees, who asked that they be killed as the
others had been because they were so tired of it all. She said the Accused told them
that there were no more bullets and that he had gone to look for more in Gitarama
but they had not yet been made available. He asked his police officers to chase
them away and said that even if there were bullets they would not waste them on
the refugees. As the refugees saw that death would be waiting for them anywhere
else, Witness JJ testified they stayed at the bureau communal.

421. Witness JJ testified that often the Interahamwe came to beat the refugees
during the day, and that the policemen came to beat them at night. She also testified

that the Interahamwe took young girls and women from their site of refuge near the bureau communal into a forest in the area and raped them. Witness JJ testified that this happened to her—that she was stripped of her clothing and raped in front of other people. At the request of the Prosecutor and with great embarrassment, she explicitly specified that the rapist, a young man armed with an axe and a long knife, penetrated her vagina with his penis. She stated that on this occasion she was raped twice. Subsequently, she told the Chamber, on a day when it was raining, she was taken by force from near the bureau communal into the cultural center within the compound of the bureau communal, in a group of approximately fifteen girls and women. In the cultural center, according to Witness JJ, they were raped. She was raped twice by one man. Then another man came to where she was lying and he also raped her. A third man then raped her, she said, at which point she described herself as feeling near dead. Witness JJ testified that she was at a later time dragged back to the cultural center in a group of approximately ten girls and women and they were raped. She was raped again, two times. Witness JJ testified that she could not count the total number of times she was raped. She said, "each time you encountered attackers they would rape you,"—in the forest, in the sorghum fields. Witness JJ related to the Chamber the experience of finding her sister before she died, having been raped and cut with a machete.

422. Witness JJ testified that when they arrived at the bureau communal the women were hoping the authorities would defend them but she was surprised to the contrary. In her testimony she recalled lying in the cultural center, having been raped repeatedly by Interahamwe, and hearing the cries of young girls around her, girls as young as twelve or thirteen years old. On the way to the cultural center the first time she was raped there, Witness JJ said that she and the others were taken past the Accused and that he was looking at them. The second time she was taken to the cultural center to be raped, Witness JJ recalled seeing the Accused standing at the entrance of the cultural center and hearing him say loudly to the Interahamwe, "Never ask me again what a Tutsi woman tastes like," and "Tomorrow they will be killed" (Ntihazagire umbaza uko umututsikazi yari ameze, ngo kandi mumenye ko ejo ngo nibabica nta kintu muzambaza. Ngo ejo bazabica). According to Witness JJ, most of the girls and women were subsequently killed, either brought to the river and killed there, after having returned to their houses, or killed at the bureau communal. Witness JJ testified that she never saw the Accused rape anyone, but she, like Witness H, believed that he had the means to prevent the rapes from taking place and never even tried to do so. In describing the Accused and the statement he made regarding the taste of Tutsi women, she said he was "talking as if someone were encouraging a player" (Yavugaga nk'ubwiriza umukinnyi) and suggested that he was the one "supervising" the acts of rape. Witness JJ said she did not witness any killings at the bureau communal, although she saw dead bodies there.

423. When Witness JJ fled from the bureau communal, she left her one year-old child with a Hutu man and woman, who said they had milk for the child and subsequently killed him. Witness JJ spoke of the heavy sorrow the war had caused her. She testified to the humiliation she felt as a mother, by the public nudity and being raped in the presence of children by young men. She said that just thinking about it made the war come alive inside of her. Witness JJ told the Chamber that she had remarried but that her life had never been the same because of the beatings and rapes she suffered. She said the pain in her ribs prevents her from farming because she can no longer use a hoe, and she used to live on the food that she could grow.

Source: International Criminal Tribunal for Rwanda, decision of September 2, 1998. Available online at http://www.unictr.org/Portals/0/Case/English/Akayesu/judgement/akay001.pdf.

Commentary

The trial of Jean-Paul Akayesu, the former mayor of the Rwandan village of Taba, was the first genocide trial in history. Initially, Akayesu was charged with encouraging the killing of Tutsis, directly ordering the killing of numerous individuals, and supervising the interrogation, beating, and execution of people from Taba. Ultimately, three additional counts of genocide and crimes against humanity were added to the charges, alleging that he had ordered and condoned the rape and sexual mutilation—and then, the murder—of hundreds of Tutsi women.

Akayesu pleaded not guilty on all counts. His primary defense was that he had played no part in the killings, and that he had been powerless to stop them. His essential claim was that at the time of the genocide, he had not been in a position of authority. His attorneys argued that Akayesu was being made a scapegoat for the people of Taba who did commit crimes.

The trial judges found that, in his role as mayor, Jean-Paul Akayesu *was* responsible for maintaining public order and executing the law in the municipality of Taba, and that he had effective authority over the police. On September 2, 1998, Akayesu was found guilty on 9 of the 15 counts with which he had been charged, regarding genocide and crimes against humanity (extermination, murder, torture, rape, and other inhuman acts). This made him the first person convicted of the specific crime of genocide in an internationally accredited courtroom. The guilty verdict also marked the first time the 1948 UN Convention on Genocide was upheld as law. On October 2, 1998, Akayesu was sentenced to life imprisonment for each of the nine counts, with the sentences to run concurrently.

The testimony of a woman known only as Witness JJ played a large part in Akayesu's conviction. Witness JJ, a Tutsi resident of Taba, was called to the stand as a "secret witness"—that is, one who could give evidence but who, for security reasons, kept her identity hidden.

A child in a family of ten, she was raised in two one-story mud brick homes, with a large outdoor kitchen and a barn. She had a basic education, and, when she came of age, she married a salesman and raised a family.

When the genocide came to Taba, Witness JJ's father and brothers were killed almost immediately. Witness JJ tried to escape with her sister and children, but her sister, who had already been injured by machete wounds, became so weak that she could not proceed. After a short time, Witness JJ lost her sister and three of her children, leaving her with only her youngest child, a baby. A Hutu farmer hid them, but when he learned that those hiding Tutsis were being caught and punished (or worse—he did not know what their fate would be), he told Witness JJ to go to the mayor's office in Taba. And with that, her fate was sealed.

After spending that first night in the rain in a field, she returned to the *bureau communal* (municipal chambers). With a group of ten others representing all those endangered, she approached Akayesu and asked that they be killed by bullets rather than have to suffer a more horrible death by machete. Akayesu's attitude was that bullets were in very short supply, and that, in any case, the perpetrators would not waste them on Tutsis. With nowhere else to go, Witness JJ and her fellow Tutsis decided to stay at the *bureau communal* and await developments.

After this, the *Interahamwe* came into the *bureau communale* during daylight hours to beat the refugees. Police repeated the exercise at night. When the *Interahamwe* came in, they also seized young girls and women—including Witness JJ—took them into the forest nearby, and raped them repeatedly. Often, the victims were then killed.

After Witness JJ had been raped for the third time, she described herself as "feeling near dead." She was later raped on two other occasions that she knew of; in all, she said, "she could not count the total number of times she was raped."

Jean-Paul Akayesu's role in all of this horror was one of leadership for the killers. Although the women sought the protection from their mayor, he was seen by the victims to stand to one side and encourage the *Interahamwe.* On one occasion, which will long be remembered as the quintessence of Akayesu's evil, he was overheard saying: "Never ask me again what a Tutsi woman tastes like." While Witness JJ's account relates that she never saw Akayesu himself rape anyone, his encouragement of those who did so made him equally guilty. He also held informal authority, as he was a senior leader of the community whose word would likely have been respected had he sought to intercede on the victims' behalf. Witness JJ concluded that Akayesu was "talking as if someone were encouraging a player"— in effect, "supervising" the acts of rape.

This testimony also includes an example of an all-too-frequent decision Tutsi mothers had to make during the genocide, namely whether to surrender their children to Hutu mothers or couples, in the hope that doing so would improve each child's chance of survival. Witness JJ gave up her one-year-old child to a Hutu couple, only to learn that this did not save his life. It was they, in fact, who killed him later.

In 2005, a made-for-television movie about the Rwandan genocide, *Sometimes in April* (directed by Raoul Peck), premiered, to critical acclaim. In the film, a female character named Valentine, played by Rwandan actress Cleophas Kabasita, took the role of Witness JJ. The testimony Valentine presents was scripted directly from Witness JJ's evidence, including the statement, "I never saw him rape anybody ... but he didn't protect us. He would tell the *Interahamwe*: Don't ever ask me again how a Tutsi woman tastes! He was encouraging his players." Here we see art imitating life in a popular medium, reinforcing and spreading the substance of Akayesu's malevolence.

Questions

1. Witness JJ was a victim of beating and vicious rape at the hands of the police and *Interahamwe*. Why do you think she was treated in such a maliciously cruel manner?
2. In light of Witness JJ's accusations, on what grounds do you think the International Criminal Tribunal for Rwanda should have charged Jean-Paul Akayesu?
3. Now that you have read about Witness JJ's ordeal, if you had the opportunity to ask her one question, what would it be?

HUTU KILLERS

Following his interviews with Rwandan Genocide survivors, which were first published in French in 2000, author and journalist Jean Hatzfeld (b. 1949) took his project in a different direction. He interviewed a number of génocidaires *from the area bordering the Nyamwiza marshland, south of Kigali. The seven short statements reproduced here discuss candidly the killers' recollections about the first time they undertook their grisly work, and they depict what, upon reflection, killing meant for each* génocidaire *on that occasion. The men Hatzfeld interviewed, all in jail serving various sentences, hailed from similar backgrounds, having come from the same region and grown up together. It is a chilling document.*

FULGENCE:

First I cracked an old mama's skull with a club. But she was already lying almost dead on the ground, so I did not feel death at the end of my arm. I went home that evening without even thinking about it.

Next day I cut down some alive and on their feet. It was the day of the massacre at the church, so, a very special day. Because of the uproar, I remember I began to strike without seeing who it was, taking pot luck with the crowd, so to speak. Our legs were much hampered by the crush, and our elbows kept bumping.

At one point I saw a gush of blood begin before my eyes, soaking the skin and clothes of a person about to fall—even in the dim light I saw it streaming down. I sensed it came from my machete. I looked at the blade, and it was wet. I took fright and wormed my way along to get out, not looking at the person anymore. I found myself outside, anxious to go home—I had done enough. That person I had just struck—it was a mama, and I felt too sick even in the poor light to finish her off.

PANCRACE:

I don't remember my first kill, because I did not identify that one person in the crowd. I just happened to start by killing several without seeing their faces. I mean, I was striking, and there was screaming, but it was on all sides, so it was a mixture of blows and cries coming in a tangle from everyone.

Still, I do remember the first person who looked at me at the moment of the deadly blow. Now that was something. The eyes of someone you kill are immortal, if they face you at the fatal instant. They have a terrible black color. They shake you more than the streams of blood and the death rattles, even in a great turmoil of dying. The eyes of the killed, for the killer, are his calamity if he looks into them. They are the blame of the person he kills.

ALPHONSE:

It was before the decision about vast total killings. A group of Tutsis had retreated into the forest of Kintwi to resist. We spotted them behind clumps of trees—they were standing with stones and branches or tools. Grenades from some of our leaders showered onto them. Then came a big to-do. The Tutsis scattered, and we followed them. In the stampede an old man, not so sturdy anymore, was knocked down as he ran. He fell in front of me. I hacked him across his back with my *inkota*, a sharp blade for slaughtering cattle—I had snatched it up that morning.

A youth next to me helped out silently with his machete, as if the victim were his. When we heard the old man finish, my young colleague indicated to me that he had known him for a long time. His own house was just up the hill from the old man's. He said he was well rid of him this way—you could see he was pleased. Me, I knew this old man by name, but I had heard nothing unpleasant about him. That evening I told my wife everything. She knew only routine details about him, we did not discuss it, and I went to sleep.

It had gone smoothly, with no need for me to struggle. Basically, that first time I was quite surprised by the speed of death, and also by the softness of the blow, if I may say so. I had never dealt out death before, never looked it in the face, never considered it. I had never tried it on a warm-blooded animal. Since I was well off, on wedding days or Christmas I used to pay a boy to kill the chickens behind the house—and just avoid all that mess.

JEAN-BAPTISTE:
We were on a path coming back from the marshes. Some youths searched the house of a gentleman named Ababanganyingabo. They frowned on him because this Hutu from Gisenyi was known to consort with Tutsis and might well lend them a hand. They discovered he had helped some Tutsis getaway their cows—behind his house, in a pen, I think. They surrounded the man and pinned him down helpless. Then I heard my name.

They called me out because they knew I was married to a Tutsi. The news about Ababanganyingabo's fix was spreading, people were waiting, all fired up because they had been killing. Someone said to the audience: "Jean-Baptiste, if you want to save the life of your wife Spéciose Mukandahunga, you have to cut this man right now. He is a cheater! Show us that you're not that kind." This person turned and ordered, "Bring me a blade." Me, I had chosen my wife for love of her beauty; she was tall and very considerate, she was fond of me, and I felt great pain to think of losing her.

The crowd had grown. I seized the machete, I struck a first blow. When I saw the blood bubble up, I jumped back a step. Someone blocked me from behind and shoved me forward by both elbows. I closed my eyes in the brouhaha and I delivered a second blow like the first. It was done, people approved, they were satisfied and moved away. I drew back. I went off to sit on the bench of a small *cabaret,* I picked up a drink, I never looked back in that unhappy direction. Afterward I learned that the man had kept moving for two long hours before finishing.

Later on we got used to killing without so much dodging around.

PIO:
I had killed chickens but never an animal the stoutness of a man, like a goat or a cow. The first person, I finished him off in a rush, not thinking anything of it, even though he was a neighbor, quite close on my hill.

In truth, it came to me only afterward: I had taken the life of a neighbor, I mean, at the fatal instant I did not see in him what he had been before: I struck someone who was no longer ordinary anymore, I'm saying like the people you meet every day. His features were indeed similar to those of the person I knew, but nothing firmly reminded me that I had lived beside him for a long time.

I am not sure you can truly understand me. I knew him by sight, without knowing him. He was the first victim I killed; my vision and my thinking had grown clouded.

ÉLIE:

As a retired soldier, I had already killed two civilians during some protest agitation in 1992. The first one was a social worker from the Kanazi area. She was of pleasant reputation and modest renown. I shot an arrow wildly and hit her. I saw her fall, though I did not hear her cries because of the great distance between us. I about-faced and strode off in the opposite direction, seeing nothing of her last moments. Subsequently, I was penalized with a fine. I also heard distant admonitions from her family and threats of jail, but met with no troublesome consequences.

In 1994, during the killings in the marshes, I thought myself very lucky because I could use my former army gun. It's one of our military traditions, to let a non-commissioned officer keep his weapon at the end of his career. Killing with a gun is a game compared to the machete, it's not so close up.

ADALBERT:

The first day, I did not bother to kill directly, because at the start my work was to shout orders and encouragement to the team. I was the boss. Here and there I threw a grenade into the tumult on the other side, but without experiencing the effects of death, except for the shrieks.

The first person I killed with a machete, I don't remember the precise details. I was helping out at the church. I laid on big blows, I struck home on all sides, I felt the strain of effort but not of death—there was no personal pain in the commotion. Therefore the true first time worth telling from a lasting memory, for me, is when I killed two children, April 17.

That morning we were roaming around, looking to rout out Tutsis who might be hidden on plots of land in Rugazi. I came upon two children sitting in the corner of a house. They were keeping quiet as mice. I asked them to come out; they stood up, they wanted to show they were being good. I had them walk at the head of our group, to bring them back to the village square in Nyarunazi. It was time to go home, so my men and I set out, talking about our day.

As leader, I had recently been given a gun, besides the grenades. Walking along, without thinking, I decided to try it out. I put the two children side by side twenty meters away, I stood still, I shot twice at their backs. It was the first time in my life I had used a gun, because hunting is no longer customary in the Bugesera since the wild animals disappeared. For me, it was strange to see the children drop without a sound. It was almost pleasantly easy.

I walked on without bending over to check whether they were really dead. I don't even know if they were moved to a more suitable place and covered up.

Now, too often, I am seized by the memory of those children, shot straight out, like a joke.

Source: Excerpt from "The First Time" from Jean Hatzfeld, *Machete Season: The Killers in Rwanda Speak,* translated by Linda Coverdale. Translation copyright © 2005 by Farrar, Straus and Giroux, LLC. Reprinted by permission of Farrar, Straus and Giroux, LLC, and Profile Books.

Commentary

The act of killing innocent people in large numbers calls for an inversion of the accustomed social order. Genocide requires that men and women engage in acts of destruction they would ordinarily view with abhorrence. Extensive studies conducted by psychologists, criminologists, and sociologists seem to indicate that human beings naturally resist killing members of their own species. When they succumb, most pay a psychological price for doing so.

In wartime, one of the problems faced by soldiers relates to the humanness of their enemy, which renders the object of their hostility all the more difficult to kill. In situations of genocide, however, in which ideology often transforms "the other" into something less than human, killing can be made easier.

In Rwanda, Tutsis were continually referred to as *Inyenzi,* or "cockroaches," rather than human beings, a clear instance of dehumanization being employed to prepare a population to commit genocide. The process of dehumanization does not itself cause genocide, but it is certainly one of a number of steps on the road to it. Perpetrators of genocide can thus degrade the "other" to justify their actions or convince their followers that the "other" is less than human. In Rwanda, for example, Hutu perpetrators would often refer to the Tutsis as something dangerous, filthy, or less than human. From the Hutu perspective, these denunciations also allowed the Tutsis to be portrayed as not worthy of living.

Genocidal killers often report feeling repulsed, sickened, and guilt-ridden about the acts they have performed. We see these responses in the accounts collected by French author Jean Hatzfeld for his compilation *Machete Season: The Killers in Rwanda Speak,* published in English in 2005. For Hatzfeld's study, he interviewed 10 Hutu killers, all friends from the same village. They spent day after day together during the genocide, fulfilling orders to kill any Tutsis within their territory. Together, they helped to kill 50,000 out of their 59,000 Tutsi neighbors. Hatzfeld interviewed them in prison, where they were either serving out their sentences or awaiting execution. What they revealed was how ordinary people living everyday lives in a farming village could transform into genocidal killers.

The accounts provide extraordinary insight into the actions and thoughts of the killers, as related by the men themselves. At least initially, when the murders began, there seemed to be some recognition by the killers that what they were doing was a violation of the basic rules of society. Any concerns they might have had, however, were quickly forgotten or overcome by repetition of the act of killing within a group that supported and rewarded performance of that act. Some of the killers note how surprised they were that it was so easy to kill.

As the men discuss their first kill, for example, Fulgence demonstrates how difficult it was for these "ordinary men" to accomplish the task demanded of them by the *Interahamwe* militias that had come into their village. In many situations, the militias would sweep through a locality and order the local men to join them in their deadly work, threatening that if the men refused, they would themselves be deemed suspect. As everyone thus became caught up in a nationwide project of slaughter, genocide became a civic virtue; to be a good citizen meant being able to kill those considered to be outside the dominant Hutu group. Fulgence notes that he had to engage in the killing—and did so—but he was not particularly good at it.

Similarly, Pancrace comments that he does not remember his first individual kill. We get the impression that he went into a gathering of Tutsis with his machete in hand, swinging wildly: "I was striking, and there was screaming, but it was on all sides, so it was a mixture of blows and cries coming in a tangle from everyone."

Alphonse, by contrast, needed assistance from a youth next to him. They had seen a group of Tutsis in the Kintwi Forest, where the Tutsis were presumably preparing to resist. As the Hutus charged them, "an old man, not so sturdy anymore" was knocked down and Alphonse "hacked him across his back with my *inkota,* a sharp blade for slaughtering cattle." The young man alongside Alphonse indicated that he had known the old man for a long time, yet another example of the localization of killing that can take place during genocide. Alphonse said that he knew the old man by name, and "had heard nothing unpleasant about him." Alphonse was surprised by the speed with which he could kill and death could come—"and also by the softness of the blow." In a matter-of-fact manner, having never before killed "a warm-blooded animal," he states that he felt rather satisfied that it had all gone so well.

Jean-Baptiste was a Hutu who had married a Tutsi. His testimony relates a choice given to him: either he could kill an innocent Tutsi man named Ababanganyingabo, or Jean-Baptiste's wife would be killed. In an excruciating example of "choiceless choices," Jean-Baptiste chose to kill the man, after which, shaken, he sat quietly with a drink in his hand. Later on, he says, "We got used to killing."

Pio, who had also never killed larger animals before, recognizes that "my vision and my thinking had grown clouded" at the time he killed his neighbor. Élie, who had killed before and knew what it was like to do so, preferred to use his gun because "killing with a gun is a game compared to the machete, it's not so close up." Another of the killers, Adalbert, describes the ease with which he shot two children, but admits that he is often "seized by the memory" of those he murdered, "shot straight out, like a joke."

The accounts collected by Jean Hatzfeld are chilling. They offer insights into the minds of the killers at the time of genocide. At the same time, they challenge us to try to place ourselves in their situation. It is an impossible task, to be sure, but considering it allows us to recognize how it was that presumably normal people allowed themselves to be swept up in a horrific series of events.

Questions

1. Can any general conclusions be drawn regarding the nature of the killing process, as it was viewed by the killers themselves?
2. In what ways do the murderers explain their attitudes toward killing? How do they differ from each other?
3. From your perspective, which of these accounts is the most distressing? Why?

DON MACNEIL AND JEAN DAMASCENE NDAYAMBAJE

Major Don MacNeil, a Canadian soldier serving as an operations officer for the United Nations Assistance Mission for Rwanda (UNAMIR), arrived in Kigali on April 18, 1994, nearly two weeks after President Juvénal Habyarimana's plane had been shot down. Jean Damascene Ndayambaje, head of the Department of Psychology at the National University of Rwanda, Butare, survived the genocide. In this account he questions Major MacNeil about the presumed abandonment of the Tutsis by UNAMIR forces in a specific incident involving the St. André Church. He also inquires about the general situation in the Nyamirambo District of Kigali.

DON MACNEIL:
I will outline some of my memories of Kigali in April through July 1994. I remember, upon my arrival on 18 April 1994, meeting some of the military observers and foreign troops involved in the evacuations and seeing the drawn expressions on their faces as they carried out their duties while civilians were being killed all around them.

I was present at formal discussions where high-ranking members of the (former) Rwandan government gave their guarantee for the safe passage through the city of Rwandan civilians under UNAMIR escort. In one such situation, we were given this agreement by the highest-ranking authority within the (former) government, but the convoy was stopped by drunken militia thugs at a roadblock in complete disregard of the agreement. We would then have to negotiate with one of the

Interahamwe militia while the others waited to kill the people we were trying to evacuate. No matter who the highest-ranking authority was or what assurance they gave, it meant nothing to the militias on the roadblocks.

Agreements for the safe passage of civilians could not be negotiated with the (former) government leadership alone, but rather required the agreement of the heads of various extremist militia and self-defense groups dressed in various uniforms. Each one of them represented a small cell of some self-defense group of a neighborhood.

At one of these meetings, a high-ranking official of the (former) Rwandan gendarmerie was shouted down by local members of the *Interahamwe* during discussions on a plan to evacuate Rwandan civilians trapped in Nyamirambo. The evacuation had to be canceled as the authorities could not guarantee security.

On many occasions, we received requests from people outside of the country that we rescue their friends and family from areas of the city where they were trapped. We received many of these requests, and most of them involved going to extremely dangerous areas of the city. We realized that there were up to 20 or 30 roadblocks to negotiate, and that, with only 250 armed soldiers in the entire country, we did not have the forces to go in and ensure their passage to safety. We often heard, after going to a certain home and not finding people there, that the militia and the *Interahamwe* would follow up and enter the house just after the departure of UN troops.

While the RPF had insisted upon a cessation of the massacres as a prerequisite for a cease-fire, on one occasion I had to inform the deputy force commander, who was chairing the meetings, that in fact another massacre was taking place as the negotiations were in progress.

Armed youths at roadblocks guarded neighborhoods and were on many occasions drunk by 1:00 in the afternoon. As a result, operations after this time were limited due to the unpredictability of what might happen at the roadblocks. We were stopped at one roadblock and a boy only eight or nine years old leaned into the truck with a fragmentation grenade in each of his hands. His task was to be part of the "fighting force" of that particular roadblock.

The phrase *"C'est la guerre, il faut comprendre, c'est la guerre"* (This is war, you must understand, this is war) was an excuse for any form of senseless killing throughout the city.

Also at this time, the former prefect of Kigali's bodyguards was disarmed in Nyamirambo by the militia, who then used the arms to shoot into an orphanage.

There were 24 roadblocks in the Nyamirambo area, and as I tried to negotiate my way through them I was often accused, as a Canadian, of being Belgian and then summarily harassed.

One particular source of frustration was the lack of consistent criteria for passage at the roadblocks. A group of military observers on their way out of town on patrol would negotiate their way through three roadblocks and be turned back at the fourth, only to then have to renegotiate back through the roadblocks they had just passed. Military observers sometimes had to bribe their way through roadblocks. Since the military and the United Nations do not provide soldiers and observers with bribe money, the troops had to use their own money.

Radio RTLM announced over the airwaves that the UNAMIR force commander was an RPF mercenary and also accused him of personally shooting down the president's aircraft on 6 April 1994.

The Ghanaian troops were constantly shot at while evacuating people by convoy. Although endangered and frustrated, the Ghanaians would always show up to continue with the operation the next day.

The International Committee of the Red Cross (ICRC) informed UNAMIR and the local authorities that wounded Rwandan civilians who were being taken by ambulance to the ICRC compound were being dragged from the ambulance and hacked to death in front of the ICRC drivers. This had a significant effect on the force's ability to transport Rwandan civilians in UNAMIR vehicles.

Finally, I must admit that on 4 July, when Kigali city finally fell to the RPF, I felt a great sense of relief. It was amazing to watch how Kigali, after only 72 hours under RPF rule, returned so quickly to a sort of normalcy. There was an immediate change.

JEAN DAMASCENE NDAYAMBAJE:

I was among a group of people who were hiding from the former government troops at Saint André Church in Nyamirambo. We tried to call UNAMIR many times requesting evacuation and yet they did not respond. We wrote a letter to UNAMIR on 1 May—about 100 people signed the letter. On 8 May, the soldiers came and killed 30 people. As the war continued, government soldiers came in and set up a mortar that they fired at the RPA. The RPA would, of course, respond. In early June the soldiers came and killed everyone they could find. Why didn't UNAMIR help the hundreds of people who were trapped at Saint André Church?

DON MACNEIL:

UNAMIR was aware of the request from Saint André Church and was also aware of the situation in the Nyamirambo district. It is important to remember here the size of the UNAMIR force left in Rwanda. There were about 250 armed UNAMIR troops who were already deployed protecting Rwandan civilians who had taken shelter at UNAMIR installations at the Amahoro Stadium, the Mille Collines Hotel, the Hotel Meridien, the King Fayçal Hospital, and the Kigali Airport.

Negotiations with the authorities had been conducted to arrange an evacuation from Saint André Church. Many *Interahamwe* and militias in the area were against the evacuation, and a previous rescue operation at the Mille Collines Hotel had almost resulted in a disaster. A UNAMIR military observer had visited the site with a representative of the prefect of Kigali's office. Upon arrival, the official's bodyguard was disarmed by drunken militia members who then used his gun to fire into an orphanage in the area, as they thought an evacuation operation was in progress. A foreign journalist accompanying the party was shot and seriously wounded.

It is important to remember that the Nyamirambo district had 24 roadblocks manned by armed militias. The district is congested and very narrow—in other words, an excellent ambush area for a convoy. Fighting was also raging at close quarters between the opposing forces. Any decision for an evacuation operation had to be based on its chances of success. We felt that it would require an entire armed force of UNAMIR if we had to fight through the area to evacuate these people. There was also a requirement for a truce in the area that we were unable to obtain. The decision not to deploy was based not only on the risk to the force, but also on the possibility that the passengers in the vehicle would be killed in any attempt to fight through the district to safety.

JEAN DAMASCENE NDAYAMBAJE:
My point is that even at the time that the letter was written by those stranded in Saint André, the UNAMIR forces had come to evacuate the white missionaries who were next door. Is this Chapter 6 applied to some and not to others when it comes to evacuation?

DON MACNEIL:
I knew of no operation planned by UNAMIR to rescue only the white missionaries from Saint André Church. UNAMIR knew that there were two white priests in the area when the fighting began. One of my colleagues, a military observer, was with the representative from the prefect's office on the day the journalist was shot. A white missionary helped the UNAMIR military observer place the wounded journalist in a UNAMIR vehicle and remained in the vehicle when it left the area. This missionary stated that when Saint André Church was attacked, two other white missionaries fled to the ICRC hospital, from where they were brought to UNAMIR headquarters the next day. Both were subsequently interviewed by the international press at UNAMIR headquarters. This is all that I know about the white missionaries who escaped from Saint André Church.

I would also like to add a point on the force commander, General Dallaire. When his force was to be reduced from 2,500 to 400 people, he had two choices. He could have barricaded his troops in the headquarters at the Amahoro Hotel, sandbagged the building, and done nothing but watch what was happening. His other option was to do what he could with the limited forces available to him. He chose the latter.

The force arranged for a transfer of endangered Rwandans between the front lines, attempted to negotiate a cease-fire, guarded citizens who had sought protection at UNAMIR installations, and monitored the security of endangered Rwandan civilians, as guaranteed by the authorities, in areas of the city threatened by *Interahamwe* and militias. The international community must remember that there were only 400 UN troops covering the entire country of Rwanda. The force commander had been promised additional troops, and the troops in place eagerly awaited their arrival, but none arrived until the war was over.

Source: John A. Berry and Carol Pott Berry (eds.), *Genocide in Rwanda: A Collective Memory* (Washington, D.C.: Howard University Press, 1999), 145–149.

Commentary

Within ten days of the outbreak of violence throughout Rwanda, UNAMIR had created what was termed a "Humanitarian Assistance Cell," comprising six military staff drawn from the Military Observer unit. During and after the genocide, Major Don MacNeil worked closely with the humanitarian community, providing advice and (wherever possible) the resources to support the safe delivery of humanitarian aid from all UN and nongovernmental organizations then operating in the country. He planned and coordinated the evacuation of displaced Rwandans through opposing forces' front lines, and negotiated with senior military and civilian representatives from all sides of the conflict. MacNeil was also the person in charge of drafting ceasefire agreements and plans for refugee evacuation and transportation. He was thus an important actor in the tactics adopted by UNAMIR force commander General Roméo Dallaire (b. 1946).

One of the key points of contention in the operation of UNAMIR related not to what it achieved, but, in the eyes of many, what it failed to achieve. UNAMIR, the United Nations Assistance Mission for (often, inaccurately, "in") Rwanda, was a UN peacekeeping operation established by Security Council Resolution 872 to help implement the Arusha Peace Agreement, which had been signed by various parties on August 4, 1993, for the purpose of establishing a lasting peace between the government and the rebel Rwandan Patriotic Front. Its initial mandate was to assist in ensuring the safety of Kigali, monitoring ceasefire and security agreements throughout the country and coordinating humanitarian intervention and relief activities. But during the genocide, between April and July 1994, the mandate was amended to focus on UNAMIR's acting as an intermediary between the killers and victims, and assisting in humanitarian activities.

With this change (by Security Council Resolution 912), the number of troops in UNAMIR was reduced from 2,548 to 270. As the killing intensified, the UN altered the mandate of UNAMIR once again. In Security Council Resolution 918 of May 17, 1994, it imposed an arms embargo against Rwanda, called for urgent international action, and increased UNAMIR's strength to 5,500 troops. None of these arrived in time to make an effective contribution to ending the killing, however.

In one of his last cables to UN Headquarters at the end of the genocide, General Dallaire wrote scathingly of the UN's failure to upgrade UNAMIR's mandate at the time when its military help was most needed to save lives. Summing up, he wrote that the international community and UN member states, with only a few exceptions, had done nothing substantive to help the situation. Debate has since raged over how effective UNAMIR could have been with a more wide-ranging mandate, and with the capacity to use force to reach peace in Rwanda.

The account from Major MacNeil addresses a number of issues pertaining to the problems facing UNAMIR, but it focuses on a specific confrontation, which took place at the St. André School in Nyamirambo, a suburb of Kigali. When the killings started on April 7, 1994, thousands of Tutsis took refuge at the nearby Charles Lwanga Church. After *Interahamwe* militias attacked refugees in the church, the survivors ran into the school compound. Some of those survivors later reported that, in desperation, they contacted the military authorities in Kigali, begging them to send troops. When soldiers did arrive, they joined the militias in the killings. By April 8, hundreds had been massacred in and around the school.

The upshot of this was a murderous cat-and-mouse game—though hardly a game, indeed—over the next month, during which people would come to the school for refuge and hide when they could. More frequently, they would be found out and murdered by marauding militia gangs. Professor Jean Damascene Ndayambaje states, "We tried to call UNAMIR many times requesting evacuation and yet they did not respond," and, "We wrote a letter to UNAMIR on 1 May," with some 100 people signing the letter they hoped would deliver them. Yet all that happened was that, within a week, more soldiers had come and more killings had taken place. Ndayambaje's question is thus one of the most pertinent imaginable: "Why didn't UNAMIR help the hundreds of people who were trapped at Saint André Church?"

MacNeil's response acknowledges that UNAMIR knew about the request from the people at St. André, but he is quick to point out that logistics prevented UNAMIR from doing much that could save lives. The tiny UNAMIR force that remained in Rwanda was desperately trying to provide shelter for Tutsi refugees at the Amahoro Stadium, the Mille Collines Hotel, the Hotel Meridien, the King Faisal Hospital, and the Kigali Airport, and was stretched beyond its capacity to send out any more troops. In one of the more soul-searing dilemmas of the Rwandan tragedy, MacNeil's account shows plainly that there was simply nothing more that could be done, other than to negotiate in the hope that an evacuation from St. André could be arranged. As far as simple tactics, planning, and execution went, wholesale rescue was physically impossible under the circumstances.

The dialogue in the account provides crucial opportunities for reflection on the helpfulness or otherwise of UNAMIR, and brings up serious questions relating to intervention in a genocide. As MacNeil testifies, "Any decision for an evacuation operation had to be based on its chances of success"; such success "would require an entire armed force of UNAMIR if we had to fight through the area to evacuate these people." This was plainly not an option. Moreover, he points out that if an evacuation were to have taken place, a truce would have had to occur too. Any such truce would have risked the safety of the UNAMIR soldiers and the evacuees, should there have been a firefight in an attempt to break through by force.

This account is a valuable documentation of what could and could not be done in the most trying of times. It clarifies why there is, perhaps, a need to reconsider a rush to judgment when assessing the records of would-be rescuers during a period of genocide.

Questions

1. What, in your view, were the major impediments for Major MacNeil as he tried to safeguard lives during the Rwandan Genocide?
2. What criticisms does MacNeil make of the *Interahamwe* as a negotiating partner?
3. Do you think Jean Damascene Ndayambaje's criticism of UNAMIR, over their inability (or was it failure?) to do anything positive to assist the people at St. André School, is justifiable?

FERGAL KEANE

Fergal Keane (b. 1961), an Irish writer and broadcaster, is highly decorated within his profession. In 1990 he was appointed to be the BBC's correspondent in Southern Africa; in this role he covered the collapse of apartheid in South Africa and the Rwandan Genocide of 1994. In Season of Blood, *his book on the postgenocide situation in Rwanda after the journalists were permitted to return, he relates how he and his colleagues reported on a society that had been completely shredded by genocide. Below is a riveting account from his journal, in which he describes his emotions on being confronted with the carnage at the church of Nyarubuye, where an estimated 20,000 people were murdered from April 15 to 17, 1994.*

This was always going to be the hardest part, this remembrance of what lay ahead in the dusk on that night in early June. My dreams are the fruit of this journey down the dirt road to Nyarubuye. How do I write this, how do I do justice to what awaits at the end of this road? As simply as possible. This is not a subject for fine words. We bounce and jolt along the rutted track on an evening of soft, golden light. The air is sweet with the smell of warm savannah grass. Clouds of midges hover around the cars, dancing through the windows. Although I can sense the nervousness of everybody in the car, we are exhausted and hungry from the long day's travelling, and we are too tired to bother fighting off the insects. Moses shifts down into first gear as we face into a long climb. The wheels begin to lose their grip and they spin in the loose sand of the incline. "Oh, shit," mutters Moses. We climb out and begin to shove and push, but the car rolls back down the hill and we have to jump out of the way. The countryside is vastly different to the deep green hills around Byumba. From the top of the hill we can see a great expanse of yellow savannah grass, dotted here and there with thornbush and acacia. Glenn says it reminds him of home. He is right. This could be the bushveld around Louis Trichardt in the far Northern Transvaal. After about fifteen minutes of maneuvering Moses eventually gets the car going again and we move off. Frank has become very quiet and he is fingering the stock of his assault rifle. After about another fifteen minutes we come to a straight stretch of track, wider than before and with a line of tall trees on either side. Up ahead is the façade of a church built from red sandstone. "This is Nyarubuye," says Frank. Moses begins to slow the car down and Glenn is preparing his camera to film. As we drive closer the front porch of the church comes into view. There is a white marble statue of Christ above the door with hands outstretched. Below it is a banner proclaiming the celebration of Easter, and below that there is the body of a man lying across the steps, his knees buckled underneath his body and his arms cast behind his head. Moses stops the car but he stays hunched over the wheel and I notice that he is looking down at his feet.

I get out and start to follow Frank across the open ground in front of the church. Weeds and summer grasses have begun to cover the gravel. Immediately in front of us is a set of classrooms and next to that a gateway leading into the garden of the church complex. As I walk towards the gate, I must make a detour to avoid the bodies of several people. There is a child who has been decapitated and there are three other corpses splayed on the ground. Closer to the gate Frank lifts a handkerchief to his nose because there is smell unlike anything I have ever experienced. I stop for a moment and pull out my own piece of cloth, pressing it to my face. Inside the gate the trail continues. The dead lie on either side of the pathway. A woman on her side, an expression of surprise on her face, her mouth open and a deep gash in her head. She is wearing a red cardigan and a blue dress but the clothes have begun to rot away, revealing the decaying body underneath. I must walk on, stepping over the corpse of a tall man who lies directly across the path, and, feeling the grass brush against my legs, I look down to my left and see a child who has been hacked almost into two pieces. The body is in a state of advanced decay and I cannot tell if it is a girl or a boy. I begin to pray to myself. "Our Father who art in heaven . . . " These are prayers I have not said since my childhood but I need them now. We come to an area of wildly overgrown vegetation where there are many flies in the air. The smell is unbearable here. I feel my stomach heave and my throat is completely dry. And then in front of me I see a group of corpses. They are young and old, men and women, and they are gathered in front of the door of the church offices. How many are there? I think perhaps a hundred, but it is hard to tell. The bodies seem to be melting away. Such terrible faces. Horror, fear, pain, abandonment. I cannot think of prayers now. Here the dead have no dignity. They are twisted and turned into grotesque shapes, and the rains have left pools of stagnant, stinking water all around them. They must have fled here in a group, crowded in next to the doorway, an easy target for the machetes and the grenades. I look around at my colleagues and there are tears in Tony's eyes. Glenn is filming, but he stops every few seconds to cough. Frank and Valence have wandered away from us into a clump of trees and the older man is explaining something to the boy. I do not know what he is saying, but Valence is looking at him intensely. I stay close to David because at this moment I need his age and strength and wisdom. He is very calm, whispering into Glenn's ear from time to time with suggestions, and moving quietly. The dead are everywhere. We pass a classroom and inside a mother is lying in the corner surrounded by four children. The chalk marks from the last lesson in mathematics are still on the board. But the desks have been upturned by the killers. It looks as if the woman and her children had tried to hide underneath the desks. We pass around the corner and I step over the remains of a small boy. Again he has been decapitated. To my immediate left is a large room filled with bodies. There is blood, rust coloured now with the passing weeks, smeared on the walls. I do not know what else to say about the bodies because I have already seen too much. As we pass back across the open ground in front of the church I notice Moses and Edward standing by the cars and I motion to them to switch on the headlights because it is growing dark. The sound of insects grows louder now filling in the churchyard silence. David and the crew have gone into the church and I follow them inside, passing a pile of bones and rags. There are other bodies between the pews and another pile of bones at the foot of the statue of the Virgin Mary. In a cloister, next to the holy water fountain, a man lies with his arms over his head. He must have died shielding himself from the machete blows. "This is fucking unbelievable," whispers Tony into my ear. We are all whispering, as if somehow we might wake the dead with our voices. "It is just fucking unbelievable. Can you imagine what these poor bastards went through?" he continues. And I answer that no, I cannot imagine it because my powers of visualization cannot possibly imagine the magnitude of the terror. David and Glenn say nothing at all and Frank has also lapsed into silence. Valence has gone to join the drivers. I do not know the things Valence has seen before this and he will not talk about them. I imagine that the sight of these bodies is bringing back unwelcome memories. Outside the church the night has come down thick and heavy. Tony shines a camera light to guide our way. Even with this and the car lights I nearly trip on the corpse of a woman that is lying in the grass. Moths are dancing around the lights as I reach the sanctuary of the car. While we are waiting for Glenn and Tony to pack the equipment away, we hear a noise coming from one of the rooms of the dead. I turn to Moses and Edward. "What is that? Did you hear that?" I ask. Edward notices the edge of fear in my voice and strains his ear to listen. But there is no more sound. "It is only rats, only rats," says Moses. As we turn to go I look back and in the darkness see the form of the marble Christ gazing down on the dead. The rats scuttle in the classrooms again.

Source: Fergal Keane, *Season of Blood: A Rwandan Journey* (London: Penguin Viking, 1995), 76–81. Used by permission.

Commentary

Nyarubuye is a district in Kibungo Province, some 87 miles east of the Rwandan capital, Kigali. It was the scene of a major massacre of Tutsis between April 15 and 17, 1994. Led by local mayor Sylvestre Gacumbitsi (b. 1943), whose authority extended to the requisitioning of communal police and the national gendarmerie, *Interahamwe* attacked the parish, where Tutsi refugees and Hutus were assembled. They were armed with machetes and traditional and homemade weapons, as well as rifles and grenades. Gacumbitsi, who orchestrated the massacre's start, addressed the crowd with a megaphone, giving instructions to Hutus to separate themselves from the Tutsis. As soon as most had complied, the communal policemen and *Interahamwe* launched their assault against the refugees within the church grounds.

On April 16, Gacumbitsi went to the precincts of Nyarubuye's Catholic church, again accompanied by a group of attackers armed with machetes, spears, and bows and arrows. As on the previous day, Gacumbitsi led the attack. The *Interahamwe* finished off whatever survivors they could find before engaging in wholesale pillaging of the church compound. The next day, it has been alleged, Gacumbitsi publicly encouraged the rape of any Tutsi women and girls who were still alive. In total, an estimated 20,000 Tutsis were killed between April 15 and 17, 1994, in and around the Nyarubuye Roman Catholic Church where they had taken refuge.

After the genocide, Gacumbitsi was captured and tried before the International Criminal Tribunal for Rwanda. In the Tribunal's judgment of June 17, 2004, he was found guilty of genocide and crimes against humanity of rape and extermination, and was sentenced to 30 years' imprisonment. The conviction was upheld upon appeal on July 7, 2006, and the Appeals Chamber added to Gacumbitsi's convictions—he was additionally found guilty of murder as a crime against humanity. His sentence was increased to life imprisonment.

The Catholic church in Nyarubuye, along with the houses of the nuns and priest where the victims took refuge, is now the site of the Nyarubuye Genocide

Memorial. There are several sites throughout Rwanda where the remains of murdered innocent people, mostly Tutsis, have been memorialized. These include the Gisozi Memorial, located in the Gasabo District in Kigali; the Gisenyi Memorial site; the Nyamata memorial in Bugesera; the Bisesero Memorial in Western Province; and the Ntarama Memorial, about 30 kilometers south of Kigali.

Fergal Keane (b. 1961), a BBC correspondent who was in Rwanda in late May and early June 1994, visited Nyarubuye with a team of other journalists. During the genocide, he kept detailed diary notes; these were later incorporated into his published memoir of the period, *Season of Blood: A Rwandan Journey* (1995). The entries drew from his most intimate reflections of what he had witnessed, and they were written with an immediacy that makes them all the more authentic. While they appear throughout Keane's book, the account here focuses specifically on his visit to Nyarubuye.

Once again, in his testimony, we see firsthand how it was that scenes of mass murder so often took place in churches. Through this one case study, we can begin to see the enormity and horror of genocide. The victims, trusting in the solace of religion and the inviolability of the church, sought shelter in the one place they thought would provide them with sanctuary. In Nyarubyue, the church was a community hub; people would congregate from around the district for services, and children attended school there. Once the genocide began, many of those who would soon become victims immediately flocked to the church of their own accord. After Sylvestre Gacumbitsi began to mobilize the Hutu extremists, those who remained in their homes went to the church, having been directed to do so by their own mayor.

Keane's descriptions of the bodies—especially those of the children—are gruesome, and as he walks around the church complex, almost treading on bodies with every step, we see the universality of the genocide. The response by Keane's colleague from Johannesburg, Tony Wende, expresses the emotions of all present as they roamed around the site: "This is fucking unbelievable. . . . It is just fucking unbelievable. Can you imagine what these poor bastards went through?" In an admission of helplessness, Keane answers, "No, I cannot imagine it because my powers of visualization cannot possibly imagine the magnitude of the terror."

One of the other main features that stands out in Keane's touching reflection relates to the sensory nature of witnessing. While his description of what he *sees* is highly evocative, it is his descriptions of the *smells* of genocide that leave a haunting impression: "Closer to the gate Frank [Ndore, a lieutenant from the RPF guiding the journalists] lifts a handkerchief to his nose because there is smell unlike anything I have ever experienced. I stop for a moment and pull out my own piece of cloth, pressing it to my face. . . . The smell is unbearable here. I feel my stomach heave and my throat is completely dry."

As for the victims, Keane depicts both their innocence and their pain. "In front of me I see a group of corpses. They are young and old, men and women," he writes. Their bodies, as he sees them, "seem to be melting away"; their "terrible faces" display "horror, fear, pain, abandonment." "Here the dead have no dignity," he concludes, as they are "twisted and turned into grotesque shapes."

The scene at the church begins and ends with Keane's reference to a large statue of Christ, with arms outstretched, above the doors of the church. This is one of a number of direct references to Christianity, such as when Keane prays, "Our Father who art in heaven . . . " Later, after he has witnessed the aftermath of even more unimaginable atrocities, he says, "I cannot think of prayers now," as if the horror has made it impossible to invoke God in such a place.

The church building has been cleaned up since that awful visit by Fergal Keane and his colleagues. A memorial and a museum have been established within the former school and convent complex, and the sanctuary remains a functioning church. The local bishop refused to give permission to have the church itself turned into a memorial. It stands as a witness to innumerable horrors, and as a testament that faith is ongoing—it defies the forces that would otherwise destroy decency and righteousness.

Questions

1. As more and more bodies are revealed during his walk through the church compound, how does Keane describe the unfolding horror?
2. What are the reactions of the Rwandans (Frank, Valence, Moses, and Edward) to the Western journalists they are guiding?
3. Can you identify two or three specific incidents or sentences in Keane's account that made a special impression on you? Why did they leave such an impression?

9. The Bosnian Genocide

Bosnia-Herzegovinia was, and remains, a much-disputed region at the crossroads of empires. The Romans, Byzantines, Ottomans, and Habsburgs all sought to gain control of this strategic Balkan territory. All left their mark, especially in the form of a multiethnic population consisting of Croats (Catholics), Serbs (Orthodox), and Bosniaks (Muslims).

During World War II, some Bosniaks collaborated with the Croatian fascist *Ustashe* organization in the formation of a Nazi puppet state called Greater Croatia. The event was accompanied by anti-Serb persecution and mass murder. The memory of this was not lost on future generations of Serbs, especially when Yugoslavia began to disintegrate in the early 1990s.

Under the communist regime of Marshal Josip Broz Tito (1892–1980), the region became the heartland of former Yugoslavia's military industries, the engineers and managers for which were largely drawn from the urban Bosniak population, rather than from the more rural Croat and Serbian populations. At the same time, Bosnia's population became the most ethnically integrated and assimilated of all the Yugoslav republics. This was not enough, however, to stem the tide of hostile ethno-nationalism, especially when it was whipped up by Serbia and Croatia's leaders, Slobodan Milošević (1941–2006) and Franjo Tudjman (1922–1999).

The war for the partition of Bosnia was fought so ferociously that it became a three-way war of atrocities and counter-atrocities involving Milosević, Tudjman, and Bosnian president Alija Izetbegović (1925–2004). Vicious, fratricidal warfare resulted in the deaths of up to 200,000 Bosnian civilians, and in the worst massacres in Europe since the end of World War II. (The most notorious of these was the Serb massacre of some 8,000 Bosnian Muslim men and boys at Srebrenica, in July 1994.)

Characterizing the conflict was the introduction of policies that would become known as "ethnic cleansing," a term used to describe attempts to force minorities off their lands. The many offensives to drive out minority populations intensified with the formation of paramilitary units. While the end goal was the "liberation" of land from its "alien" inhabitants, greater and greater emphasis was placed on killing as a means of ensuring that those displaced would never return. Ethnic cleansing of non-Serb populations became the norm rather than the exception, and it was accompanied by the physical destruction of cultural and religious sites.

Typically, the policy of ethnic cleansing would begin with the harassment of local citizens of an unwanted group, who would be terrorized and intimidated (often in fear of their lives) into leaving their homes. Such terrors could include torture, rape, beatings, mutilation, or the murder of others as an example to the wider population. Sometimes, wholesale murder in large numbers took place. Once an area had been "cleansed" of its unwanted population, the perpetrators moved in their own people, altering the character of the region as though the original owners had never existed. In this way, they laid claim to the region as if of right, with no one able to claim pre-existing title through prior occupation. Genocidal violence characterized the Bosnian Serb tactics meant to destroy the entire Muslim population in Srebrenica and other UN-designated "safe areas."

Particularly during 1992 and 1993, Serbian forces were known to commit mass rape of Bosniak and Croat women in officially created detention centers, or "rape camps." As mass rape became institutionalized, groups of women were enslaved in ethnically cleansed schools, homes, restaurants, and other places, which served as brothels for the Serb fighters. In many cases, the victims and their rapists knew each other before the war. Officers often ordered stimulants for the men in their military units to use.

There were two essential reasons for this strategy. The first was that it would add to the climate of fear, encouraging the forced mass departure of Bosniaks from towns and villages throughout Bosnia and Herzegovina. As part of the campaign of ethnic cleansing, it was meant to instil sufficient fear so that people would leave, coerced by the prevailing climate of terror. It put all women on notice that if they did not leave, they could be subject to rape.

The second reason for the institutionalization of rape was its introduction as an instrument of genocide. Bosniak women of child-bearing age were systematically gang-raped, and not simply to terrorize them. They were subjected to repeated rape in order to destroy their ethnic identity; because they had been raped, upon returning to their communities they would be ostracized. Young women would never marry, and those already married would be divorced. Rape permanently stigmatized them, pushing them to the fringes of society and making them pariahs. Were they to become pregnant—an objective of the rapes, in many cases—they would be doubly "tainted." Children born of rape would be perceived as being of mixed ethnicity, and would not be considered members of the communities into which they were born.

The express purpose of genocidal rape was to humiliate and disgrace the victims and their families, weakening the fabric of the Muslim community. In that sense, mass rape, as practiced in the camps, was part of a genocidal campaign. Additionally, by rendering raped Muslim women "untouchable" and unfit for marriage within Bosniak society, the Serbs reduced the available pool of women from whom the next generation could be born. The rapes reduced the number of Muslim children and increased the number of Serb children.

By way of response to the Serbs' ethnic cleansing operations, the United Nations established a number of what it referred to as "safe areas" during the conflict. UN humanitarian relief efforts to deliver food, medical supplies, and the like to the safe areas were, however, constantly hampered by Serb interference. Frequently, the safe areas became little more than besieged towns and cities that were poorly guarded by UN troops with inadequate mandates.

In the spring of 1993, the UN named six locations as safe areas: Bihać, Goražde, Sarajevo, Srebrenica, Tuzla, and Žepa. As a city under siege, Srebrenica found itself constantly suffering from privation. The Serb army tested the resolve of the United Nations Protection Force (UNPROFOR) troops guarding the city by blocking UN aid convoys. By holding out like the capital city Sarajevo, Srebrenica became a symbol of Bosniak resistance, but on July 6, 1995, its defiance came to an end.

Encouraged by UN equivocation over whether or not to maintain the "safe areas" initiative, Bosnian Serb general Ratko Mladić (b. 1942) led a 10-day campaign to take over the town. As the campaign was getting underway, thousands of Srebrenica's men and boys fled the city in order to reach Muslim fighters beyond the hills, presumably hoping to lead the fighters back to defend their loved ones. Women, children, and the elderly were for the most part loaded onto Serb-chartered buses and evacuated. Mladić's troops took over the city and overran the UNPRO-FOR base at nearby Potočari, where a group of Dutch peacekeepers had been sheltering thousands of Bosniaks. Then the troops began hunting down Bosniak men. They captured their targets in small groups and concentrated them in larger numbers in fields, sportsgrounds, schools, and factories. There, the Bosniak men were slaughtered by the thousands.

It is impossible to arrive at anything but an approximation of the number killed. Many mass graves are even now yet to be located, and population figures from before the fall of Srebrenica are imprecise because of the large number of uncounted refugees who had earlier flooded into the city. Best estimates indicate that at least 8,000 were killed. Srebrenica has become an emblem of the brutality of the Serb war against Bosnia's Muslims, and of the UN's failure to stand up to genocide. The latter is especially evident given the fact that the safe zone was not defended, and was instead simply allowed to be taken with the connivance and assent of the Dutch peacekeepers and their NATO commanders, both on the ground and elsewhere.

Later, in July, Žepa was also overrun, though without the accompanying slaughter that took place at Srebrenica.

The Bosnian War lasted for three years, until a settlement was negotiated under the U.S.-sponsored and UN-supported Dayton Agreement of November 21, 1995. The treaty, to be supervised by NATO, divided Bosnia (which would still be considered a unitary state) into two separate ethnic enclaves.

"A SARAJEVO MOTHER AND DAUGHTER"

The experiences of families during the Bosnian tragedy took multiple forms, but they almost always involved some form of separation from loved ones. In August 1994, American professor Julie Mertus (b. 1963) and feminist playwright Eve Ensler (b. 1953) interviewed a number of Bosniak women who had found refuge in Islamabad, Pakistan. Among them were the mother and daughter in this account. The daughter, aged 18, had never before heard her 41-year-old mother's story. After a year and a half in Pakistan, they reached their destination, Canada, in December 1994.

MOTHER:

I know too much now. The best thing is that we're now all together. I don't know where to start.

DAUGHTER:

We all knew that war was coming. My father was in Libya working to support the high cost of my younger brother's expensive medical care for his chronic illness. So my mother was taking care of all of us—me and my three brothers and sisters. One day, Mother came in and said, "Kids, wake up! We must go now." I helped gather my brothers and sisters and we all went down into the basement.

MOTHER:

We spent two and a half months in that basement. There were over fifty people in my basement.

DAUGHTER:

She tried to move us somewhere else, where there would be more room, but there was no place to go. I was the biggest problem for my mother. She was afraid that I would be raped.

MOTHER:

I knew that somehow I had to get my children out of there. One day, I found two cars that worked and I found some gas. Then, I saw a Serb in the street. He was about thirty years old and he had a long scar on his face—he was pretty ordinary looking. I had never seen him before and I didn't know his name, but he had a good face, a kind face. I approached him and asked for help. He said, "Come tomorrow and pack your things."

DAUGHTER:

The next day, we went to this man with my brothers and sisters. He was waiting in the car. All of us kids got in, but Mother had to stay behind because there wasn't any room. . . .

We were all crying, but when we passed by the Serb soldiers, we had to pretend that we were happy. We had to sit and wave at them like we were going on a holiday. That was the hardest part. The man drove the car through the sector controlled by Serbs. We went about twelve kilometers and then were at the edge of the Croatian side. The man stopped the car and said, "Get out. I can't go any further." As soon as we got out of the car with our bags, soldiers appeared out of nowhere. We were afraid but they helped us. We went to the house of a friend we knew there. He brought us to the "children's embassy," where they gave us food and then said, "Go alone."

I used all of the money my mother had given me to buy tickets for all of us for Croatia. The bus ride was a nightmare—twenty-four hours and thirty people on a small bus. First we went to Split, then Makarska, then Promajna. That first month, we had nothing. Just one room and three beds for six people. We didn't even have sheets. As the oldest, I tried to take care of everyone. I didn't hear anything about my mother.

After a month, I met a Croatian soldier who said he would take a letter to my mother. A cousin got the letter and contacted me. He kept saying that everything was OK, but I felt that everything wasn't OK. He couldn't say anything precise about Mother. When I finally heard that she really was OK, I was so happy that I danced in the streets. My heels were broken on my shoes, but I kept dancing. I was so happy, but somehow, I still couldn't believe it. I wanted everything to be fine, but without hearing my mother's voice, I couldn't believe anything.

MOTHER:

I kept a phone in the fireplace of my house, so that I could make calls and no one would hear. When my daughter got to the Croatian side, she called to say that she was OK, and our Croat friends called to say that they had left for Croatia. But then nothing. I kept the phone in the fireplace but I didn't hear anything after that.

DAUGHTER:

My mother saved at least forty people. She found food for everyone when there was no food. She wore a very big skirt. Whenever people came into the basement in our house, she would make them give her their guns, and she would hide them in her skirt. Then, she would take them from her skirt and bury them in the yard. So there would be no weapons in the house if soldiers came. . . .

The Serbs came and caught her brother and brother-in-law and put them in prison. And then she stopped helping other people. Then she just tried to get them out of prison. You could pay the Serbs and they would bring food to the prison.

MOTHER:

Over 480 men on our street were captured; until this day, we haven't heard from 130 of them. After the men were rounded up, they started gathering up the women. One Serb friend came to my house and said, "You must go to an interview."

DAUGHTER:
I knew him too; he was my classmate from high school.

MOTHER:
They put me in a prison in a basement. There were ten women in one room—two were older women, and the rest were between the ages of thirty and forty.

DAUGHTER:
This is the first time I'm hearing this!

MOTHER:
From then on, every day was the same. We had one meal a day and we had one chance to go to the bathroom a day, and we were never allowed to shower. They gave us nothing for menstruation. The women who were bleeding would sit in a corner. Like animals . . . there was nothing else we could do.

There was no light in the basement so we all sat in darkness. And it was so cold, we all began to get sick. They would put smoke bombs in the prison just to scare us and they would eat in front of us, just to tease us. But, maybe because one of the prisoners was married to a Serb, they didn't do anything really bad to us. . . .

I kept thinking that at least my children were in a better place. I wasn't sure where they were, but I knew it was better. . . .

After two months in the basement like that, I was saved. The Serb who had helped my children came in the middle of the night and stole me from the prison. He threw me in the trunk of a car and drove me off. I still don't know his name. . . .

I don't know why he helped me. Maybe it was because they all knew that my husband wasn't a soldier.

DAUGHTER:
What did you do?

MOTHER:
I hid in the trunk of my car by our house. There was shooting all around. Another neighbor gave me petrol. I got in the front seat of my car and waited, but the shooting didn't stop. I was sitting, slouched in the seat with men on one side of me shooting at men on the other. There was a Serb soldier's car right in front of me. He started driving and I began following him. I just kept driving until I was on the other side [the Croatian side]. Now, when I think about it, I must have been crazy; but I wasn't thinking. I was like a crazy one.

When I got to the other side, I went to my Croatian friend's house, and I waited until nightfall.

DAUGHTER:
She was ashamed. She didn't want our friend to see her in the light—she had been wearing the same clothes for two months and she had never had a shower.

MOTHER:

I had a bad fever. As soon as I rang our friend's doorbell and he opened the door, I fainted.

DAUGHTER:

She had pneumonia and arthritis and who knows what else.

MOTHER:

I stayed for five days, but I couldn't wait any longer. My friend gave me some money and some clothes. I still had a fever when I got in my car again and drove to Croatia. . . .

I was alone. I kept fighting off hitchhiking paramilitary groups who wanted a ride. It was too dangerous to have anyone in the car with me. I had to fight to be alone.

DAUGHTER:

Our friend called me to say that my mother was coming. I almost died with joy. But when, after two days, she didn't arrive, I began to think he was lying.

MOTHER:

It took a long time because I could only travel at night and the car was very slow.

DAUGHTER:

But she came! When I first saw her, I didn't recognize her because she looked so bad. We started weeping and holding each other. We both thought, "We must find Dad."

MOTHER:

He didn't have a passport, but even without one, he crossed into nine countries, weaving his way to Croatia. He went to Malta, Turkey, Italy, Germany, Austria, and who knows where else, on his way to Croatia.

DAUGHTER:

When my father called from Zagreb, the first thing my mother said was, "Where are you?" Then she started to cry. She didn't even ask, "How are you?" Just, "Where are you?"

MOTHER:

He came down to Promajna but stayed for only two weeks. Then, he put on a soldier's uniform and went back to Bosnia to buy all of our family members' freedom. He used all of the money he had made in Libya to bring everyone out. He got stuck in Croatia when they closed the border. Then, two months later, they sent us all to Pakistan.

DAUGHTER:

We're trying to get to Canada, but we're too sick. Our family can't pass the physicals necessary for entry. My mother is still sick from the prison. Four months ago, she had a heart attack and now she has kidney problems. And my brother has his chronic illness, and at least another one of us is very sick whenever we try to test healthy.

MOTHER:

We're waiting. . . .

How did I sustain myself through all this? When I closed my eyes, I just thought of my daughter's eyes. She has such lovely, large brown eyes. Doesn't she? Everything is OK because we're alive.

Source: Julie Mertus, Jasmina Tesanovic, Habiba Metikos, and Rada Boric (eds.), *The Suitcase: Refugee Voices from Bosnia and Croatia* (Berkeley and Los Angeles: University of California Press, 1997), 23–28. Used by permission of University of California Press and Julie Mertus.

Commentary

An illusion people sometimes have of genocide victims is that they are helpless before the onslaught facing them. While it is certainly true that *génocidaires* target those who are defenseless, innocent, or noncombatant, it is equally true that victims rarely just wait around passively to be murdered. Knowing what might happen if they do is, in most cases, a spur to action, provided there is time to act. This is an important qualification, as all too often time is not available.

In the case of the family represented in this account, they had sufficient warning that war was imminent, and they were thus able to make some preparations to meet the challenge. While we do not know the details of the arrangements they made before the onset of war, or of the discussions that took place, it is apparent from the account that some form of refuge was created in the family basement, possibly with precautions similar to those of a fallout shelter in the 1960s. Whatever the arrangements, the family—a mother and four children—swung into action immediately when danger appeared. They were able to spend two and a half months undetected. Ultimately, the basement proved capable of housing more than 50 people.

From time to time the mother would go above ground to see if there had been any developments. Her main focus was preventing her daughter from being raped; she was conscious of the need to get her daughter away from the danger zone. It was on one of her forays above ground that she found two workable vehicles that could help evacuate at least some of those in the basement. A Serb was on the street, and he offered to help. As the daughter explained, "The next day, we went to this man with my brothers and sisters. He was waiting in the car. All of us kids got in, but Mother had to stay behind because there wasn't any room." Because of the man's actions, the daughter was able to reach safety and escape into Croatia.

Remaining behind, the mother had to make do as best she could. As is so often the case in situations of genocide, her vulnerability was compounded by the fact that there were no men in the area to defend the defenseless. Nearly 500 men from the street had been captured by the Serbs and taken away to unknown destinations, making it much easier to attack those remaining. As the mother put it, "They started gathering up the women." That was the real start of the mother's ordeal.

The Serb militiaman who came for the mother was known to the family. This local intimacy is seen all too frequently in genocide situations. The militiaman told the mother she "must go to an interview." She was taken away and "put in a prison in a basement," which she shared with ten women in one room.

In an interesting sidelight to the mother's description, the daughter—who was saved, and ultimately survived the war in Croatia—had been completely unaware of her mother's experience. She responds, "This is the first time I'm hearing this!" It is entirely possible that the mother kept the details of her experiences from her daughter to protect her emotionally; on the other hand, she might have wished to suppress them until now. But once she begins to relate what happened to her, the words flow. She describes having had one meal and one opportunity to use the bathroom each day, no chance to bath or shower, and no access to facilities for women who were menstruating. Moreover, there was no light in the basement, "so we all sat in darkness," and there was no heating, so in the cold "we all began to get sick."

Remarkably, given the nature of the conflict and the enormous amount of sexual violence accompanying it, the women in the basement were not assaulted sexually. In her interview, the mother attributes this to the possibility that it was "maybe . . . one of the prisoners was married to a Serb." It was difficult to find an explanation for the absence of that form of viciousness, though other types of harassment did take place, such as the detonation of smoke bombs throughout the prison "just to scare us," or small forms of psychological torture, like the habit the guards had of eating in front of the prisoners. The mother concludes, "They didn't do anything really bad to us."

After two months of confinement in the basement prison, the same Serb soldier who had helped her daughter and other children to escape unexpectedly released the mother. He came in the middle of the night and basically "stole me from the prison," throwing her into the trunk of a car and driving her away. It was an incredible set of circumstances, all around. Her only possible explanation for her release was that it was known that her husband, who was overseas at the time of the war, was not a soldier.

After her escape, she initially hid in the trunk of her car. She then managed to get to the Croatian side of the front line by driving right through the combat zone. She was in poor physical condition, not having bathed or changed her clothes for two months, and she had a bad fever, pneumonia, and arthritis. She stayed with a Croatian friend for five days. Her friend gave her some money and clothes, and she left again in her car. She drove to sanctuary in Croatia, at every step doing her best to avoid "hitchhiking paramilitary groups who wanted a ride." Ultimately, the mother reached Croatia—and reunion with her family.

The very idea of a Serb soldier—a militiaman, no less—helping Bosniak children to escape, then rescuing their mother months later, is, indeed, inexplicable, though not impossible. There are always anomalies of this kind; several have been identified in this volume. The one thing that needs to be borne in mind is that genocide is a human enterprise, and that, as such, it is as subject to the full range of human behaviors (and incongruities) as any other social endeavor.

Questions

1. What was the nature of the mother's ordeal while she was imprisoned by the Serbs? Do you think she is holding anything back from her daughter as she relates her story?
2. What were the circumstances that led to the mother and daughter's separation?
3. In your own words, describe how the family unit was reunited over time.

BORISLAV HERAK

"Genocidal rape" is a recently developed term that suggests the use of mass rape as a weapon against perceived enemies. Genocidal rape degrades, demoralizes, and humiliates victims and their families, and causes physical trauma. It can also lead to forced impregnation, which, in some societies, results in the victim becoming a social pariah. Rape was frequently employed during the Bosnian War as an instrument of ethnic cleansing, used by Serbian armed forces against Bosniak women and girls. Borislav Herak (b. 1971), a Bosnian Serb soldier, was the first Serb to be put on trial for war crimes in Bosnia-Herzegovina. He was interviewed by George Rodrigue for the Dallas Morning News *in May 1993; what follows are parts of that confrontational conversation.*

GEORGE: In general they say that you have killed many men, women, and children with guns and with knives, and that you raped many women. Is that true?

BORISLAV: It is true, but I did not kill any children.

G: I would like to talk about the women you raped. I believe you have listed their names before. Could you do that again for me please?

B: Amara, Sabina, Sumbula.

G: Okay. Any more? Who was the first woman you raped?

B: Amara.

G: Tell me what happened.

B: We had an order to go to Restaurant Sonja in Vogosca. We were told that we were going to rape girls there.

G: Who told you this?

B: My captain. The commander of our unit. So as to increase the morale of our fighters.

G: What was the name of your captain?

B: I do not know his last name. His first name was Borov, and he came from Breza [thirty kilometers northwest of Sarajevo]. He was working as a captain there too, and he came to Sarajevo as a refugee and became a captain there.

G: Was this good for your morale?

B: Not at all. And before that and after that I had to go to the front lines, so it was the same for me.

G: How do you mean?

B: It was just a stupid thing to do. We hadn't any fights, and that is why it was worthless.

G: So what did you think of this order?

B: I had to obey it.

G: What would have happened to you if you had not?

B: They would have sent me to the worst front line in Trebinje in Herzegovina, or sent me to jail.

G: They would not have killed you?

B: I cannot say that. But I knew they would have taken away the house that they had given me.

G: They had given you a Muslim's house.

B: Yes.

G: Was it nice?

B: Yes. It had two floors, and it was white. There was a place to keep cows. A building for them, behind the house.

G: So you got to the restaurant, and what did you see?

B: It had a guard in front of it, and the girls were in the room.

G: What room?

B: The girls were in a room just inside the door.

G: How many girls?

B: Sixty.

G: How did they look? Clean, dirty, beaten, not beaten, young, old?

B: They were young, twenty to twenty-five years. They were looking normal, with normal clothes on them. They hadn't any bruises on them.

G: Did they look well fed or hungry?

B: I didn't notice.

G: What happened next?

B: I know that they were killed afterward.

G: I want to ask who did the very next thing. Who said the next thing?

B: They found Mordrag Vukovic and Dragan Damjanovic, they were in Seselj's army [a paramilitary group]. And they worked there. It was their work to guard the women.

G: What happened then?

B: We told them that we were sent by Borov, and they knew what to do. They brought the girls to us from the room. . . . They picked girls for us.

G: And which one was picked for you?

B: That Amara girl . . . she was tall, black hair, about twenty.

G: Did you say anything to each other?

B: No

G: What happened then?

B: We went up to the room. On the second floor. That guy Miro showed us the way. And there we raped her, the four of us.

G: They picked out one girl for the four of you?

B: Yes.

G: You were all in the room when she was raped?

B: Yes.

G: Didn't this seem strange to you?

B: Just a little bit.

G: Why did you do it?

B: Because I had those guys with me. I had to listen to the order, or I would have to face consequences if I did not.

G: Did you say anything to each other this whole time?

B: We told her to take off her clothes. . . . She didn't want to. And that guy Misa Damjanovic started to beat her.

G: Did he beat her with his rifle butt or his hands?

B: With his hands. And then she took her clothes off and we raped her. And she put her clothes back on, and we took her away.

G: Did you feel good about this, or guilty?

B: I felt guilty. But I didn't want to say anything or to show it to the others.

G: You did not kill this one?

B: Damjanovic did.

G: How do you know?

B: I went with him. We went together to Zuc [a mountain in Sarajevo].

G: You and Damjanovic?

B: Three of us. They took her out of the car, the two of them, and I sat in the car. I saw that they had guns. One of them shot her in the head. They took her into some bushes; they sort of hid her there and then they killed her. . . . Then they came back.

G: Did they say why they did this?

B: When they finished and we were still in the restaurant, Miro Vukovic told us to kill her. Because they did not have enough food or space, and they wanted to bring new girls into the restaurant. So we should kill her.

G: What did you think of this?

B: I just kept my mouth shut. I was standing by the side.

G: I did not ask what you did. I asked what you thought.

B: I thought that what they were going to do was bad.

G: That is all you thought?

B: Yes.

G: Were you surprised?

B: I had already heard the stories about that. About killing girls. It was known to me already.

G: When they came back from shooting her the first time, were they laughing or sad or just very quiet?

B: They had music turned on in the car as we went back, and there was no conversation.

G: What was the music?

B: Serbian folk music. The usual folk music. . . .

G: When you [yourself] killed [Sumbula] . . ., what were you thinking?

B: I can't remember. It was a long time ago.

G: I'm sorry, but I cannot believe that you don't remember. How many unarmed women have you shot in the back?

B: Three.

G: Do you remember what you were thinking while you shot any of them?

B: I knew that those were my orders. I knew I had to obey the orders.

G: If someone had told you before the war that if you did not rape and kill a Moslem girl they would have taken away your money and sent you someplace dangerous, would you have raped and killed the girl?

B: I would not have believed it. And I would not have done it.

G: Why would you do it now?

B: I had to do it.

G: Isn't that rather a bad excuse? You did not argue with these orders. You didn't even say that you didn't feel like it. You never said, Why don't we just let them go? Isn't this a bad excuse, "orders?"

B: We all had to obey the orders.

G: Let me ask you this. You have heard a lot of propaganda about how the Serbs are in danger and the Muslims want to slaughter them. Did you believe this?

B: Yes, I believed it. I had been told that in Sarajevo terrible things are going on. That they have prisons and whorehouses. That they rape little girls from five to seven years. That they throw babies and women to the lions in the Sarajevo zoo.

G: Now you grew up there, right? You had Muslim friends?

B: Yes. My brother-in-law is a Muslim.

G: Now before the war started would you have ever believed that Muslims could do such things?

B: No.

G: Had a Muslim ever hurt you in any way?

B: No. No. They only helped me. They were helping me all the time. I once had an accident, fell down and hurt my head. And a Serb neighbor was afraid. He ran away. A Muslim neighbor picked me up and took me to the hospital.

G: So how did you come to believe this propaganda about the Muslims?

B: I don't know.

G: Are you incapable of thinking for yourself? Do you believe everything that people tell you?

B: No. I don't believe everything that I hear. I can think for myself. But when I came to Vogosca, to the Chetniks, they told me that they had phoned to Sarajevo and were quite sure that my father had been killed at his house, on the street, in Sarajevo, and that my house had been burned. So that is why I believed them, and I started to think in a different way.

G: Your father is ashamed of what you have done.

B: He told me, I am your father and you are my child. And I can forgive you, but others cannot.

G: Do you feel ashamed?

B: It is hard for me to look in his eyes.

G: How could somebody who grew up with Muslim friends, who had Muslims in his family, how could he grow up to treat Muslims this way?

B: I don't know. But while I was in Sarajevo my cousin came to my house and told me that the Muslims had put me on a list of people to be killed. And because we are close relatives, I believed him. When I escaped they told me a lot of stories about what the Muslims had done. Raping, slitting throats. And my thinking began to change.

G: What do you think now about the Serbs' claims to be great warriors and victims of the Muslims?

B: I think that they do not know what they are doing. As a matter of fact, because they act like this and fight like this they are going to ruin themselves. They are going to destroy themselves. It is easy for them while they are up in the hills. And it is easy for them while they have artillery and the Bosnians have just guns. But they will never be able to come down from the hills and visit the town. And that will be hard for them.

G: You know that by talking to so many people you have perhaps condemned yourself to death. Why have you done this?

B: They should know what they are doing on the other side.

G: What will happen to you now?

B: They will kill me. . . .

> Source: Alexandra Stiglmayer, "The Rapes in Bosnia-Herzegovina," in Alexandra Stiglmayer (ed.), *Mass Rape: The War against Women in Bosnia-Herzegovina* (Lincoln: University of Nebraska Press, 1994), 148–154. Used by permission.

Commentary

Borislav Herak, a textile worker from Sarajevo, was born on January 18, 1971. During the Bosnian War he fought as a Bosnian Serb soldier with the Army of Republika Srpska. He was the first person to be convicted of the crime of genocide following that conflict, and the only person convicted of genocide by a local court before the establishment of the State Court of Bosnia and Herzegovina.

During his courtroom appearance, Herak was charged with 32 murders and 16 rapes, including the murder of 12 of his rape victims. He confessed that the soldiers in his group were told to rape in order to improve unit morale, as they would fight better if they were united through the shared experience of rape of their female captives. Accordingly, he and his fellow soldiers frequented Cafe Sonya (*Kod Sonje*), one of several alleged "rape camps" outside Sarajevo. During various periods of the early part of the war, Cafe Sonya held up to 70 Bosniak women and girls at a given time. Those who were killed, or who died as a result of their experience, were replaced as a matter of course.

In February 2000, the Human Rights Chamber for Bosnia and Herzegovina ordered that Herak's death penalty be commuted to 20 years' imprisonment.

The interview presented in this account has Herak's confession to having raped three women. His "explanations" for his actions are classic and instructive of how otherwise normal, moral men can become rapists and murderers. He justifies his actions on the basis that he was given an order he had no choice but to obey. If he did not commit the rapes, he explains, he would have been sent "to the worst front line in Trebinje in Herzegovina, or sent to jail." The municipality of Trebinje, in southeastern Herzegovina, lies within Republika Srpska, the Serb-controlled part of Bosnia-Herzegovina, and was the scene of vicious guerrilla fighting in the early part of the war.

When asked whether he would have been killed for disobeying the order to rape, Herak says he did not think so, but he certainly would have lost the large double-story Muslim house he had been given. Upon reflection, he did not think the exercise improved his morale at all—and he was sent to the front lines, anyway. Nonetheless, although he considered the order "stupid" and "worthless," he "had to obey it," and that was that.

What, other than "obeying orders," would make a young man—who was seemingly quite ordinary before the war—become a multiple murderer and rapist once war removed the conventions of peacetime society?

Prior to the war, he states, he could never have imagined himself raping or killing women. He would not have believed it possible of himself, and would not have done it. But when war broke out, he says, he had to do it. "We all had to obey the orders," he explains to rationalize his actions. Herak had been told terrible things about Muslims as part of a propaganda campaign. He believed the propaganda about the Serbs being endangered by the Muslims, who, he was allegedly told, wanted to slaughter them, and who ran "prisons and whorehouses" in Sarajevo where "little girls from five to seven years" were raped and near which "babies and women [were thrown] to the lions in the Sarajevo zoo."

He believed all this, we are told, despite having grown up in Sarajevo and known many Muslims prior to the war—and despite having thought highly of them. Even his brother-in-law was a Muslim. Moreover, before the war he never would have believed that Muslims could do such things. When asked how it was that he came to believe the anti-Muslim propaganda, he responds simply, "I don't know," "I don't believe everything that I hear," and "I can think for myself."

Before the war, some 44.5 percent of the population of Vogošća, a suburb of Sarajevo, was ethnically Serb. Although the Serbs controlled that part of the city during the war, it was heavily damaged during the siege of Sarajevo, and then as the Serbs left in large numbers. Herak went to Vogošća while it was still occupied by the Chetniks (Serb paramilitaries), where he was told that his father had been killed and his house burned. When confronted with particularly intimate revelations such as these, he began to look personally at the war, or, as he says, "I started to think in a different way." While he was there, his cousin told him that the Muslims had put him on a death list. He also heard "a lot of stories about what the Muslims had done," such as raping women and slitting throats. Again, he says, "my thinking began to change."

This all translated into a particularly callous disregard for the lives of the Muslims he encountered.

The first victim he raped was a girl of about 20 named Amara. She (he uses the term "that") was chosen for Herak by his officer. Nothing was said; Amara was raped by Herak and three others, who were all present throughout the acts. When asked why he did it, Herak stated that it was because "I had those guys with me," and he had to obey the order or face consequences. One of the ongoing features in the justifications by *génocidaires* of their actions relates to group or unit solidarity. While this usually pertains to matters such as mass killing, in this situation rape is the focus. That sense of group solidarity is why, when Herak is asked why he did not do anything to stop the crime from taking place, he says that, although he felt guilty, he "didn't want to say anything or to show it to the others." When one of the other men murdered Amara, he again did nothing. As he says, "I just kept my mouth shut," even though "I thought that what they were going to do was bad."

It is clear from his account that Borislav Herak was a very confused *génocidaire,* who knew what he was doing was wrong, but participated in the most appalling acts anyway because he felt he had something personal to lose if he did not. Trying to justify his actions on the grounds of private loss—of his new house, of his safety from the front line, of his standing in the group—he went along with the orders given to him not because he was a racially driven zealot, but because it suited him to do so. In his narrative, perhaps, we find a problematic explanation for genocidal behavior that has nothing to do with ideology and everything to do with personal ambition, a factor that might well be more widespread than usually acknowledged.

Questions

1. This interview is a very thorough interrogation of a genocidal rapist. If you could ask Borislav Herak one question not asked here, what would it be? What response do you think you would get?
2. Do you think Herak showed any remorse for his behavior during the Bosnian War?
3. Why do you think Herak went so quickly from being one who knew many Muslims before the war, to one who could readily commit the acts related in this account against Muslims from his own community?

NIHADA HODZIC

Between April and June 1992, Serb forces attacked dozens of Bosniak villages in the district of Srebrenica and the neighboring municipalities of Bratunac, Vlasenica, Rogatica, and Višegrad. One of these villages was Zaklopača. On May 16, 1992, Serb forces approached the village and demanded that the Bosniak residents hand over their weapons. Other than a few hunting rifles, there were no weapons in the village. Upon learning that the residents were effectively unarmed, the Serbs blocked all the exits and massacred at least 63 Bosniak men, women, and children. Nihada Hodzic, a survivor of the massacre, was interviewed about her experience by Daniel Toljaga of the Institute for the Research of Genocide Canada. This account is part of that interview.

NIHADA HODZIC:
First of all, I would like to sincerely thank you for the opportunity to share my experiences and broader knowledge about the events of May 16, 1992, that would

befall Zaklopača and much of eastern Bosnia as the Serb aggression progressed into the heartland of Bosnia and Herzegovina. . . . Generally people were assured that nothing would ever happen to us—when we heard automatic weapons being fired in the distance, we were told that it was only routine "training" by the armed forces. . . . [W]e had a well trusted Serb neighbor Milenko Đurić (Gorčin) reassuring our safety time and time again, telling us "not even a hair will be missing from your bodies." Unfortunately, we had trusted our Serb neighbors; we believed their deceitful lies to keep us grounded in the village. Prior to the massacre we had attempted to flee to a safe haven in Zivinice, however we were sent back with the same type of reasoning by the Serb neighbor. . . .

DANIEL TOLJAGA:
What were the first signs that the massacre was about to happen?

NIHADA HODZIC:
One week prior to the massacre two of my uncles and my father were arrested and brought for questioning to the Police Station in Milići. At the time my father was working in Boksit Transport, in Milići, where upon one day he along with his relative, on their way home, were taken by the reserve police and brought to the Milići police station. First however, they had asked for their identification cards, and made sure they were Muslim. Whoever had a Muslim name, they told them to form a line and to follow them to the station. When they finally reached their destination, for hours they interrogated them with petty questions. Questions regarding personal family backgrounds to some other questions to which no one could give any answers to. For example they would point to a machine gun and ask whose it was—obviously no one could have known—when my father answered "I don't know" the interrogator said "you will know" and shoved him off. At the police station my father along with hundreds of other Muslim men were shoved into a small room where he witnessed some very gruesome acts being performed on these defenseless civilian men. They were beaten beyond recognition, some defecated out of fear and it was simply a gruesome and frightening atmosphere. Shortly thereafter, though it seemed much longer to my father, our long time neighbor Gorčin, whom I have mentioned before, came to his "rescue." Gorčin was responsible for my father's release from the police station, and he was brought back home that same day. . . . Of course, other men were not so lucky, they were left behind at the station, and we are not sure what happened to them.

There are however other smaller indicators of the massacre coming our way. About the same number of days prior, Serbs were adamantly cruising through our village in search for weapons, and demanded that everyone who had any type of weapon even "hunting guns"—that they should hand them over. In other words, they were demilitarizing our village days before the actual massacre, making sure we had no way of defending ourselves, even though no one had claims to any type of lethal weapons anyway.

Also, just about when the massacre was to occur, my mother (Najla Hodžić) was in her vegetable garden just outside of our home, when Police jeeps and cars came flooding into our small town. It was noon, on a very beautiful and sunny spring day on May 16, 1992. There were a few cars (she could not recall the exact number as they were driving back and forth through the village), in front of them a police car and following them a white jeep with the slogan "pokolj" (slaughter) written in Cyrillic across the vehicle. Our house was located right next to the main road, so my mother saw everything in clear view as they were rolling into the village, coming from the main road leading from the town Milići. She recalls that the vehicles had been packed with Chetniks, with long beards, some with nylon socks covering their heads, and loaded Kalashnikovs across their broad chests. Upon seeing this, my mother hurriedly motioned my oldest uncle Bećir Hodžić (who was helping my mother around the garden) to run, yet his last words to my mother were "don't worry sister-in-law everything is going to be alright—don't be afraid" when he was spotted by the Chetniks and taken away, not to be seen alive again.

DANIEL TOLJAGA:
At this point, you and your mother were also in immediate danger of being killed. Can you tell us what happened next?

NIHADA HODZIC:
Once the vehicles moved further into town, my mother ran into the house and frantically began to pack the bare essentials (some clean clothes, food and a few family pictures) and get my sisters and I ready for the worst possible situation. I was only a small child then, but I remember, in the midst of this frightful situation I was so obnoxious as to whine about which clothes I was going to wear—obviously I was not fully aware of the seriousness of what was about to happen. At this time, we had no idea where my father was, and thus we would remain clueless of his whereabouts until almost one year later, when we finally found out that he was alive. . . . My mother, my two older sisters and I ran across the yard to one of my other uncle's homes (Haso Hodžić), at which time almost all my other aunts and their kids were gathered. Just as we, along with my other five aunts and their children and a few other neighbors gathered inside, the lightning bolts began to fly, and the sound of thundering bullets began to ring on all sides. My mother was with me all the time—cuddling me inside her lap and shielding me from all the harm. The bullets whizzed through the house, creating big cratered holes as they made a full impact with the concrete walls. At one point, a bullet pierced through my mother's light denim jacket, as I was still cuddling in her lap. The bullet missed us both by a hair. For another fifteen to twenty minutes, the showers of deadly bullets filled the suffocating air, killing anything that was moving—anything that was alive would have met its final death. As it calmed down, we heard my second uncle (whose house we were all in) calling upon my aunt to come out. We all did, and from the porch we

saw my uncle standing at gunpoint. A Serb was aiming at him, ready to pull the trigger any time. My dear uncle looked pale, and afraid. He asked for a cigarette, and as he reached for the lighter in his pocket, the ringing sound of Kalashnikovs went off once more, and as we were all standing on the porch, we all saw my beloved uncle murdered in front of our very own eyes. His body was thrown up into the air at least a few feet from detonation and came back crashing onto the hot asphalt, motionless and lifeless. My grandmother saw her son mercilessly killed in front of her sorrowful, teary eyes. As she frantically yelled out "My son is Dead," the Serb (Chetnik) opened fire again, chasing us back into the house, shocked, dismayed and still in disbelief of what we had seen. But my grandmother ran out, bewildered, lost and deeply hurt into the streets—suffering a mental breakdown. Throughout this time, we were quite unaware of the whereabouts of my father (Ekrem Hodžić). From his perspective of the story, things followed in a different fashion from ours. While we were still inside the house, my father observed everything from the woods just above my grandfather's house. As he saw the cars rolling into town, driving in the direction of the village "Gornji Zalkovik'" full of Chetniks and returning empty. Curiously, my father went north into the woods to observe where they had gone while two of my uncles went down to see what was happening in town. Just as he reached into the woods the shots began to fly. He remained in a state of shock as he began running deeper into the woods, however, unaware of where he was going he returned to the outskirts of the woods in dismay—unable to comprehend what was going on.

DANIEL TOLJAGA:
When the shooting stopped, I can only imagine the shock and horror you and your family had to endure. Would you mind telling us what happened immediately after the massacre?

NIHADA HODZIC:
As the thunder of bullets finally stopped, our small town was gasping for air—it was gasping for life. The Serbs left, the same way they came in, completing their heinous job with blood on their hands. The blood of innocence—the blood of Zaklopača. We dared to step out again, to witness that inferno, the death and destruction of this inevitable storm which plundered our town and raped it of its virtues and good life. We saw dead bodies everywhere. The smell of death permeated the entire town. Dead children, women, men. Bodies everywhere. We were in shock. The tears seemed to have almost dried up, nothing was coming out. It was like a nightmare! A terrible nightmare you desperately wished to wake up from, but never did. We covered my uncle with a blanket, and proceeded to go further into town—hoping to find survivors. We saw my eldest uncle (Bećir Hodžić) again—in a kneeling position with a cigarette still burning in between his index and middle fingers, his head bowed to the ground, and a puddle of blood next to him—he was dead too.

We saw small children with their mothers lying side by side on the ground, motionless, very still—in an eternal sleep. We were told that my father was among the dead too. We couldn't go on. My family and I decided to give our selves in (to "surrender" to the Serbs)—we thought we had no one left alive, in this highly emotional moment we were ready to die too. My father, on the other hand, was met by other men who survived and fled into the woods. Among them was my uncle Bećir's son Amir (seventeen at the time), who told my father, that everyone in town was dead—that they were the only survivors. My father also witnessed during this time, after the massacre, Serbs came back to the village to bury their crimes into yet another mass grave. My father saw everything. From this point onward, my father's path diverged from my mother's, sisters' and my own. It is a long story. . . . We later learned that my father was indeed alive, in March of 1993 we were reunited in Zagreb, Croatia.

> Source: "Interview with Nihada Hodzic, Survivor of the Zaklopača Massacre," Institute for Research of Genocide Canada. Accessed at http://instituteforgenocide.org/en/wp-content/uploads/2012/01/Interview-with-Nihada-Hodzic.pdf. Used by permission of the Institute for Research of Genocide.

Commentary

On May 16, 1992, Serb forces approached Zaklopača, a small Bosnian village located in the municipality of Vlasenica, on the border of the Srebrenica municipality. In what was to become a standard format for ethnic cleansing, they demanded that the village's Bosniaks hand over their weapons; other than for a few hunting rifles there was none. Upon realizing that the residents were unarmed, the Serb invaders closed down all entry points to the village, effectively blockading it and ensuring that no one could leave. They then committed a massacre of the villagers. Numbers of those killed vary: while some accounts give a figure of just over 60, others reach as high as 80. What is certain is that the victims were Bosniak men, women, and children.

The massacre took place some three years before the Srebrenica Genocide of July 1995. Pro-Serb apologists claim that Naser Orić (b. 1967), the commander of Bosniak forces in and around the city of Srebrenica between 1992 and 1995, was responsible for starting the violence in the region in 1992. He and his small group of militiamen began attacking the Serbs as early as April 20, 1992, when his forces successfully ambushed a number of vehicles of local Serbian police at Potočari. Immediately thereafter, regular troops from the Yugoslav People's Army (*Jugoslovenska Narodna Armija,* or JNA) started artillery assaults against Orić's stronghold in Potočari and the surrounding villages. In early May 1992, Bosniak forces began to assault the Serbs in and around Srebrenica, who fled or were driven out. Bosniak forces retook control of the Srebrenica regional district on May 9.

Orić then proceeded to enlarge the area under his control by attacking Serb villages around the town.

Against this backdrop, the massacre at Zaklopača has sometimes been explained as a reaction on the part of the Serbs to Bosniak provocation. In Nihada Hodzic's account, however, we see that Bosniaks in the Srebrenica region were persecuted and killed from the first weeks of the Bosnian War, well before Naser Orić's attacks against the local Serb villages.

Nihada provides us with a first-person account of the massacre, starting with what happened to her father: in a classic case of ethnic cleansing, he, along with the rest of the men, was separated from his family. Some of the men were tortured. During this initial assault, a Serb neighbor, Gorčin, intervened in order to save her father's life. As Nihada relates, Gorčin "was responsible for my father's release from the police station, and he was brought back home that same day." As we learn, though, her father then went into the woods, and his survival was unknown to Nihada and the rest of the family for a very long time, until they were finally reunited in March 1993 in Zagreb, Croatia. In what has become a frequent motif in the study of genocide, a survivor once more has a member of the perpetrator group to thank for his survival. This does little to exonerate the entire perpetrator cohort, of course, but it does show that there were often good people whose sense of common humanity overrode the ideologies that led to the mass murder of neighbors.

Nihada's descriptive details of the massacre are told with a finely drawn sense of recall. As she notes, the Serbs killed openly and with impunity. The extent of the killing is shown clearly in her account: "We saw dead bodies everywhere. The smell of death permeated the entire town. Dead children, women, men. Bodies everywhere." She leaves her audience in little doubt as to the terrifying actions committed by the Serbs. Once the shooting stopped, she relates, the town was "gasping for air—it was gasping for life." Upon their return from their hiding places, the villagers "were in shock," as they were in a situation that was "like a nightmare" that "you desperately wished to wake up from, but never did."

They saw her eldest uncle, who had been killed, as well as small children "with their mothers lying side by side on the ground, motionless." As they could not find her father and presumed him to be dead, the family decided to surrender to the Serbs. They no longer had the will to live.

After the Zaklopača and Vlasenica massacres, a large number of captured Bosniaks were transferred to a Serb-run concentration camp at Sušica, near Vlasenica. Between late May and October 1992, it has been estimated that up to 8,000 Bosniaks of both genders and all ages, mostly from the Vlasenica region, passed through the camp. Overcrowding was severe, and atrocities were common, particularly against women, who were often raped or sexually assaulted. Detainees were compelled to work as forced labor (and often died as a result of mistreatment). Some were murdered by camp guards.

The camp was closed down in late September 1992, but on the night of September 30, 1992, a final massacre occurred, during which about 150 inmates were driven out of the camp and executed. The few remaining prisoners were transferred to the larger Batković camp near Bijeljina, in northeastern Bosnia.

The testimony offered by Nihada Hodzic is a vitally important description of the massacre at Zaklopača, although there were other survivors, including members of her own family. Several trials of Bosnian Serb leaders before the International Criminal Tribunal for the former Yugoslavia have since used these testimonies as evidence, as they are relevant to charges of genocide, persecution, extermination, murder, deportation, and other inhumane acts.

The attacks against Zaklopača and other villages in the region have been held up as archetypes of ethnic cleansing, particularly given the attendant expulsion and murder of Bosniaks and the subsequent expropriation of the lands upon which they had lived. Nihada Hodzic's testimony stands out among the detailed depictions of ethnic cleansing, as it offers the perspective of a victim who experienced firsthand the worst of anti-Bosniak measures.

Questions

1. Describe, in your own words, what happened at Zaklopača during the massacre of May 16, 1992.
2. What indications did Nihada see in advance that the Zaklopača massacre was part of the Serb campaign of ethnic cleansing in the broader Srebrenica region during the spring of 1992?
3. Do you think Nihada is a credible witness of the Zaklopača massacre? Why or why not?

KEMAL PERVANIĆ

Kemal Pervanić (b. 1968) is a Bosniak who grew up in a thoroughly mixed community of Muslims, Serbs, and Croats. When his village was overrun by Bosnian Serb forces, all the men, including Kemal and his brother Kasim, were rounded up and sent to a Serb concentration camp at Omarska. He was to spend seven months there, followed by another period of incarceration in a camp at Manjaca. After horrific experiences, Pervanić was released. He managed to find sanctuary in the United Kingdom. The account here, from his memoir, details some of his and Kasim's encounters at Omarska.

Among the early victims was a group of men from Garibi. When the Serb army attacked the Kozarac region, the small village of Garibi resisted. A bunch of villagers armed with Kalashnikovs fired at the approaching army. They refused to surrender until their resistance was crushed. Amongst the survivors were all six Garibovic brothers and their three neighbours, Ferid Garibovic, and the Jukic brothers, Mujo and Hamed. There was a special reason for them to come first on the waiting list. Zeljko Meakic had been their neighbour, and he was the man who ran the show in the camp. During the guards' "training period," he kept the men from Garibi in anxiety. They were not ill-treated, but they knew it wouldn't stay that way for long. They knew he was preparing something for them.

Eventually, four of the six brothers and their neighbour Ferid were taken out at night. We heard screams and the sounds of beatings. After a while, the screaming stopped. Some of those from the "pista" saw the guards throw the men's broken bodies on to the trailer tractors. They were still alive. The tractor moved behind the camp buildings. Minutes later continuous gunfire was heard in the distance. Their lives had been extinguished forever.

During one of the evenings following their deaths, Djemal, the oldest of the Garibovic brothers, ended up inside the central building. It was raining and the guards herded everyone from the "pista" inside the buildings. Djemal saw Kasim inside our room, and he came up to talk to him. His other living brother, Hilmija, was in the small room in the garage together with some guys from our village. Djemal told us what had happened in Garibi village and about his sense of foreboding. He knew that he and Hilmija could not be safe with Zeljko around. They were not. Soon after, they were executed, too. Mother Garibovic had lost all six of her sons.

The Jukic brothers ended up very much the same way. Hamed was killed early on in the camp. Mujo faced a more brutal death. Rumours spread that he had been taken to the police station in Omarska village where he was hanged. What he had had to endure before his death remains a secret.

After this group exercise, there was nothing else the guards could learn. They became professionals. Beating and killing was now their job. They rested only during their lunch hour and during coffee breaks. From then on the "White House" became like a sinister bus station. Many people passed through it, but for most of them it was the last stop of their lives.

Sometimes the guards killed to celebrate. June 28 was St. Vitus's Day—the anniversary of the Battle of Kosovo, where Serbia lost to the invading Turks back in 1389. For many Serbs, it is the most sacred day in their lives. On June 28 1992, when the guards came on duty, they were spruced up, clean-shaven, and wearing smart civilian clothes. A fire was lit in front of the "White House." They roasted a pig—a traditional meal on this day—and ritually carved it with a dagger. They garnished it with the customary corn bread and plenty of home-made plum brandy. The radio played music which ominously suggested it was going to be an unforgettable night.

Ustashe, Ustashe
A deep pit awaits you:
Its width is one metre
Its depth one kilometre . . .

The guards drank. The first "sacrifices" were brought out—followed by the sounds of beatings, the screams of the victims, and the torturers' uncontrollable laughter. The "Turks" who survived will never forget that St. Vitus's Day.

· We also had visitors from outside who came into the camp in order to take their revenge and settle old scores. One day, about sixteen Chetniks died in the Kozara Mountain while trying to capture armed groups that were still refusing to surrender. A group of survivors, led by a tank driver from Orlovci named Zoran Karlica, arrived at the camp to take their revenge. Karlica entered our room and asked the people by the door where they were from.

"From Kevljani." Everyone was suddenly from Kevljani because everyone knew that we had not resisted, and it was therefore the safest place to be from.

Without explaining who he was, or why he was here, Karlica shouted: "All men who possessed guns stand up!" Everyone remained nailed to the floor. He went berserk and threatened all of us.

"Shall I stand up?" Kasim asked me. I was petrified. He was scared, too. I could not say a word. Somebody had to stand up, so Kasim did.

"Tell him you only had a legal automatic pistol," I whispered while he was getting up. From the other part of the room, closer to the door, my old schoolmate Damir stood up, too. A few more people followed. Karlica asked them what kind of weapons they had owned.

"Legal pistols," they said.

"Show me your permits." Kasim explained he had already handed it in on Monday, May 25. Karlica did not accept this. He was not interested in weapons, legal or illegal. He had come to seek revenge.

"You are a liar," he said to Damir, belting him across the face. Damir fell on the floor. Blood poured from his nose.

Karlica then pulled out his pistol and hit Hamdija Balic on the forehead. Blood flowed down Hamdija's face in huge spurts. At this point, a guard named Jovan, who had let Karlica in, told him to stop. But he made no actual effort to prevent him. Only when Pirvan entered and told him to stop did Karlica actually leave—moving on to repeat the same performance in other rooms.

A few days later, another group of soldiers came to the camp for some "fun." They weren't looking for anyone in particular. It was evident that in their eyes we were all guilty of something—no matter who we were. One of them, Prevara, a local character, was hitting everybody over the head and the back with a mountaineer's axe. When we returned from our meal, he came to the door of our room.

Zaim Klipic, a young man from my village, went to talk to him. Kasim said: "We used to be colleagues. I'm going to talk to him, too."

"Don't be a fool. Stay where you are. You used to know him, you don't know him now." Kasim took my advice.

When outside visitors came looking for a specific target, those left alive after their departure would wonder what might happen on the next such occasion—and whether next time they would be one of the chosen. The most appalling of these orgies happened around June 17. It was late afternoon. Terrible screams penetrated the walls of our room. They could be heard in every corner of the camp. They were screams of fear and of great pain. My hair stood on end. All talk in the room died out. The screams were mixed with laughter: obviously somebody was being tortured. Only later did we hear what had happened.

Several outside visitors had gone to the two rooms next to the garage. They called out Enver "Eno" Alic, Jasmin "Jasko" Hrnic, and Emir "Karaba" Karabasic. Eno's father Meho was taken to the garage to find his son and bring him out. When the beating started, he could not bear to watch his son being tortured—and he left without asking for permission.

At least two other inmates had been forced to take part in this brutal game. One of them, E.J., a young boy from the northern part of my village, had been ordered to drink motor oil—both from a ditch running through the garage and from a beer bottle given to him by one of the Chetniks. He was then ordered to kneel before Eno Alic, and they forced him to bite off his testicles.

The Chetniks experimented with all kinds of cruelties which arose from a sickened mind, but the nightmare of this particular cruelty will never end for the boy who was made to carry it out. Eno died in terrible agony, but at least it was swift. E.J. will have to live with this horror for the rest of his life. For the Chetniks, it had all been great fun.

Back in his room, E.J. remained in a state of shock for days. Jasko and Karaba had also been killed.

Source: Kemal Pervanić, *The Killing Days* (London: Blake Publishing, 1999), 78–82. Used by permission of Kemal Pervanić.

Commentary

Garibi is a small town in Republika Srpska, some 107 miles northwest of Sarajevo. In this account from Kemal Pervanić, we learn that among the early victims of the Bosnian War was a group of men from Garibi, the location of small-scale Bosniak resistance to the Serb incursion. Some of the villagers, armed with Kalashnikovs, fired at the approaching Serbs. They refused to surrender until their resistance was crushed. Pervanić says that the survivors included all six of the Garibovic brothers as well as their three neighbors, Ferid Garibovic and the Jukic brothers, Mujo and Hamed.

After recounting how the war affected these families—and how so many of the village's sons were lost—Pervanić contextualizes the torture and killing by referring to the history of the region. First he mentions St. Vitus's Day (Vidovdan), held on June 28 (June 15 in the Julian calendar), a feast day sacred to Serbian Orthodox Christians. St. Vitus's Day is normally celebrated by the Serbian Orthodox Church as a memorial day to Saint Prince Lazar (c. 1329–1389) and his Serbian fighters, who were killed during the Battle of Kosovo against the Ottoman Empire on June 28, 1389. The battle became the focus of Serbian romantic tradition during the period of national renewal in the nineteenth century, and the date resonated in Serbian, Yugoslav, and world history throughout the twentieth century. For many Serbs, it has taken on an aura of profound sanctity.

Pervanić relates that on this day in 1992, when the guards in Omarska came on duty, they were "spruced up, clean-shaven, and wearing smart civilian clothes." During the evening, after the guards enjoyed a traditional meal of roast pork, the radio played music that ominously suggested it was going to be an unforgettable night. This music referred to the Ustashe, the Croatian ultranationalist, separatist, fascist, and terrorist organization opposed to Serbs, Jews, Communists, Roma, and non-Catholics, created in 1930 by Ante Pavelić (1889–1959). The guards then brought out captive Bosniaks, whom they beat and tortured to the sounds of the persecutors' laughter.

The Omarska camp can best be described as a concentration camp run by Bosnian Serb forces in the town of Omarska, near Prijedor in northern Bosnia. During the Bosnian War, the Bosnian Serbs established a concentration camp network, the purpose of which was to concentrate in designated areas large numbers of Bosniaks and, in some instances, Bosnian Croats. The camps varied in size and style. Some were rudimentary, temporary structures such as guarded warehouses, schools, or factories that had been pressed into service; others were more developed and ranged across a number of buildings surrounded by barbed wire, displaying what are now typical, accepted characteristics of all such camps.

At Omarska, terror was the order of the day. Murder, torture, rape, and violence were common. Hundreds of prisoners died of starvation, beatings, and ill-treatment such as that highlighted by Kemal Pervanić.

In one incident, for example, Pervanić describes a revenge killing, when Serb soldiers came into the camp to murder Muslim men after a battle in which 16 Chetniks had been killed at Kozara, a mountain in western Bosnia. What made the soldiers even more enraged was the fact that these losses had been incurred while they were attempting to capture armed Bosniaks who refused to surrender. The visitors came into Omarska to take their revenge.

It was therefore always a matter of great concern when outside visitors arrived at the camp. Amidst what Pervanić describes as orgies of killing, one date stands out: June 17, 1992. On that day, a guard in the Omarska camp, later identified as

Zdravko Govedarica, along with four other guards whose names are not known, took a prisoner, Serif Velic, to a room in the administration building. They stripped Velic to his underwear, kicked him in the testicles, repeatedly beat him with a baton and rifle, and kicked him in the ribs, causing him to lapse into and out of consciousness.

Later, as Pervanić recounts, several outside visitors came into the camp and engaged in what can best be described, in a perverse sense, as "sport." One prisoner, Meho Alic, was forced to watch as his son Enver, known as Eno, was beaten. Two other inmates were also compelled "to take part in this brutal game"; one was made to drink motor oil, after which "he was then ordered to kneel before Eno Alic, and they forced him to bite off his testicles." As Pervanić recalls, "The nightmare of this particular cruelty will never end for the boy who was made to carry it out." He "remained in a state of shock for days." Pervanić's concludes that the boy "will have to live with this horror for the rest of his life," while for the perpetrators of the crime, "it had all been great fun."

This atrocity is reminiscent of one attributed to Dušan Tadić (b. 1955), a Bosnian Serb who was the first person to be indicted by the International Criminal Tribunal for the former Yugoslavia. At the Serb concentration camps at Omarska and Keraterm, Tadić was notorious for his alleged brutality, even though he was not a guard, nor did he have any formal role. Beatings and mutilations were common, and frequently led to death. On one occasion he supervised a torture in which an inmate was ordered to bite off the testicles of a fellow prisoner; on another, he reportedly sprayed the contents of a fire extinguisher into a victim's mouth.

Kemal Pervanić's shocking testimony could lead one to the view that the guards were nonhuman monsters or psychopaths, and yet the study of genocide shows that every human being is capable of killing. Pervanić spent the whole time he was in Omarska in a state of terror, but in order to survive he had to keep a cool head—and keep his head down. What we do not learn in this account is the fact that Pervanić already knew some of the guards. One had been a teacher, and another was a former classmate. We have seen this local intimacy many times before. Pervanić found himself having to ask why this was the case. In response to his own question of how it is possible for people to turn so suddenly on those they know, he concludes that it takes a long time to prepare people for the slaughter of their neighbors. Preparation for genocidal killing is a long-term project; it is not something that takes place spontaneously.

Questions

1. What was the nature of the concentration camp at Omarska?
2. How does Pervanić describe some of the tortures that took place at the camp? Which, if any, made an impression on you? Why?
3. Why was it often more dangerous for prisoners when visitors came to the camp?

"AMER"

In July 1995 the eastern Bosnian city of Srebrenica became the scene of the greatest massacre on European soil since the Holocaust. Both Srebrenica and its neighbor, Žepa, had been guaranteed by the United Nations as "safe areas," but the reality was anything but safe for those living there. Amer (only his first name is used here), who spent much of the war alternating between the two towns, was one of the survivors of the siege and betrayal of Srebrenica and Žepa. He is now a taxicab driver in Melbourne, Australia. This is the first time his account has been related in any format.

I was born in 1973, in the village of Godomilje, a small community in eastern Bosnia within the municipality of Rogatica—between the cities of Višegrad and Žepa. Before the war in 1992, the population was about 80 percent Serbian and 20 percent Muslim. As far as I can remember, there were no Croats in the town. The community was thoroughly integrated; we went to the same schools together, and did not see any real differences between us.

I finished high school at the age of 18 and should have gone into the army for my national service year, but because [of] the war I held back from joining the army. I went and hid when they came for me. We all had an idea that something bad was going to happen. In 1991 Yugoslavia was starting to collapse, and war was taking place between the Serbs and Croatia. The government in Belgrade gave the Bosnian Serbs weapons to help the fight against Croatia, and many volunteered to go and fight.

In April 1992, Borike, a small town about twenty kilometres from Rogatica, was the first community the Chetniks began to infiltrate. The Serbs were heavily supplied with guns, uniforms, bullets—everything they would need as an army of occupation. Living in the general district between Žepa and Godomilje, we were very worried. We knew we would be targets if we stayed where we were, so we went undercover and lived in the bush. We would only come back to the village for food, when we could be sure the Chetniks weren't around. When they finally did come into our village and took over—under the command of Captain Rajko Kusic and four other officers—they demanded that the villagers hand over all the guns and weapons in the village. Of course, there was hardly anything there, just a few rifles for hunting. In the hills, watching what was happening, we saw a huge pall of smoke coming from the direction of the village around 4:00 o'clock in the afternoon. Our house, and that of other Muslims in the village, had been destroyed. From then onwards we had no other option but to sleep in the forest.

My parents were with me throughout all this. My dad found the whole thing confusing, because we knew that those who had handed over their weapons, or stayed, were killed anyway. It was a good lesson for us: there could be no opportunity for compromising or negotiating with the Chetniks, because whatever we did could only have one possible outcome.

We made it to Žepa on June 4, 1992. During the second half of 1992, and then throughout 1993, the Serbs surrounded Žepa with tanks and troops. It became difficult to supply the city, because Serbs surrounded all approaches. It was next to impossible for us to break through to help the city, as we only had hunting guns and hardly any ammunition. We had maybe twenty bullets, if that. Our aim was to provide local protection for Žepa, but our effectiveness was limited. I was on duty to guard against a Serb attack, whenever I was needed; day or night, it didn't matter. I worked both shifts. We sure couldn't mount an offensive or anything like that. The Serbs never took the city until July 1995, but that was because of the UN troops giving in, not because we lost the city ourselves.

In 1992 I went over the mountains to Srebrenica, with my parents. We found sanctuary in a house that had previously been Serbian on the outskirts of the city. The previous residents had fled to Serbia, and left their house empty. I then alternated between Srebrenica and Žepa for the rest of the war.

Srebrenica is close to the border between Bosnia and Serbia, near to the Drina River. Because of its location it was very difficult to feed the city. There was hardly any food there. Between 1992 and 1995 I did not see any sweets, candies—or salt. The main way we got food was to pinch it from farms around the local area. In February and March of 1993 NATO planes made food drops which contained small lunch boxes, but this was never enough because more people kept flocking into Srebrenica as refugees.

In April 1993 the United Nations declared Srebrenica and Žepa to be "safe havens," and peacekeepers from Ukraine were sent to protect Žepa. We considered them to be totally corrupt. We felt betrayed by the United Nations, and in particular French general Philippe Morillon, who was in command of the UN troops, because he did not give a true report to the UN of what was happening at Srebrenica. They made money out of selling things to the civilians—their uniforms, their boots (200 Deutschmarks), coffee (100 Deutschmarks for a kilo), gasoline, stovetops on which the civilians could cook, and many other things. They would help themselves to the humanitarian convoys, and then sell items to the population. This, of course, made it even harder to feed the people. There was no work of any kind, so the only way to supplement our lives was through offering our labor on local farms in exchange for food.

In June 1995 a Ukrainian officer told me that the fall of Žepa was imminent, and that the UN troops would be unable to prevent it. He anticipated that the Serb forces were about to occupy the town. We had nowhere to go, and although we tried to get away by going up to a hill above the town, we watched as nearly 5,000 Serbian soldiers and paramilitary groups entered and took over Srebrenica. There were

500 men in our group, but we were under-equipped and unable to do anything to stop the occupation. The only bonus for us was that while we couldn't hit the Chetniks, we thought they couldn't get at us, either.

This was until my cousin, Mujo Durmišević, was shot and killed just ten metres away from me. He had tried to show us where cover could be found, and was hit by Serbian grenades. We panicked, and everyone ran deeper into the bush. I ran about 600–700 metres, and saw a friend of mine who had been shot up. He was dead, his stomach and guts hanging out. Throughout all this time, the UN troops were not helping; we heard that they were back in Žepa, drinking with the Serbian army.

The commander of the Bosnian government forces in Žepa throughout the siege was Colonel Avdo Palić. When the Serbs, commanded by General Ratko Mladić, finally took over the town in July 1995, Palić tried to negotiate a settlement with the Serbs that would protect civilians. We were still hiding in the forest, but Mladić showed that he was not interested in negotiating. He had Palić murdered. The time we gained through the negotiation helped us to get away, however. We tried to circle around the Serbs, and reach more established Bosniak positions. The women and children remained in the town, however, under Chetnik control.

We remained in the bush for five days, before we were ordered to go to the Red Cross for sanctuary and a possible population exchange. During this time my brother-in-law was severely wounded, shot in both legs. Nevertheless, we took him with us, as we crossed the Drina into Serbia—in my case, as I could not swim, clutching a plank of wood. Dead bodies were in the water all around us. Others made the crossing over the next ten days; some people remained in the forest, in some cases for up to four months.

Soon after I crossed the river, a Serb soldier on a hill saw us, and leveled his gun in our direction. Motioning for us to remain where we were, we put our hands on our heads and waited for other Serbian troops to come. One guy, who didn't act as instantly as the Serbs demanded, was shot right there, in front of us. There were 14 of us, and we had been arrested by members of the White Eagles paramilitary group. They took us to a camp. Once we arrived there, one of them said angrily, "I fucked your mother," and began to bash and hit us. Another asked us, "How many people have you killed?" after which two more of us were shot dead on the spot.

After two and a half hours of this, radio orders came in that we were to move to Jagoštice. By now we were a group of about 20. One of the Chetniks said, "No, I'm going to kill them all here, now," though luckily he didn't do it. What we did have to do, however, was crouch down with our hands on our heads, and hop along like ducks. He said that if he touched any of us on the shoulder and we fell over, he would shoot us. At random, he then said, "I'll kill number 17." This was our friend Semso Hodzic, who was then beaten. He wasn't killed, though.

On 2 August, when we came to the school where they were taking us, everyone had to take off their clothes and give up anything that could be considered valuable—especially our watches and any gold or money we had. We had to run a gauntlet of beatings for maybe half an hour. Robbed of everything I had, I was then beaten again. I lost consciousness, and was in a state of shock for some time after I came to. At around 2:00 or 3:00 a.m., they woke us up with more beatings and the barking of vicious guard dogs. By 7:00 a.m. they brought up covered army trucks that could hold maybe 20 people. They packed 40 of us into this space, and we set off to who knew where. One man died on the journey. At about midday we stopped and were ordered down from the trucks. We came to a camp at Slivovica, where we remained for five days. Here, we were subjected to continuous interrogations. I was questioned for two or three hours for each of the next two nights, beaten all the time. All the men were tortured and one man I knew, who went into the camp weighing about 120 kilos, came out a month later at maybe 60 kilos. Myself, I went from 91 kilos to 65 kilos in the same period.

After our time in Slivovica, we were sent to a camp at Mitrovo Polje, where I was to spend the rest of the war. This was one of many camps in Serbia—not in Bosnia, but in Serbia itself. We travelled all night, were beaten throughout the trip, and as soon as I arrived I was hit hard on the chest. Immediately I felt one of my ribs break. As I fell, the guard also hit me hard on the back of my neck with a heavy piece of wood. I couldn't move for a month after this.

Again, questioning all night, every night. Every person was given a Serbian name, to replace their Muslim name. To the guards, I became "Novak." They also demanded that we sing Chetnik nationalistic war songs.

I remained in that camp until March 1996, three months after the war ended. I had been registered with the Red Cross as a prisoner back in August 1995, and was on a list to be sent to Denmark, but when the Red Cross representative came to the camp nothing happened. It seemed to him as though I was being looked after, but after he left I was beaten again, as the Serbs accused me of complaining about my treatment.

In January 1996 the repatriation and release process began, and people began to leave the camp. I didn't leave. It turned out that Denmark didn't want to take me, after all. In April 1996, though, I made it back to Zvornik in a prisoner exchange, not far from where my journey began four years earlier.

Source: Interview, Paul R. Bartrop and "Amer," July 31, 2012, Melbourne, Australia. Used by permission.

Commentary

The beginning of Amer's testimony is a reminder that before the Bosnian War there had been a good deal of integration between the Serbs and Muslims in Bosnia, and that the communities had lived together in peace and harmony for many years. The three main nationalities—Bosniak, Serb, and Croat—lived in inextricably mixed communities, and coexisted relatively peacefully. Before the 1990s these communities were characterized by widespread intermarriage.

Rogatica is a municipality and town in eastern Bosnia, about 35 miles northeast of Sarajevo. It lies about halfway between Goražde and Žepa. In the last prewar census, held in 1991, the municipality had 21,812 residents, which included 15,374 (60.38 percent) Bosniaks and 10,169 (30.48 percent) Serbs. The town of Rogatica had 8,930 inhabitants, including 5,662 (63 percent) Bosniaks and 3,062 (34 percent) Serbs. Amer came from Borike, a village in the municipality.

When the war began in April 1992, the Serbs began their assault on the region in Borike, a small town about 16 miles from Rogatica. As Amer relates, they were heavily armed, and the Bosniaks in the area were fully aware of what this portended. Amer and his family left their home and hid in the bush, coming back from time to time only for food. Eventually, the village was put to the torch, while the family watched. They then moved, as refugees, to Žepa, which soon came under siege from Serb troops.

Žepa is located in eastern Bosnia, not far from Rogatica. In 1993 the town was declared a United Nations safe area (one of three in eastern Bosnia, along with Srebrenica and Goražde). A small Ukrainian Army unit of UNPROFOR peacekeepers was stationed there. With a population of only about 15,000, Žepa was one of the smallest of the UN safe areas, though its size was offset to some degree by its natural advantage of being situated on high ground that could be well defended. Given its isolation, however, a credible defense was always an unlikely proposition. Supplies were difficult to acquire because of the siege, and local defense, as Amer indicates, could only use the few available hunting rifles, for which there was practically no ammunition. As he says, though, when the town fell in July 1995, it was because the UN troops handed Žepa over to the Serbs, "not because we lost the city ourselves."

He is referring to the conquest of Žepa by Bosnian Serb forces led by General Ratko Mladić in July 1995. While the town's defenders put up a strong resistance, the 79 Ukrainian peacekeepers—whom Amer holds in very poor regard—were powerless to influence developments in any direction. The negotiated evacuation of women and children from the town began around July 21, 1995. There was no similar agreement to evacuate the men of Žepa.

The military commander of the enclave was Colonel Avdo Palić (1958–1995), who refused to surrender his forces, or the town, until he had an agreement from Mladić concerning a safe evacuation for Žepa's inhabitants. On July 25, the Serbs entered the town. Its defenders had already left for the nearby hills, either to regroup in defensive formations or to make their way to Bosniak-controlled areas on foot. Unlike earlier at Srebrenica, there was no accompanying slaughter of Muslim men by the victorious Serb forces. Palić himself disappeared soon after the town was captured. He is believed to have been murdered on Mladić's orders.

Amer's account relates that during the war, he alternated between Žepa and Srebrenica, about 16 miles apart. In Srebrenica, he and his parents found sanctuary in
a house from which the previous residents, Serbs, had fled. He recalls that throughout the siege it was difficult to obtain food or any creature comforts ("sweets,
candies, or salt"), and the only way to supplement daily needs was to go out of the
city on what, during World War II, would have been referred to as food raids.
A major difficulty was caused by the continuous arrival of more and more refugees
from outlying areas, which swelled the population and created even greater de-
mand for resources and supplies that were already being stretched to the
maximum.

With the fall of Srebrenica in mid-July 1995, Amer returned through the forest
to Žepa, but when the Serbs closed in on the town later in the month, most of the
men fled. As Amer's testimony relates, he was captured by Serb soldiers and imprisoned, first in holding locations, then in a succession of concentration camps
including Omarska. Amer describes how the prisoners at Omarska were subjected
to a regime of starvation, torture, and murder.

He was then sent to the Sljivovica camp in Uzice, Serbia, outside Serb-controlled Bosnia, after which he was sent on to another camp at Mitrovo Polje, also
in Serbia. There, members of the Serbian police, state security service, and army
committed war crimes against prisoners, including Amer, between July 1995 and
April 1996. In 2011 the Belgrade-based Humanitarian Law Centre filed criminal
charges against a number of policemen for the killing, torture, and inhumane treatment of prisoners that took place at Sljivovica and Mitrovo Polje. Amer, as it turned
out, had been one of more than eight hundred prisoners from Bosnia detained in
the two camps.

At Mitrovo Polje the prisoners were forced to change their Bosniak identity to a
specifically Serb one. This comprised changing their names—as Amer informs us,
he became "Novak"—singing nationalistic Serbian ("Chetnik") songs, and (although
he does not mention this in his testimony) reciting Orthodox Christian prayers.

Amer was finally repatriated in March 1996, well after the war ended with the
signing of the Dayton Agreement on November 21, 1995, and its ratification in Paris
on December 14, 1995. Although the war officially ended at that time, a number of
anomalies remained. The siege of Sarajevo, for example, only came to an end on
February 29, 1996, when Bosnian Serb forces left positions in and around the city.

For Amer, even though he had been registered with the Red Cross as a prisoner
back in August 1995, nothing happened to hasten the process of his release until
January 1996. Even then, there were delays. His original sponsoring country, Denmark, had undergone a change of heart, and without a country of refuge he was
unable to leave the camp. As we read, it was only in April 1996 that he managed to
return to Zvornik as part of a prisoner exchange, "not far from where my journey
began four years earlier."

Questions

1. Was there any significance to the fact that Amer was able to alternate between Srebrenica and Žepa during the war? What might that be?
2. How does Amer characterize the Ukrainian UN troops sent to safeguard the people of Žepa? Why does he feel this way?
3. Why do you think it took until long after the war was over for Amer to be released from the Serbian camp at Mitrovo Polje?

PIERRE SALIGNON

Between 1992 and 2008, Pierre Salignon worked for Médecins Sans Frontières (MSF) as head of programs and director general. In 2001 he gave testimony to the French Parliamentary Hearing into the Srebrenica Tragedy. A lawyer by profession, Salignon's initial role with MSF was that of senior field coordinator for the former Yugoslavia, an office that placed him in an ideal position to observe wartime developments firsthand. In 1994 and 1995 he visited Srebrenica, where he was able to report on events both there and in other parts of Bosnia. His report to the French Parliamentary Hearing provided important testimony regarding the abandonment of the Bosniak population by the United Nations.

In July 1995, when the Serbian forces in Bosnia launched their offensive against Srebrenica, the massacre of the local inhabitants was foreseeable, no matter what is said by certain French leaders who have appeared before you. . . .

Everyone, not just the French authorities, was well aware of the methods being used by General Mladic and his troops [who] launched their attack on Srebrenica in July 1995. . . .

I first went to Srebrenica in March 1994. What I saw was literally a ghetto, an open-air prison. The United Nations had established the Muslim enclave in Srebrenica as a "protected zone" in April 1993. It had been put under the protection of an UNPROFOR contingent after the Bosnian soldiers had been disarmed.

More than 40,000 civilians, mostly women, children and elderly, were living in terrible conditions. They were subject to both the Bosnian-Serb militia's blockade and the controls of the UN soldiers. At the time, my impression when I entered Srebrenica was that the law of the aggressors prevailed, and the UN forces simply complied. Although the UNPROFOR presence initially curbed cease-fire violations, what it was mainly doing was playing into the hands of General Mladic's forces by prohibiting the Bosnians from entering or leaving Srebrenica.

The inhabitants were caught in a trap. Access to Srebrenica was controlled by the Bosnian Serb authorities, who at whim refused entry or exit to aid organisations and confiscated the contents of convoys. UNPROFOR was unable to intervene.

The civilian population received the bare minimum to survive. The situation was particularly difficult in the city, where more than 20,000 people were concentrated into an area where only 5,000 inhabitants had lived before the war.

In 1994, action by the UN peacekeepers consisted solely of maintaining the military status quo. No consideration was ever given to using force to end the siege. UNPROFOR's Canadian battalion was trapped for several months before being relieved. I remember talking with the Canadian forces, who were subjected to daily ridicule and who were disgusted by their mission. I also remember the emaciated refugees, their fear that Srebrenica would be attacked, that they would be slaughtered and their memories of the ethnic cleansing in eastern Bosnia in 1992 and 1993.

The situation continued to deteriorate in the months that followed, which led MSF to question the usefulness of its operations in the eastern Bosnian enclaves. Despite ourselves, we had become "prison doctors." I remember writing in the MSF newsletter in June 1994 that "the lack of international political will means that we are now providing social services for the occupying forces while waiting for the civilian population to be displaced and the ethnic cleansing in eastern Bosnia to be completed." The UN forces were not given adequate resources for their mission. There were too few of them, they were poorly equipped, they were trapped and had become hostages.

On October 20, 1994, in an opinion column published in the French daily *Libération,* I also wrote about the future of the inhabitants of Srebrenica, Gorazde and Zepa. I said that their future "was dependent on the will of the international community to see them survive." Without support from the international community, I was convinced that Srebrenica and Zepa would soon fall and that the worst would then happen. That is why MSF worked so hard to keep its medical teams in Srebrenica. We hoped that the presence of foreign witnesses would make the murderers hesitate. . . .

During another visit to Srebrenica in March 1995, I had to negotiate for several hours with the local authorities in Bratunac before being able to enter the enclave. The militia were arrogant and mocked us. They made no secret of the fact that— I quote—"When the time comes, they would kill all the Muslims. . . ."

On 14 June 1995, right in the middle of the hostage crisis, our representative in Pale, Stéphan Oberreit, still confronted with the authorities' refusal to let us into Srebrenica and Gorazde, sent us a message. . . . Military preparations against the enclaves were taking shape and it was becoming increasingly clear that the military did not want to see us there if there was to be an offensive and slaughter, which he felt to be relatively certain. He also asked us some questions: "What should we do? Should we leave Srebrenica and Gorazde for safety reasons and is it impossible for us to bring in new teams? Should we stay there despite the risks. . . ?"

This was the background to my visit to Pale from 17 to 26 June 1995. . . . A small medical team—a nurse and a doctor—were allowed to go to Srebrenica on 24 June 1995. The Pale authorities however refused to allow an expatriate surgeon to join them. The ICRC and UNPROFOR were also negotiating permission to enter the enclaves, but were still being refused.

With the Bosnian Serb forces entering the Srebrenica safe area on July 6, 1995, the question of protection became essential. The massacres were predictable and all men of fighting age were in danger of being killed. . . .

We could not imagine that the UN troops would hand the population over to the Serb militias. Right up to the end, the MSF team in Srebrenica refused to believe that the UN would fail to react. We were wrong. . . .

While part of the terrified population of Srebrenica fled to the UNPROFOR base in Potocari to seek the protection of the United Nations, the Peacekeepers barred base access to trucks loaded with wounded and Bosnian medical personnel who had just evacuated Srebrenica hospital. Only the determination of the Bosnian doctors and refugees who mobbed the gates of the United Nations base, forced them to let them in. . . .

The wounded were not spared and on 14 July 1995, when the list of wounded received in the UNPROFOR base in Potocari was drawn up by the MSF team and Bosnian staff, it was above all to protect them and prevent them simply disappearing during the evacuation. To our horror and stupefaction this list, which was then handed over to UNPROFOR, was to enable General Mladic's men to select their victims more easily, without those in charge of the UNPROFOR force in Potocari being able to do anything about it.

By July 13, 1995, in Tuzla, under the control of the Sarajevo authorities, news was beginning to circulate about a column of refugees who were attempting to flee the enclave through the forest. Nothing however was planned to help them. While the escaped women spoke of the columns of prisoners they had seen leaving the forests near Bratunac and Koljevic Polje, the United Nations and the Western governments did and said nothing. The massacres continued for several days in complete impunity. More than 7000 victims, mostly men, were then executed and thrown into mass graves. More than 2000 were taken prisoner in Potocari, with the others captured as they attempted to escape through the forest.

I find it hard to believe that it was not possible to help them. . . .

On 24 June 1995, with the first Serb incursion into Srebrenica, we in Paris were sure that a large-scale Serb attack had been launched. We were then in contact with the field and with many journalists in Europe, with representatives of the United Nations and the UNPROFOR, to warn them of what was about to happen.

We were constantly on the phone to MSF volunteers in the field, in Belgrade, Zagreb, Pale and Srebrenica, but also with the HCR and the ICRC in Geneva, Mr. Kofi Annan in New York, and many others.

As the news from Srebrenica reached us, we made it public. Starting on 6 July 1995, MSF issued almost daily press releases describing the tragedy and expressed its greatest concern as to the fate of the civilian population. On 12 July, MSF denounced the separation of the men and women, in plain view of the UN peacekeepers, and the transfer of the prisoners to the Bratunac stadium. Several calls for protection of the population were issued. With the arrival of the first escapees in the Tuzla region, our personnel in the field bore witness to the clear signs of ill treatment shown by many women and girls. The escapees also spoke of the massacres in progress. On the evening of 13 July, the Serbian forces had finished deporting most of the population, which had sought refuge with the UNPROFOR in Potocari, some 30,000 people, two thirds of whom were inhabitants of the enclave. However, in a release published on 14 July, MSF already stressed the fact that if the majority of the refugees in Potocari came from the south of the Srebrenica enclave, there was still no news of the several thousand civilians from the villages further to the north. In Tuzla, in Bosnian territory, there were already rumours of a column of more than 10,000 people trying to break through the Bosnian Serb army's defensive lines. The escaped women explained that most of the men had preferred not to go to Potocari, as they were convinced that they would not be protected by the peacekeepers. They were mostly, although not exclusively, men, refugees, unarmed adolescents, protected by a few Bosnian soldiers. . . .

Despite this information, UNPROFOR stood passively by. The European states, including France, simply protested without doing anything. . . . The promise of protection made to the inhabitants of Srebrenica was not kept and the lack of political will to defend them contributed in leading them to the massacre. They were abandoned.

Source: Pierre Salignon (*Médecins sans Frontières* Program Coordinator in 1995 for the former Yugoslavia), during the French Parliamentary Hearing into the Srebrenica Tragedy, 2001. Accessed at http://www.doctorswithoutborders.org/press/release. cfm?id=1347&cat=press-release&ref=tag-index. Used by permission of Doctors Without Borders.

Commentary

Srebrenica is a town and municipality in eastern Bosnia. In 1995 the town became the scene of the greatest massacre on European soil since the *Shoah* of World War II. The United Nations had declared Srebrenica a "safe area" in the spring of 1993, along with five other Bosnian Muslim cities (Bihać, Goražde, Sarajevo, Tuzla, and Žepa) then under siege at the hands of the Bosnian Serbs. During the siege, Srebrenica found itself constantly suffering privation, as the Serb army tested the resolve of the UN troops guarding the city by blocking UN aid convoys.

UNPROFOR was an acronym for the United Nations Protection Force, a UN peacekeeping operation for the former Yugoslavia established by Security Council

Resolution 743 on February 21, 1992. The purpose of UNPROFOR was to create conditions conducive to peace negotiations and to safeguard the peace in certain designated regions. The mandate was broadened from time to time while the conflict unfolded, with UNPROFOR being given responsibility for such areas as border control, the demilitarization of certain areas (by mutual negotiation with the parties involved), protection of Sarajevo Airport, provisioning and safeguarding of humanitarian aid, protection of civilian refugees, and, ultimately, defense of the six UN-designated safe areas.

UNPROFOR was also responsible, with NATO support, for ensuring that agreements entered into by the parties would be respected. On occasion, commanders called in NATO air strikes and other expressions of deadly force for the purpose of compelling compliance. At its maximum strength, UNPROFOR maintained a foreign complement drawn from 37 different countries. It was frequently criticized for its inability (interpreted by many as unwillingness) to do more to protect lives throughout the war. The fall of Srebrenica in July 1995, with its attendant massacre of up to 8,000 men and boys, represented the nadir of UNPROFOR's mandate in Bosnia, from which the force's already battered reputation never recovered.

Srebrenica has become a symbol of the brutality of the Serb war against Bosnia's Muslims, and of the failure on the part of the United Nations to stand up to genocide. This is especially the case given that the safe zone created by the UN was not defended, and was instead simply allowed to be taken with the connivance and assent of the Dutch peacekeepers and their NATO commanders, both on the ground and elsewhere.

Pierre Salignon, who was working with Médecins Sans Frontières during the Bosnian War, has provided his recollections of the massacre, which show the perspective of a witness whose major interest was in providing aid and succor to refugees and noncombatants. Much of the early part of his account deals with the period leading up to the massacre, during which time he observed the ongoing deterioration of conditions in Srebrenica. Even in March 1994, when he first arrived, his impression was that the town was "literally a ghetto, an open-air prison." Of note is his observation that the town had been placed under the protection of UNPROFOR in April 1993, "after the Bosnian soldiers had been disarmed," an often-overlooked aspect of the Srebrenica tragedy.

By the time Salignon arrived, more than 40,000 civilians, mostly women, children, and the elderly, were somehow eking out a living in the town, "living in terrible conditions." His impression was that "the law of the aggressors prevailed, and the UN forces simply complied." He notes that the presence of UNPROFOR played into General Ratko Mladić's hands, as those in the town "were caught in a trap." Access to Srebrenica was controlled by the Bosnian Serb authorities, "who at whim refused entry or exit to aid organisations and confiscated the contents of convoys." What was most galling was that, in this environment, "UNPROFOR was unable to intervene."

Once the invasion of Srebrenica had taken place, the main observations in Sa-lignon's account relate to the betrayal of the town and its inhabitants by the UN forces. The Serbs' intent, after all, was well-known, and only outside intervention—or, at least, a commitment to defend the enclave—could have prevented what was clearly going to be a major assault on human rights. His account shows him to have been obviously shocked when the Dutch troops handed over the city to Mladić, and he condemned UNPROFOR for its passivity in the face of what would become geno-cide. His position is clear, as he states: "I find it hard to believe that it was not possible to help" the residents of Srebrenica.

Foreseeing what was likely to happen, he notes that an air of panic enveloped the aid workers. In Paris, Médecins Sans Frontières was in constant contact with del-egates in the field, as well as with journalists, UN representatives, and high-ranking officers from UNPROFOR, all with one aim: "to warn them of what was about to happen."

As the news from Srebrenica arrived, Salignon and his team made it public, and over the next few days they provided a running commentary on developments. At every turn, MSF called for the population to be protected. In his account, Salignon raises the most critical question of them all: Why was the response from the inter-national community so negligible? It is, unfortunately, a question he could not an-swer. Despite all the information being spread, he notes, "UNPROFOR stood pas-sively by"; all that happened was that the European countries, including France, merely protested. He states, "The promise of protection made to the inhabitants of Srebrenica was not kept and the lack of political will to defend them contributed in leading them to the massacre." There was only one possible conclusion to draw: the people of Srebrenica "were abandoned."

Pierre Salignon's account of the fall of Srebrenica, and of the massacre that fol-lowed, is a definitive statement from a witness who based his descriptions on both firsthand observation and reports from those with whom he was coordinating in the field. He leaves little room for doubting that what happened at Srebrenica was a humanitarian and moral catastrophe of the greatest magnitude.

Questions

1. As the leader of a major international aid agency, can Pierre Salignon rightly be described as a witness to genocide? Give reasons for your answer.
2. Was Salignon's team at the Médecins Sans Frontières office in Paris successful in generating international recognition of the reality of the Srebrenica massacre?
3. Do you think the actions of organizations like MSF are helpful in a situation such as that at Srebrenica? Or do they only allow the global community to feel that it is making a worthwhile difference?

10. The Darfur Genocide

In the first years of the twenty-first century, the Government of Sudan (GOS), aided by Arab militias known as *Janjaweed*, carried out a campaign of terror, economic destruction, rape, and murder against the non-Arab "black Africans" of Sudan's Darfur region. Initially, the GOS and *Janjaweed* retaliated against rebel groups of Sudanese blacks who had attacked government installations and the provincial capital of Al Fasher. The rebel groups had committed the attacks out of frustration over the fact that the Sudanese blacks had been, and were being, discriminated against, marginalized, and subject to injustice at the hands of the GOS. Between 2003 and 2007, instead of merely confronting the rebel groups, the GOS and *Janjaweed* carried out wholesale attacks on the villages and farms of Sudanese blacks in Darfur.

A region roughly the size of France, Darfur is located in the western part of Sudan, bordering Libya, Chad, and the Central African Republic. Prior to the outbreak of violence in 2003, Darfur's population was approximately 6 million people, comprising dozens of different tribal groups. Thirty-nine percent of the population was considered "Arab" and 61 percent was considered "non-Arab" or "black African." Because of intermarriage, the distinction between the two peoples relates more to lifestyle differences and cultural affiliation than race. Darfuri Arabs tend to lead nomadic lives, herding cattle and camels throughout the region, while non-Arabs are often sedentary farmers.

Beginning in 2003, the regime of Omar Hassan Ahmad al-Bashir (b. 1944) engaged in a scorched-earth campaign against the black Africans of Darfur. For years, the Fur, Masalit, and Zaghawa ethnic groups of Darfur had been calling on the government in Khartoum to use monies from the taxes they paid to help them develop their region, especially through the building of roads, schools, and hospitals. They also called for better treatment of black Africans by the police and judicial system. Further, they complained bitterly that Arabs in the region were given preferential treatment over black Africans.

When it seemed that the complaints were falling on deaf ears, a rebel group, the Sudanese Liberation Army (SLA) was formed, and in early 2003 it began carrying out attacks against government and military installations. Short-handed because of a much bigger and more destructive civil war in the south of the country, al-Bashir hired nomadic Arabs to join forces with GOS troops to fight the rebels. However, instead of focusing their attacks solely on the rebels, the GOS and *Janjaweed* militias carried out a scorched-earth policy against all black Africans in Darfur. The GOS and *Janjaweed* killed men, women, and children; raped young girls and women; and, prior to burning down hundreds of entire villages, plundered what they could. By 2006, estimates of those killed ranged upward to 400,000, with over 2 million Darfuris internally displaced and another 250,000 uprooted to refugee camps in Chad.

Much of the blame for the intensity of the violence rested on the shoulders of the Arab militias, the *Janjaweed*. The name is colloquially used to mean "devils on horseback" (or sometimes, depending on the context, camels are substituted for horses). The government brought in the *Janjaweed* to help counter the attacks by the rebels and to track the rebels down, but instead of simply focusing on the rebels, the GOS and *Janjaweed* systematically and ruthlessly attacked village after village of ordinary citizens and noncombatants.

Eyewitness accounts describe how the Sudanese government forces and *Janjaweed* would sweep into villages on horse- or camelback, wielding automatic weapons and firing indiscriminately at civilians. Homes, grain stores, and crops were destroyed, while women, children, and the elderly were whipped, raped, tortured, and, frequently, murdered. These tactics were designed to terrorize victims, forcing them to flee their homelands. Once they were gone, Arab populations would resettle the land, effectively eradicating the rebels' power base.

Initial reactions to the conflict were inadequate, as bystanders such as the United Nations, the United States, and the European Union chose to prioritize other foreign policy issues over the escalating crisis in Darfur. In particular, a painfully slow negotiating process was taking place between al-Bashir and the leader of the Sudan People's Liberation Army (SPLA) of Southern Sudan, John Garang (1945–2005), to try to bring to an end the devastating civil war in the south. In May 2004 a provisional agreement was signed between the GOS and SPLA. A comprehensive peace agreement, the Naivasha Agreement, was signed on January 9, 2005. In order not to rock that boat, many actors in the international community deliberately preferred not to notice what was happening in Darfur.

Al-Bashir and his government continually denied that a campaign of genocide was occurring, and argued that the casualty and death figures were grossly inflated. They rejected accusations that they were supporting aggression by the *Janjaweed* against the black African rebel groups, claiming that foreigners had "fabricated" and "exaggerated" the conflict.

Following an investigation conducted by the U.S. government in Darfuri refugee camps in Chad, and based on analysis of the data, U.S. Secretary of State Colin Powell (b. 1937) declared, on September 4, 2004, that the killing in Darfur constituted genocide. The United Nations subsequently carried out its own investigation between

December 2004 and January 2005, for the express purpose of ascertaining for itself whether, in fact, genocide had been or was being perpetrated in Darfur. The investigation determined that while serious crimes of humanity had been perpetrated, there were no findings to prove that the GOS and *Janjaweed* had committed genocide. By the same token, the United Nations did not rule out that genocidal acts had been committed, and maintained that an analysis of additional evidence in the future would be considered. The UN inquiry recommended that the Security Council place 17 individuals from the Sudanese government on targeted sanctions, with 5 others, including al-Bashir, listed as potential targets. In 2005 the International Criminal Court (ICC) also began an investigation into the atrocities committed by the GOS and *Janjaweed* for possible future trial proceedings.

In July 2008 the prosecutor of the ICC, Luis Moreno Ocampo (b. 1952), accused al-Bashir of having committed genocide, crimes against humanity, and war crimes in Darfur. On March 4, 2009, the court issued a warrant for al-Bashir's arrest on counts of war crimes and crimes against humanity. Genocide was not included in the indictment. On July 12, 2010, however, this was overturned on appeal, and a charge of genocide (on three counts) was added to the indictment. Al-Bashir became the first sitting head of state to be indicted by the ICC, and the first to be charged with the crime of genocide. By 2013 he was still at large, and there seemed to be little chance of him being arrested or brought to trial.

"SULEIMAN"

Buried deep in the notebook of independent filmmakers Jen Marlow, Aisha Bain, and Adam Shapiro, a note about "Suleiman" (b. 1947) can be found. He was listed as a key humanitarian affairs contact for the Sudanese Liberation Army (SLA), a rebel group founded—as the Darfur Liberation Front—by members of three indigenous ethnic groups in Darfur: the Fur, the Zaghawa, and the Masalit. Interviewing him in English, the filmmakers found Suleiman to be articulate, intelligent, and an astute commentator on the affairs of the region and the objectives of the SLA. In this account, he discusses his own experiences at the hands of the Sudanese government forces. Although the worst killing of the Darfur Genocide has now hopefully come to an end, in many respects there remains a legacy of silence among the survivors. This is not helped by the fact that Sudanese president Omar Hassan al-Bashir (b. 1944), who was indicted for genocide by the International Criminal Court in July 2010, remains at large. The account that follows, therefore, is intended to be illustrative of the situation that prevailed in Darfur. It is unequivocally far from being the last word on the matter.

I was born here in North Darfur, in a place called Anka, in the year 1947. I went to Khartoum for technical secondary school in 1964. I spent fourteen years working for the government, in the Ministry of Industry. I worked in a factory that specialized in making paper bags, and cartons. . . .

I was about eight years old when the British left. I don't remember the faces and the activities, but so many of our elder people say that the British period was better than the national period. At least the colonials oppressed us all equally and no Sudanese had power to dominate the others. The people who have been governing Sudan since 1956 until now are only from a few tribes. Since independence, the government of Khartoum has been trying to marginalize the bigger tribes of African origin in Darfur.

Until now, we are missing power and participation in the government in ruling Sudan. We are missing education. We are missing health. We are missing any kind of development for the area. Since you crossed the border until you came here, what kind of civil life have you found? Nothing, except what was created by nature.

In the south of Sudan, they were fighting since 1955 to claim their rights, the same exact rights as we are fighting for. From 1972 until 1983 they stopped the war, and then they started again. For thirty-eight years, they struggled for their rights and they did not find them. And the international community was deceived by our government of Sudan who prolonged the period of talk. We started this fight in Darfur in 2000 to claim our rights. The marginalization that created the war in the south is the same cause as the war in the west. If the government continues on the same track, there will be wars in other areas, as has already started in the Nuba Mountains. The Darfur war will not be the last for this government, if they remain in power. I have known some of the political leaders since they were students . . . if this government does not change, Sudan will not be settled. . . .

Previously, we and the Arabs exchanged marriage. Some of the Zaghawa are married with the Arabs. Some of the Arabs are married with Zaghawa, with the Fur, with the Masalit. It was a complete community life. In the past, in peacetime, the Arab nomads moved from south Darfur to the north of Darfur after the rainy season. They would spend the whole winter in the north with us, with Fur, Masalit, with any tribe. We would help each other. When someone lost some of his livestock, everyone came and helped seek the lost animals. We built good relations between us. Definitely, some conflicts happened between individuals, and then the tribal leaders and the elders sat together and solved the problem. Someone gave some money, cattle, or camels from someone to the other, and the thing was resolved. After the livestock grew bigger and the number of citizens themselves grew larger, the farmers needed a wider area of land to plant for their food, and the herders also needed a wider area for their livestock. The needs of the life for the herders and farmers came into conflict, and the government found the chance to wedge between the two, keep them separate, and push them to war. The war is taking place on behalf of the government.

For the Arab tribes, the idea of this war is to get land. Not all the Arabs. I'm only speaking about the Janjaweed. Janjaweed is the combination of *jeen*, which is evil, *jawad,* horse, *jeed*, a kind of weapon. The Arab nomads tried to frighten the farmers off their land in order to feed their cows. The government joined their efforts. The government called for other nomadic Arabs from neighboring countries, mainly from Chad, Mali, Central Africa Republic, Cameroon, and sometimes from Niger, a collection of nomads moving from the west to the east. The government told them there is a good life and easy to find unowned livestock. Please, come and take. They came in heaps and big numbers, and they found themselves in the middle of some kind of war. So they participated in it.

The government itself, why is she coming to our area and what is she seeking? If she left us with the Janjaweed, either of two options would happen. Either we would defeat them and they would flee back to their countries, or we would come to negotiations and agree to live with each other. But the government is trying to prolong the war. We don't deserve for this conflict to be extended. But what can we do? If the government wants to cleanse the area and replace us with the Arabs, we have two options: Either fight to survive, or grab our hands and sit until we are killed. So, we are fighting for survival, to defend our lives. We have nothing else to do. They cannot defeat us. They cannot clean us.

We and the Arabs are compelled to this war on behalf of the government. You passed Muzbat yesterday, I think. Have you seen the holes made by the bombs? Do Janjaweed have fighter planes? The government is backing the Janjaweed and the Janjaweed are fighting on behalf of the government. Our true enemy is the government of Sudan. We are not fighting the Arabs. We are fighting against the government who is using the Arabs to clean us out of the area and pressing them to replace us in our lands.

The Arabs are not using their minds because they feel that the government is backing them. If the government stops supporting them or giving them ammunition and guns, I think they would come to their senses and we would seek a way with each other to make peace and to continue to live peacefully, as it was before they started this conflict. We spoke to Arabs and we need to speak more, but they did not come to the realization that they are fighting on behalf of the people in power in Khartoum. . . .

In February 2000, the government started to detain and imprison me. I spent about four months in jail in Port Sudan. Then I was released. I had two months out of jail; then I was arrested again the same year in September. I sat about five months in jail and was released again. In 2001, I was again detained for about six months. When I was released the third time, I tried to come out and join the SLA. But I didn't find the chance. I was detained for the fourth time in 2003 and spent another six months in jail.

Instead of giving us food three times a day, they fed us once or twice, to make us complain. But we didn't. Even if we would die of starvation, we refused to complain. They tried to beat me. I called their people and they were afraid to repeat it again. I was left just to sit in prison. The last three times I was not asked anything. No one interrogated me, no one accused me, no one told me why I was in jail. They said they feared I may be killed by some enemies whom I don't know. They said, "The people of Darfur may harm you, so we are trying to keep you safe." I know the real reason. They thought that I had relations with the SLA in Darfur, but they hadn't the evidence.

When the thing became bigger and the government participated as a partner in this war, we elders felt compelled to go back. I spent forty years of my life in Khartoum, living an easy civilian life there, with my house and my family and my children. Nothing to be compared to the harsh life we are living now, these hard rocks. . . .

Nothing could attract me to come here except the feeling that if I stayed there and did nothing while my tribe is being cleaned from the area, I will lose some of . . . I will feel ashamed. Finally, I escaped prison. I came to stand beside my tribe, the Zaghawa, and help. . . .

Any kind of war affects children and women, definitely very badly, but if it is our fate and there is no other choice, what should we do? We just try to minimize the effect of war on our citizens and continue fighting, until we come to our rights or at least to secure our lives. Our choice is to fight so that they may survive. . . .

We do not want to secede from Sudan. If we make a country within the borders of Darfur, we will make a small country, without prospects. Sudan, as its borders are now, can be ruled by small, federal governments with a central base of power. We can make a federation. Sudan cannot be governed by only one central government. . . .

The door to peace is to disarm the Janjaweed. But the government delegation includes the ministers who created and backed the Janjaweed. If those militias are not disarmed, peace will not ever come to Darfur.

Source: Jen Marlowe with Aisha Bain and Adam Shapiro, *Darfur Diaries: Stories of Survival* (New York: Nation Books, 2006), 106–112. Used by permission.

Commentary

During the late nineteenth century, Britain extended its control over Egypt southward into Sudan, a region nominally part of the Egyptian domain. The British effectively treated the country as their own colony. After the Egyptian Revolution of 1952, it seemed to be only a matter of time before Sudanese independence would occur, although Britain attempted to maintain its control of the region. After a period of carefully planned decolonization, a Sudanese nationalist, Ismail al-Azhari

(1900–1969), was elected the country's first prime minister, and on January 1, 1956, independence was proclaimed and recognized. This placed Sudan's Arab population in a position of ascendancy within the largely Muslim country.

Darfur, a region in western Sudan, is populated mainly by three related ethnic groups, the Fur, Zaghawa, and Masalit peoples. It was incorporated formally into Sudan during the colonial regime in 1916. Under colonial rule, the region was left as a backwater. Because of the difficult nature of Britain's colonial acquisition of the territory, Darfur's development was somewhat neglected as the British attempted to pacify and appease the more militant population of central Sudan, near the capital, Khartoum.

After continued neglect, rebel groups of Darfuris (known in the vernacular as "Sudanese blacks") coalesced into a movement called the Sudan Liberation Army. They attacked government installations and the provincial capital of Al Fasher, acting on their frustration over the region's ongoing discrimination. The population had long been marginalized at the hands of the Government of Sudan (GOS).

Between 2003 and 2007, in retaliation, GOS troops and *Janjaweed* carried out widespread ethnic cleansing and genocide against the Sudanese blacks in Darfur. Wholesale attacks on the villages and farms of Sudanese blacks took place, with the indiscriminate killing of men, women, and children. Girls and women were raped, and, before burning down hundreds of entire villages, GOS and *Janjaweed* engaged in extensive acts of plunder.

Suleiman's testimony provides a personalized history of Sudan and Darfur in summary form. He describes how in earlier times, the Darfuris and Arabs enjoyed relatively harmonious relationships. Intermarriage was not uncommon between the Arabs and all three of the local groups. As he notes, "It was a complete community life." The nomadic Arabs would follow the seasons, moving from south to north with the rains. "They would," he recalls, "spend the whole winter in the north with us, with Fur, Masalit, with any tribe," and they "would help each other."

What, then, went wrong? In Suleiman's view, the war is government-directed, and it is in the government's interest only. It is a war for Arab supremacy, conducted in order to obtain land. In particular, he levels an accusing finger at the *Janjaweed*, the Arab nomads who, with the support of the government, have attempted to frighten the local farmers off their lands. Moreover, Suleiman considers that many of those he refers to as the "nomadic Arabs" have come from neighboring countries such as Chad, Mali, the Central African Republic, Cameroon, and Niger. As he sees it, the conflict is basically a territorial war between the herders and the farmers, driven by the government but fought by *Janjaweed* on its behalf, with the object of "cleansing" the area.

Suleiman considers that the complete responsibility of the government for the conflict has led to its attempting to prolong the war in order to totally rid the area of black Sudanese. He believes the conflict to be a racial one, which the locals must fight in order to survive. It is that simple: "[W]e have two options: Either fight to survive, or grab our hands and sit until we are killed. So, we are fighting for survival, to defend our lives. We have nothing else to do."

Without the prompting of the GOS, he maintains, the local population could reach an accommodation with the *Janjaweed*. Either "we would defeat them and they would flee back to their countries, or we would come to negotiations and agree to live with each other." As he sees it, the *Janjaweed* do not possess the military capabilities to wage a successful war by themselves. The campaign of aggression would collapse quickly without the government. "We are not," he says, "fighting the Arabs." His view is that "we are fighting against the government who is using the Arabs to clean us out of the area and pressing them to replace us in our lands." The "true enemy" is "the government of Sudan," he states succinctly.

Suleiman had lived in Khartoum with his family for over four decades before the war began in Darfur. His statement that when the war escalated and government complicity became more and more obvious, "we elders felt compelled to go back," says a great deal about the normal impulses found in many populations at risk. Nothing could have made him return to Darfur "except the feeling that if I stayed there [in Khartoum] and did nothing while my tribe is being cleaned from the area, I will lose some of . . ." His words trail off into deep reflection, but his next remarks are equally evocative: if he does nothing, "I will feel ashamed." The prison of a comfortable life in Khartoum became too much for him, so "I came to stand beside my tribe, the Zaghawa, and help."

One of the key points in the ongoing discussions during the mid-2000s concerning Darfur's future focused on the objectives of the Darfuri rebels. Some, particularly in Khartoum, argued that the rebels were seeking secession and independence. This was explicitly rejected by rebel leaders such as Abdul Wahid Muhammad al-Nur (b. 1968) in favor of a liberal, secular, and democratic state for all of Sudan, to ensure that religious differences could not be used to kill and oppress the country's citizens. The irony, of course, is that the people of Darfur were being victimized for their skin color, not their religion, which was the same as that of the majority Arab population ruling in Khartoum.

Suleiman is aware of this. In his account he states quite clearly that "we do not want to secede from Sudan," as that would only make for "a small country, without prospects." What he is looking for is a federation of states in which power is decentralized and the *Janjaweed* are disarmed. Without that, he concludes, "peace will not ever come to Darfur."

Questions

1. What, according to Suleiman, is the main objective of the Government of Sudan (or, in lieu of that, those he describes as the Arabs) in pursuing the war in Darfur?

2. Why did Suleiman decide to leave his comfortable life in Khartoum and return to the war zone in Darfur? Why are Suleiman and many others like him engaged in the conflict?

3. Does Suleiman hold out any hope for a favorable resolution to the Darfur crisis?

Bibliography

The literature of genocide is vast, and cannot possibly be replicated in a work of this size. The following list, therefore, is intended as a starting point only, and a bare minimum of the types of works represented in the academic literature. It should be noted that, in many cases, the sources of the accounts throughout this volume can also be employed as bibliographical references.

The Herero Genocide

Bley, Helmut. *Southwest Africa under German Rule 1894–1914.* Evanston, IL: Northwestern University Press, 1971.

Bridgman, Jon M. *The Revolt of the Hereros.* Berkeley: University of California Press, 1981.

Drechsler, Horst. *Let Us Die Fighting: The Struggle of the Herero and Nama Against German Imperialism (1884-1915).* London: Zed Books, 1980.

Erichsen, Casper and David Olusoga. *The Kaiser's Holocaust: The Forgotten Genocide of the Second Reich and the Colonial Roots of Nazism.* London: Faber and Faber, 2010.

Gewald, Jan-Bart. *The Angel of Death Has Descended Violently amongst Them: Concentration Camps and Prisoners-of-War in Namibia, 1904–08.* Leiden, South Holland: African Studies Centre, 2005.

Hull, Isabel V. *Absolute Destruction: Military Culture and the Practices of War in Imperial Germany.* Ithaca, NY: Cornell University Press, 2006.

Sarkin, Jeremy. *Germany's Genocide of the Herero: Kaiser Wilhelm II, His General, His Settlers, His Soldiers.* Melton, Woodbridge, Suffolk: James Currey, 2011.

Silvester, Jeremy and Jan-Bart Gewald, eds. *Words Cannot Be Found: German Colonial Rule in Namibia: An Annotated Reprint of the 1918 Blue Book.* Leiden: Brill, 2003.

Zimmerer, Jurgen and Joachim Zeller, eds. *Genocide in German South-West Africa: The Colonial War of 1904–1908 and its Aftermath.* London: Merlin Press, 2007.

The Armenian Genocide

Akçam, Taner. *A Shameful Act: The Armenian Genocide and the Question of Turkish Responsibility.* New York: Metropolitan Books, 2006.

Akçam, Taner. *From Empire to Republic: Turkish Nationalism and the Armenian Genocide.* London: Zed Books, 2004.

Akçam, Taner. *The Young Turks' Crime Against Humanity: The Armenian Genocide and Ethnic Cleansing in the Ottoman Empire.* Princeton, NJ: Princeton University Press, 2012.

Balakian, Peter. *Black Dog of Fate: A Memoir.* New York: Basic Books, 1997.

Balakian, Peter. *The Burning Tigris: The Armenian Genocide and America's Response.* New York: HarperCollins, 2003.

Dadrian, Vahakn. *The History of the Armenian Genocide: Ethnic Conflict from the Balkans to Anatolia to the Caucasus.* Providence, RI: Berghahn Books, 1995.

Graber, G.S. *Caravans to Oblivion: The Armenian Genocide 1915.* New York: Wiley, 1996.

Hovannisian, Richard G., ed. *The Armenian Genocide: History, Politics, Ethics.* New York: St. Martin's Press, 1992.

Hovannisian, Richard G., ed. *The Armenian Genocide in Perspective.* New Brunswick, NJ: Transaction Publishers, 1987.

Hovannisian, Richard G., ed. *Looking Backward, Moving Forward: Confronting the Armenian Genocide.* New Brunswick: Transaction Publishers, 2003.

Hovannisian, Richard G., ed. *Remembrance and Denial: The Case of the Armenian Genocide.* Detroit: Wayne State University Press, 1999.

Melson, Robert. *Revolution and Genocide: On the Origins of the Armenian Genocide and the Holocaust.* Chicago: University of Chicago Press, 1996.

Miller, Donald E. and Laura Touryan Miller. *Survivors: An Oral History of the Armenian Genocide.* Berkeley: University of California Press, 1993.

Suny, Ronald Grigor, Fatma Muge Gocek, and Norman M. Naimark, eds. *A Question of Genocide: Armenians and Turks at the End of the Ottoman Empire.* New York: Oxford University Press, 2011.

The Holocaust

Bauer, Yehuda. *A History of the Holocaust.* New York: Franklin Watts, 1982.

Bauer, Yehuda. *Rethinking the Holocaust.* New Haven, CT: Yale University Press, 2002.

Berenbaum, Michael and Abraham J. Peck, eds. *The Holocaust and History: The Known, the Unknown, the Disputed, and the Reexamined.* Bloomington: Indiana University Press, 1998.

Bergen, Doris. *War and Genocide: A Concise History of the Holocaust.* Lanham, MD: Rowman and Littlefield, 2002.

Browning, Christopher. *Ordinary Men: Reserve Battalion 101 and the Final Solution in Poland.* New York: HarperCollins, 1992.

Browning, Christopher. *The Origins of the Final Solution: The Evolution of Nazi Jewish Policy, September 1939–March 1942.* Lincoln: University of Nebraska Press, 2004.

Dawidowicz, Lucy S. *The War Against the Jews: 1933–1945.* London: Weidenfeld and Nicolson, 1975.

Desbois, Fr. Patrick. *The Holocaust by Bullets: A Priest's Journey to Uncover the Truth Behind the Murder of 1.5 Million Jews.* New York: Palgrave Macmillan, 2008.

Dwork, Deborah and Robert Jan van Pelt. *Auschwitz: 1270 to the Present.* New York: W.W. Norton, 1996.

Dwork, Deborah and Robert Jan van Pelt. *Holocaust: A History.* New York: W.W. Norton, 2002.

Friedländer, Saul. *Nazi Germany and the Jews: The Years of Persecution, 1933–1939.* New York: HarperCollins, 1997.

Friedländer, Saul. *Nazi Germany and the Jews, 1939–1945: The Years of Extermination.* New York: HarperCollins, 2007.

Gilbert, Martin. *The Holocaust: A History of the Jews in Europe During the Second World War.* New York: Henry Holt, 1986.

Goldhagen, Daniel Jonah. *Hitler's Willing Executioners: Ordinary Germans and the Holocaust.* New York: Random House, 1996.

Gutman, Yisrael and Michael Berenbaum, eds. *Anatomy of the Auschwitz Death Camp.* Bloomington: Indiana University Press, 1994.

Hilberg, Raul. *The Destruction of the European Jews.* (3 vols.) New Haven: Yale University Press, 2003.

Hilberg, Raul. *Perpetrators, Victims, Bystanders: The Jewish Catastrophe 1933–1945.* New York: Harper, 1993.

Klee, Ernst, Willie Dressen, and Volker Riess, eds. *"The Good Old Days": The Holocaust as Seen by Its Perpetrators and Bystanders.* New York: Free Press, 1988.

Laqueur, Walter, ed. *The Holocaust Encyclopedia.* New Haven: Yale University Press, 2001.

Levin, Nora. *The Holocaust: The Destruction of European Jewry, 1933–1945.* New York: Thomas Y. Crowell, 1968.

Longerich, Peter. *Holocaust: The Nazi Persecution and Murder of the Jews.* New York: University Press, 2010.

Yahil, Leni. *The Holocaust: The Fate of European Jewry, 1932–1945.* New York: Oxford University Press, 1990.

The Cambodian Genocide

Dith Pran. *Children of Cambodia's Killing Fields: Memoirs by Survivors.* New Haven, CT: Yale University Press, 1997.

Etcheson, Craig. *After the Killing Fields: Lessons from the Cambodian Genocide.* Westport, CT: Praeger, 2005.

Haing S. Ngor, with Roger Warner. *Survival in the Killing Fields.* London: Chatto and Windus, 1988.

Hinton, Alexander Laban and Robert Jay Lifton. *Why Did They Kill?: Cambodia in the Shadow of Genocide.* California Series in Public Anthropology. Berkeley and Los Angeles: University of California Press, 2004.

Kiernan, Ben. *Genocide and Resistance in Southeast Asia: Documentation, Denial, and Justice in Cambodia and East Timor.* New Brunswick, NJ: Transaction, 2007.

Kiernan, Ben. *How Pol Pot Came to Power: Colonialism, Nationalism, and Communism in Cambodia, 1930–1975.* 2nd ed. London: Verso, 2004.

Kiernan, Ben. *The Pol Pot Regime: Race, Power, and Genocide in Cambodia under the Khmer Rouge, 1975–79.* 3rd ed. New Haven: Yale University Press, 2008.

Ponchaud, François. *Cambodia Year Zero,* London: Allen Lane, 1978.

Schanberg, Sydney. *Beyond the Killing Fields.* Dulles, VA: Potomac Books, 2010.

Short, Philip. *Pol Pot: The History of a Nightmare.* London: John Murray, 2005.

Vickery, Michael. *Cambodia, 1975–1982.* Boston: South End Press, 1984.

The Guatemalan Genocide

Archdiocese of Guatemala. *Guatemala: Never Again!* Maryknoll, NY: Orbis Books, 1999.

Garrard-Burnett, Virginia. *Terror in the Land of the Holy Spirit: Guatemala under General Efrain Ríos Montt, 1982–1983.* New York: Oxford University Press, 2011.

Higonnet, Etelle and Marcie Mersky. *Quiet Genocide: Guatemala 1981–1983.* New Brunswick, NJ: Transacation Publishers, 2009.

Jonas, Susanne. *The Battle for Guatemala: Rebels, Death Squads, and U.S. Power.* Boulder, CO: Westview Press, 1991.

Montejo, Victor and Victor Perera. *Testimony: Death of a Guatemalan Village.* Willimantic, CT: Curbstone Books, 1995.

Nelson, Diane M. *Reckoning: The Ends of War in Guatemala.* Durham, NC: Duke University Press, 2009.

Perera, Victor and Daniel Chauche. *Unfinished Conquest: The Guatemalan Tragedy.* Berkeley: University of California Press, 1995.

Sanford, Victoria. *Buried Secrets: Truth and Human Rights in Guatemala.* London: Palgrave Macmillan, 2004.

Simon, Jean-Marie. *Guatemala: Eternal Spring, Eternal Tyranny.* New York: W.W. Norton, 1987.

The East Timor Genocide

Aubrey, Jim, ed. *Free East Timor: Australia's Culpability in East Timor's Genocide.* Sydney: Vintage/Random House Australia, 1998.

Fernandes, Clinton. *The Independence of East Timor: Multi-Dimensional Perspectives— Occupation, Resistance, and International Political Activism.* Eastbourne, UK: Sussex Academic Press, 2011.

Fernandes, Clinton. *Reluctant Saviour: Australia, Indonesia and the Independence of East Timor.* Melbourne: Scribe, 2005.

Gunn, Geoffrey C. *East Timor and the United Nations: The Case for Intervention.* Lawrenceville, NJ: Red Sea Press, 1997.

Nevins, Joseph. *A Not-So-Distant Horror: Mass Violence In East Timor.* Ithaca, NY: Cornell University Press, 2005.

Robinson, Geoffrey. *"If You Leave Us Here, We Will Die": How Genocide was Stopped in East Timor.* Princeton, NJ: Princeton University Press, 2010.

The Kurdistan Genocide

Aburish, Said K. *Saddam Hussein: The Politics of Revenge.* New York: Bloomsbury USA, 2000.

Al-Bayati, Hamid. *From Dictatorship to Democracy: An Insider's Account of the Iraqi Opposition to Saddam.* Philadelphia: University of Pennsylvania Press, 2011.

Black, George. *Genocide in Iraq: The Anfal Campaign Against the Kurds.* New York: Human Rights Watch, 1993.

Galbraith, Peter. *Unintended Consequences: How War in Iraq Strengthened America's Enemies.* New York: Simon and Schuster, 2008.

Hiltermann, J. R. *A Poisonous Affair: America, Iraq, and the Gassing of Halabja.* New York: Cambridge University Press, 2007.

Karsh, Efraim and Inari Rautsi. *Saddam Hussein: A Political Biography.* New York: Free Press, 1991.

Kelly, Michael J. *Ghosts of Halabja: Saddam Hussein and the Kurdish Genocide.* Westport, CT: Praeger, 2008.

Moore, Robin. *Hunting Down Saddam: The Inside Story of the Search and Capture.* New York: St. Martin's Press, 2004.

The Rwandan Genocide

Barnett, Michael. *Eyewitness to a Genocide: The United Nations and Rwanda.* Ithaca, NY: Cornell University Press, 2002.

Dallaire, Roméo, with Brent Beardsley. *Shake Hands with the Devil: The Failure of Humanity in Rwanda.* Toronto: Random House Canada, 2003.

Des Forges, Alison. *Leave None to Tell the Story: Genocide in Rwanda.* New York: Human Rights Watch, 1999.

Fujii, Lee Ann. *Killing Neighbors: Webs of Violence in Rwanda.* Ithaca: Cornell University Press, 2009.

Gourevitch, Philip. *We Wish to Inform You That Tomorrow We Will Be Killed with Our Families.* Farrar, Straus and Giroux, 1998.

Mamdani, Mahmood. *When Victims Become Killers: Colonialism, Nativism, and the Genocide in Rwanda.* Princeton, NJ: Princeton University Press, 2001.

Melvern, Linda. *A People Betrayed: The Role of the West in Rwanda's Genocide.* London: Zed Books, 2000.

Melvern, Linda. *Conspiracy to Murder: The Rwandan Genocide.* London: Verso, 2004.

Prunier, Gérard. *The Rwanda Crisis: History of a Genocide.* New York: Columbia University Press, 1997.

Rusesabagina, Paul. *An Ordinary Man.* New York: Viking Penguin, 2006.

Straus, Scott. *The Order of Genocide: Race, Power and War in Rwanda.* Ithaca: Cornell University Press, 2006.

The Bosnian Genocide

Allen, Beverly. *Rape Warfare: The Hidden Genocide in Bosnia and Herzegovina and Croatia.* Minneapolis: University of Minnesota Press, 1995.

Filipović, Zlata. *Zlata's Diary: A Child's Life in Sarajevo.* London: Viking, 1994.

Honig, Jan Willem and Norbert Both. *Srebrenica: Record of a War Crime.* New York: Penguin Books, 1997.

Leydesdorff, Selma. *Surviving the Bosnian Genocide: The Women of Srebrenica Speak.* Bloomington: Indiana University Press, 2011.

Malcolm, Noel. *Bosnia: A Short History.* London: Macmillan, 1994.

Nuhanović, Hasan. *Under the UN Flag: The International Community and the Srebrenica Genocide.* Sarajevo: DES Sarajevo, 2007.

Rohde, David. *Endgame: The Betrayal and Fall of Srebrenica, Europe's Worst Massacre since World War II.* New York: Farrar, Straus and Giroux, 1997.

Silber, Laura and Allan Little. *The Death of Yugoslavia.* London: Penguin Books and BBC Books, 1995.

Simms, Brendan. *Unfinest Hour: Britain and the Destruction of Bosnia.* London: Allen Lane, Penguin Press, 2001.

Stiglmayer, Alexandra. *Mass Rape: The War Against Women in Bosnia and Herzegovina.* Lincoln, NE: University of Nebraska Press, 1994.

Vulliamy, Ed. *Seasons in Hell: Understanding Bosnia's War.* New York: St. Martin's Press, 1994.

The Darfur Genocide

Flint, Julie and Alex de Waal. *Darfur: A New History of a Long War.* 2nd ed. London: Zed Books, 2008.

Hamilton, Rebecca. *Fighting for Darfur: Public Action and the Struggle to Stop Genocide.* London: Palgrave Macmillan, 2011.

Mamdani, Mahmood. *Saviors and Survivors: Darfur, Politics, and the War on Terror.* New York: Pantheon, 2009.

Prendergast, John and Don Cheadle. *Not on our Watch: the Mission to End Genocide in Darfur and Beyond.* New York: Hyperion, 2007.

Prunier, Gérard. *Darfur: A 21st Century Genocide.* 3rd ed. Ithaca, NY: Cornell University Press, 2008.

Reeves, Eric. *A Long Day's Dying: Critical Moments in the Darfur Genocide.* Toronto: The Key Publishing House, 2007.

Steidle, Brian, with Gretchen Steidle Wallace. *The Devil Came on Horseback: Bearing Witness to the Genocide in Darfur.* New York: PublicAffairs, 2007.

Totten, Samuel and Eric Markusen, eds. *Genocide in Darfur: Investigating the Atrocities in the Sudan.* New York: Routledge, 2006.

Index

Note: page numbers in **bold** indicate main topics in the volume.

About the Author

PAUL R. BARTROP, PhD, one of the world's leading scholars of the Holocaust and genocide, is Professor of History and Director of the Center for Judaic, Holocaust, and Genocide Studies at Florida Gulf Coast University. He was the 2011–2012 Ida E. King Distinguished Visiting Professor of Holocaust and Genocide Studies at Richard Stockton College, New Jersey. Prior to this appointment, he was head of the Department of History at Bialik College, Melbourne, Victoria, Australia between 2003 and 2011, where he taught a range of subjects in history, Jewish studies, international studies, and comparative genocide studies. He is a former member of the International Association of Genocide Scholars and a past president of the Australian Association of Jewish Studies, and is currently vice-president of the Midwest Jewish Studies Association in the United States. Among his many published works is *A Biographical Encyclopedia of Contemporary Genocide: Portraits of Evil and Good* (ABC-CLIO, 2012).